TOTAL LATIN AMERICAN ARCHITECTURE

LIBRETTO OF MODERN REFLECTIONS AND CONTEMPORARY WORKS

BROAD PERSPECTIVE_ LONG PERSPECTIVE / Performance, Buenos Aires 2007.
2010_ Image specially composed for this book by A. de Brea.

"Not a few readers will notice various transgressions of literary convention here. To give only a few examples: the Argentine characters switch from one familiar form to another whenever it suits the dialogue; a Londoner who is only starting his study of French begins to speak it with amazing fluency (and even worse, in a Spanish version) as soon as he crosses the Channel; geography, the order of subway stations, freedom, psychology, dolls, and time obviously cease being what they were in the realm of Cynara. (...) The subtitle, A Model Kit, might lead one to believe that the different parts of the tale, separated by blank spaces, are put forth as interchangeable elements. If some of them are, the framework referred to is of a different nature –sensitive sometimes on the writing level, where recurrences and displacements try to be free of all causal fixedness, but specially on the level of meaning, where the opening for combinatory art is more insistent and imperative. The reader's option, his personal montage of the elements in the tale, will in each case be the book he has chosen to read."

Julio Cortázar, foreword of his book *62: A Model Kit*, New York, 1972.

TOTAL LATIN AMERICAN ARCHITECTURE

LIBRETTO OF MODERN REFLECTIONS AND CONTEMPORARY WORKS

POETICAL STRUCTURES OBSERVED

TOPICS UNDER CONSIDERATION

A LOOK OVER LABORATORIES

TERRAIN / LANDSCAPE / TOPOGRAPHY

COVERING FOLK FACTORS

THE VOLUMETRIC REASONING (REVIEWING PHYSICAL FEATURES)

ANNEXES

LATIN AMERICAN ARCHITECTURE

César Pelli

In the early years of my professional life, I saw myself as a Latin American architect. Now that I have been living and practicing for some 58 years in the United Sates I cannot any longer call myself just such. But my early interests, affinities and my understandings remain with me although now I also see what happens in the region as from the outside.

As I think about Latin America the common thread of all of the many buildings and the many architects practicing in the region there, I conclude that what distinguishes them from other architects in other parts of the world is an emotional affinity. There is almost every architectural tendency reflected today in Latin America and its architects are just as individualistic as those in other parts of the world. But still I know in my veins that there is such a thing as a Latin American architect. Those that practice there are affected by similar cultural environments and most importantly by similar traditions. The ideas and visions about city buildings that the Spaniards and Portuguese brought to the Americas were quite different than those of the Anglo Saxons. As I say this, the image that comes to my mind is that of the central plaza: the very public space at the ancient core of our cities. There is something quite marvelous in this gesture of conceiving a new city with an empty space, a public space, at its core. Unquestionably the cathedral and the government house were also there, but the very center was dedicated to the public and as the city grew many other plazas appeared, reestablishing with them this affirmation of the great value for the public sphere that Latin Americans share.

Although my practice is now quite North American, I know that this simple and powerful idea has affected my architecture deeply. I still believe that the public is more important than the private and this is apparent to some degree in all of my buildings. In Latin America when one thinks of the public space, one also thinks of a very much used and active space where we come together with our neighbors and other citizens. The plaza is where discussions, manifestations and protests take place.

When I think of Latin American architects those that first come to my mind are the great architects that left their mark in the early and middle 20th century, our predecessors. I think of architects like Luis Barragan who brought poetry to his designs in Mexico using other traditional Latin American elements such as the bare wall, privacy and silence. I also think of Eladio Dieste in Uruguay and his love of the common brick, another traditional Latin American element, and how Eladio infused the modest brick with extraordinary technical and artistic power. The other two architects that also come to my mind are not so easy to define: one is Oscar Niemeyer and the other is Amancio Williams; both were strongly influenced by Le

Corbusier and both tried to absorb, interpret and execute Le Corbusier's ideas in their own countries: Niemeyer in Brazil and Williams in Argentina and they both did it very successfully, creating some extraordinary pieces of architecture. In Niemeyer's hands, Le Corbusier's architecture became playful, joyous and exuberant; that is very Brazilian. In Williams" hands, particularly in his most iconic building, La Casa de Puente in Mar Del Plata, Le Corbusier's forms and principles are treated with great respect and tact, but they are also somehow misinterpreted so as to create a very Latin American example of the International Style at its best.

Repsol-YPF Tower in Buenos Aires, Argentina.
Courtesy of Pelli Clarke, Pelli Architects

I am quite familiar with the architecture and culture of Argentina and Mexico and a bit less so with that of Brazil, but I have never been to other dynamic countries such as Peru, Columbia or Venezuela. They have had some very good architects and perhaps this is another quality shared by architects in Latin America; that is, everyone knows what everyone else has done or is doing.

Some of Latin American countries also have very strong architectural examples of pre-Columbian architecture still affecting the character of their cities. I believe it is impossible to design in a place such as Mexico City if one is not aware of what the Aztecs have done there, or in Peru and Bolivia without recognizing that the best architecture in the country is that of the Quechuas and Aymaras who created magnificent and daring structures before the Spaniards came. These indigenous precedents are well known throughout Latin American, although in countries such as Argentina and Brazil that have no built examples their presence is rather remote. Today, of course, the world has shrunk and continues to shrink at great speed and we are as apt to be as influenced by the work of an architect in the city where we practice as with that of an architect at the opposite end of the globe. If this trend continues, it will be difficult to talk about Latin American architecture. We may be able to talk about the work of specific groups in some regions or in some countries or of the work of individual talented architects that may or may not be nourished by the traditions of Mayans, Aztecs or Incas or by those of the Spanish settlers and founders. What I do expect with confidence is that good, excellent and great architects will keep on flourishing in Latin America and that they will keep on influencing other architects all over the world.

MOVING / People Crossing 9 de Julio Avenue, Almost at Any Time.
2010_ Image specially composed for this book by María de Brea Dulcich.

Disparos de aproximación
(RECKONING THE TARGET)

Alfonso Corona Martínez

In this continent, landscape is the monument.[1]

1. What is Latin America?

This book is not about a folk or typical Latin American architecture. Latinoamérica is not some faraway, isolated region. Yes, it has white sandy beaches, mountains and glaciers, yes. Impressive ruins from Pre-Columbian civilizations ruthlessly destroyed by our Spanish ancestors, yes.

Ana de Brea shows here a different Latin America through its recent architecture. One that flourishes in our time of global communications. An architecture of the present and designed for the next future.
It does have roots in the past; but does not appeal to nostalgia.

Latin America is not a single region, but many. The common trait of these nations is that they were colonies of Spain, with the exception of Brazil and the Guianas. We all then speak the same language, with many different inflections and vocabularies. All received the Spaniards (or the Portuguese) for a ruling class in the sixteenth century. Most of them received migrants from other European countries in the nineteenth and twentieth centuries; in a few of these countries European migrants became a large part of the population. That is the case of Argentina, Uruguay and Chile. Pay attention to the surnames of the authors shown here and you will agree that "other Europeans" integrated smoothly with the grandchildren of Spanish *conquistadores*.

Geography is not a common trait. Our continent stretches from the tropical shores of the Caribbean, across the Equator down to Antarctica. It has jungle, desert, the flat pampas and the mighty Andes, with some of the highest mountains on Earth. Political divisions among these nineteenth century republics mirror the divisions devised by the Spanish for their colonial empire.

A few parts were established over the dismembered Inca Empire; others were sparsely populated by tribes and groups barely out of the Stone Age.

As is aptly said by Ana Fernández in her essay, these geographical differences "are expressed by widely varying manners of inhabiting the territory."

2. Latin American architecture in the age of globalization

Most of the houses in this book appear to be the scenario of a conflict: that of adapting the single volume house in the "natural" landscape, which is the form willed by the architect, with local or traditional features as the "patio" or internal courtyard.

1. Cazú Segers, Chilean architect, at the *Mundaneum* meeting in Mendoza, Argentina, 2011.

The problem of fitting the building into the landscape is sometimes tackled by characterizing the building as just another large stone among others in the barren landscape. This is made easier if you use reinforced concrete –an artificial stone. This is the case of works by the Peruvian architects, Barclay&Crousse, or the Argentine Claudio Ferrari in Uruguay. Others solve the problem of geometry versus landscape by simply perching their white boxes cantilevered more or less atectonically in the Modernist tradition.

This volumetric emphasis shows that the works displayed belong to the global preferences of late twentieth-century architects in all the Western World. Another international feature, if it can be called that way, is the desire for flat, continuous surfaces for the simple volumes of the building. This also makes buildings difficult to adapt to local climate. Gone are the prominent sunbreakers of Brazilian architecture of mid-twentieth century. Gone also are the rough and contrasting surfaces of Brutalism. And with this last trait, the traditional recourse of the discreet allusion to Classical systems of architectural elements. Most of the examples are buildings whose appearance drifts away from Classical tectonics, by ignoring the differences between supporting and supported elements.

With this stance, the outer surface is likened to the smooth surfaces of later-day curtain wall. Flat roofs of the 1920s defy tropical rains, just like it happened in Latin American Modernism of the 1950s, only that contemporary technology enables architects to bring that old dream to a safe reality.

These esthetic preferences call into question another value that the Modernist era tried to maintain, even if reinterpreted, from the Academic tradition: that is, the idea of character[2] as the quality that identifies for the passerby the use intended for the building, its "function." The sleek, enigmatic prism is the new prototype, and it is "globalized."

Perhaps these contradictions generate the esthetic tension that attracts our attention to this collection of works. Protecting the volume from the scorching sun and inclement rain displaces most of these designers" attention from the concern with distribution (an old functionalist obsession) to the "skin' that has to solve relations with the site without using heaps of ineffective air-conditioning.

That would also be incorrect in the present ecological mood.

Latin American architecture, as I can see, is really globalized.

"This (different regionalism) is the result of a complex interaction between modern international capitalism and various national traditions ingrained in institutions and attitudes. We should not expect to find, in this sort of regionalism, any differences of a fundamental kind, or complete survivals. Rather it manifests itself in the form of nuances. The materials of culture are similar in all cases, but each country tends to interpret these materials in a slightly different way. It is precisely because the ingredients of contemporary architecture are so similar all over the "developed" world that the slight differences of intepretation to which they are subjected in different countries are so interesting."[3]

3. Identity (Finale)

The main adavantge that we discovered working in those projects was that Latin American architects could simultaneously work with sophisticated technology from industrialized countries and build with a low-tech craftamship that was of a good quality. That specific position allowed us to propose particular solutions adapted to our environment, without submitting ourselves to the rigid, industrialized building requirements that we constantly had to follow in Europe.[4]

2. See Colin Rowe, "Character and Composition' in his first book of collected essays, *The Mathematics of the Ideal Villa.* M.I.T. Press, Cambridge MA, 1982.
3. See Alan Colquhoun, in "Regionalism and Technology" from his book *W.* M.I.T.Press, Cambridge MA, 1991.
4. Extracted from "The Desert Workshop," by Barclay&Crousse in this volume (segment *F. Terrain / Landscape / Topography).*

They also write: *The chronic economical, conceptual and material shortage that our country (Peru) suffered in the past taught us how to be ingenious so as to reach our architectural objectives with few resources. In Latin America these resources can be hi-tech or low tech, sophisticated or basic, or even exist together side by side. All those means can be used as freely as one uses a tool, rather than as an imposed necessity.*

"Local identities –says Mauro Bianucci in his essay "Authenticity or Death," do not exist in isolation." Perhaps the different geographies provide distorting mirrors for one another. However, the search for local identity is not new; it had been put to test before, in the stylistic manner of architects academically trained in that long epilogue of Beaux-Arts training that was usual in our (then) few Schools of Architecture well into the 20th century.

Many architects in the sub-continent tried enthusiastically in the 1920s and "30s to revive their local Colonial architecture, and some of their efforts were suitably adopted by national governments of a more or less authoritarian inclination as "the National Style." Perhaps the last effort was made by our Argentine trend of Las Casas Blancas, a brave effort of the late 1950s to sincretize the "poor" church architecture of Colonial northern Argentina with Modernist Elementarism and béton brut. (The difficulty of trying this synthesis was subtly observed by Alan Colquhoun in 1982)

This concern for a local or regional architecture is somehow still present. Witness this phrase by the same Mauro Bianucci, also in his essay: "Even though none of these artists (he refers to different groups all over the continent) would claim that their work is a traditional example of their native country (and most of them live abroad) their work is deeply pervaded by their local identity."

The concern exists; but the quotation I"ve selected shows us something else. These men and women consider themselves as Latin American architects even when "most of them live abroad." This was more usual for writers like Julio Cortázar, who wrote a large part of his very Argentine stories living in Paris, a voluntary exile. The same holds for architects of earlier generations, some of them very successful in their profession, so much as to have their works reunited in books like "Argentine Architects Abroad," by Luis Grossman and Daniel Casoy.

Architects and artists living and prospering out of their country are nothing new; it is something that begins at least with Serlio in France in the 1500s. However, Serlio never ceased to be an Italian architect. The authors in this volume decide consciously to remain being Latin American but, unlike Serlio, the sources of the art they practice, the models they follow, are not to be exported to less favored lands, as was the case of the Italian Renaissance. It is just the opposite.

They have been trained as architects in our universities, almost without exception; and that training was largely based in the reverence of the "Great Masters of Modernity," mainly Le Corbusier and Mies van der Rohe.

Possibly, what makes interesting the works of this younger generation is that they do not imitate the work of those Masters, a trait that was for several decades the proof that our architecture was already "Modern." Perhaps this is the first genuine Latin American contemporary architecture.

Quality of the form does not exist in the form itself but the effect.
(2007_Paul Puzzello).

Checking out Unlimitedness

Ana de Brea

Architecture - A Latin American Fragment (Recording Modern Reflections and Contemporary Works).

Creation is a Patient Search
Le Corbusier[1]

By *design*, the title of this publication intends to communicate to the reader the targeted objective. It intends to circumscribe a segment, a series of observations and actions in architecture. However, it is a selected, fully open, and deep fragment, that carries the explicit intent of outlining conceptual and practical verifications on critical views and concrete projects, concerning the actual, extensive world of architecture in the Latin American territory.

Therefore and intentionally from the very beginning, this work, as discreetly as possible declares to be a highly, intensely elaborated *fragment*.

Getting Started

It is appropriate to remark here that the qualificatory condition of being a fragment is set in this project as exclusively relevant to architectural expressions of the Latin American field of Architecture. There are three distinct evidences for this claim:

1. A geographical location. This limit also means an understanding of geography not just as a natural setting. It should be understood as an action that could be translated as 'position,' 'situation,' or a set of circumstances that clearly show validation of the particular way in which a belief, a theory, or a philosophy is placed and established (*the site / frame / parti* [2]);

2. The significance of being modern architectural pieces as opposed from those relating to the remote past (*the state / predicament*[3]), in order to help portray a more truthful locus; and

1 From Wikipedia, the free encyclopedia: Charles-Édouard Jeanneret, better known as Le Corbusier (October 6, 1887 – August 27, 1965), was an architect, designer, urbanist and writer, famous for being one of the pioneers of what is now called modern architecture. He was born in Switzerland and became a French citizen in 1930. His career spanned five decades, with his buildings constructed throughout Europe, India, North America and South America. He was a pioneer in studies of modern high design and was dedicated to providing better living conditions for the residents of crowded cities. Le Corbusier adopted his pseudonym in the 1920s, allegedly deriving it in part from the name of a distant ancestor, "Lecorbésier."

2 *parti (in French) /* partido (in Spanish): Popular and widespread Spanish expression in architecture schools, particularly in the southern part of South America (probably originated in the middle 60's). Partido *relates to the essence of the 'main idea' or 'idea synthesis,' that gives rise and makes sense to an architectural project. Also* associated to the notion of 'taking and playing decisions,' as well as to connecting to the action/process of 'deciding the project methodology,' habitually through a formal judgement (conceptualization). Also: decisiveness.

3 From Mac Dictionary: predicament – noun - archaid Philosophy (In Aristotelian logic) each of the ten 'categories,' often listed as: substance or being, quantity, quality, relation, place, time, posture, having or possession, action, and passion. ORIGIN late Middle English: from late Latin *praedicamentum 'something predicated' (rendering Greek Kategoria 'category'), from Latin praedicare (PREDICATE).*

3. The unambiguous desire to belong in the contemporary[4] world thanks to the precise facts of the "here and now" (*the present time*).

Regarding the character of the elements that compose this publication, I want to call the whole work an *opus*. I will explain it this way: it is like a large umbrella that covers many subjects and separate pieces. At the same time, it focuses in detail, like a zoom lens, on a purposive structure. In that structure it does not matter if the works are large or small; the tangible sizes of the architectural objects in display –dimension, scale and other traits, are not the sole important ones. Every aspect of these objects (*or architectures*) was considered in this book as what it really is: *a relative magnitude*. The stance I adopt in this research is centered in becoming a positive conversational instrument for a much wider international architectural discussion.

From that intelligible rationale, the publication would try to belong to a sort of "yes, but" generation instead of a "what if" peer group, to use the words of Winy Maas.[5] In his writings Maas invites to reflect about one of the possibly latest notions of open topography (*frame*) in architecture. He says, '*the post-geographical city is one with no real physical place: an endless, virtual sea of encounters. But we are still bound to geographical places: to meet, to connect, to exchange, even if they are more and more temporal. Maybe it is a new geography. It begs us to discuss an implementation of urban space beyond classical planning tools of 2D zoning.*'

It is undeniable that accepting conjectural approaches is also crucial in Winy Maas' architectural work, as he states in the same essay for Volume: Counterculture, '*I hate the prefix "re-": reinterpretation, renewal, renegotiation... "Re-" is killing everything. I think the word 'evolutionary' is the better goal. It suggests an evaluation of the trajectory that lies ahead of us without discounting that which came just before.*'

Clearly, the intentional motivation of fashioning a book about Latin American architecture, a very specific subject, by bringing a series of ingredients together in *a broadly open exploration* brought back the study to observations, to nomadic reasoning.

As described by Brian Massumi,[6] '*Nomad thought does not immure itself in the edifice of an ordered interiority: it moves freely in an element of exteriority. It does not repose on identity; it rides difference. It does not respect the artificial division between the three domains of representation, subject, concept, and being; it replaces restrictive analogy with a conductivity that knows no bounds. The concepts it creates do not merely reflect the eternal form of a legislating subject, but are defined by a communicable force in relation to which their subject is only secondary, to the extent that they can be said to have one. They do not reflect upon the world but are immersed in a changing state of things.*'

By all means, it became stimulating to think of an approach for the book project exactly divergent from any form of *didactic method*.[7] Instead of it the organizing system should be Socratic.[8] In that

4 From Mac Dictionary: contemporary – adjective – 2. Belonging to or ocurring in the present: ...*of our contemporary society. / Following modern ideas or fashion in style or design: contemporary architecture. ORIGIN mid 17th* cent: from medieval Latin *contemporarius, from con -'together with' + tempus, tempor -'time' (on the pattern of Latin contemporaneus and late Latin contemporalis).*

5 Winy Maas is one of MVRDV co-founders, Rotterdam –a global operating architecture and urbanism practice with a progressive ideal engaged in solving global issues. He authors the essay Yes, But published by *Volume Counterculture, 2010#2 that is referred in this piece.*

6 See 'Translator's Foreword: Pleasures of Philosophy,' *Brian Massumi, p. xii.* A Thousand Plateaus by *Gilles Deleuze, Felix Guattari. University of Minnesota Press, Minneapolis (third printing) 1991.*

7 From Wikipedia, the free encyclopedia: A didactic method (Greek: didáskein, *to teach; lore of teaching) is a teaching method that follows a consistent scientific approach or educational style to engage the student's mind. The didactic method of intruction is often contrasted with dialectics and the Socratic method; the term can also be used to refer to a specific didactic method. Didactics is a theory of teaching, and in a wider sense, a theory and practical application of teaching and learning. In demarcation from "Mathetics" (the science of learning), didactics refers only to the science of teaching.*

8 From Wikipedia, the free encyclopedia: A Socratic method (also known as method of elenchus, elenctic method, Socratic irony, or Socratic debate),

sense, as a different alternative, this work is just a multiplex construction, built out of interrelated, scholastic theories as well as of innovative events and experimental ventures on the architectural discipline in the region.

In essence, it is physical and conceptually a very challenging but simple project: the creation of an operational *vernacular-opera* through all central pieces. It is intended to be a potential future reference-tool for a chronicle of what goes on in Latin American architecture, at the very first decades of the third millennium.

Action. Movement. The book was based on the idea of *walking the topic* towards the intended goal; once again the reflection itself was a very much-constructed process. A process built by personal encounters, online convocations, and visits to offices, studios, and ateliers. Then evoked in individual analysis. The whole experience was like a massive discussion but operating at full pace. Many times a very enthusiastic cyber colloquy, many other times it was a stirring, more concrete dialogue.

Blueprint.[9] *Action + Variety*

Yes, variety counts.

> A sequence of topical segments *(organized as an unsystematic series and through a number of different projects in each case)*: a. the single family house (looking at the way people *live in* or *occupy* a place or environment / b. searches on bigger scales (does scale have a direct relation to dimension?) / c. poetical structures observed *(just that)* / d. topics under consideration *(invited compositions)* / e. a look over *laboratories*[10] (investigation, not just research) / f. terrain / landscape / topography (geography all around) / g. covering folk factors (*traditional* (adj.) *society* (n.)) / h. the volumetric reasoning *(reviewing physical features)*.

In communicational expression, along with taking into consideration the primacy of the Spanish tongue in that specific part of the world, the decision of writing a book about Latin culture in the English language firmly underpins the purpose of bringing to this stage other additional components –the Latin American ways of thinking of / building of architecture, to the more global architectural discourse.

To be honest, for some time before the genesis of this project, I frequently had begun questioning myself about the effective value of getting into a more inclusive architectural dialogue. To what extent would that purpose be more than just an extravagant, ambitious, or even an unnecessary compendium? Was the idea of *a global architecture dialogue* going to be fairly possible? In what ways/aspects if any, the completion of this project would contribute to the mainstream understanding of architecture? I became intellectually curious about finding the explicit, proper answers to those

named after the classical Greek philosopher Socrates, is a form of inquiry and debate between individuals with opposing viewpoints based on asking and answering question to stimulate critical thinking and to illuminate ideas. It is a dialectical method, often involving an oppositional discussion in which the defense of one point of view is pitted against the defense of another; one participant may lead another to contradict him in some way, strengthening the enquirer's own point. The Socratic method is a *negative method of hypothesis elimination, in that better hypotheses are found by steadily identifying and eliminating those that lead to contradictions. The Socratic method searches for general, commonly held truths that shape opinion, and scrutinizes them to determine their consistency with other beliefs. The basic form is a series of* questions formulated as tests of logic and fact intended to help a person or group discover their beliefs about some topic, exploring the definitions or *logoi (singular logos), seeking to characterize the general characteristics shared by various particular instances. The extent to which this method is employed to bring out definitions implicit in the interlocutors' beliefs, or to help them further their understanding, is called the method of maieutics.* Aristotle attributed to Socrates the discovery of the method of definition and induction, which he regarded as the essence of the scientific method.

9 From Mac Dictionary: blueprint – noun – a design plan or other technical drawing. figurative something that acts as a plan, model, or template. – verb – (trans.) draw up (a plan or model) : (as adj.) (blueprinted) ORIGIN late 19th cent.: from the original process in which prints were composed of white lines on a blue ground or of blue lines on a white ground.

10 From Mac Dictionary: laboratory – noun – a room or building equipped for scientific experiments, research or teaching. ORIGIN early 17th cent.: from medieval Latin *laboratorium*, from Latin *laborare 'to labor.'*

inquiries. This book could be a very classic working-model to continue exploring, and nurturing those interrogations and uncertainties.

(Theorems + Verifications) x More

> All material in nature, the mountains and the streams and the air and we, are made of Light which has been spent, and this crumpled mass called material casts a shadow, and the shadow belongs to Light. [11]

Apart from wanting to talk over the architectural field with a wider audience, as a Spanish speaker I pondered if it was not superfluous to engage in processing a critical piece of work on Latin American architecture that would demand using the English language. Maybe that was a welcome challenge and an indispensable tool for me. Far from stressing here the challenge of working with different languages at the same time, the really difficult task was the need of acquiring a permanent, high-degree research method, not only to define which was the substantial material that should be gathered but it was also important to learn *how to* revise, contrast, and edit that significant matter. It has been truly inspiring; almost the entire process was driven by an endless self-request of mirroring both cultures. Definitely, the whole project was deeply focused at paying attention to the two sides; and the inquiry technique has been a vital instrument to affirm every piece of the investigation, as well as to exchange the truly appropriate considerations, and to assemble them.

At different moments, the project also demanded to devote extra weight and additional responsibility to achieving a very clear visual-statement for the total narrative. Straightforward, since the very first sketches —almost at the end of fall 2009, the investigation had allowed me to understand better that the visual report should be almost a newly composed lexicon, one that could grant the opportunity of being acknowledged by an audience formed of more than a single culture. I was unquestionably aware that it was most likely that this prospective aspect of the book could be seen critically, or taken as a superficial slant. It is very right to state that the search of the *new language* disclosed itself as an indispensable quality to complete this book project. Not completely unexpected, perhaps it was by that vision that the project began reinforcing its objectives, keenly framing its determined firmness of being a book on architecture where visual communication is honestly meaningful and direct. Also in every aspect of this effort my scholastic aim was to assemble a book intended to encourage an extended and assorted range of cases for discussion.

Surely that was the exact position from where I started the means to this publication.

Architecture as Writing Philosophy[12]

> There is a great difference between writing history of philosophy and writing philosophy. In the one case, we study the arrows or the tools of a great thinker, the trophies and the prey, the continents discovered. In the other case, we trim our own arrows, or gather those, which seem to us the finest in order to try to send them in other directions, even if the distance covered is not astronomical but relatively small. We try to speak in our own name only to learn that a proper

11 From Wikipedia, the free encyclopedia: Louis Isadore Kahn (February 20, 1901 or 1902 – March 17, 1974) was an American architect, based in Philadelphia, Pennsylvania, United States. After working in various capacities for several firms in 1935. While continuing his private practice, he served as a design critic and professor of architecture at different American universities. Influenced by ancient ruins, Kahn's tends to the monumental and monolithic; his heavy buildings do not hide their weight, their materials, or the way they are assembled. Louis Kahn's works are considered as monumental beyond modernism. His work infused the International Style with a fastidious, highly personal taste, a poetry of light. His few projects reflect his deep personal involvement with each. The Japanese American artist and landscape architect, *Isamu Noguchi nameed him "a philosopher among architects."*

12 From Mac Dictionary: philosophy: ...the study of the theoretical basis of a particular branch of knowledge or experience. ORIGIN Middle English: from Old French *philosophie, via Latin from Greek philosophia 'love of wisdom.'*

> name designates no more than the outcome of a body of work –in other words, the concepts discovered, on condition that we were able to express these and imbue them with life using all the possibilities of language. [13]

I decided to include Paul Patton's quote since I first read it. It was a sort of *mantra* for this book project. It helped me to stay apart from creating just a compendium fragment of projects.

* * *

In order to get to an interesting range of testimonies, it was predictable that the research had to expand to give an exact dimension of features, of enough evidence to guarantee the probable, future assumptions/interpretations. In regard to succeed in that endeavor, this book makes visible a large number of carefully chosen architectural projects. According to the intention of following the predetermined purpose for the book not naively, but categorically from the comprehension that the discipline of architecture does not mean exactly the same as buildings, or just constructions, I worked with the profound conviction that it is equivalent to a reflective process of thinking. The *architectural projects* considered for publication were not only references to built examples but also to various types of approaches and strategies.

Almost all of these *oeuvres* are being published for the first time –in any language; and all of them have been done by architects and designers (*thinkers*) from Argentina, Brazil, Chile, Colombia, Ecuador, England, Mexico, Paraguay, Peru, Spain, the United States, Uruguay and Venezuela. In addition, the book includes several mentions of other artistic works as well as additional architectural proposals thought for, or performed in other countries: Bolivia, Costa Rica, Holland, Italy, Nicaragua, and Panama –in the majority of cases, developed by Latin American firms.

Weaving as a Course of Action

> A book is more than a verbal structure or a series of verbal structures; it is the dialogue it establishes with its reader and the intonation it imposes upon his voice and the changing and durable images it leaves in his memory. …Literature is not exhaustible for the simple and sufficient reason that no single book is. A book is not an isolated entity: it is a relationship, an axis of innumerable relationships[14].

Surprisingly, in the course of the exploration the spectrum of analysis multiplied its magnitude by itself, and in geometric progression. Among other aspects, the study spiraled up through a sort of an intuitive rational praxis of interlacing previous knowledge, connecting advised references and associations to the main topic, as well as recorded memories, involving broadened team projects, collaborative research, and related types of academic work. It has been exceptionally thought provoking to see the almost natural development of a very compact woven process, in which analogous architectures as well as notably similar approaches to it appeared occurring in parallel time but in very different territorial settings not only of the Latin American region but also of the rest of the world.

In that way, it was comfortably agreeable to assume the book narrative was echoing some of the *whys* meant for this publication. A wide-ranging line of projects was going to demonstrate the efficiency of mapping the argument for a unique and logical architecture connection. It was clear to see along the route of the project how emphatically that link could show an ongoing crusade, a concerted effort, perhaps something equivalent to what the long-established term 'movement' could connote as it historically did in the architectural field. However, the notion of effusively validating the existence in the region of a perceptible replication of a traditional 'architectural movement' would seem a fallacious statement. In any event, it was not an interesting search either. On the contrary, it gave me the

13 See 'Preface to the English Edition,' xv. Difference & Repetition/Gilles Deleuze: *translated by Paul Patton. Columbia University Press, New York, 1994.*

14 Jorge Luis Borges, essay 'A Note On (toward) Bernard Shaw,' 248-9.

impression that a natural panoramic fragment, in the manner of an introspective *potpourri*,[15] would flexibly articulate a more proper interpretation of that linked record of modern reflections and contemporary works on Latin American architectures.

In point of fact this publication was defining a deed to architecture: a deed sketched out by a resolute group of people working nearly at the same time, almost on identical subject material but in contrasting terrains. In addition to having performed a great contribution to document this project, the providers of writings and projects saw that the endeavor brought about the notion that it could stand itself as a significant channel, skillful enough to advance the profession they shared and to give a new impulse to their artistic ideas to the next level of experimentation.

A notable series of international institutions and universities associated to the architectural domain, together with a succession of correlated companies also supported in some way this publication. Likewise, from the early steps of the project, this last individual stance had been conveying to the surface another fascinating facet for the promised text. The scope of the designed actions comprised in the publication would be putting on display not merely precedents of what (*postulatory and physically*) is being produced in the region –programs, typologies, traditions, innovations, technologies, values... created by architects in their effective role of practitioners. The book would also get across to a detailed fruition of a generous amount of work that is being done by most of the same architects in their key responsibility as academics.

Yes, 360 degrees of observation –today more than ever. And the objective of paying attention to both, theory and practice together without taking one over the other.

The Academic World & the Empirical Arena

It is conventionally known that in the respected architectural setting, Latin America has constantly presented a very strong relationship between the orbit of ideas –the academic world, and the explicit realm of the construction of those ideas –the empirical arena. With the possible exception of a few isolated instances, most of the recent history of the architectural domain in the territory clearly displays some eloquent role models of the vibrant appreciation of that link. In fact, it has become very evident that this liaison has not been constructed only at a national level in each separate country. There are countless architectural examples/events that have been further endorsing that connection pushing it to an international stage, predominantly within South American countries, outlining a more 'regional' framework. Very probably this South American linkage is also underlined by a prevailing, well-spirited political discourse that has been lately occurring in the southern zone of the Latin American region.

Thus, it is right to acknowledge this book would not be excluded from that demarcated background.

* * *

> We (Latin Americans) are more about geography than fundamentally equivalent to history. Basically in South America what makes us countrymen is the geography, not the history. The exploration (the future) is geographical; the experience (the past) is historical.[16]

Without the intention of trivializing any possible methodology, the genesis of this book moved away from being just a romantic topography picturing a selected type of ideal views of reality through numerous architectural pieces. In opposition to that kind of strategies, (and *by a resolute, solemn promise*) this volume brings closer several acts of examining the strengths of architecture, as well as of experiencing its resistances.

15 From Mac Dictionary: potpourri – noun – a misture of things, especially a musical or literary medley. ORIGIN early 17th cent. (denoting a stew made of different kinds of meat): from French, literally 'broken pot.'

16 Rafael Iglesia, Argentinean architect. From his invited talk: *When the Problem is the Solution, inaugurating the Spring Lecture Series 2008, at the BSU College of Architecture and Planning, on Monday January 28th.*

It was understood then, that by doing that, the elements of the required *new-composed lexicon* would maintain the focus of looking at architecture entirely as a tool of action (*the qualifier*), instead of looking at architecture as if it were just the same as any regular noun, able of being qualifiable.

Once again and probably not totally unexpectedly the assembly of all these years devoted to a process of intensely learning about Latin American architecture, has been beneficial for me to clearly realize that I had begun acquiring a more and more pronounced interest in finding *a philosophical scheme*, perhaps *a humble theory*, that could likely be named as "no labeling."

In just one sentence, conveying a statement, even if it looks just as tautology architecture is architecture.

This statement, in a humbly respectful manner, suggests a possible parallelism to the 'everything is architecture' testimonial that *Corbu*[17] steadily claimed and maintained. I believe both declarations not only open the door with freedom towards architectural interests and architectural approaches but also demand a deeply serious conceptualization of what we architects understand by architecture.

The whole process pushed me to find a very solid evidence to activate the always precise and relevant principle I had set myself: it was not about characterizing the architecture (*the 'Latin,' the 'Good,' the 'Great...'*). The central essence was deeply connected with discovering the set of circumstances and particulars that allow architecture to have granted distinctive merits (*the character*) to a place, a region. Yes, geography.

* * *

Whom to call?
In the words of Oriol Bohigas: "those who make real things, the doers"
And that is what I have done.

Grupo R (*or a joint energy*)

My work is based on an ontology that believes in the existence of 'Being' as a non-finished structure. This structure is almost a permanently occurring circumstance, like a continual origination. Philosophy looks for the essence only in the same mode as (Martin) Heidegger[18] adopts a meaning for the German word 'Wesen.' He discusses 'Wesen' is not a noun (nature, being, essence, creature, character, entity, thing, person, soul, temper, quiddity, grain) but a verbal infinite: 'to be present.' Heidegger argues that philosophy is preoccupied with what exists but it forgets the question of the 'ground' of being. (Joseph) Quetglas[19] also refers *to that*

17 Commonly and familiarly reference to 'Le Corbusier' in the world of (*at least South American) architecture.*

18 From Wikipedia, the free encyclopedia: Joseph Quetglas Riusech (Palma, Balearic Islands, 1 May of 1946) is an architect and professor at the Balearic Politechnic University of Catalonia. Primary school and pre-university in the French Lycée in Barcelona. He studied architecture at the School of Architecture, title of architect, 1973; project manager Final: Rafael Moneo. Interested in teaching has been a professor since 1974 at the School of Architecture, starting teaching in the areas of Planning, Health and History of art and architecture, with professors Manuel Ribas i Piera, Xavier Rubert de Windy and Josep Maria Sostres. Title Ph.D., 1980, director of the doctoral thesis: Rafael Moneo. Since 1988, professor at the Polytechnic University of Catalonia, having their specialized teaching and research in the fields of art history and modern and contemporary architecture. He organized and directed a series of magazines and book collections on architecture. He has been typically recognized for "his tireless research and dissemination of studies on Le Corbusier built-in Massilia, corbusénnes Annuaires d'études" and his carreer as an architecture critic.

19 From Wikipedia, the free encyclopedia: Joseph Quetglas Riusech (Palma, Balearic Islands, 1 May of 1946) is an architect and professor at the Balearic Politechnic University of Catalonia. Primary school and pre-university in the French Lycée in Barcelona. He studied architecture at the School of Architecture, title of architect, 1973; project manager Final: Rafael Moneo. Interested in teaching has been a professor since 1974 at the School of Architecture, starting teaching in the areas of Planning, Health and History of art and architecture, with professors Manuel Ribas i Piera, Xavier Rubert de Windy and Josep Maria Sostres. Title Ph.D., 1980, director of the doctoral thesis: Rafael Moneo. Since 1988, professor at the Polytechnic University of Catalonia, having their specialized teaching and research in the fields of art history and modern and contemporary

exact belief in his work. We (architects) *should say 'entering,'* 'exiting,' 'connecting,' 'closing…' in preference to refer to just 'a door.' I do trust the reflection must be on the verb 'to inhabit,' and not on the noun 'house.' This mode of understanding has nothing to do with making the world more reasonable; it is about stepping out from the unblended contemplation, and getting involved in daily life. I search for an architecture that has the power of saying by virtue of leaving behind the naïve easiness of its own language.[20]

Globally acknowledged as one of the noteworthy leading architects in Latin America, Rafael Iglesia has been imbuing the current international disciplinal discourse of architecture with new vitality, essentially through his dialectical approach to architecture. Born in Entre Rios, but based in Rosario, Iglesia stands out in the Latin American sphere with a work that becomes exceptionally personal, in which the *structure* reveals the fundamental conceptualization for his architecture, and *weight* and *heaviness* the interpretational cogency to dispute the orthodox understanding of gravity. All with the sole use of stones, brick, logs, planes of concrete…

Especially in the South American architectural circle, any reference to Rafael Iglesia's theoretical or physical projects undoubtedly gravitates towards the highly concentrated work done by the Grupo R (*R Group*), a movement originated by a team of very young architects, in 1991, in Rosario –considered together with Cordoba the second most important cities of Argentina. Worthy of note, the members of the Grupo R did not have the objective of emerging by playing the role of imperative individuals for the architectural scene. Since almost all of them were at the initial phase of their careers, it was clear there was no intentionality either to actively show off their own architectural work. There was no 'architectural truth' to campaign for. As a matter of fact, each member of the team has worked independently from the others since the beginning of the group, and has advanced from very different slants and viewpoints. One could say that surely the focal motive for the creation of this alliance was generated over a very conducive *Latin* manner: the crew moved forward just from passion, based on their affinity of interests, and inspired by a fervent desire of changing the latent architectural *status quo* that was prevalent at that time in the city.

Those were the first years of a welcome reinstated democracy in the country –with a rhythmical replication in other nations of the Latin region, very predominantly in South America. The effervescence of a revived freedom as well as the ebullient need of expression became tangible symptoms manifested through diverse lines of artistic work –essentially, the vertiginous proliferation of different types of graffiti[21] and murgas.[22] Needless to say, as one of the arts, the architecture was not behind those indicators.

Informally formal, the members of the Group R associated to mold a singular strategy to channel a series of concerns and initiatives identified with the world of architecture, to primarily reestablish the disciplinal discourse of the city, and to make it known at national and international levels. Rafael Iglesia is one of the eight founder members of the Grupo R.[23] His work as well as the work done by most of his fellows are part of this book.

architecture. He organized and directed a series of magazines and book collections on architecture. He has been typically recognized for "his tireless research and dissemination of studies on Le Corbusier built-in Massilia, corbusénnes Annuaires d'études" and his carreer as an architecture critic.

20 Rafael Iglesia, Argentinean architect. From his invited talk: *When the Problem is the Solution, inaugurating the Spring Lecture Series 2008, at the BSU College of Architecture and Planning, on Monday January 28th.*

21 Graffiti is the name given to spontaneous inscriptions made on a wall or other surface in a public spaces.

22 Expression and connection drive the motor of the murgas in most of the principal cities in the region, creating an event that is unique to South American culture. Similar to the North American 'parade,' the murgas are groups of people that march through the streets with chants of pride and passion. The groups are diverse, comprised of members from local schools, neighborhoods (*barrios*), *and other organizations as well as volunteers from the general community. Whenever the murgas find it necessary, they gather together, sometimes joining with neighboring murgas -or even with murgas from bordering countries, for collective performances. After marching through the streets of the quarter or city, they ussually gather in a theater or plaza where they continue their performance on stage and interact with the audience. Each murga is a popular representation of its neighborhood and people, developing its own style and identity through poetry, music, and colorful costumes. Their songs are often artistic expressions of social and political situations in the city or in the country. The murgas typify the emphasis that South Americans place on community and publicly open popular art.*

23 Created 1991 Grupo R was composed of eight architects: Gerardo Caballero, Jose Maria D'Angelo, Rubén 'Pitufo' Fernández, Rafael Iglesia, Rubén Palumbo, Augusto Pantarotto, Gonzalo Sanchez Hermelo, and Marcelo Villafañe. All of them resided in Rosario, Argentina.

With schedules well organized, self-sponsored, and solid theoretical agendas the *Grupo R* began developing annual lectures series and other events that motivated the architectural discussion in the city of Rosario. The starting point was in 1991, with a one-week long conference: La Construccion del Pensamiento ("Constructing Critical Thinking in Architecture") with keynote speakers such as Mario Gandelsonas, Enric Miralles, Mario Corea, Clorindo Testa, and Justo Solsona among others.

The list of visitors became very large with the years. The same applies to the discussion that widened taking an international dimension. In the beginning there was a strong Spanish presence, mainly Catalonian from Barcelona. That connection was notoriously strong: Rosario, home of the Grupo R has many traits in common with Barcelona. Perhaps this is the reason why Oriol Bohigas[24] was one of the first guests of the Group. Bohigas' stance has always been strong in the theoretical debate and in his practice as an architect and urban designer. His work was already wellknown in South America. There is also the fact that the renewal of Barcelona for the Olympics[25] was at that moment a recent and very interesting model of urban actions based on the architectural discipline. Also from Spain the list of invited architects to Rosario grew in the years that followed, including Luis Peña Ganchegui (San Sebastian), Manuel Gallego (La Coruña), Antonio Ortiz (Cruz y Ortiz Architects, Sevilla & Amsterdam), Ignasi de Sola-Morales (Barcelona), and Jose Antonio Martínez Lapeña (J. A. Martínez Lapeña & E. Torres Architects, Barcelona).

I met by chance again Alberto Campo Baeza[26] a short time after I began this book project. Campo Baeza had been another Spanish professional who visited South America to take a part in the architecture discussion organized by the Grupo R. 'In Argentina there has always been first class architecture, he said. That's because Argentina is a profoundly cultured country. I would say that in terms of Modern Architecture it is comparable to any European country. Le Corbusier's only house project in the Americas, the Curutchet House (*Casa Curutchet*), is in La Plata, the Capital of (the province of) Buenos Aires. The same as in almost any other Latin country, in Argentina there are great modern architects like Clorindo Testa, and Mario Roberto Alvarez, or Kurchan and Ferrari Hardoy, partners in the Grupo Austral[27] (*Austral Group*) with Antonio Bonet. All of them are comparable to any of the European figures of the period. I believe the same is also valid about contemporary architecture of this time. I am sure there will always be interesting architecture discussion in Latin America; there are many examples'.

In the mid-nineties Grupo R raised its bet and gathered to discuss conceptual practices inviting

24 Oriol Bohigas i Guardiola (Barcelona, 20 December 1925) is a Catalan Spanish architect and urban planner. He is partner in the architecture office MBM. From 1980 until 1984 he has been the Director of Planning of the City of Barcelona. Among numerous awards, he has been distinguished with the Urbanism Medal of the *Academie d'Architecture de Paris*.

25 From Wikipedia the free encyclopedia: The 1992 Summer Olympic Games, officially known as the Games of the XXV Olympiad, were an international multi-sport event celebrated in Barcelona, Spain, in 1992.

26 Alberto Campo Baeza was born in Valladolid (1946); first saw the light in CADIZ (Spain) and the Architecture in Madrid (Degree 1971), P.H.D. in 1982. He became chairman and professor of design in Madrid in 1986. He taught in E.T.H. Zurich in 1989-1990, in Dublin (1992), Naples (1993), Copenhagen (1996), in EPFL Lausanne in 1997, in University of Pennsylvania (1986 and 1999), BAUHAUS in Weimar (2002), and Kansas S.U(2005). He has been visiting scholar and has lectured at Columbia, Harvard, Miami, Washington, and Chicago (USA), Palladian Basilica in Vicenza, IUAV in Venice and in Roma, and in Mendrisio (Italy), as well as in Portugal and Asia (China and Japan). In Latin America he was invited professor at universities in Argentina, Panama, and Mexico. His work has been vastly awarded. Among the most recent: First Award for the Spanish Pavilion in the Biennale of Venice (2000), the Award of the Bienal de Miami (2000) and the COAM Award (2002) for the Blas House. The COAB Award (2003) for the Centre BIT in Mallorca, the COAAO Award (2003) and Eduardo Torroja Award (2005) for the headquarters of the *Caja de Granada* and the Award Architecture in Stone (2003), in Verona, for the Almería Offices, as well as having been awarded in the BA Buenos Aires International Biennial and at the Biennial in Ponzano, Venice. A book of his collected writings 'La idea Construida' (*The Idea Built*) has become the 15th edition and monographs on his work have been published in different countries and languages. His architectural work has been exhibited in many major cities.

27 Campo Baeza's reference to the Grupo Austral (*Austral Group*) in Buenos Aires, Argentina; which in 1938 designed the known widely BKF chair. The partners of the group were Antonio Bonet, Juan Kurchan and Jorge Ferrari Hardoy, so the chair was named "BKF" after them. The BKF chair is a modern update of the *Paragon chair*, which was first made for use as campaign furniture in the 1870s. A later version of the design was known as the *Tripolina chair*, a portable chair introduced in the early 20th century. Jorge Ferrari Hardoy along with Antonio Bonet and Juan Kurchan developed the BKF in 1938 for an apartment building they designed in Buenos Aires. On July 24, 1940, the chair was shown at the 3rd *Salon de Artistas Decoradores* exhibition where the Museum of Modern Art discovered it. At the request of MoMA design director Edgar Kaufmann Jr., Hardoy sent three pre-production chairs to New York. One is in the MoMA collection and one is at the Frank Lloyd Wright house Fallingwater, but no one knows where the third chair went. Naming the BKF as one of the "best efforts of modern chair design," Kaufmann accurately predicted that it would become extremely popular. Likewise, Hans Knoll recognized its commercial potential and added it to the Knoll line in 1947 (extracted from Wikipedia, the free encyclopedia).

personalities beyond the limits of the Spanish language and similar background. Pablo Beitía from Buenos Aires, Eduardo Souto de Moura[28] (Portugal), Wiel Arets (Holland) and Carme Pinos (Barcelona) took a part in these meetings. The content of the discourse amplified the margins, edges, or frontiers. There was no outside or inside nor a front and a back. There were no factions or sides. There was a common topic and it was architecture.

Álvaro Siza (Portugal), Jhan Erickson (Finland), Per Olaf (Sweden), Carlos Ferrater (Spain), Ben Edman (Norway), Jens Arnfred (Denmark), Juhani Pallasmaa (Finland), Gonzalo Byrne (Lisbon), Pep Llinas (Spain), Joao Carrilho de Graca (Lisbon), Eduard Bru (Spain), and Adalberto Días (Porto) were the guests in symposia from 1996 until 2000. Even if Rosario was the city where "everything happened" the debate widened. The initiatives of Grupo R were replicated in Buenos Aires and lectures extended to the CAyC[29] two days after Rosario. The audience kept growing. Whether in Rosario or Buenos Aires Latin Americans joined the lectures: Uruguayans, Paraguayans, Chileans, Colombians, Venezuelans…

In the following years other groups appeared such as Paralelo 35[30] (Buenos Aires, 1997) or mxdf an urban research center, dealing with the production of space, its occupation, its defense, and the city as a theme: it was founded in Mexico DF by Tatiana Bilbao along with architects Derek Dellekamp, Arturo Ortiz and Michel Rojkind, among others. (Different segments of this book include the work done by many of the "Paralelos" –*Parallel 35*, as well as several projects designed by most of the members of the Mexican team).

Another recent association of a younger generation, *SuperSudaca* is presented as an architectural manifesto without a precise geographical location by forming an international network centered in South America displaying temporary partnerships. Some of these are international, brought together by a common interest in the content of the project. They establish another form of communication.

In several segments of this 'fragment' it would be interesting to see projects originated from countries extremely opposed in the map of Latin América (*rojkind architects* from Mexico + Dieguez Fridman Architects & Associates from Argentina, is only an example). In these partnerships, geography does not isolate offices but makes them near. That happens in the case when two or three offices in the Latin American region join forces to propose an architectural solution for Asian countries. Perhaps the heritage of the Grupo R –that somehow is akin to that group R (*Revolution*) of Barcelona, present-day shows a more modern version of cooperative action. One which values diversity as much as individuality.

* * *

The Structural Platform

The plan of creating an *open framework* as a supporting structure for the inquiry on Latin American architecture was, step by step, defining a wholly more interesting exploration. Again, there was not just one line to be communicated; there was a fabric of lines deserving attention.

Focused on one of the primary aims for this project –to achieve a fragment of modern architecture pieces, the process was indicating in every phase the need of a book rooted in transcending any dogmatic categorization. Accordingly, the investigation was embedded in going beyond any

28 On 28 March 2011, it was announced that Eduardo Souto de Moura is the 2011 Pritzker Prize winner, architecture's highest honor. He is the second Portuguese architect to win the honor, after Álvaro Siza.

29 The Art and Communication Centre (*Centro de Arte y Comunicación,* CAYC) in Buenos Aires was initially established as a multidisciplinary workshop in August 1968 by Víctor Grippo, Jacques Bedel, Luis Fernando Benedit, Alfredo Portillos, Clorindo Testa, Jorge Glusberg and Jorge González. From 1968 until his death in early 2012 Jorge Glusberg was the Director of the Center for Art and Communication. In 1972 the "Scuola de Altos Estudios del CAYC" was founded. In the seventies CAYC became an international center for the Pop art-culture and the famous Architecture Museum (*Museo de Arquitectura*). Well-known teachers at CAYC have included Justus Dahinden and Mario Botta.

30 Paralelo 35 was componed in its inception (1997) by Luis Bruno, Ana de Brea, Fabian de la Fuente, Claudio Ferrari, Pablo Ferreiro, Oscar Fuentes, Adrian Sebastian y Marcelo Vila. The group established for several years a kind of an architectural board for the Museo de Arte Moderno de Buenos Aires (MAMba), a place where the group every two weeks used to organize architectural presentations and discussions.

notion of cataloguing "one side" or "the other." Instead, it has aspired to highlight the synchronized seriousness of both the conceptualization and the materialization of an architectural idea.

In parallel to their full-time occupation as design specialists of architecture, practically all the professionals whose work has been gathered to be a part in this publication, have considered and dedicated time and vocation to education, in most instances without interruption for many years. All these erudite efforts have engaged their interest at distinct regional architecture schools, as well as having played the role of a pivotal change in prominent workshops, lectures series, conferences, or study-abroad programs all over the world.

The tangible notion of conceiving a book that would juxtapose theory and practice appeared to be spelling still another stimulating approach for the entire endeavor. From that explicit point of view, the publication transparently would gravitate in favor of placing itself as a tool-stratagem to inquiry about thoughts and facts. In other words, it would create a very indispensable and desirable fervor to re-embark on the large-scale architectural debate. In the same way, it would motivate the continuity of an international forum including both stages: the framework conceived with speculative and hypothetical propositions (*the academic world*), and the very conclusive text pertaining to the apposite actuality (*the empirical arena*).

A Blog-scenario

As an additional characteristic item, and not just regarding matters of certainties, it becomes imperative to state, the cutting-edge digital agoras currently accessible to interact in cyber forums have been a definitely helpful *modus operandi* to materialize this book. This is not a redundant consideration either. The availability of those communal, virtual assemblies have allowed the flexibility and congruous rhythm that are necesary to work in the world of today, especially in collaboration with a vast number of participants from widely differing locations.

It is not new; since several decades ago, the scheme of networking has been showing a very quick and close relationship to the architectural universe. Without any difficulty, and with gigantic, never-ending steps that trade-net has been producing a massively bonding series of fresh subsystems that any architectural process must diligently absorb. Moreover, it evidently has been making people approachable to operate interactively, and in a very comfortable and easy manner. Seriously taken, the networking system has been positively redefining the meaning of teamwork in architecture. A joint effort.
Emphatically, that procedure also unveiled a singularly attractive but intensely demanding aspect of the project: its basic dynamic of a permanent motion. I have already mentioned that; it seemed consistent with the principal goals of the exploration, to vividly detail its *ongoing-narrative* dimension in a graphical composition as well. In that regard, the purpose of displaying this complete analysis in a *blog*[31] manner, showed the best signs of invigorating that force in architectural literacy. Also, the blogging configuration pointed to the possibility of stimulating progress within the process of reading the book.

As I said before, there has not been in this project any direct intention of involving one dimension only. Certainly, in the creation of this libretto there was not a desire of 'linearity,' or of 'a final saying,' but a laborious set of formulations as an agreed substitute.

Again, this is not a traditional textbook. It is not a regular investigation. I do esteem to see it as a working, interpretational tool.

31 From dictionary.com: blog –*noun, verb, blogged, blog-ging. 1. noun a Web site containing the writer's or group of writers'own experiences, observations, opinions, etc., and often having images and links to other Web sites. An online diary; a personal chronological log of thoughts. 2. verb to mantain or add new entries* of a diary and to make them accessible to others. Also related to update.

Curious Asymmetry

Without vagueness, I could say that from day one of the book process all those earlier determined affirmations unexpectedly positioned this architectural essay in an increasingly expansive domain of questions. Conceptualizations and disquisitions on the topic germinated in every academic reunion I was part of; it was like a uniform journey involved in a strong pensive manner. Colloquially or conventionally, I have largely discussed those terms over the years of this project. In the more global and far-reaching world we live in, where every single thing gives the impression of rising or evaporating in just one second, how truly central does the notion of defining adjectives become? As it happens, I realized how difficult it was for me to get to an engrossing possible answer. At the end of the day, I was responsible to draw up a published work on Latin American architecture. For unknown reasons, by doing that I cultivated the idea of putting the accent on encapsulating, encircling, or all the more confining the architecture (*the modern, the contemporary*) to a species of type. On second thought, there are signs that it was more sensible to privilege looking at architecture (*the modern, the contemporary*) as a full entity, as a discipline with a distinct and independent existence, without keeping it within bounds. Architecture understood as a self-governing, nonaligned tool of action strongly capable of optimizing the world around us.

That was when I began noticing the absence of "Latin" thought and works in the international architecture scene. Only some isolated architects were known out of the continent.

I also wanted with strong determination to avoid any "kitsch" overtones, any apparently sensible or logical explanation. I did not want to restrict Latin American architecture to colour, form, technology or geographical situation. I did not believe such traits were meaningful enough. Neither did I want to restrict my research to comparative studies; I did not find similarities and differences interesting enough.

Could I do it directly from architecture as such?

I based my research on this stance; I wanted to cross-examine the real value –if any, of assigning "adjectives" in architecture. Now, thinking of how wonderfully uplifting the whole process has become, I would say once again that I pleasantly found evidence to claim that an inquisitive route is invariably better than a descriptive one.

Thus, it would be also central not to expect at this stage any precise backdrop of instructions that would help explain 'the Latin American architecture type/style.' Even more, it would not sound correct to use those words (*type/style*) for works that are explicitely contemporaneous. It would probably contradict any twenty-first century reflection (*progressively modern*) to vigorously voice that there is a set up prescription, a fixed doctrine, or any kind of "isms" that would apply to architecture. As far as I know, the elucidation of architecture as a tool of action in place of just only a question of form has been one of the most inspiring and conspicuous revelations of the discipline, as has been corroborated with the most solid string of examples all over history.

Then, instead of a list of descriptive points, this project congregates a collection of interpretations on the subject that potentially would assist the reader to understand the differences and similarities in culture(s) and in usage(s) of a prospective enclave that –particularly in South America, is in possession of much more than a common idiom, a reciprocal historical background, and a mutual physical zone in the concrete map of the world.

Indeed, this line of argument led to abstracting and materializing a collage book, in the manner of a potpourri or a patchwork. A book that would be constantly mapping complementary visions, as well as networking similar strategies. This fired a further enthusiasm in the author for this architectural platform.

Encouraging an Open Discussion

Just like the book by Orlando Barone 'Dialogues Borges – Sabato,'[32] inspired me to write a book of conversations of Mario Roberto Alvarez and Clorindo Testa –Señores Arquitectos, *Ubroc* 1999, this time it was not very different from that earlier book. Frankly speaking, one must admit at the time of the very first steps of this involvement, just a few years ago, two other thought-provoking *bibles*[33] had become a strong part of the series of intentional readings and willful exercises I habitually engage in my theory seminars or in the design studios I am responsible for, in my performance as an architecture professor. I should also add that I have been considering them while preparing a lecture or a presentation. Naturally the two books had happened to be a truly vehement cornerstone of my individual research investigations as well as very relevant for my corporeal architectural projects, and even in any other artistic piece I might generate. With authentic conviction I would say those books have been a manifest influence in bonding the layers of the present work together.

On one side, the ethical honesty of continuing to cross-examine the role of the architecture discipline in today's society, and that one inherent of its hero (*the architect*) as the central subjects of the *Berlage Institute* forum had equally captivated both my academic and my professional attention. It was also substantially interesting that the text was presented as the result of a fusion of a significant number of meanings, understandings, actions, reactions, and conversations. In my observation, that logic of multiplicity of angles visibly rendered the very attractive gesture of flexibility that I observe characterizes markedly our blunt modern times. On top of that, once again by virtue of discussing architecture, one could perfectly sustain the vivid impression that variety and tolerance might be defined as always-welcome symptoms of an every day more solid absence of uniformity.

Evidently contrasting in graphic mode of expression but maintaining a keen intellectual curiosity, any project with the signature of Rem Koolhaas is generally stimulating. *Content* –at that moment his most recent literary work performed for the present a function like that of the Berlage Report by having a broad amalgamation of approaches to a main architectural topic. *Content*'s seventy or eighty sections in the manner of magazine stories also helped strongly to activate Julio Cortázar's thought-provoking suggestion[34] of creating a book that could be read in a non-linear fashion; a book that would also challenge the notion of scale as prevalent aspect in the orbit of values.

Yes, quite unexpectedly, two European architectural publications were beginning to give their attention to the process that leads to fostering a book on Latin American architecture to be written in English. I thought that was a good omen. Since then, the interaction of cultures became a seriously motivating-force in the project, along with the emphasis on collaging that highlighted the 'motion side' of the book, emphasizing its three-dimensional quality.

I have to report that repeatedly in discussions, classes, and lectures, I found myself experiencing a coherent and a more robust necessity of reflecting once again on what architects explore –in every curve of the present global scene, when they look at architecture and produce architecture. Invariably, the notion of paying full attention to the large picture to contrast knowledge seemed to be essential if we wanted to be able to identify, if that was possible, Latin American architecture.

32 Argentine journalist, writer and university lecturer, in late 1974, Orlando Barone (1941-) arranged several meetings between Jorge Luis Borges and Ernesto Sabato, where these writers shared their different perspectives on various matters. These conversations were published in 1997, in the book Dialogues Borges-Sabato. The first edition quickly sold out, as did its following two editions. In 2007 it was re-edited.

33 Author's reference to the Berlage Institute Report, Hunch 6/7: 109 Provisional Attempts to Address Six Simple and Hard Questions About What Architects Do Today And Where Their Profession Might Go Tomorrow, by Jennifer Sigler and Roemer Van Toorn (episode publishers, 2003), and to the book Content, by Rem Koolhaas (Taschen, 2004.)

34 Author's reference to the foreword by Julio Cortázar for his own book: 62: A Model Kit (New York, 1972) also chosen to be a part in the intro of this book.

Becoming Latin

> ...You cannot connect dots looking forward; you can only connect them looking backwards. So you have to trust that the dots will somehow connect in your future.[35]

Identity as a trait began to appear strongly in my mind. In particular, what does identity mean in architecture?

Identity is not an atavism; it is not really inherited.

I do believe identity is deeper than singing the remembered lyrics of a tango or dancing a *cueca* or a *carnavalito*. Identity is projected to the future; identity wants to establish strong foundations for our children and beyond.

I began developing comparative studies; they were positive at the very start of my book project. Not long after I thought they were a set of very commonplace observations. Trying to unravel the sense of identity and meaning gave an impulse to research projects. Such projects were more interesting; I have to confess, than purely comparative research.

* * *

> A man sets out to draw the world. As the years go by, he peoples a space with images of provinces, kingdoms, mountains, bays, ships, islands, fishes, rooms, instruments, stars, horses, and individuals. A short time before he dies, he discovers that the patient labyrinth of lines traces the lineaments of his own face.[36]

I always found it unnatural to be called "Latina." If I remember correctly, I had always developed any variety of analysis from very direct topical focuses, in which geography was always pertinent but never understood only as setting. If there was something that defined being "Latin" I thought there were many aspects involved; honestly I thought that exceso probably would produce a loss of many subtle details. But, in generational terms, it was a widlely accepted, firm conviction that geography meant site but also situation; geography was the mathematical locus that defined a series of conditions of a particular subject. That was precisely the same as what happened in the immense, simple world of architecture.

Nevertheless, I wondered during the process of this project also about the "descriptive typology." It is known that in many studies about cultural topics, one, spontaneously, tends to give a value to the "typology" facts. As such, for a long time, I paid attention to contrasts and similarities in the organization of space, to the relationship of the use of those spaces, as well as the definition of the borders and composition of structure and much more; they become descriptive aspects of such. However, after a long meticulous period, my search demanded to follow only those parameters: architecture as a matter of relationships.

The intention of 'here and now' instead, was from the beginning of the undertaking one of the important objectives of this work. With that, I have proposed a global context in terms of relationships and focuses, and in terms of geography: the local, the regional. From this perspective, 'typology' in reference to 'stereotype' was shown keeping an eye in the second half of the last century. I have found out that in the Latin American regions, there were more diverse and interesting points of view in each case.

With the self-imposed, academic responsibility of learning better about the significance of 'Latinity,' I found myself more and more inclined towards a 'no type' type of investigation. The process to achieve this project guided me to notice this book could have been an ample fragment instead of just a segment. Through an exhaustive journey about what is being produced here and now, I had started to realize that

35 Extracted from Steve Jobs' Stanford University Commencement Address, May 2005.

36 Jorge Luis Borges, Afterword to *El Hacedor, 1960*

the identity in architecture does not differ from what it is said to be 'honesty in architecture.'

Also, and maybe there are too many objectives here but the modern times conceptually requires it, I did not want to define a book only for intellectuals related to the architecture discipline. I have tried to always create a piece of work, in which content could be appreciated beyond the academic world (from the very first moment I have been motivated to sum the 'Pop'[37] into the project; absolutely motivated).

Again, maybe from excessive pretentiousness, I did not think the work exclusively would be exposed for an academic validation but instead, on the contrary, I thought it would be more interesting to see the book as a tool of action, a working instrument to continue questioning and discussing what I mean when I refer to 'Latin-American architecture.'

In that regard, I had begun feeling responsible of understanding better the significance of culture. I started questioning the awareness of being Latin, and did it through a series of academic ventures and professional works. All those undertakings were put up in one way or another –exhibits, competitions, talks, papers, artwork, architectural projects, installations, studio-class subject of explorations. It becomes clear to me the book has been the result of a deep, observational process. It has been compounded as if it were an interpretation.

I must confess for good or bad –and it is not even important to define it, I had never been intrepidly interested in the regional or local. The interest of my architectural or art investigations has always had a very liberal spectrum. I have never thought of limiting myself. That point was something that caused great controversy of course in both, my academic work and my professional trajectory. Generally speaking it is thought 'the superficial' is something without content, vulnerable, and without value. I have even thought that adding the pop-concept would contribute to the perception of a massive book, vast and without strength. But even then I have set the bar in producing a conversational tool more than constructing a discursive book instead.

An extensive, copious, open and inclusive examination is not an easy task. In my work, that vision was crucial: to open up, to reflect upon, and to project. That necessity of a sufficient, inclusive view grew more and more by nature as I developed the process, becoming evident almost physically (in graphic terms) as the most solid objective of the work.

I became aware this libretto had to include visions from 'here' and 'there'. It should be a total libretto.

* * *

What is the vision of architecture in Latin America if somebody has never been there? Or, maybe has been in the region only from an academic point of view; or, just through the approximation you get from working and being part of a project; or, from just presenting a proposal from 'here' to 'there?'

Is it possible to give credit to that vision?

How should that be evaluated?

I would include the vision of those 'others' as well, those from Latin America, who now for professional or academic reasons practice the discipline in other lands. I thought the book should be put together in that manner without a doubt, and I have developed it with that conviction.

As such, my investigation manifested itself without prejudice of being inclusive of observations and

37 From Mac Dictionary: pop [2] |päp| adjective (attrib.)
1 of or relating to commercial popular music: a pop star | a pop group.
2 often derogatory (esp. of a technical, scientific, or academic subject) made accessible to the general public; popularized: pop psychology.

without stereotypes. I would like to say that it began to be (and continues to be) a modern investigation. From that point of view, I did not draw limits in the kind of readers I was expecting for this work. I have been interested in those objectives as challenges. My investigative work allowed for possible mistakes. We all know how much we can learn from them but we also know that when 'everything' is a success, one can make the mistake of not reviewing rigorously what has been done or is being done.

The academic observation from the 'inside' should be included as much as the one from the outside. The makers and the theorists should also be included; and of course, more.

Once again, I remember Corbu, and the importance of his 'seeing is a cognitive tool, not just a rethinal phenomena.'

Because of all those points, I am not presenting a single-minded selection. There is not a single color, or gender, or genre, or only one generation. The selection of works shows no unanimity of scale or size, it is not restricted to "green" architecture. Maybe the selection is somehow seen as colorful, and certainly displays a different geography. Perhaps this book can be read as a contribution to help us (*architects*) reflect about the meaning of geographical determination. Does it still mean physical limits or boundaries? In any case, it can renew the debate about what we call physicality.

At this point I had began being interested in "no limits" as in "no labels" or rather in the boundless.

Architecture is here a Latin American libretto in that direction, the direction of not having limits.
And in this ensemble my zoom focuses on some intended segments, where I find a series of works to be reflected on, and to analyse.

So here it is that simple. A total, colloquial libretto on Latin American architecture to evoke the dialogue, to meeting the conversation.

* * *

It is also important for me to say that since the beginning of my quest for Latin American Architecture, I was certain that three deep matters that the reader has to be aware of, to have in mind before entering this selection of works: materiality, art and clear concepts. These subjects led the inception of my work, and they are still my guide. This *fragment* mirrors the same notions, valid for the present in architectural thought. Any researcher could easily compile a list of names relevant for modern theory and design, belonging to most of the countries in Latin America. I thought important to provide a reference to architects of an earlier generation. The reader will understand that my professional background led me to interview three renowned Argentine architects. Trying to be coherent with my intention of not giving adjectives any special attention I started immediately my meetings and informal talks with Mario Roberto Alvarez, Clorindo Testa and Justo Solsona to incorporate them to the discussion.

Yes. Lets discuss about LATIN AMERICA and its ARCHITECTURE.

Following pages:
Just a few images of a lengthy succession of actions trying to questioning and contrasting knowledge and pieces of information to finally understand better the meaning of Latin American architecture + From shows at the Buenos Aires Museum of Modern Art as well as at other international venues and the membership in several groups of discussion to an even more responsible expedition including different studio settings and languages + Personal or group visits to projects [in many cases together with the authors] + Independent professional investigations along with academic affairs + Multinational workshops & studio talks... And MORE. It has been a seemingly endless junket. And will not stop here.

thoughts / reflection / projects
architectural graffitti from latin america

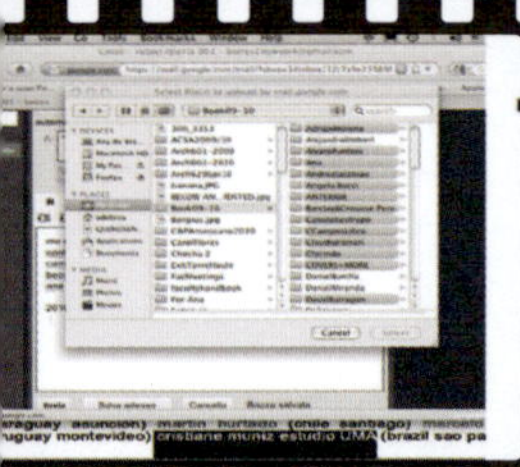
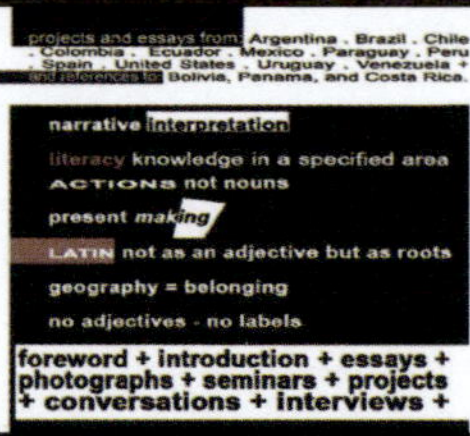
projects and essays from: Argentina . Brazil . Chile . Colombia . Ecuador . Mexico . Paraguay . Peru . Spain . United States . Uruguay . Venezuela +
and references to: Bolivia, Panama, and Costa Rica.
narrative interpretation
literacy knowledge in a specified area
ACTIONS not nouns
present making
LATIN not as an adjective but as roots
geography = belonging
no adjectives - no labels
foreword + introduction + essays + photographs + seminars + projects + conversations + interviews +

LATIN AMERICAN ARCHITECTURE exhibit

american architecture
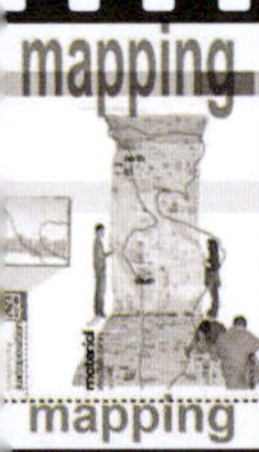
mapping
mapping

there is a
COMMON
THEME.
theSINGLEhabitation

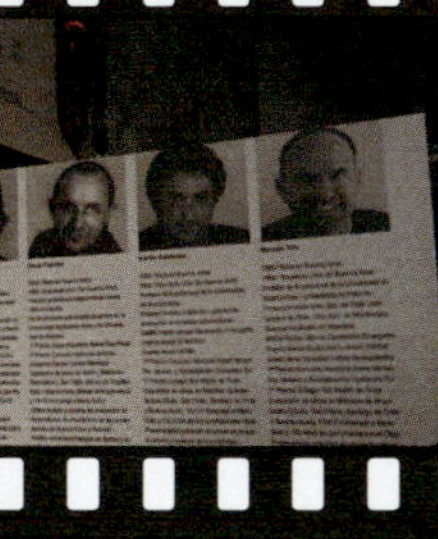
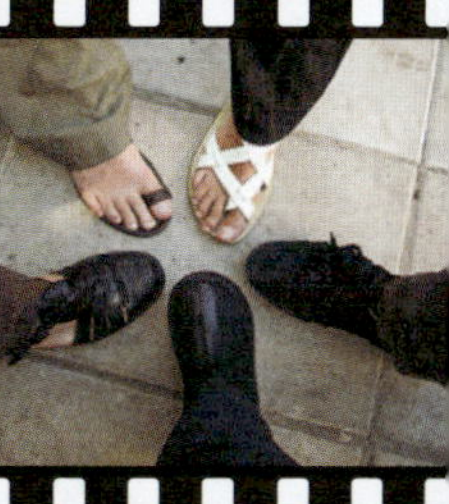

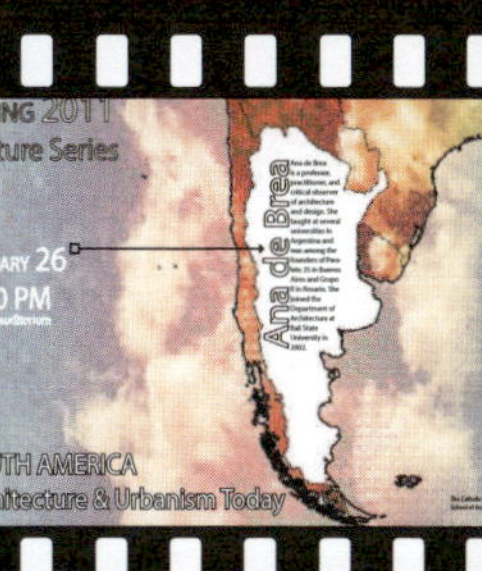
PRING 2011
ecture Series
ANUARY 26
5:30 PM
Ana de Brea
OUTH AMERICA
rchitecture & Urbanism Today

wall placement restricts views to historic port
...block out work...
...block out the street...
PORT
...el mayor trabajo de
...hecho por el hombre...
...language itself, the city remains man's greatest
...of art."
Lewis Mumford

VOLUMETRIC
LA CASA DE
PARAMETERS
CLORINDO TESTA
BUENOS AIRES
LINA BO BARDI
TOGETHER

From above to below / Left to right: Aqualina, Madero Office, Libertador 350 & Optima Business Park by Mario Roberto Álvarez.

Estética de la estática
(THE AESTHETIC OF PHYSICAL LAWS)

Interview with Mario Roberto Alvarez[1]

Four years ago, in Buenos Aires, Mario Roberto Alvarez received this chronicler in his office, very early, in a winter morning. Prosperously, the extensive experience gathered by dint of working as architecture columnist had allowed me the opportunity to meet Mario Roberto Alvarez long years back, at several times, and at very different types of events. I realize now writing these lines, we first met almost twenty-five years ago. It was the beginning of a close, collegiate relationship, which we had been developing since then, even including several publication projects done in collaboration. This time was the unique occasion to talk to him about Latin American architecture. With absolute certitude, I became aware of the fact that in any scenario, Alvarez and I had always communicated merely under the wider umbrella of architecture, through long discussions on its appreciations and values. In all those dialogues, Alvarez was up to date, with the latest knowledge of what was currently coming about the small, great domain of architecture from all over the world. In all those conversations, he had devoted appropriate references to architectural actions he agreed, or disagreed with –I lucidly recall Alvarez used to say "I do not understand it," principally in reference to architectures that did not follow the Miesian principles, in all planes of thoughts, ethics, logics, aesthetics… Alvarez masterly constructed the concept of physical sophistication in architecture, with a large list of projects of different kinds. However, without doubt, it must be said that physical sophistication stands as the common shape for any of his buildings. I would assume it was not just with me; but I should say Alvarez has never spoken about architecture employing "Latin American," or "not Latin American," terms. It was just about architecture. I remember I captured that testimonial memory, thinking of it as a possible, other piece of evidence for this publication, towards affirming that architecture should not be qualified only by an oblivious use of shallow adjectives. I deliberately put myself on the side of looking for a discussion on Latin architecture that would be based on an interpretive manifesto, not on a descriptive one. That would be a skeptical consideration in relation to architectures by Mario Roberto Alvarez; he had developed (and expanded) a singular, disciplinal exegesis, showing firm and constant support of that understanding. In the Latin American sphere, his work is strongly seen as synonym of a linear performance in architecture. The same as I had done almost once a year since residing in the United States, I paid a visit to Alvarez's office that morning. We had concerted the meeting by phone. I sincerely admit the vivid conversation had already started whith that phone call, a week before. I felt privileged of having shared that exceptional relationship with Alvarez, but mostly from discovering (one more time), how openly, and in the habitual elegant manner, he had answered to a new architecture voyage I was putting forward. From the very beginning of this book venture, (even after irrefutably defining its focus on questioning the most recent set of reasons, and logical lines of thinking in the region) I knew I must discuss the topic also with Alvarez. Any book on modern architecture in Latin America would not avoid his work as a prominent precedent for the new generations. One could positively say, a large number of professionals conceive of Mario Roberto Alvarez as an architecture trademark, an emblem of solid rationalism, strong convictions,

1 Mario Roberto Álvarez (November 14, 1913 – November 5, 2011) was an Argentine architect. Alvarez was considered one of the most productive and emblematic representatives of the rationalist approach to architecture in Argentina.

and vigorous discourse. Alvarez and I based our friendship on that seriousness; I have learned enormously from him. Thousands of architects have learned immensenly from the work of his office. He was ninety-seven years old that morning, in Buenos Aires. I would say I could see him expressing his analyses for the exact, meticulous notions about how discipline and professionalism are compelled to the architecture field, in the same way as he did in every earlier encounter. Particularly in South America, Mario Roberto Alvarez symbolizes the head of a line of thinking; he represents a singular architectural doctrine based on modern paradigms. "Come in, let's talk about architecture," he said to me pointing the seats around the table. That was the way we had started the conversation. *Our last dialogue*[2].

AdeB. In this global world, should we look at architecture as a noun (*object*)? Or is architecture an action (*a verb, a tool*)?

MRA. Since men abandoned the caves, when they left the caverns behind, architecture has been an object, a tool, and a verb. The evolution of humanity has had obvious transformations, and architecture has helped through heroic periods of action, as well as of theoretical discussions. The Modern Movement has been one of those episodes of daring, in which architecture was trying to adapt to the world through declaring new paradigms, discussing different social issues, as well as dissimilar economic and political frames from the ones inherited from the Industrial Revolution.

AdeB. Is it possible to speak of Latin American architecture in terms of objects of production?

MRA. It depends where that *object* is inserted. If the site is an urban location, and the project is an office building, or a housing complex, or even a single-family house the answer would be "no." I would say that very probably all those projects would have a number of common aspects in any urban setting, situated in any metropolis of the planet. Perhaps the suburban, or more rural environments, show more opportunities to see more legitimate factors that could relate to any of the particulars of culture, maybe accentuated through technological differences mainly because of typical climatic backgrounds. The peripheral areas are where the landscape might appear. Metropolitan cities are more cosmopolitan; they have a specific rhythm, a unique dynamism... Anyways, I do not believe there is a type that could be defined a "Latin' American architecture.

AdeB. Have you seen yourself reflected in the architecture work done by other Latin American architects? Luis Barragan[3]... Laureano Forero[4]...

MRA. I did not have the opportunity to know them personally, but I do know their work. I suppose that if there is a possible relationship, it arises in some common points of a modern architectural vision.

AdeB. Does the type of technology used in a project influence the architectural identity?

MRA. Yes, but it is not a determinant. Projects can be generated with diverse technologies without losing their identity or contemporary spirit.

AdeB. Is there a new identity for architecture? Has architecture become more global?

MRA. Yes, and in many cases. As a rapid example, just consider the office buildings... Over the last decades architectural fashions, or architectural manners, have emerged, and they tend to create more and more eccentric buildings in order to become unique, and isolated from the common factors or identical, constructive components found all over the world. In this way the mode of refuge is the form as the goal, and the most unconventional form possible. This is the disability of architecture, opposite to other disciplines, such as aeronautical engineering where the result must be a plane that "must fly." Could you imagine the approaching of eccentric forms applied to aeronautics? I believe I would never travel by air again.

2 Mario Roberto Alvarez died the 5th of November, 2011 in Buenos Aires, Argentina, nine days before his 98th birthday.

3 From Wikipedia, the free encyclopedia: Luis Barragan (Guadalajara, March 9, 1902 – Mexico City, November 22, 1988) was a Mexican architect. He studied as an engineer in his hometown, while undertaking the entirety of additional coursework to obtain the title of architect.

4 Laureano Forero. Born in Medellin, Colombia. He obtained his degree with honors in Architecture from the *Colombia National University*, at Medellin District, in 1962, and a *Technical Principles in Buildings Diploma*, by the Milan Polytechnic, Italy, 1964. His post-professional studies took place at the Architectural Association, London, England, 1965.

AdeB. Does architecture have to have an identity? Is that related to a type of components? Or is it to the replication of modes, of manners?

MRA. I am going to answer with a known saying, but I believe it is a very effective example. We all have two eyes, a nose, a mouth, two ears, ... Nevertheless, we all have our own identity. The same concept should be applied to architecture. In analogy with my previous response, I would say the problem appears with architecture that shows two mouths, three eyes, and other distortions…

AdeB. Do you believe there are certain aspects that communicate the Latin condition in reference to the concept of "belonging"?

MRA. Perhaps, particularly in Argentina, the Latin American setting relates to history; we have developed through immigration, big ships crossing the Ocean… If in addition to history you sum the current globalization… We understand the possible Latin-American identity is composed of a diverse series of aspects.

AdeB. Is it sufficient to say that there is a way of thinking of the architecture in Latin America? In this case, how is it framed?

MRA. Architectural production is not related to a region. It depends on varied factors: economic, social, political, climatic… All these factors are not even the same, in fact very dissimilar, in different areas of the Latin American territory. Probably these are all subjects that are analyzed and discussed at different levels of the architecture education. It is good that discussion probably exists. But to me architecture is a tangible, built concept. It emerges as a phenomenon of several factors and variables working together, but those conditions could come from distinct realities of the region. We could probably find affinities between projects, and may be they relate to the concept, or to the essence of the project. But even in this case, a building in Buenos Aires, Mexico DF, or Sao Pablo could have more points in common with another building in Tokyo than with other pieces located in the same city.

Mario Roberto Alvarez in his office.

This overlapping color and spontaneous compositional beauty is a phenomenon based in place. There is a spirit to these moments that are not designed or staged, but happen through cultural forces. (2007_Paul Puzzello).

para vos
la ciudad que queremos.
Hay un lugar para vos
en la ciudad que
PARTIDO SOCIALISTA
El progresismo en la ciudad
Hay un lugar para vos

From above to below /Left to right: 1. Clorindo Testa gave life and vitality to the Brutalist movement with his headquarters for the *Banco de Londres y America del Sur.* His interpretation of the beton brut style of concrete construction was refreshing among the many copycats if his age. 2. Testa's Biblioteca Nacional de la Republica Argentina shows the artistic and fun side of brutalism by elevating the entire building in the air and by playing with color, shapes, and impressive monumentality. 3. Vivienda en Pinamar by Clorindo.

The Relation with Art

Interview with Clorindo Testa

It was in June 2009, in Buenos Aires. I arrived to the office around 9:00 in the morning. I saw the very familiar picture: Clorindo seated at his desk, with his classic suit and tie attire, and a regular pencil in his hand immediately on top of a big piece of tracing paper. Once again Clorindo Testa, the singular artist, the personal architect, was sketching ideas. If I remember correctly, he had received an invitation to participate in a collective art exhibit that was being organized as homage to *The Beatles*. He seemed to be as excited as in any new beginning. This is also a repeated image of him: that infectious energy towards the exploration of new ideas. Clorindo has always represented to me the values of an unusual modern expressionism, the ethic of those serious thoughts that observe deep philosophies, claim profound statements, and encompass a particular inflection in their formal vocabulary, but all of that without saying it out loud. I have at all times imagined Clorindo Testa would define an architect as someone who is responsibly in charge of telling the creative but real visions of his time –very modern, concrete fantasies. As a bonus, Testa has been able not only to tack from one project to another to develop a remarkable vocation, but also one art –*his* paintings, sculptures, and installations to another, his architecture. He has done it in a very skillful and accomplished way. In fact, he is frequent and affectionately referred to as *Maestro*, "master." I perfectly remember I knew about Clorindo Testa while in my first years as an architecture student. That was the very end of the seventies, and Clorindo (with Jacques Bedel and Luis Benedit) had won the competition for the *Centro Cultural Recoleta* "Recoleta Cultural Center," a public exhibition and artistic events complex located in Recoleta neighborhood, an area of significant historical and architectural attention. The site for the project was very important even in terms of dimension; it joined a number of formerly existing buildings that originally belonged to the Franciscan Order. In the adjacent area, buildings such as the *National Fine Arts Museum and the National Library of Argentina* (also designed by Clorindo Testa, in 1962, with Francisco Bullrich and Alicia Cazzaniga) among many relevant others, as well as the *Plaza Francia* –the French Plaza, famous since the 1960s because of its street fairs, and also the idiosyncratic *Recoleta Cemetery*[1] unexpectedly leading a district full of life and nature. I can evoke in detail various facets of the whole construction process of that project.

One day, I was very young; I asked my father what "beauty" was about. Probably, I had heard that word but did not know what it meant. My father brought a book –one I still keep, on Greek sculptures, and pointed me the Victory of Samothrace[2]. I said, *"but, Kodama, it does not have a head."* And he answers: *"who told you that beauty is a head? Look at the folds of the robe; the breeze from the sea blows the folds. The capture of that breeze, and making it*

1 Recoleta Cemetery is located in the Metropolitan Buenos Aires, next to a former monastery. As the manifestation of great pieces of nineteenth- and twentieth-century of funerary art and architecture, this cemetery becomes one of the most daily visited places in the city by a large number of local and international tourists.

2 From Wikipedia, the free encyclopedia: *The Winged Victory of Samothrace*, also called the Nike of Samothrace, is a 2nd century BC marble sculpture of the Greek goddess Nike (Victory). Since 1884, it has been prominently displayed at the Louvre and is one of the most celebrated sculptures in the world.

visible through the movement of the folds of a robe for eternity, that's beauty".[3]

One of my close college classmates was working at that moment as a junior assistant of the construction site, and that was the reason I could habitually visit the project for the Recoleta Cultural Center, before going to school. My friend and I used to spend precious time observing the meticulous aspects of the design drawings and construction documents that were displayed all over temporary spaces built for in situ meetings. I conserve a vivid impression of those moments. I would say that was probably the first time I saw the developing of a piece of architecture in which modernity was clearly shown as the thoughtful and respectful dialogue between the past and the present. In a very smart, lucid way the project communicated to the users that "respectful architecture" meant a lot more than impersonating what it is revealed across the street. More than thirty years ago, in my first studies, it felt as a revelation. I recall myself contemplating in ecstasy the originality of that composition. A number of the existing buildings involved probably some of the oldest in the city a church built around 1730, and a convent turned into a shelter for the homeless hundreds years later, were going to host the exhibition galleries together with some additional volumes, all of them rendered in pastel colors. Also, the uncut skeleton of the old private church of the abbey, in vibrant terracotta would be transformed into the auditorium required for the new program... And more. Certainly, much more. I could say that experience has been a cornerstone in my actual understanding of architecture. In a totally subjective manner, I tend to join my experience in following the process for the *Centro Cultural Recoleta* with examples such as the *Glass House*, by Philip Johnson[4], or the *Beinecke Rare Book and Manuscript Library*, created by architect Gordon Bunshaft[5], among other singular buildings from all over the world, developed around the transitional period from the first to the second half of last century, that have challenged us (professionals – educators) to think about the meaning of honesty in architecture. Architectures that appear to be more interested in paying contemporary reverence to high principles than in being defined as an individual type.

It was soon after those years that I met Clorindo Testa for first time. To my amazement he was the invited speaker in my graduation ceremony. Since then, I must say, happy and thankfully, I have had the immense fortune of accompanying Clorindo in many disciplinal events. He has been a sort of mentor in my walk of life; I have visited each of his projects, and looked for his opinion on subjects related to the world of art and architecture I was interested in. As is predictable of a modern thinker, he has been always open for discussion. Just like now, roughly three decades later from that first time, when he is seated in front of me to start our conversation.

CT. I believe we could affirm there is a Latin American architecture type... no, I would better say a Latin American architecture nature. If you look at it carefully, you find that the concept is generic in the world; the world discusses about theories, philosophies, ideas, approaches, technologies... But the sun and the landscape are the real truth, they do not show strong variations so we have to pay attention to those aspects, we need to

3 See any of the different online audio-visual or diverse types of internationally published interviews to Maria Kodama. She describes the anecdote in most of the cases to introduce the subject and/or when she directly reflects on the meaning of aesthetics. Also in some of them she refers to the moment when she shared with Borges the same story. Maria Kodama is the widow of Argentine author Jorge Luis Borges and sole owner of his estate after his death in 1986.

4 From *Wikipedia*, the free encyclopedia: Philip Cortelyou Johnson (July 8, 1906 – January 25, 2005) was an influential American architect. In 1930, he founded the *Department of Architecture and Design* at the *Museum of Modern Art in New York City*, and later (1978), as a trustee, he was awarded an *American Institute of Architects Gold Medal* and the first *Pritzker Architecture Prize*, in 1979. In 1949, inspired by Mies van der Rohe's Farnsworth House, Johnson designed the *Glass House*, in New Canaan, Connecticut; an exact geometry with exterior skin of glass walls with no interior divisions, which is considered one of the most talented works of modern architecture.

5 From Wikipedia, the free encyclopedia: *The Yale University Beinecke Rare Book and Manuscript Library* (BRBL) was designed in 1963 by architect Gordon Bunshaft (May 9, 1909 – August 6, 1990) of the firm of Skidmore, Owings, and Merrill, and is the largest building in the world reserved exclusively for the preservation of rare books and manuscripts. The six-story above ground tower of book stacks is surrounded by a windowless rectangular building with walls made of a translucent Danby marble, which transmit subdued lighting and provide protection from direct light. Extracted from SOM (Skidmore, Owings & Merrill) website. *On Beinecke Library* by Gordon Bunshaft: "...if they are handsomely done, great spaces give an emotional experience to people." Gordon Bunshaft was awarded with the Pritzker Prize in 1988, sharing it with the Brazilian architect Oscar Niemeyer.

6 See *Class Notes - Tschumi and Mori on the Education of Architects*, by Susan S. Szenasy. "Metropolis," August 2003.

produce architecture for those constant features; we need to interpret the sun and the geography, because they express different conditions in North America, or in South America, in Europe... Those are seriously singular elements that can make a difference. It is not better or worse, it is not a type, it is just about understanding differences.

AdeB. Is architecture a noun (object)? Or is it an action (a verb, a tool)?

CT. I like to think of architecture as the concretion of an idea. I believe it depends on who makes the architecture that it can be a message or a tool, or just the construction of a series of functions. Architecture itself is a serious subject; we (architects) are responsible for the architecture that we produce, and we are also more or less in command of how we use it. The same as with creativity, or with the arts, it is always subject to everyone; it is not a topic that can be easily taught or cultivated. Architecture is a discipline in constant change, and needs a lot of compromise from the people that create it.

We (as educators) have to create an atmosphere and a space where students and teachers can do their most creative work. I compare it to being a film producer instead of a director. That is the task shift from architect to chair. You produce a body of work —which may or may not be architecture— by putting people, ingredients and stories together to make things happen. Education is invisible really. So you have to make certain intellectual, aesthetic, and spiritual investments.[6]

AdeB. What is your interpretation of "identity" in architecture?

CT. I have always valued the moment. I enjoy the world of ideas, and consider it is very interesting to take that idea to the highest level possible. I have always tried to do that; I have always appreciated that fabulous instant of making the conceptual decision that would drive the whole project. That adrenalin has always been a motivation for me; it is a precise project, with specific conditions, in a particular site... There is a frame that we must interpret, and we must translate it into architecture. I believe architecture is in the comprehension of those particularities. It is in that reflection that we find architecture; it is in the way we observe the situation. And time plays an imperative role; architecture must be a reflection of the moment in which it is produced. Architecture has to be in accordance to its time, and cultural manners, and the usages of that special region. It mirrors a way of understanding lives and situations, and from there we (architects) should be able to make architecture in any part of the world. In my opinion, that is the definition of modernity. I honestly believe there is no choice, we have to be modern, and architects should be modern in agreement to the present times. If there is an identity in architecture it relates to that: the need to be modern. That is the reason I disagree with the designs of private neighborhoods, the gathering of a number of houses distributed behind a gate; it does not have anything to do with modern life, with modern cities, where dynamism, flexibility, and an explicit combination of matters are essential aspects that function together and produce the environment where metropolitan life can develop.

Image of the visit to Clorindo Testa's office in Buenos Aires, 2009.

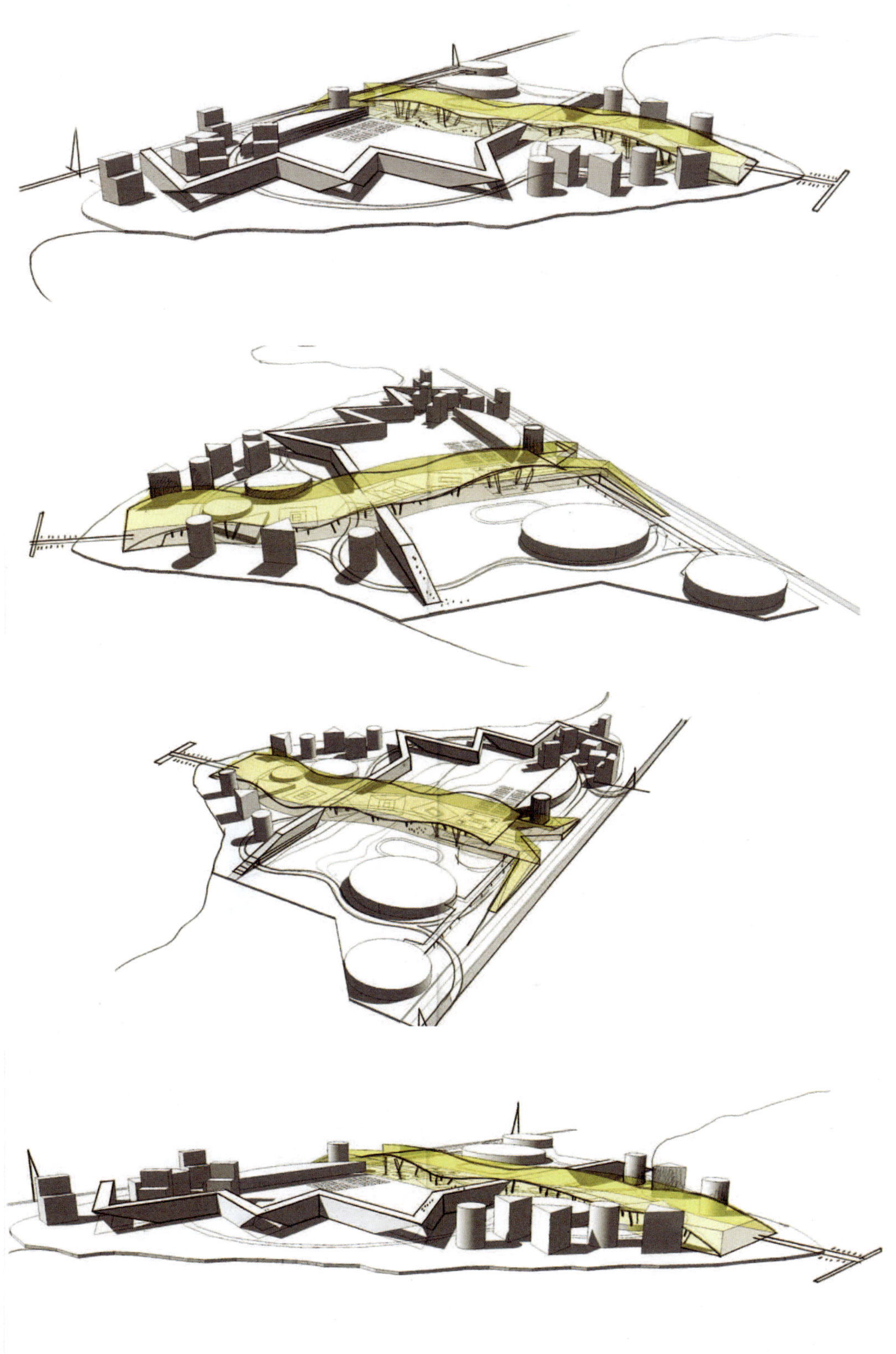

Original sketches by Clorindo Testa on his proposal _In association to H. Torcello and Studio Converti, submitted to the International Competition Rio de Janeiro Olympic Games, 2011. Cortesy by Horacio Torcello Architects.

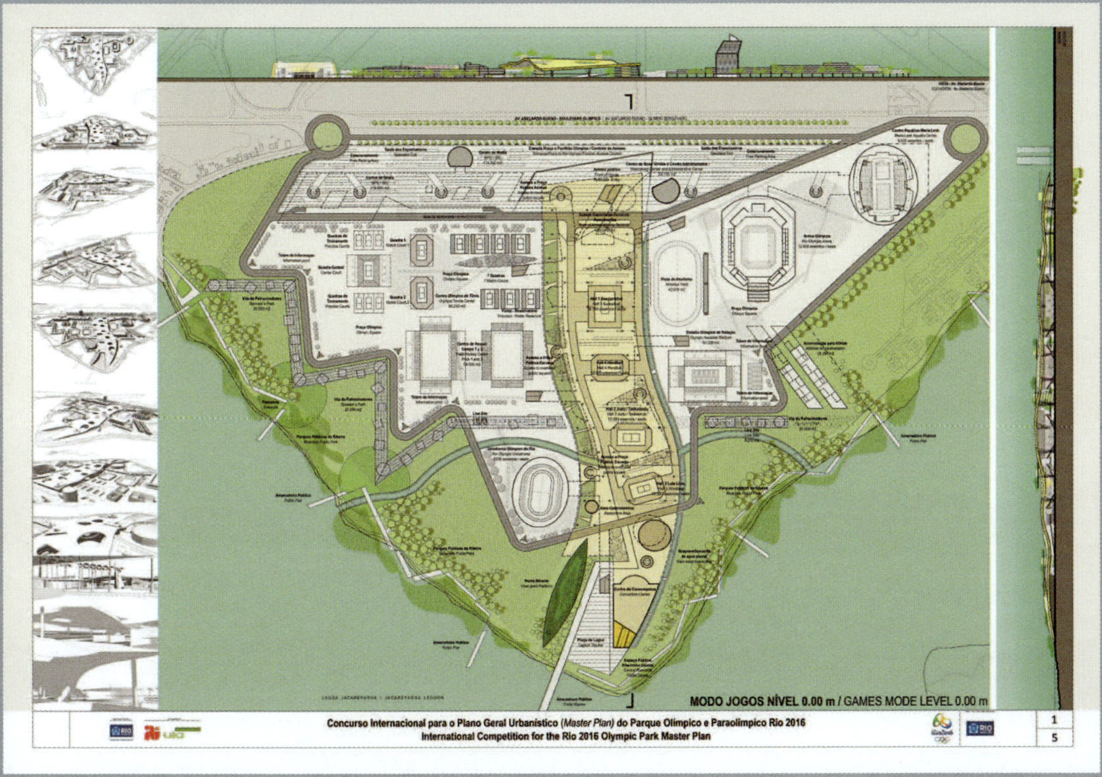

MODO JOGOS NÍVEL 0.00 m / GAMES MODE LEVEL 0.00 m

Concurso Internacional para o Plano Geral Urbanístico (*Master Plan*) do Parque Olímpico e Paraolímpico Rio 2016
International Competition for the Rio 2016 Olympic Park Master Plan

1
5

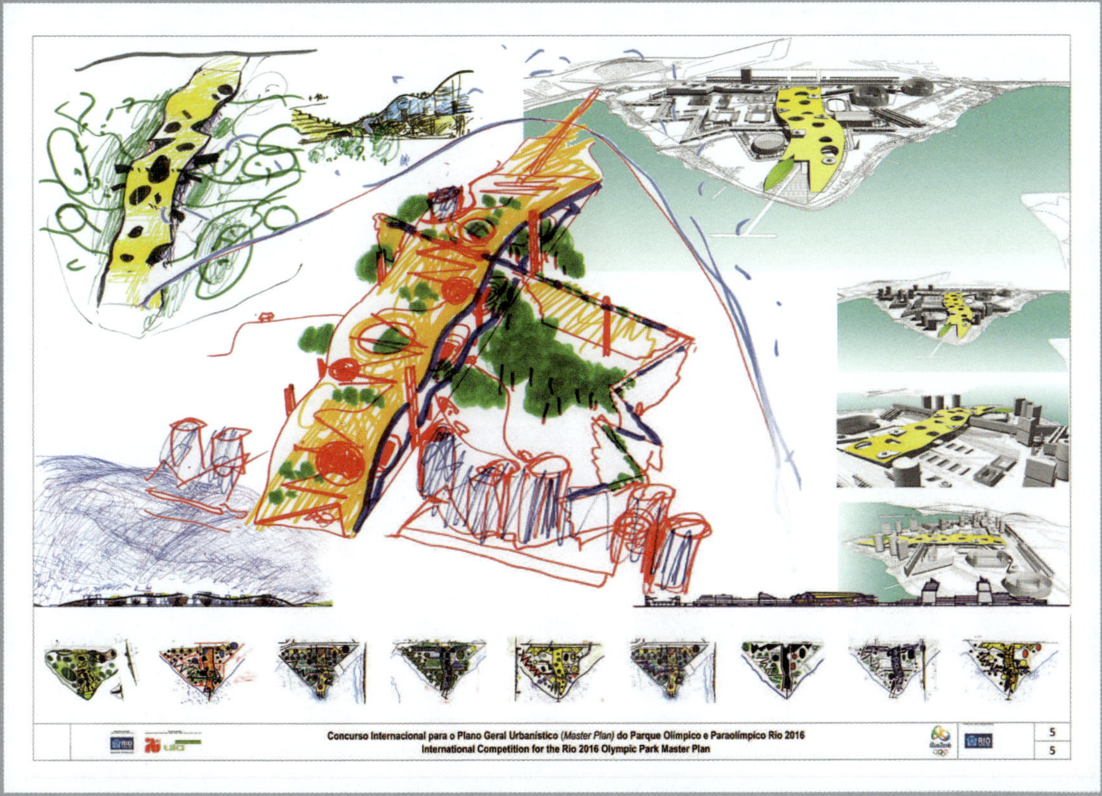

Concurso Internacional para o Plano Geral Urbanístico (*Master Plan*) do Parque Olímpico e Paraolímpico Rio 2016
International Competition for the Rio 2016 Olympic Park Master Plan

5
5

Geometry and the Clear Plan

Conversation with Justo Solsona

A few words on Latin American architecture

Manteola, Sánchez Gómez, Santos, Solsona, Salaberry Architects (M|SG|S|S|S) are working as an architecture office since 1966. All the principals have been developing academic activity at School of Architecture, Buenos Aires University (FADU UBA). Santos was an associate professor teaching design studios from 1962 to 1964; she also worked as a Torcuato Di Tella University Counselor. Manteola is a professor of architecture leading her course at FADU UBA. Sánchez Gómez is full professor at FADU UBA. Justo Solsona is full professor at FADU UBA and Director of the Master Advanced Architectural Design Programe in the same national school. Sallaberry was Head of the College of Architecture at Palermo University until 2009. Solsona, Sánchez Gómez and Manteola, also have been members of professional institutions such as the National Federation of Architects, and Central Society of Architects. Among their most important projects: Buenos Aires International Ezeiza Airport (2000); Corporate Headquarters as Industrial Union of Argentina (winning the national competition in 1967), Prourban office building (1977); sports facilities such as Mendoza Football Stadium (World Cup 1978); Manantiales Housing Building, Uruguay (1978); and the TVN National Television, Santiago de Chile, after being awarded first prize in the regional competition in 2000. The team has been awarded profusely nationally and internationally, and has been invited to lecture at the most important universities throughout the world as well. In addition, the work done by the office has been included in a great number of the most eloquent global architectural publications: Casabella (Italy), GA Global Architecture (Japan), Progressive Architecture (USA), Techniques d"Architecture (France), Der Architect (Germany), Arquitectura Viva (Spain), ELARQA (Uruguay), and projecto (Brazil) among others.

In every ocassion I have travelled to Argentina since my arrival in the USA I visited Justo Solsona ("Jujo" for almost everybody that belong to the architectural world in the region). Located very near to the Kavanagh building and the San Martin Square in Buenos Aires, his office shows always a particular sinergy. July 2010 was not the exception. At that time, when this book was being developed, the idea of including his name was unquestionably considered. By virtue of his projects, his teaching, and his writings, Jujo Solsona, undoubtably becomes a pivotal part of any architecture discussion but very specially when it relates to modern conceptualizations and contemporary thinking in South America. Informally formal our conversation covered a number of topics that afternoon; from circunstances of the everyday life to the most recent work done by graduate students at the University. It was not accidental that we also spoke about diferences and similarities that the field of architecture (education and practice) reveals in the north side or the south side of

From above to below / Left to right:
1. 1957_ Towers in La Boca Competition. City of Buenos Aires, Argentina.
2. 1964_ Houses in Santa Teresita, Buenos Aires Province, Argentina.
3. 1968_ Municipal Bank of Buenos Aires City Main House, City of Buenos Aires, Argentina.
4. 1985_ International competition "Progetto Bicocca", Milano, Italy.
5. 1995_ Swimming Pool Complex for International Competitions in Mar del Plata, Argentina.
6. 2005_ Mulieris Towers, Puerto Madero, City of Buenos Aires, Argentina.

the equator. I remember that situation because it was the starting point to tell Jujo about the book project and my uncertainties about finding a possible definition of Latin American Architecture. *We could find similitudes, geographical reasons... aspects in common* -he began describing.

JS: Imagine, both Luis Barragan and Laureano Forero are Latin architects, one from Mexico, the other from Colombia. But they both are architects with very different kind of architecture conceptions, and particularly related to different scales. So, in my opinion they don't represent only one Latin American architecture, they represent different lines of thinking and contrasting ways of elaborating ideas of a architecture, and of course coming from a European influence. Also Oscar Niemeyer would be an interesting case to reflect about. No one could deny that Niemeyer's architecture is Brazilian but indubitably Modernist at the same time.

AdeB. Could we say that in Latin America the understanding of architecture as an action is more powerful than the appreciation of object architecture?

JS. In our office we don't think in dichotomycal terms, as you say opposing *objet* versus *action*. Instead we think architecture is a matter of interaction: this means that multiple factors and problems have to be considered and solved by the moment you really construct and finish a building. Program, users, urban context, economical conditions, available techonlogy, among a long list of issues... It seems imposible to reduce architecture to two points of view. Besides, we all emphasize this broad perspective of looking at architecture in our teaching activities. Academia and practice are very much related in our studio; actually we created our office being a university team fifty years ago. In fact, in 1957 we won *La Boca Towers* (at that time our group was composed of Ernesto Katzenstein, Gian Peani, Fina Santos and I) and that project proposed for the first time in Argentina the tower tipology to solve social and economical housing complex. Then, I should say competitions, whether national or international, are another instance of interaction because usually we encourage students and young architects to participate with us in very good discussions. And perhaps La Boca Towers was a sort of premonition because we keep developing this tipology until now with *Mulieris Towers* (figure 6) in Puerto Madero; both cases are not isolate buildings but a group of two or four towers; that's the way we think this tipology acts in the development of modern, high density cities, creating scale and urban borders.

AdeB. What are your thoughts about the influence of technology in architecture?

JS. Although the relationship between architecture and technology is one of the most important factors in our discipline it doesn't mean we have to be condicionated by it. Instead we have to explore working with materials to obtain the best possible architecture with less expensive solutions and local possibilities. For instance, in our Office we solved *Mar del Plata Swimming Pools* (figure 5) using metal structure and a dome manufactured both by Argentine industry; that means we did not obtain the same proportions, as slender as an aluminum one (like European and North American buildings). Instead we had what I called "South American High Tech" proportions, and very quickly! In 1994 we had to cover the swimming pools in only few months before the Pan-American Games and we thought in those old English structures used for Train Stations at the end of 19th century and the beginning of 20th in most Latin American countries. This is a very common technical solution, which has demonstrated its quality and performance for more than a hundred of years. In 2000 we developed the same structure in the project for the *Ezeiza International Airport*, in Buenos Aires. This was another building of high spaces and public use. On the other hand, when we built *Santa Teresita Housing* in 1966 (figure10), a group of houses for tourists, we decided to use impermeable roofs made impermeable with Hypalon painting –what was a new waterproof paint in Argentina at that time. We could materialize oblique planes and rigorous lines according to volumetrical ideas; obtaining such kind of continuity between roofs and walls. Also, in 1968 we built *Municipal Bank of Buenos Aires City Main House* (figure 3) using glass brick for all the walls and mezzanines looking for transparence and reflected surfaces and effects. It was a huge challenge because all planes had to be modulated exactly as invariable brick measures.

AdeB. If you were asked to describe the most important aspects of Latin American architecture, what would you say?

JS. If something characterizes Latin American architecture is diverstity. In our office, we never think about that while we are working. We do think of getting the best building possible to be used by a particular group of people and to be built in a specific site. I believe Latin Americans share important and even unique problems such as popular housing –like Brazilian Favelas or our Villas Miseria (shanty towns)– but our ways of responding to the problem are very different. Why? Because of multiple regions, climates, materials, and toughts. As you see, there are very many differences that can alter the architectural response. At this point I would say we have to be careful with any kind of nationalism.

AdeB. So from your point of view we cannot say there is a Latin American way of thinking of architecture...

JS. Sometimes I ask myself why critics insist so much in founding Latin American architecture? Is this a matter of looking for a label? I do think it would be much more enriching to recognize our differences as a result of the virtues of so many good architects who have worked and keep working in our huge continental region. Most of the time they all do it under very difficult conditions, which finally make me think that our (Latin American) architecture seems to be *miraculous*... perhaps that would be a very good word to define it!

Justo Solsona in his office.

YESTERDAY AND TODAY. Series: Trip to South America, 2004.
2010_Image specially composed for this book by Isaac Bracher.

THE SINGLE FAMILY HOUSE

DWELLING PLACE, BODY, HABITATION, MEMORY, REFUGE, BACKGROUND, OUTSIDE, INSIDE, LINE, TRIBE, RESIDENCE, CLAN, HOME, "TO LIVE IN", OCCUPANTS, CONNECTION, RELATIONSHIP, "GET TOGETHER", CONGREGATION, ROOTS, UNDERSTANDING.

X HOUSE

Arquitectura X
Ecuador

Date: 2003-2007
Project: X House
Location: La Tola, valle de Tumbaco, Quito, Ecuador
Design Team: Arquitectura x - Adrián Moreno Núñez, María Samaniego Ponce
Construction Team: Adrian Moreno Núñez, with Carlos Guerra Espinosa
Structural Engineer: Pedro Caicedo
Electrical Engineer: Pedro Freile
Water Systems Engineer: Raúl Cueva
Site area: 14,800 SF.
Total floor area: 3,800 SF.

1. At the time of designing the house, the team did not have a chosen site. So, as a basic scheme we set out an elemental scheme that could work both in Quito and in the valleys east of the city; this meant distilling our experience into an abstract form, inspired by the work of Donald Judd, which could be placed in any of the sites we would be likely to find: an open-ended box, whose spatial limits would be the eastern and western ranges of the Andes.

2. As we had no actual place, we looked at the spaces we felt to be our own, and we saw the patio as the essential placemaker throughout our architectural history.

3. On the other hand was our fascination for the prototypical glass-house and its possibilities in our year-round temperate climate.

4. While the patio creates a sense of place it has to be enclosed in order to work, so the mountains can't become the spatial limit. The glass-house is perfect for that unlimited sense of space; the addition of a patio into the glass house gave us the chance to adapt to the different site possibilities.

5. We separated the private and public spaces defining a patio; the service spaces and circulation could be added as a plug-in as needed, depending on site conditions, further defining the patio.

6. Finally this diagram could be fit into the open-ended box according to the specific site conditions, which would define orientation, size and proportion.

Materials and Construction

Construction and the choice of materials were parallel considerations to the design concepts, and they were decided based on similar premises: a building system that could be modulated and would allow for decision making based on varying budgets and site conditions.

A light steel structure on a concrete plinth supports the rusted steel and plywood open-ended box. Circulation, service spaces, and the elements that make the house function are inserted in white and enclosed in polycarbonate for protection from the strong western sun. All services run concentrated, parallel to the circulation; rain-water is kept separate from drainage, it is surface collected and flows down the rusted ends of the box into the ground.

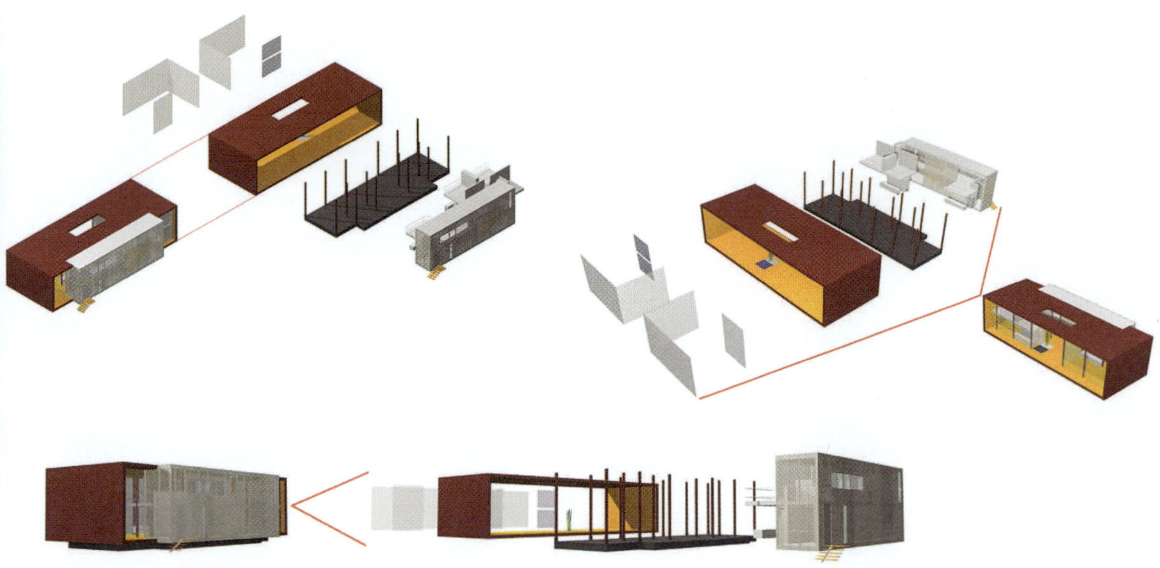

Construction concept

1 HOUSE
2 GARAGE
(UNDERGROUND)
3 GARDEN

SITE PLAN

GROUND FLOOR PLAN

1 PATIO
2 LIVING/DINING/KITCHEN
3 BEDROOM
4 FAMILY ROOM
5 ENTRANCE
6 SERVICE/STORAGE
7 LIBRARY/STUDY
8 PLAY ROOM
(GUEST-FUTURE BEDROOM)

FIRST FLOOR PLAN

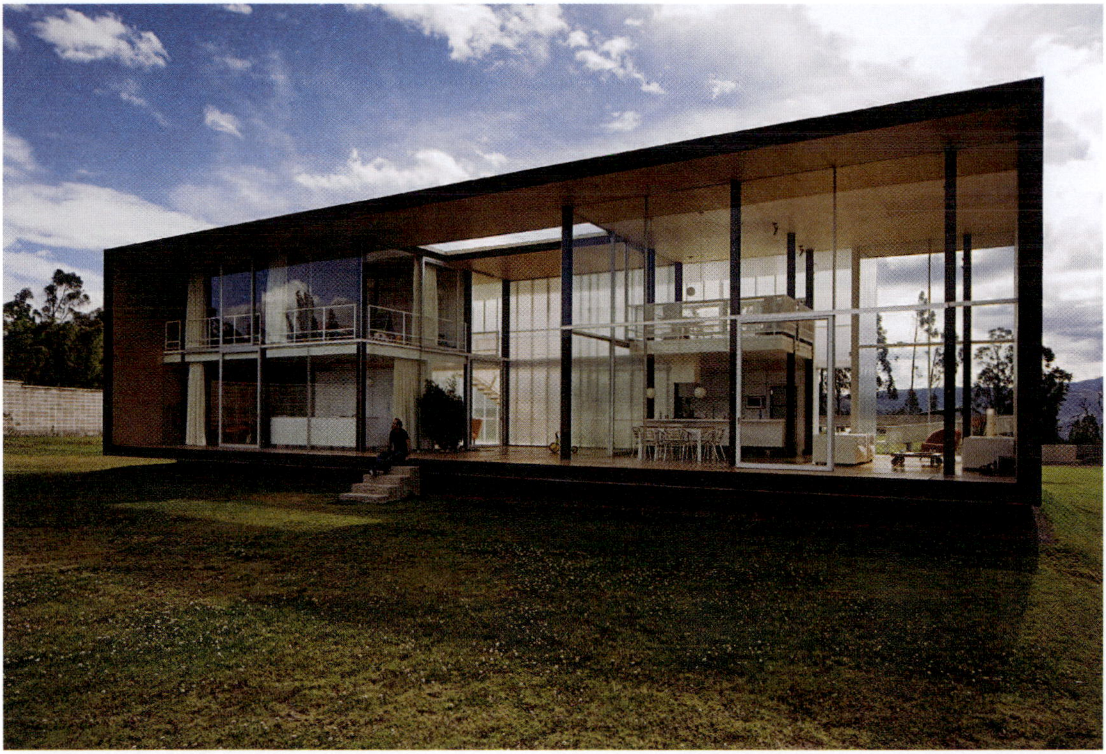

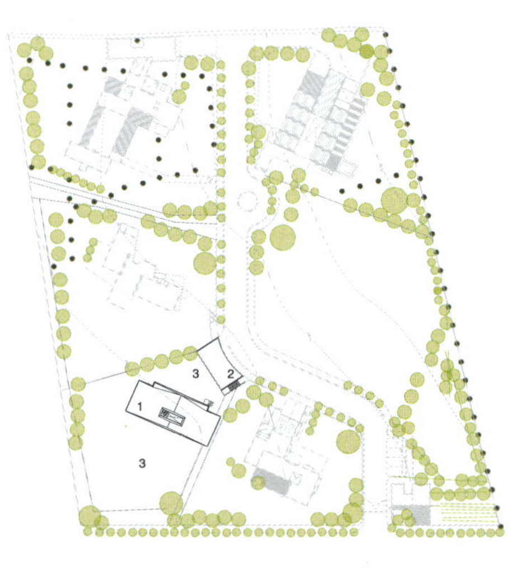

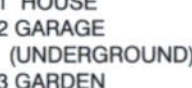

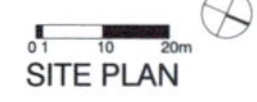

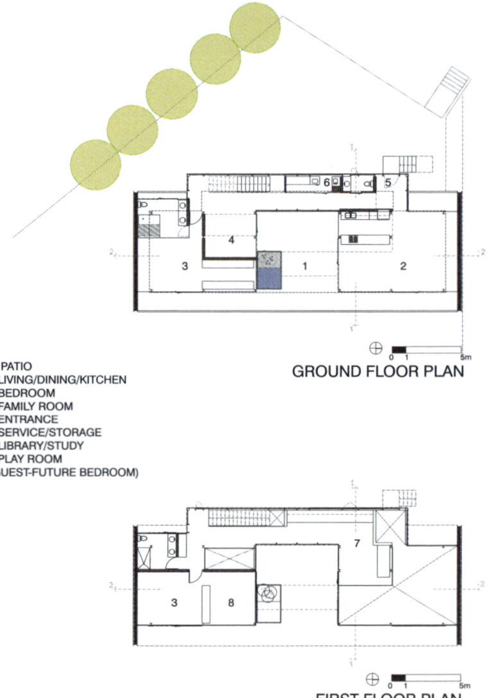

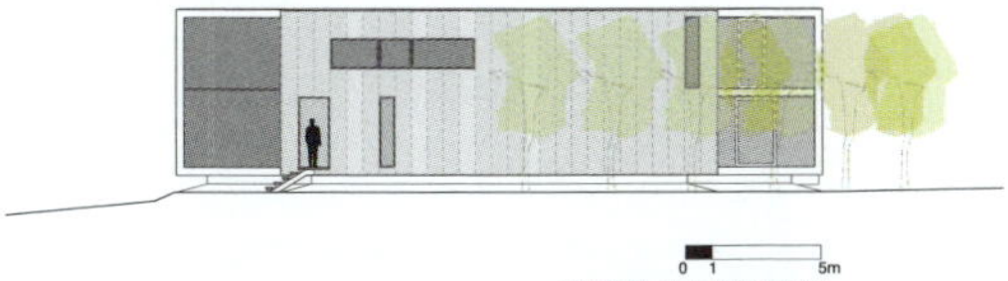

0 1 5m
WEST ELEVATION

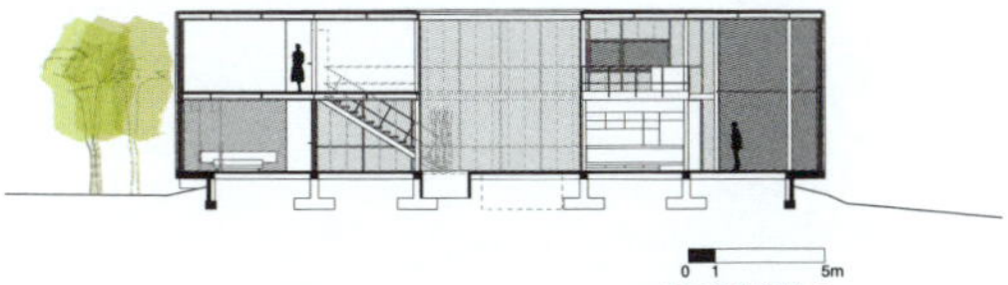

0 1 5m
SECTION 2

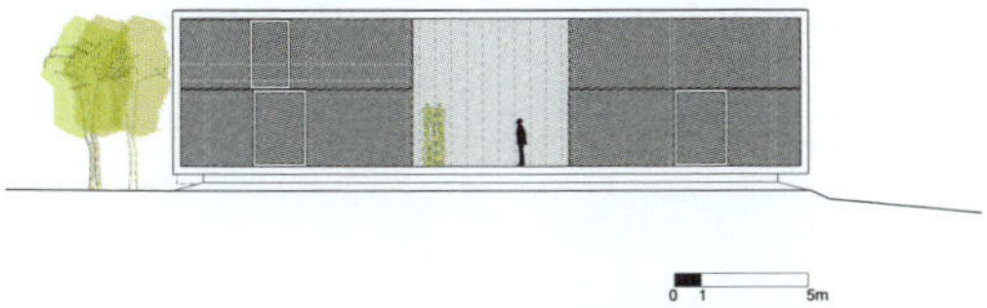

0 1 5m
EAST ELEVATION

1 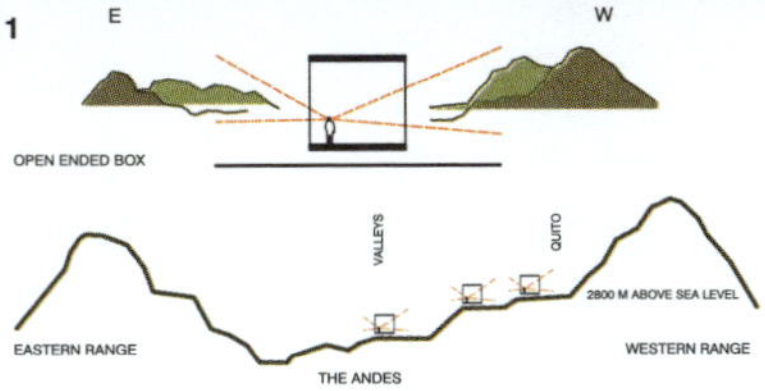
E
W
OPEN ENDED BOX
VALLEYS
QUITO
2800 M ABOVE SEA LEVEL
EASTERN RANGE
THE ANDES
WESTERN RANGE
ELEMENTAL SCHEME APPLICABLE IN QUITO & VALLEYS

2 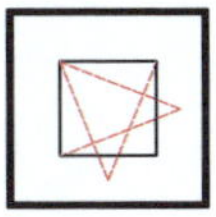
PATIO HOUSE

3 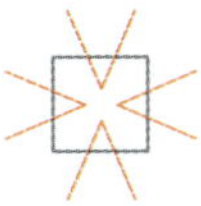
GLASS HOUSE

4 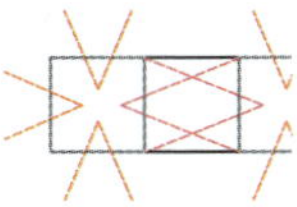
PATIO
+
GLASS HOUSE

5 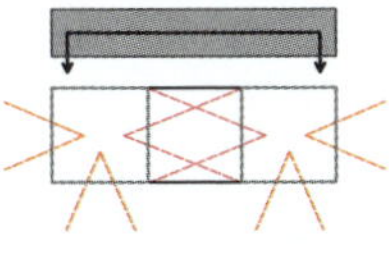
CIRCULATION
& SERVICES

6
FUNCTIONING
GLASS HOUSE
WITH PATIO
+
OPEN ENDED BOX

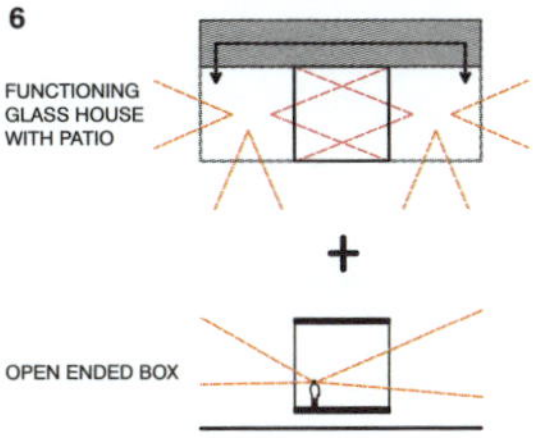

PS HOUSE

JPRCR Architects
Colombia

Date: 2009-2010
Location: La Ceja, Antioquia, Colombia
Design team: Camilo Restrepo, J. Paul Restrepo
Collaborators: Santiago Cadavid and Hugo Herrera
Site area: 3,768 SF.
Total floor area: 1,216 SF.

External desires
The family asked for a Tudor house.

Site location
A very green flat terrain near the woods and surrounded by a bluish mountain landscape.

Design principles
A very large membrane to welcome a wide range of environmental and visual relationships. Constructing a surface of rocky aspect that curves and folds to produce multiple relationships between interior and exterior spaces.

Floor plan

Schematic

MQ HOUSE

Roberto Amette
Argentina

Date: 2008
Location: Chapelco Golf, San Martin de los Andes, Neuquen, Argentina
Design team: Roberto Amette
Collaborators: Architects Maria Elena Cuppolo and Diego Scurk
Total floor area: 2,600 SF.

This house is located twenty kilometers from the center of San Martin de los Andes, in the Andean Patagonia, in the lakes circuit, on the eastern side of the Andes Mountains. The mountain landscape is characterized by an immeasurable vastness, intense, overwhelming... The climate is harsh in winter and the western winds are constant.

The production of this work participates in the old, but no-less-valid debate on the antinomy Modernity/Identity and takes as relevant the proposal by C. Fernandez Cox from more than a decade ago, "Appropriate Modernity." This idea not only marks the borders between what is ours (our belongings) and what isn't, but it also shows us the plastic qualities of culture, where what belongs to us is re-discovered and re-modeled, in a continuous and necessary process of transformation and change which gives rise to new and multiple manifestations.

That is to say that local culture is not interpreted as Folklore, but as tradition, re-shaped and represented expressing a dynamic relationship between the place and time. This approach seeks to overcome the idea of an excluding, restrictive and autistic modernity – limited to stylistic or formal aspects – and proposes itself as a rereading of Andean architecture.

The project proposes a crude and direct relationship between man and landscape. The relationship is abrupt, with no other mediation than a horizontal space that neutralizes the landscape's natural gravity, characterized by verticals and diagonals: a box resting on a podium anchored to the ground, visually and materially.

In the box, a series of operations suggest its breakage: the wall becomes transparent in its attempt to disappear and spread into the landscape; the roof rises and melts into the sky; the powerful stone wall which limits the inside space and the crafted fireplace that forms the tympanum are design operations that act on the characterization (or memory) of the domestic space and multiply the effect of the captured exterior.

The house is set on the highest part of the land (that old architecture lesson), in a dominating position and the relationship with the site is mediated with a patio, a break after a steep rise.

There, the stability of the horizontal is sought out again, like a founding act of architecture and a shelter from the dominant western winds. The two parts of the house and the natural terrain make the patio.

The two parts of the house are linked by an empty and longitudinal space (directional) that reproduces the system of movements in the mountains and organizes the architecture.

The materials are used with the mediation of geometry and abstraction as manifestations of the rational character of our culture.

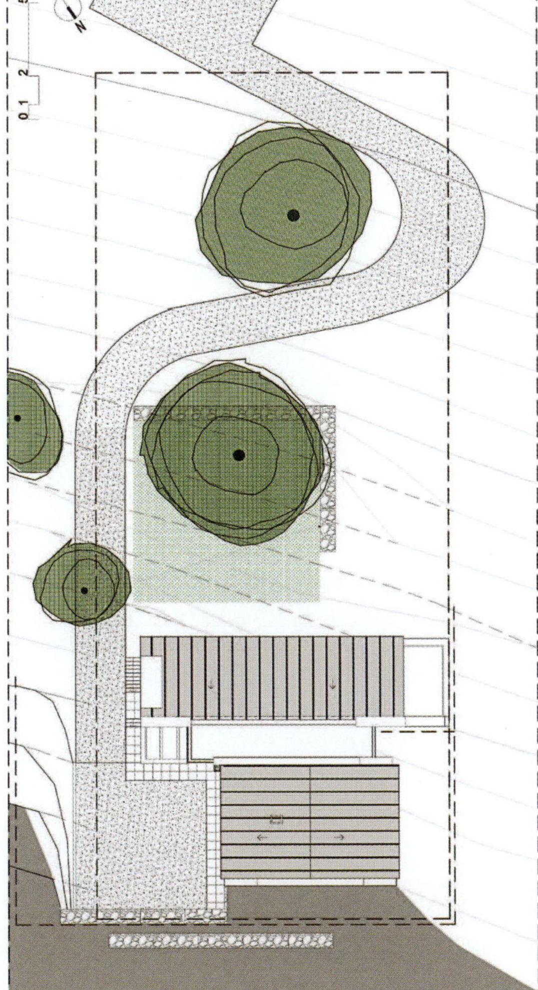

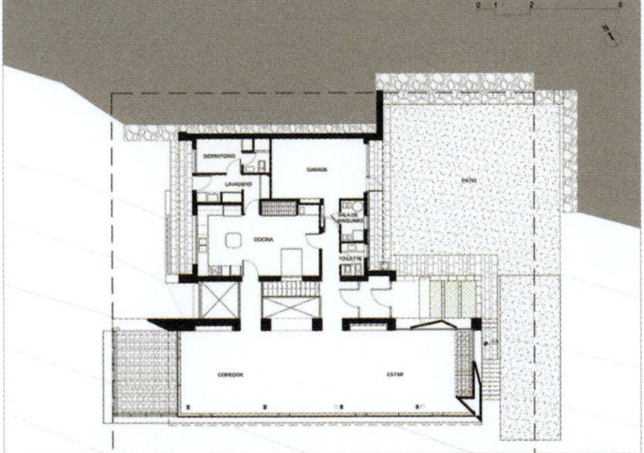

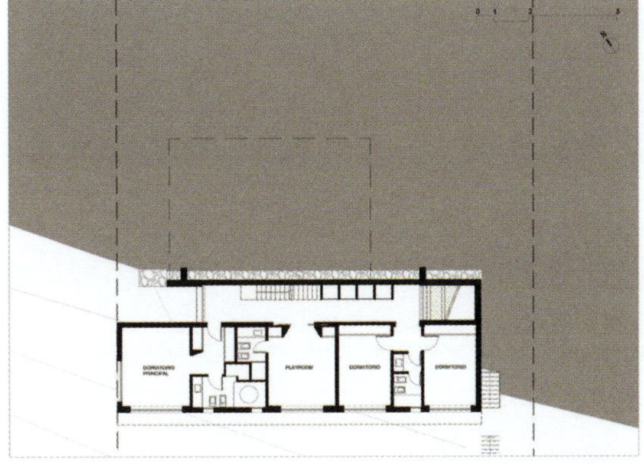

Site plan
Ground Floor
First floor (right)

FYF HOUSE

P-A-T-T-E-R-N-S
Argentina

Date: 2004-2007
Location: Rosario, Argentina
Design team: Marcelo Spina and Georgina Huljich, Principals in charge; James Vincent, Hunter Knight, En Jang, Ben Luddy, Assistants
Partners: 1st Phase: Estudio +, Alejandro Beltramone and Dalabona Arquitectos: Monia Dalabona
Total floor area: 2,000 SF.

FYF house is located on the outskirts of Rosario (the second largest city in Argentina), approximately 300 km north of Buenos Aires. The small house, approximately 2,000 square meters, is built in a new residential development adjacent to a traditional neighborhood. FYF can be described as a spatial and physical attempt to challenge the planar stability and flat homogeneity of the Pampas landscape in a domestic setting. The project was conceived as a monolithic solid, a monochromatic form punctuated only by subtle inflections that establish a complex physical relationship among the different spaces, while maintaining a sense of identity and privacy between them.

Specifically, a docile cast-on-site reinforced concrete shell constitutes the body of the house. Determined by a structuring geometry governing the shape of the house, problematic transitions are registered in the shell through local folds and bends. Perforations in those transitions produce openings where windows are located, allowing for internal conditions of interstitial luminosity, cross-ventilation and oblique views. Moreover, through shape and disposition, these openings experientially accentuate or play down the effects of the mass, while emphasizing its overall topology.

The house is organized into a basic layout of public and private spaces connected by a central corridor and articulated by a small light well. The internal atmosphere of the house offers a contrasting effect between calmness and fluidity. While all the rooms are discretely separated, they are also connected by means of strategic openings located right at the transitions, hence adding a sense of controlled endlessness to the main areas of the house.

Because one of the clients is an agricultural engineer and a landscape designer, the project offered the opportunity to incorporate a special activity into the program: a small greenhouse. Instead of isolating it from the rest of the house, we chose to situate the greenhouse in a continuous spatial sequence with interior social spaces, swimming pool and solarium, thus integrating house with garden and exploiting its expressive dynamism.

Placed in close proximity to the main public areas, a pliant pool produces a cascading physical continuum with the body of the house. By twisting the volume and merging it with the ground, the pool complicates the spatial stability of the house and activates a dynamic and oblique sequence of movement and views to the landscape beyond. Tectonically, the projecting roof of the pool area is broken down into small coffer-like compartments that allow glazing facets to be flat, while indicating the complex curvature of the hyperbolic surface.

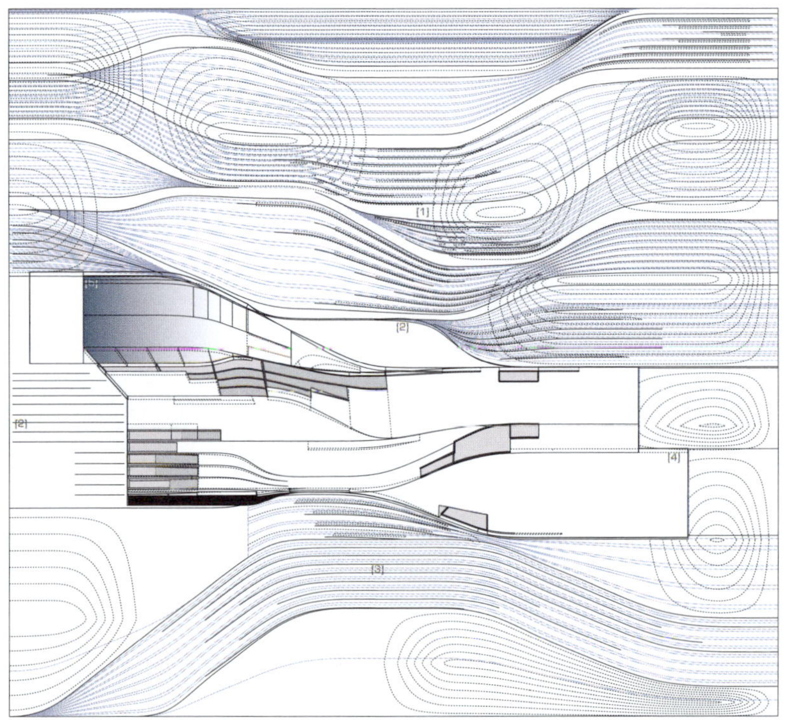

Site plan

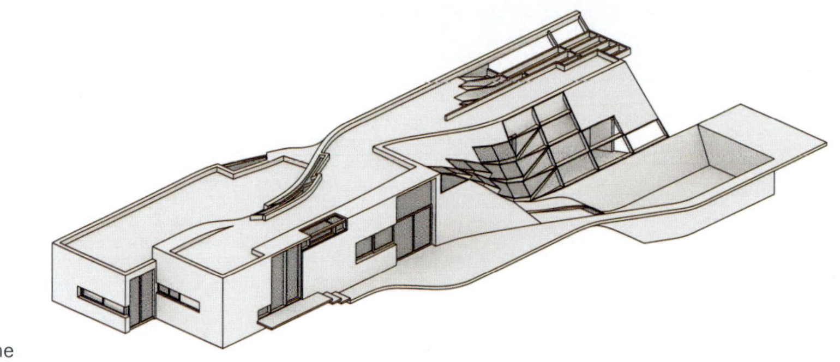

Volume

INTEGRATED SYSTEMS

[1] LANDSCAPE
Mounds and shreds demarcating vegetation activity
[2] TERRACE
[3] INTERIOR PARTITIONS
Activity flow and controled green systems
[4] CONCRETE SHELL
Framing and window systems
[5] SUBSTRATE GEOMETRY

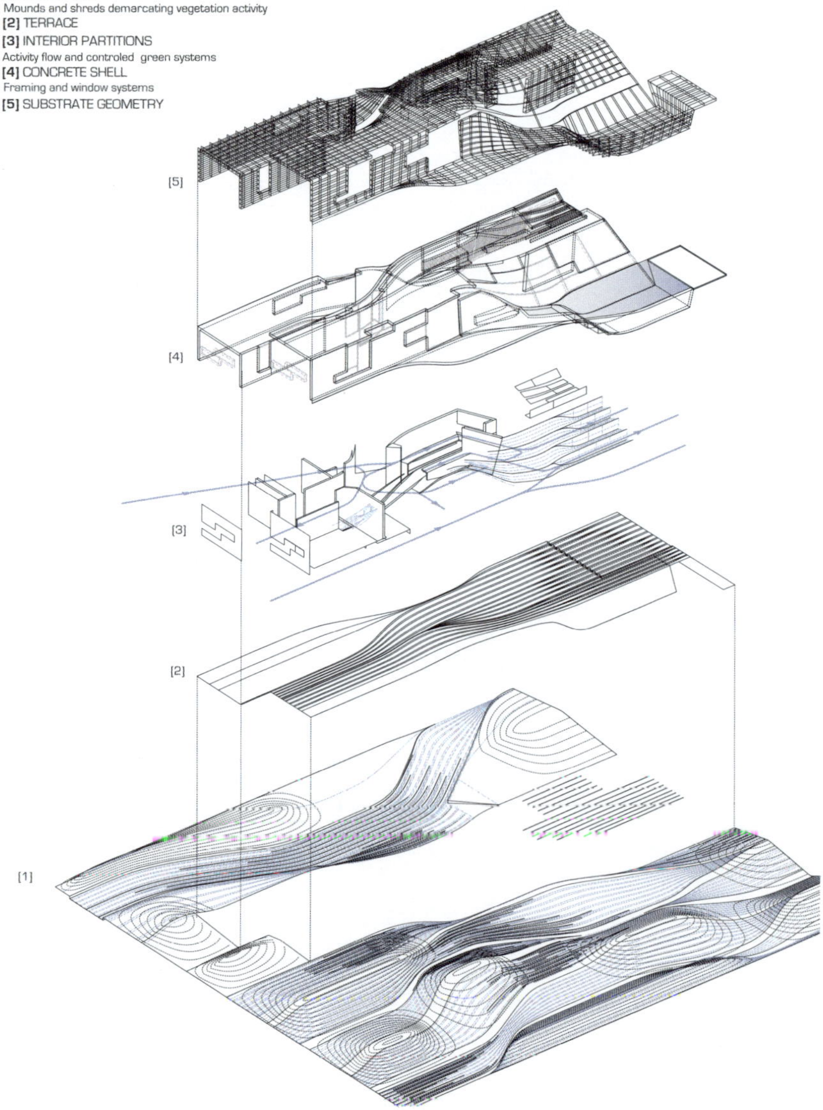

[5]

[4]

[3]

[2]

[1]

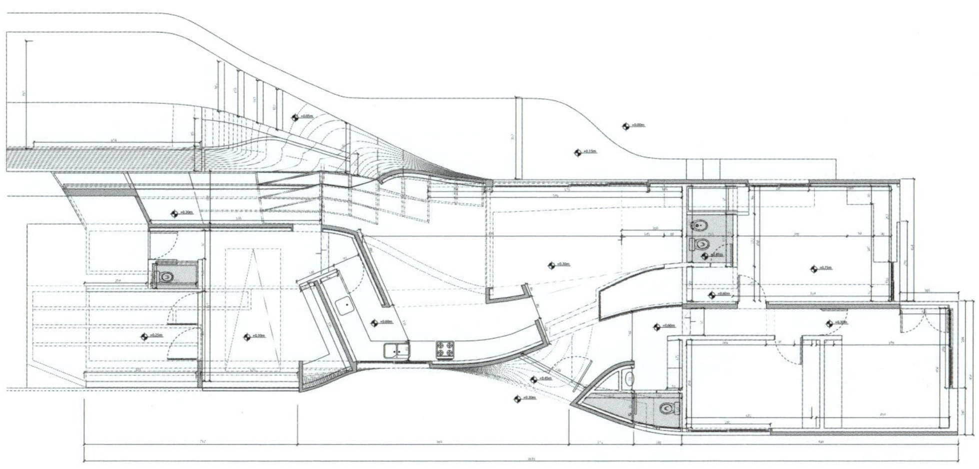

Ground floor

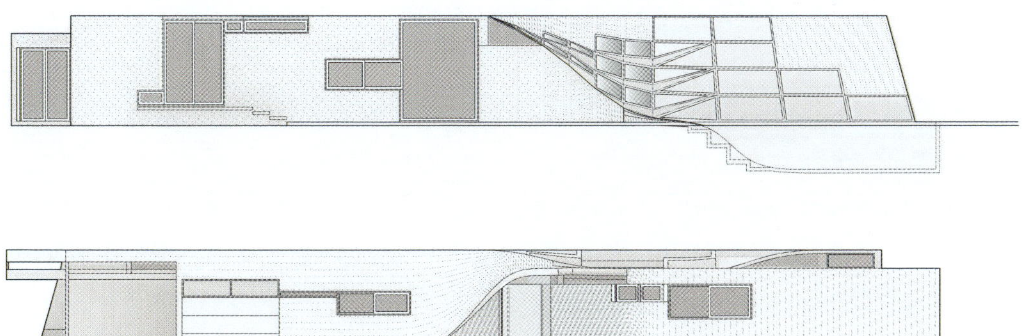

Elevations

2010_Collage specially composed for this book by Kevin Klinger.

MEDELLIN / "It is sutured together with an omni-present civil connectivity, and technology silently in service to our humanity. One no longer needs to clamor up to the top of the hill, but rather float gently upwards to opportunity. In principle, there is an opening of the municipality with civic spaces, social places, and windows to the world. One stands to learn as much gazing inward here as they do gazing out."

TAPIALES HOUSE

Zas Lavarello Architects
Argentina

Date: 2007
Location: Vicente López, Argentina
Design team: Zas Lavarello Architects: Javier Zas, Paula Lavarello
Site area: 12,000 SF.
Total floor area: 3,200 SF.

Making use of the site and particularly of the existing tree, which becomes a fulcrum for the organization of the floor plan. The presence of the tree results in this play of transparencies and reflections, the fulcrum of composition, condensation and synthesis between nature and the artificial work: the visuals converge on top of the tree, which filters the solar rays, contributing to softening the northern sun over the large windows.

The site, with a steep slope, defines two clear areas: the back zone is higher, containing a harsh change of level in relation to the front zone were the pool is located, which becomes the courtyard (pool) expansion of the bedrooms that look out towards it, taking advantage of optimum solar conditions considering the existing latitude.

Because of the high zone of the existing site, that coincides with the level of the upper floor where the pool is located, it emerges "naturally" from the heart of the existing site, without the need for expensive structural displays. This allows for proximity with the bedroom area and being able to look out without being observed.

The unfolding of the exterior and interior stairs find their reason for being in the difference of levels of the used spaces – some of which already existed in the demolished original house – and we are allowed to go through the various precincts that create this conception of house open to the phenomenological experience of dwelling.

From the beginning, our premises also consisted in being "loyal" to the modern rational tradition that flourished in Argentina since the beginning of the last century and that has produced work of notable value: including sun exposure, site and dwelling conditions, which play a fundamental role in the layout of the respective areas. In other words, in our conception, the sun passage through the different times of the day became the source of the project's concepts and ideas, which were decisive in regards to the distribution of the dwelling's different functions.

The tectonic composition of the residence achieves a climax that relates to the landscape, in the change of grade between the front zone which is ten meters lower than the rear zone. The two "L" volumes are laid out embracing the court-garden and in axis with the interior-exterior relationship. On the lower floor of one of the "L"s wings, this generates a linear living + dining sequence without wall interruptions and with ample floor-to-ceiling windows.

The continuity of the glass floor-to-ceiling skin along all the façade's perimeter accentuates the interior relationship as well as the positioning of columns, set back from the enclosure – freeing it from complex details and accentuating its unaltered rhythm.

All issues that recall the central idea of modern architecture, redeemed by Frampton, the issue of nodes, of joints, of encounters. Ultimately the tectonic, as examples that can be traced in Latin-American architecture.

ROLIM DE CAMARGO HOUSE

MMBB Architects
Brazil

Date: 2006
Location: São Paulo, Brazil
Design team: MMBB Architects: Fernando de Mello Franco, Marta Moreira, Milton Braga
Project team: Marina Sabino, Márcia Terazaki, Thiago Rolemberg, Ana Carina Costa, Marina Acayaba, Marcelo Maia Rosa
Structural engineer: Cia. de Projetos
Mechanical engineer: MBM Engenharia
Interior designer: MMBB
Landscape architect: Isabel Ruas
Consultant: Frederico Falconi Rocha
Site area: 4,810 SF.
Total floor area: 3,440 SF.

The Rolim de Camargo residence was developed from the flexibilization of its original design and the boost of outdoor/indoor relationships.

Supported by four columns only, the house rises up from the ground, liberating the land for several outdoor uses, such as leisure and services.

The columns support two reinforced concrete parallel load-bearing walls. They are the building superstructures, which are also reinforced by the transversal slabs. All technical installations are juxtaposed to the sidewalls forming the house infrastructure. Therefore, all fixed parts have been grouped on the volume's periphery.

The space between the bearing walls and the slabs shelters the other functions, which are organized according to the plan's flexible layouts. This is a response to the inevitable usage transformation that this residence has undergone over time.

A central court articulates all spaces, integrating them both visually and functionally through its multiple transparences, created by emptiness and glass surfaces.

Under the living room slab – in the semi-basement – sit the laundry and garage areas.

As an extension to the living room and kitchen areas, the garden and veranda appear, which stretch through the house's grounds. They make a single environment, which virtually comprehends the total land surface.

On the first floor, the house bedrooms and offices present a double-face feature, which relates them equally both to the indoor and outdoor environments.

Over the top slab, a garden roof allows for a glimpse of a wide horizon, something unique in the city of Sao Paulo.

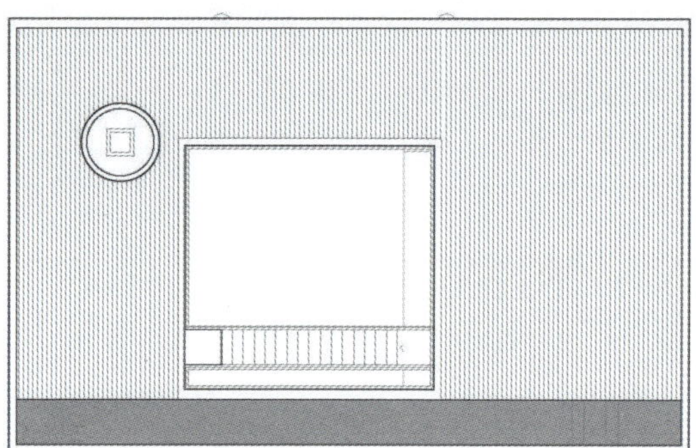

Roof plan

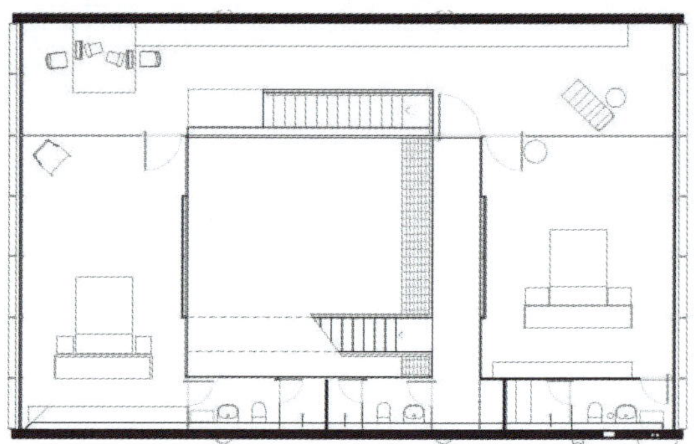

Second floor

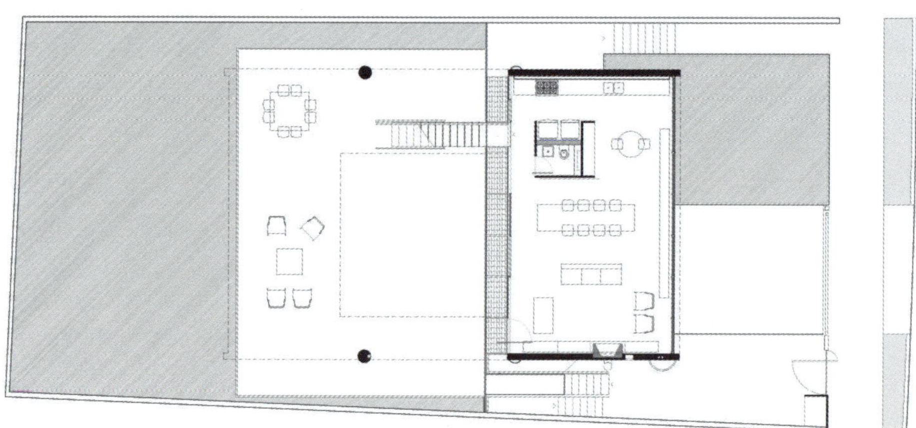

First floor

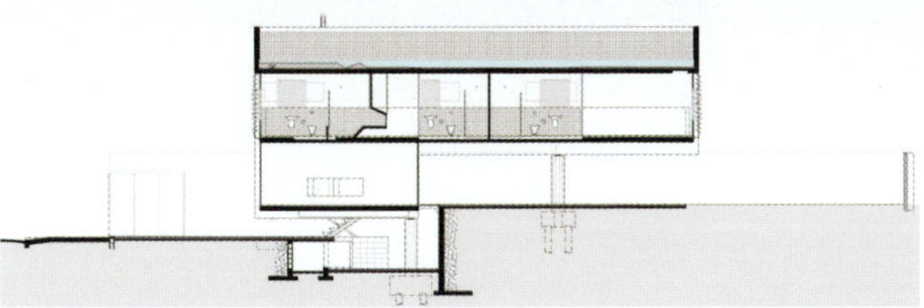

Longitudinal section

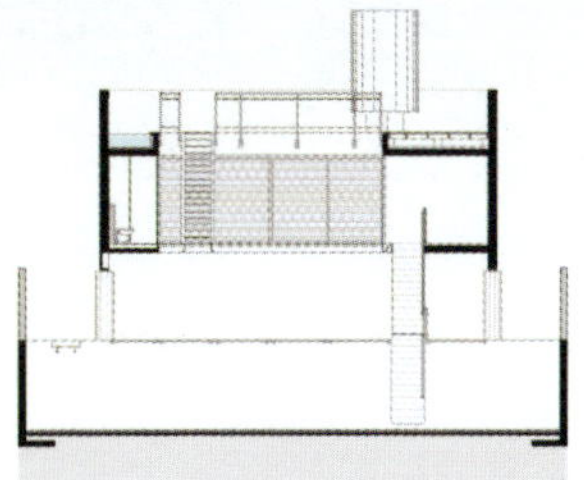

Transversal section

WINDOW OF THE WORLD / Buenos Aires, 2005. Argentina Series.
2010_ Image specially composed for this book by Gina Stahl.

DM HOUSE

Dellatorre-Oubiña-Shanahan
Argentina

Date: 2003-2009
Location: Tigre, Buenos Aires, Argentina
Construction Team: Z construcciones
Structural Engineer: Ricardo Fernández, Alicia Martínez
Site area: 8,400 SF.
Total floor area: 3,014 SF.

Flat, peripheral, impersonal, artificial and recent; these define the characteristics of the site, altered only by the presence of a pond or the view of a nearby river.

The size of the plots of land and their coding reflect the contradiction between the object, its limits and the neighbors. The party-wall, that ally, absent though latent, and the prohibition of materializing it establish a hysterical relationship between the fullness and the void of the different houses.

In this context, the quest to create own places in a no-place structures the ideas of both houses.

The program of the two houses develops from a basis of three bedrooms, public areas and utility rooms with the addition of roofed carports in the CD house, initially for two cars, finally four.

The DM house was supposed to be built in two stages, preserving the expression of a finished house even in its intermediate instance.

The spatial language employed results from the combination of the evolution of the postwar modern house and the Spanish cultural tradition, with its walls and courtyard architecture.

Space, structure and material are the principal resources of the building's character.

The choice of exposed reinforced concrete and the reutilization of its timber formwork as a non-load-bearing skin establish the field where the designers moved.

The stereotomic use of the material, in the form of wall, floor or roof in the CD house, the time elapsed between the stages, and the tectonic condition of the DM house, are the characteristics that define both works.

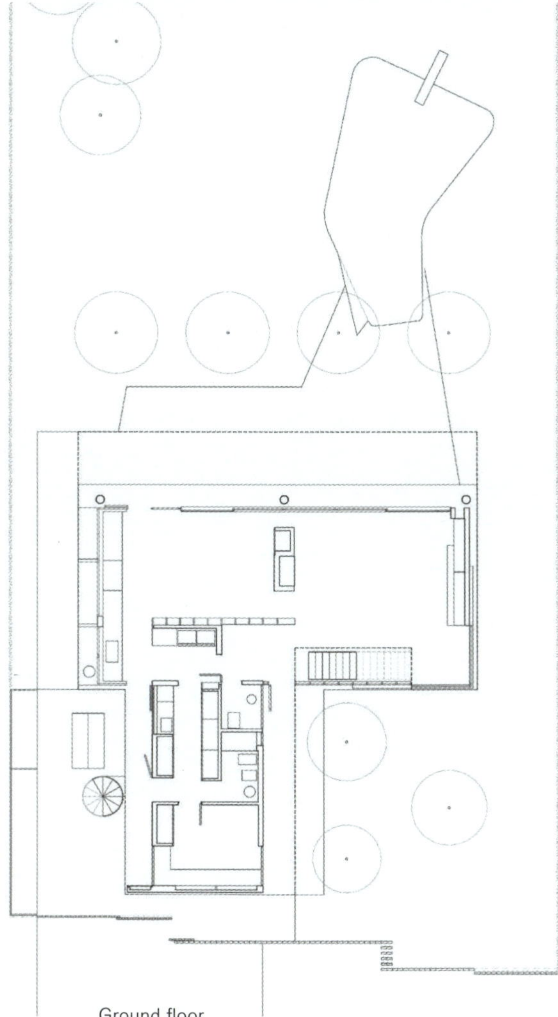

Ground floor

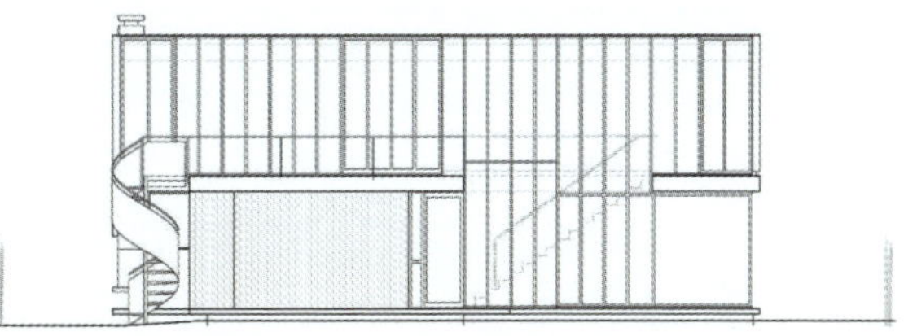

Elevation

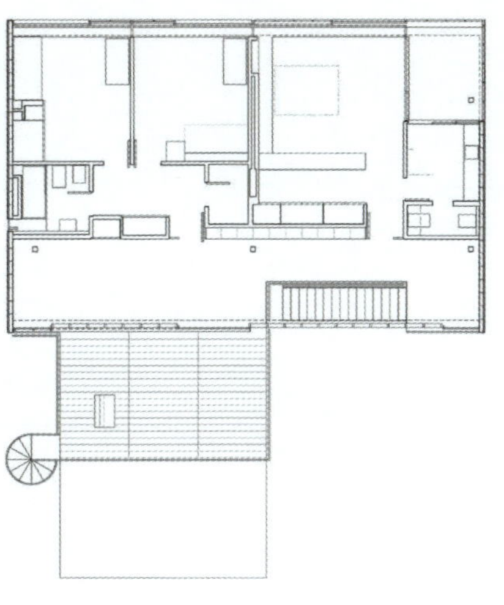

First floor

CD HOUSE

Dellatorre-Shanahan-Valverde
Argentina

Date: 2008
Location: Tigre, Buenos Aires, Argentina
Construction Team: Z construcciones
Structural Engineer: Ricardo Fernández
Site area: 11,300 SF.
Total floor area: 3,550 SF.

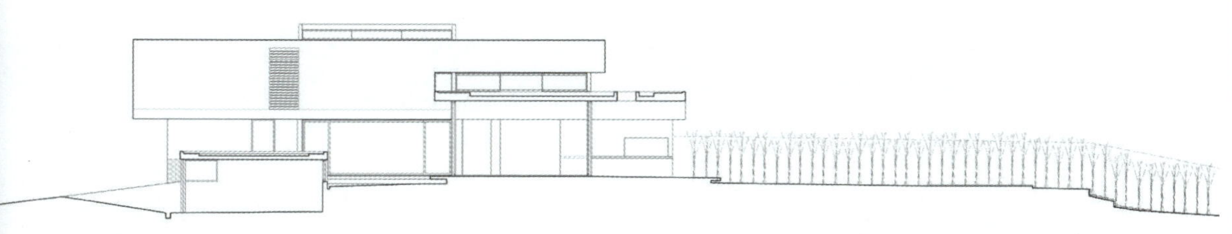

Longitudinal elevation

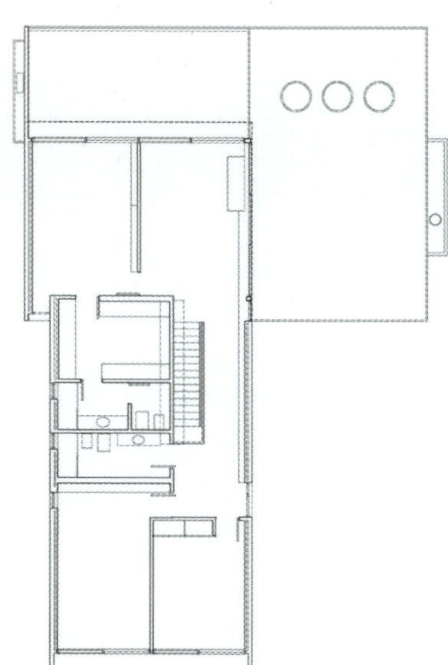

Floor plan

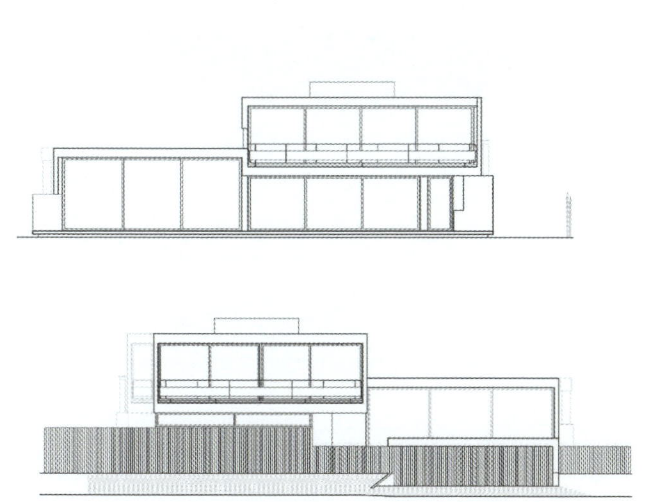

Elevations

BACOPARI HOUSE

Una Arquitetos
Brazil

Date: 2012
Location: São Paulo, Brazil
Design team: Una Arquitetos: Cristiane Muniz, Fábio Valentim, Fernanda Barbara and Fernando Viégas
Project team: Ana Paula de Castro, Carolina Klocker, Eduardo Martorelli, Fabiana Cyon, Gabriela Gurgel, Enk te Winkel, Igor Cortinove, Marta Onofre, Miguel Muralha, Sílio Almeida
Construction: Pecprana + F2
Structure: Cia de Projetos
Services: Pessoa e Zamaro
Lighting: Ricardo Heder
Waterproofing: Proassp I Weathering: Drawing
Landscape: Soma
Site area: 7,240 SF.
Total floor area: 5,040 SF.

The house is located in a neighborhood with abundant forestation. The plane ground, surrounded by houses and no distant views, is longer than the standard. The project intends to build a large garden that permeates the house and builds the landscape, in continuity with the existing vegetation. The tall trees (pau ferro trees, eight meters height) were brought at the beginning of the works. Parallel concrete walls, ten meters apart, define the supports of the suspended plans.

At ground level, the idea was to allow transparency from the street to the end of the plot. The access is made through a covered square where cars can be parked. The limits are marked by gardens with a reflecting pool, the first patio, which precedes the double-height living room, and the dining room, extending to the terrace. The second courtyard has gardens and a swimming pool, onto which the playroom opens.

After the walls, the construction is an assembly: the upper slabs supported by metallic beams between gables. Building services are located in accessible shafts in each concrete plan.

Stairs connect the wine cellar, in the basement, to the upper floor, at the treetops level. On this floor there is a library in a horizontal gallery, which opens onto the patio and the living room.

All bedrooms have the best orientation, northeast. The succession of open and closed spaces, associated with glass façades, water tanks and dark panels generates a series of reflections and transparencies, diluting the boundaries between inside and outside.

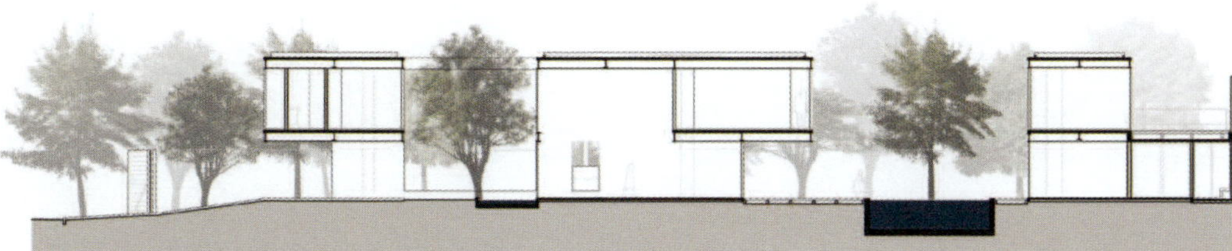

Longitudinal section

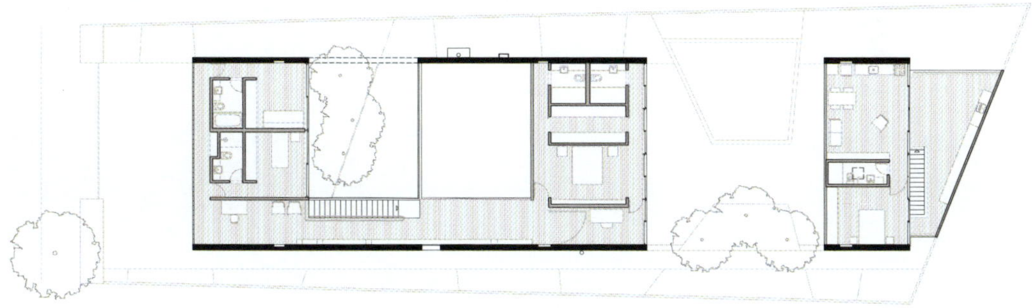

First floor

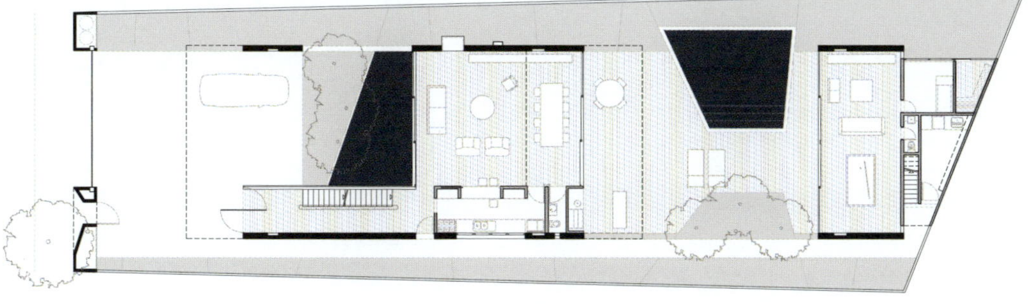

Ground floor

BOAÇAVA HOUSE

Una Arquitetos
Brazil

Date: 2011
Location: São Paulo, Brazil
Design team: Una Arquitetos, Cristiane Muniz, Fábio Valentim, Fernanda Barbara, and Fernando Viégas
Collaborators: Ana Paula de Castro, Bruno Gondo, Eduardo Martorelli, Enk te Winkel, Igor Cortinove, Marta Onofre, Miguel Muralha, Roberto Galvão Jr., and Sílio Almeida
Structural engineer: Cia de Projetos
Systems: Pessoa e Zamaro
Water systems: Proassp, Irrigam
Lighting: Ricardo Heder
Audiovisual systems: Oguri audio e video
Landscape: Soma Arquitetos

The slope where this site is located, with a six-meter difference between the back neighbor and the house, provides a large distant view from the street level. The continuity is established therefore through the neighborhood treetops and the skyline on the banks of the Pinheiros River.

The suspended concrete volume protects living areas on the ground level, with spatial variations from the design of the pavement with various heights. This wood pavement connects the entry to the pool, unfolding inside the room.

The concrete wall supports construction and divides the longitudinally, giving independence to the facilities areas. This colored block was pigmented with iron oxide. The presence of this molded wall is extended from the reflections of light and follows a transition from external to internal areas. Two concrete columns complete the supports of this level, allowing for apparent asymmetry in the regular structure.

Thinking of the structural sense as a folding, the volume of the superior level behaves differently. There is no continuity of the pillars; instead, the concrete walls support the cover slab.

In contrast with the first level, where the bedrooms are, the opacity of the volume appears. It indicates some intimacy; reentrant balconies mediate views from these rooms. These extractions ensure diagonal views, multiple light and ventilation accesses emphasizing the sun's path. A solarium on the roof completes the rising way.

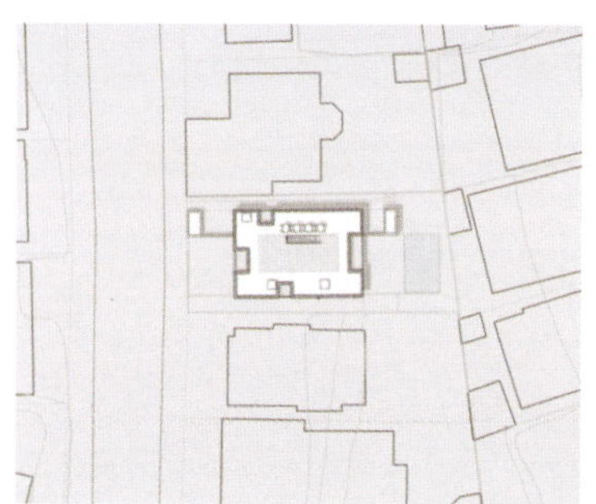

Site plan

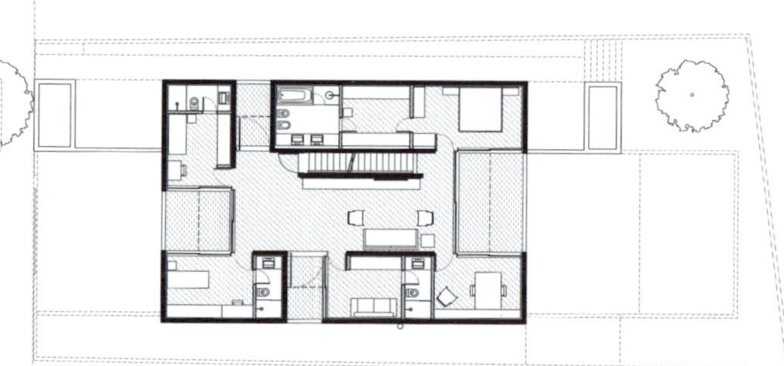

First floor

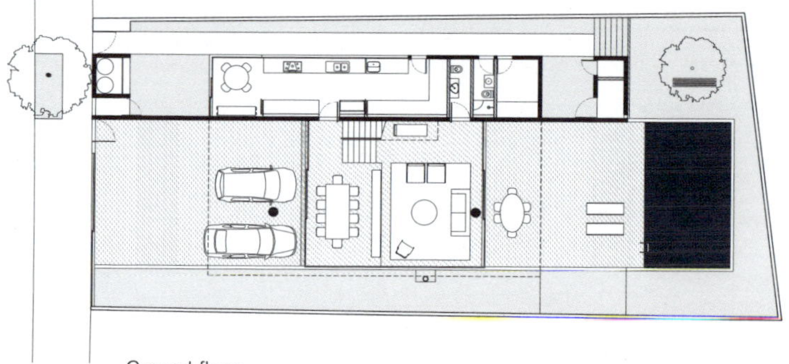

Ground floor

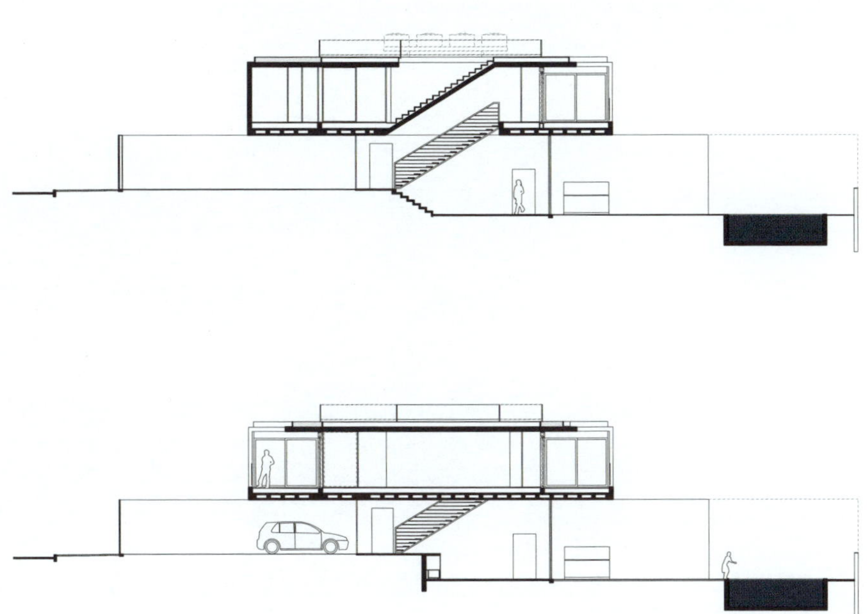

Longitudinal sections

CRENELLATIONS IN THE SKY / Buenos Aires, 2005. Argentina Series.
2010_Image specially composed for this book by Gina Stahl.

BINIMELIS HOUSE

Polidura - Talhouk Architects
Chile

Date: 2005-2007
Location: La Reserva, Chicureo, Colina, Chile
Design team: Polidura + Talhouk Architects: Antonio Polidura, Marco Polidura, Pablo Talhouk
Structural design: Daniel Stagno
Construction: Constructora Los Robles
Site area: 9,500 SF.
Total floor area: 2,600 SF.

This is a house for a young couple with two children, located in La Reserva lots in Chicureo, Colina, Chile.

The site presented three conditions that determined the actions taken by the architects to define the project. Because of the triangular shape of the site and the legal building-lines, the area to locate the house is right in the center of this form, with a steep incline of 40%, leaving the sun exposure and the views towards the valley.

The architectural idea consisted in organizing the program in two overlapping volumes parallel to the main terrain lines in a way that the two volumes relate to the landscape.

The lower volume is buried in the terrain and adopts a materiality that allows the piece to blend with the landscape; the stone-walls help to make the site more enclosed too. In this part of the house the bedrooms connect with the garden over the street level.

The upper volume lies over the lower one; by abstraction, it differs from the stone socle and the terrain.

In order to do this, the architects worked with simple geometry using just one material and a neutral color. Organizing the more social spaces, this volume breaks up to prevent views towards the quarry orienting them to the valley. In this case a big opening connects to the garden located at the upper street level.

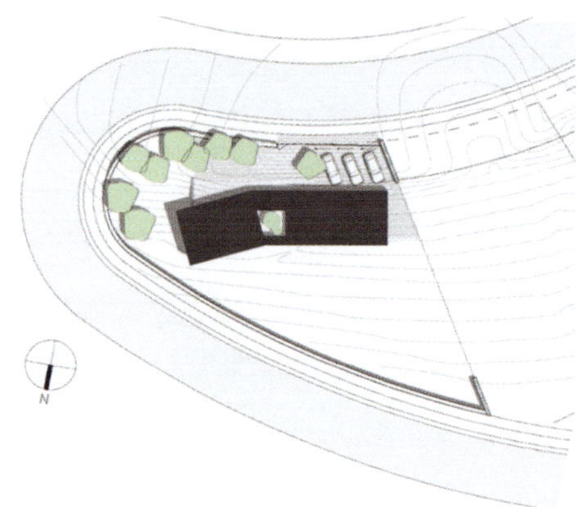

Site plan

Transversal section

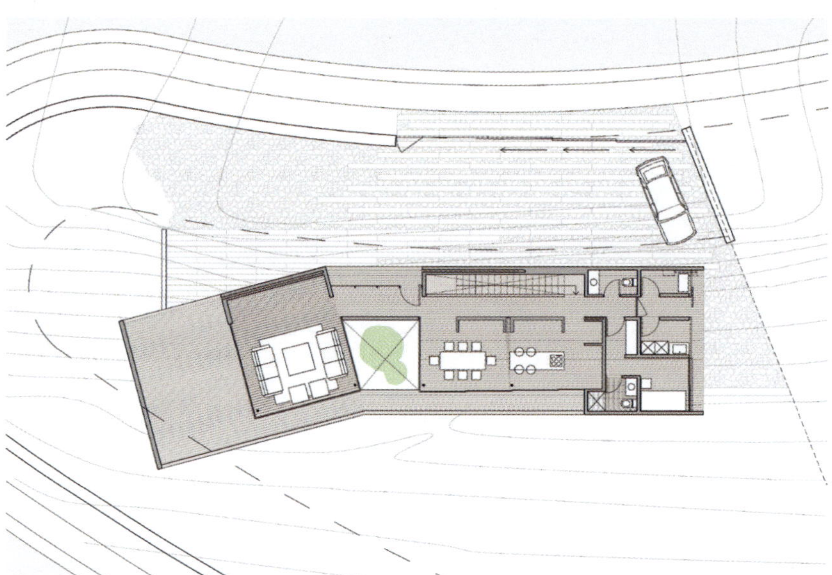

First floor

Ground floor

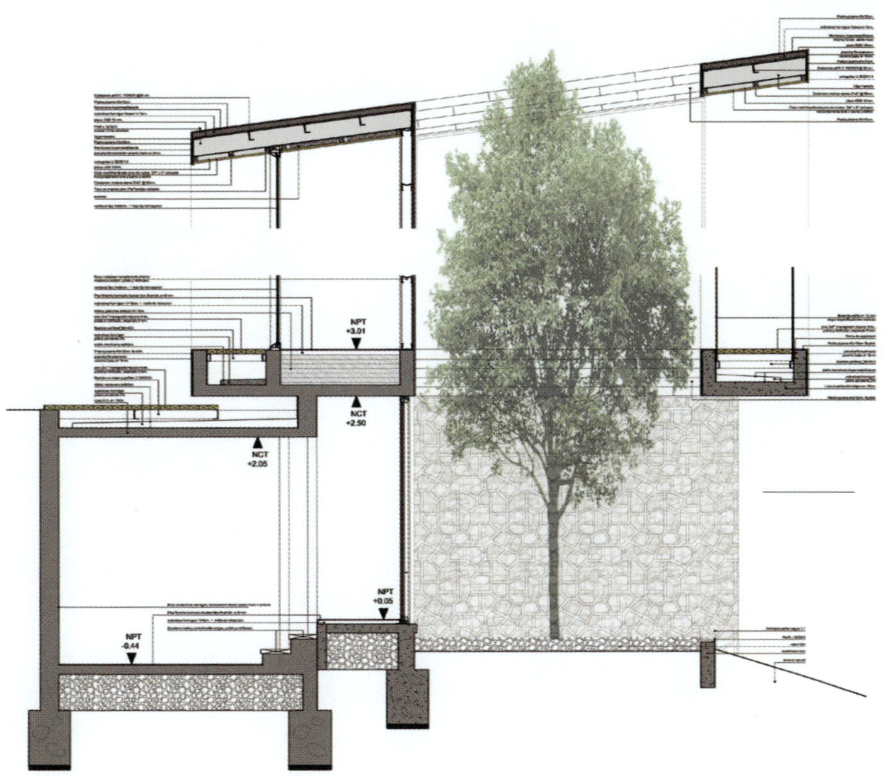

Transversal section detail

FUICA HOUSE

Polidura – Talhouk Architects
Chile

Date: 2007
Design team: Polidura + Talhouk Architects: Antonio Polidura, Marco Polidura, Pablo Talhouk
Location: La Reserva, Chicureo, Colina, Chile
Structural Design: Daniel Stagno
Construction: Constructora Los Robles
Site Area: 8,500 SF.
Total floor area: 1,400 SF.

This is a house with a low construction cost and that could be repeated in different sites with an average slope of 35%.

The strategy consisted of separating the public and private spaces into two perpendicular volumes. In section these two volumes are connected with the land in a way so that each space of the house relates to the garden.

The organization of each volume would depend on the access to the site. This architectural organization always displays one volume down facing the valley and the other one facing the site next door, allowing for open views and a considerable distance from the neighboring houses.

In this case the volume below is made of concrete, working as a structural containment for the upper terrain. This organization generates the possibility of adding a horizontal garden on the upper level. Built entirely with steel, this volume appears to be more flexible and transparent.

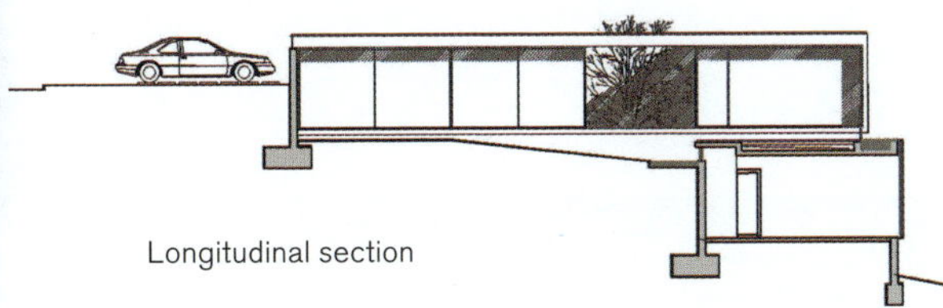

Longitudinal section

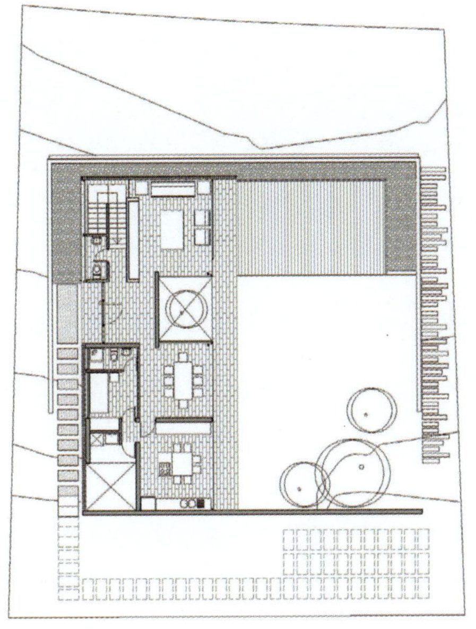

First floor

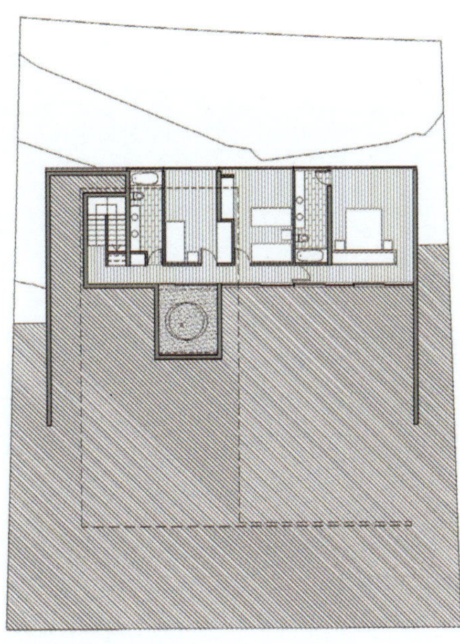

Ground floor

ENTRE MUROS HOUSE

Al Borde
Ecuador

Date: 2007-2008
Location: Tumbaco, Quito, Ecuador
Design team: Al Borde, David Barragán, Pascual Gangotena
Collaborators: Estefanía Jácome, José Antonio Vivanco
Technical advisor: Bolívar Romero, Rammed Earth Specialist
Construction: Miguel Ramos
Site Area: 50,000 SF.
Total floor area: 1,800 SF.

The wish to set up, the search for living in harmony with nature, the need of autonomy for each one of the three members of the family, the low budget (understood as the optimization of resources and spaces) and the phrase: "There is always another way of doing things and another way for living," set out by the family, were the starting point for the design.

Far from the pollution of the city, the house is set on the hillside of the Ilaló volcano in an indomitable land. Two streams open to the landscape of the valley limit it. A cut in the sloping land helps to generate a platform for the project and also to get enough raw materials to build the gravity walls. The waving form resulting from this cut in the land defines the position and order of every wall. The succession of the adobe walls and the different heights of the roof defines the division of the house for the activity or the user.

In order to get rid of the domino effect, the gravity walls break up their parallelism solving the structure and strengthening the character (spirit) of every refuge. The furniture is worked inside the thick adobe walls. The long corridor is used as an element that isolates the project from immediate neighbors and reinforces the autonomy of every space.

This architecture aims to highlight the nature of the material elements that compose it, promoting the aesthetic, formal, functional and structural qualities as well as a maximum respect for the environment.

The harmonious relationship between nature and architecture is very important for the owner and also a decisive fact in the design, the construction process and the operation of the house.

Following ancient customs, a ceremony is prepared to ask permission from the volcano. Gifts and good omens are buried, creating an energetic center in the space that divides the social area from private areas. The house is cleaned of bad energy during the ceremony, and finally an offering is put into the energetic center, which works as a meeting point between the users and the volcano.

Gray water is directed into processing pools so it can be reused for irrigation. A dry bath and a solar system for heating water are designed. The wood and reed-grass have been cut under a "good moon" to avoid using chemical products to treat them against pests.

The land as a building material ensures the project's low environmental impact. The raw material comes from the cut generated in the sloping land. It does not produce rubble, stores heat and regulates the interior climate by having the capacity to absorb and eliminate dampness more rapidly and in a larger quantity than other materials.

LADRILLO MAMBRON
36X16X7CM
CADENA DE REFUERZO
DE HORMIGON
TAPIAL - ALTO 100CM, ANCHO
60CM, LARGO 430CM
MALLA ELECTROSOLDADA
150X150X6
CHICOTE VARIILA
CORRUGADA Ø12MM
ESTRUCTURA DE ARRIOSTAMIENTO
PINGOS DE EUCALIPTO Ø10CM
LATILLA DE CAÑA
GUADUA
TIERRA CON PAJA
PICADA
ENLUCIDO DE CEMENTO
MALLA ELECTROSOLDADA
150X150X6
REPLATILLO
LOSA DE HORMIGÓN 210
KG/CM2 - 10CM DE ALTO
VIGA DE MADERA ROLLIZA
DE EUCALIPTO Ø16CM
VIGA DE MADERA ROLLIZA
DE EUCALIPTO Ø14CM
PARED DE BAREQUE
0 10 50 100CM
LOSA DE HORMIGÓN 210
KG/CM2 - 10CM DE ALTO
CIMIENTO HORMIGON
CICLOPEO
SUELO COMPACTADO

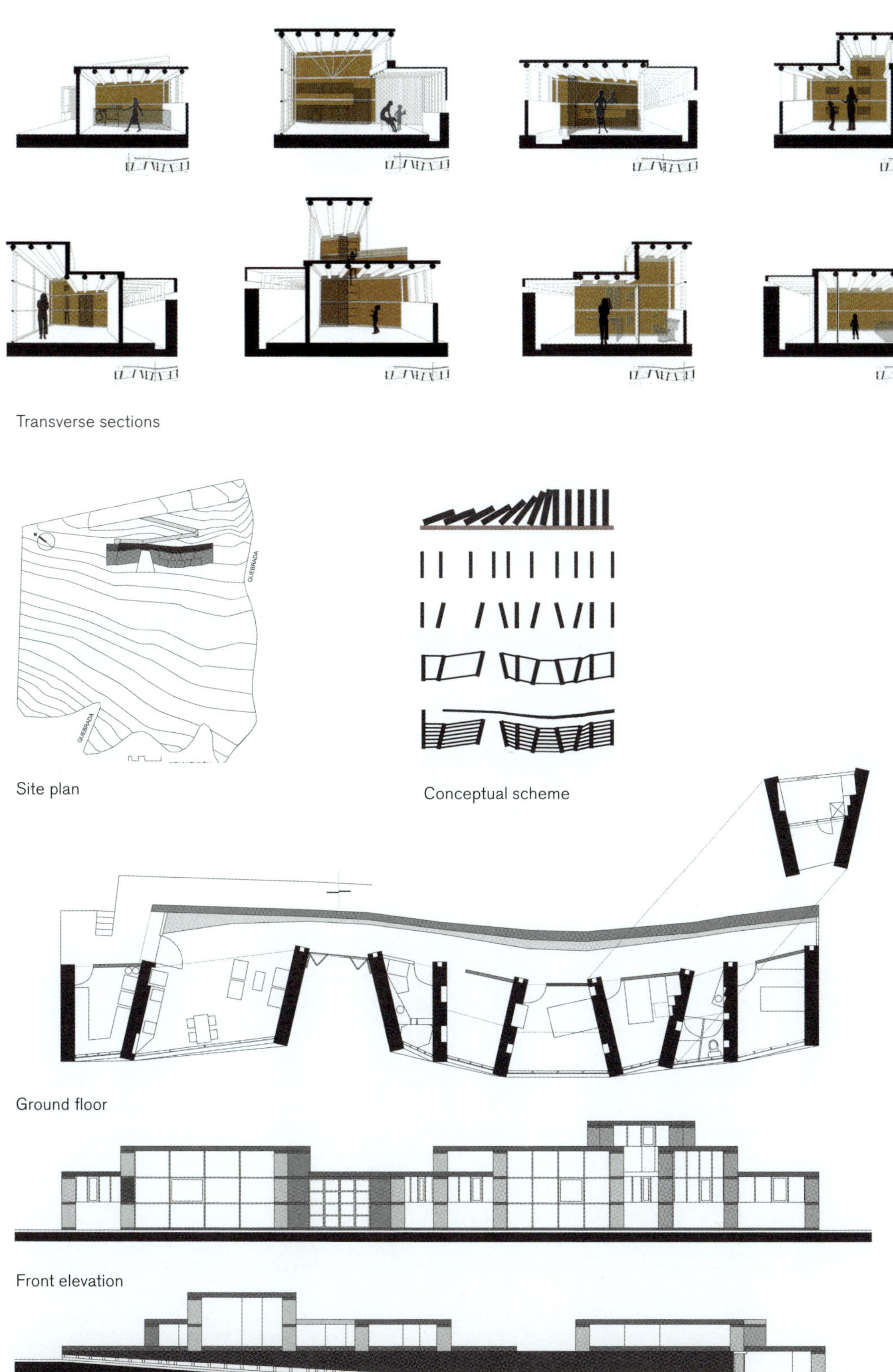

Transverse sections

Site plan

Conceptual scheme

Ground floor

Front elevation

Back elevation

PENTIMENTO HOUSE

José María Sáez + David Barragán
Ecuador

Date: 2006
Location: La Morita, Tumbaco, Quito, Ecuador
Design team: José María Sáez, David Barragán
Collaborator: Alejandra Andrade
Construction: Jaime Quinga
Prefabricated pieces: Héctor Sánchez, architect
Structural Engineer: César Izurieta
Site Area: 50,000 SF.
Total floor area: 2,340 SF.

A garden and a fearless client. Architecture has to be naked to connect with its surroundings. The house is built with a single piece of prefabricated concrete; it can be placed in four different ways (assembly), which resolves structure, walls, furniture, ladders, even a garden façade that served as the origin of the project. The exterior is a neutral grid that is camouflaged as a fence or hedge. Inside, each wall is different and is adjusted to its needs in terms of scale, function, position, and so on.

A concrete platform serves as its foundation and adapts to the topography, bypassing the trees or incorporating them. The prefabricated system is set up on top of the platform. Each piece is mounted onto steel rods that are anchored with epoxy glue onto the platform. These rods and the fastening elements between the pieces create a tight structure of small columns and lintels, which is well-suited to the seismic conditions in the area.

The interstices between prefabricated pieces are left open in some places and closed in others, using transparent or translucent acrylic and wooden strips, which act as filters for vegetation and light. On the inside, those cracks help to support a number of wood pieces that serve as shelves, seating, tables and stairs.The house does without finishes as far as possible.

The foundation slab is coated with black pigment and hardener to create the finished floor. The prefabricated concrete elements are left visible both on the interior and the exterior. The interior wood and the exterior vegetation remain an important part of the project. The open overlook on the top floor is stripped of any secondary elements, allowing for air and light to pass through, framing the views of the distant mountains. Its serves to link the user with the surrounding environment.

The blessing of a low budget leads to economy, simplicity and clarity. Pushed to look for the answer from within the project, the budget limitations led us in that direction: stripping accessory elements, going after intensity through reduction, simplifying the building processes. Working with light, nature, the temperate climate and the available materials. The use of few materials and clarity in their use.

Liberating austerity, allowing for enjoyment, a sensory experience and a connection with nature. Architectural synthesis, which is held in a small number of its own laws. A single piece, a single constructive action of stacking the flowerpots. An architecture diluted in nature: the outside is a vertical extension of the garden and the minimalist furniture inside. A flowerpots wall, which brings together environment and user.

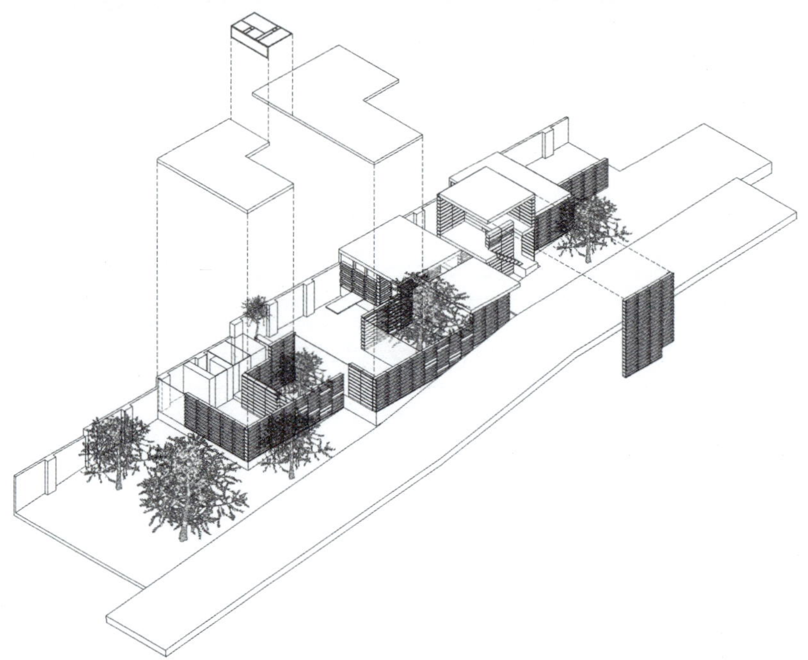

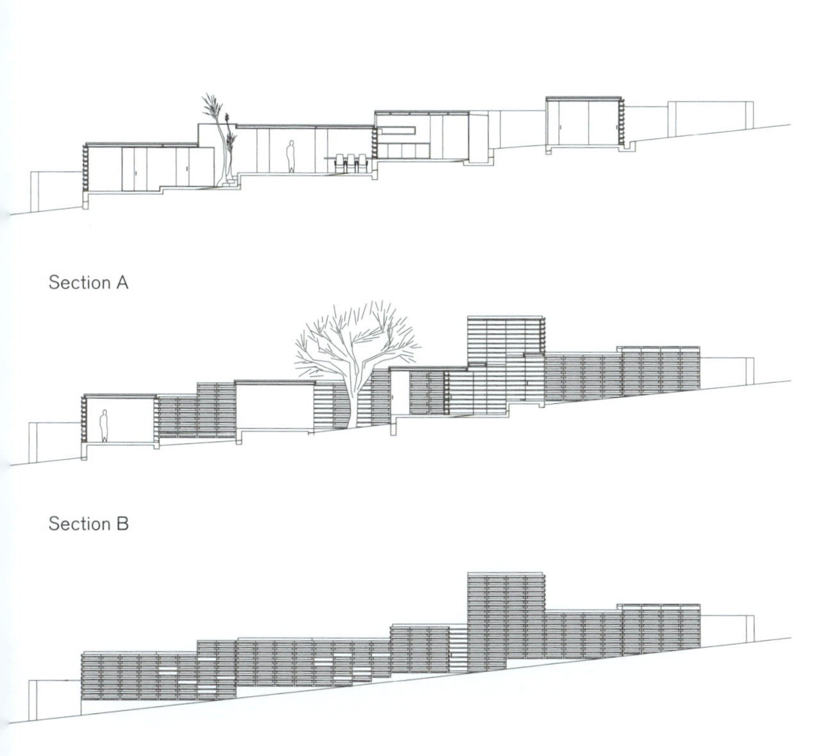

Section A

Section B

East elevation

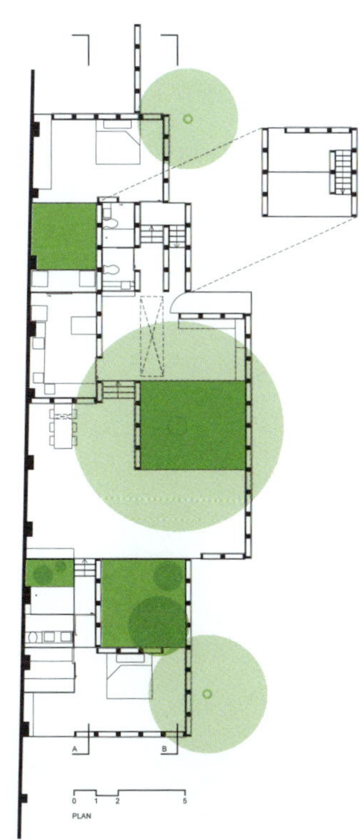

Floor

A WINDOW ONTO THE WORLD OF LE CORBUSIER. Series: Trip to South America, 2004.
2010_Image specially composed for this book by I. Bracher.

SAN JUAN HOUSE

José María Sáez + David Barragán
Ecuador

Date: (renovation), 2007
Location: Quito historic downtown, Ecuador
Design team: José María Sáez
Collaborator: David Barragán
Engineering: Herberto Novillo
Construction: Jaime Quinga and Luis Pillajo
Total floor area: 7,270 SF.
Site area: 11,250 SF.

A house in Quito's historic Old Town turns its gaze toward a private garden. On the old terrace, the new hall becomes a connector between the interior and the exterior. A continuous steel girder reaffirms the vocation of opening to the landscape, while its horizontality unifies the façade facing the garden. The extremes of the beam are delicately separated from the adobe (sun-dried mud brick) wall, barely brushing them. The mobile gallery allows for a wide range of openings toward the garden; the user can decide if the room regains its original condition as a terrace.

Inside, the hall is an internal connector, the heart of the house. Massive, substantive, timeless; it is the extreme expression of the materiality of a house. Its verticality relates only to the sun and the other rooms. The thick and irregular perforations are aligned with internal views, creating a primitive and non-obvious order.

The constructive system is the principal actor of this original house and its land: Hanging an 18-meter-long beam, placing a ceiling on structural walls, digging a crack in the ground to negotiate the sharp drop.

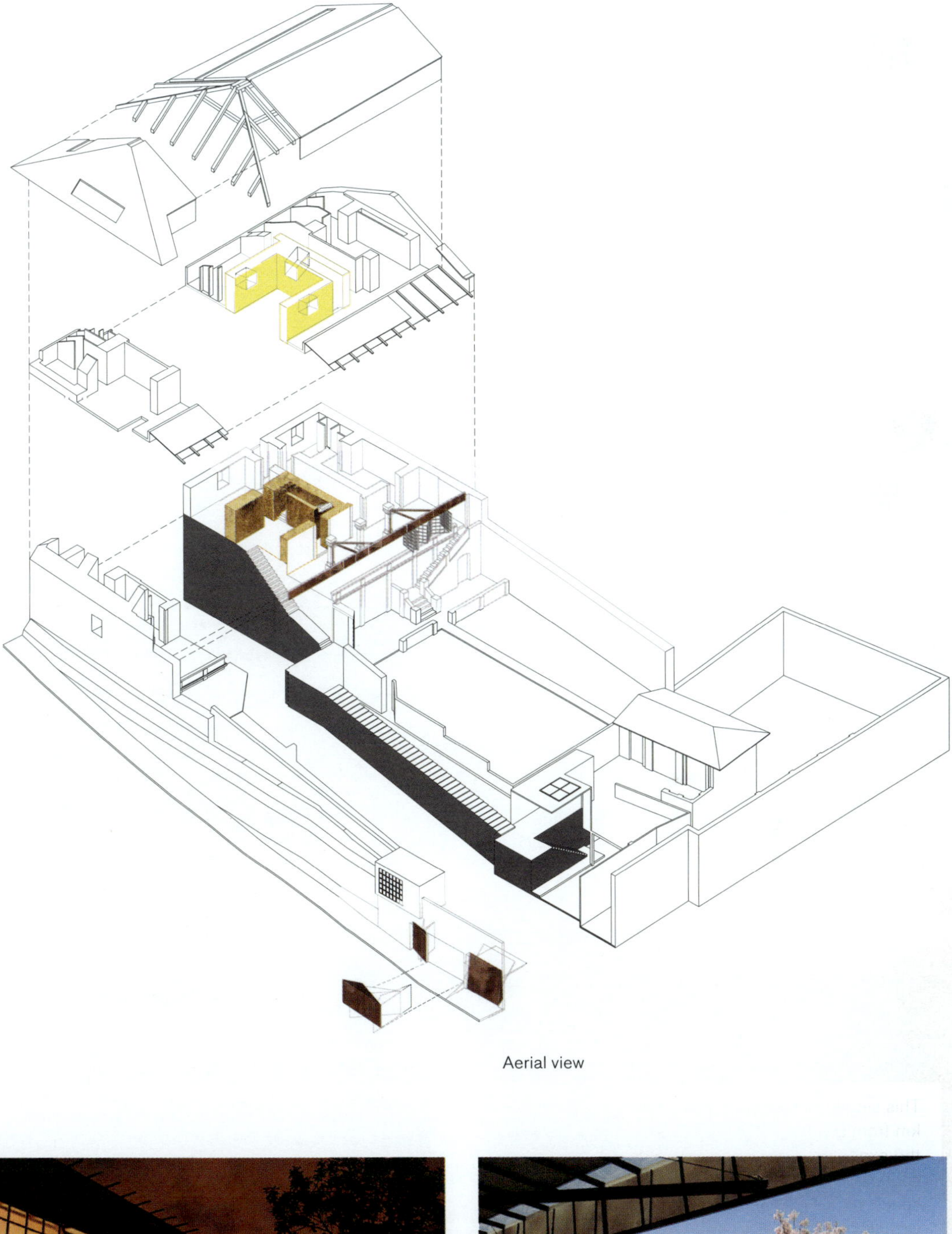

Aerial view

M HOUSE

Fernando Fritz - Eric Fritz Architects
Argentina

Date: 2010
Location: Lujan, Argentina
Design team: Fernando Fritz & Eric Fritz Architects
Collaborator: Ana Messina
Total floor area: 2,000 SF.

This single-family house is projected in Luján, 40 km from Buenos Aires, and aims to move toward the experimentation of bringing into realization the spatial ideas of folding in order to acquire a dynamic space where infinite possibilities, processes and virtuality can unfold across a diverse architectural landscape with no definable beginning or end; rather, an evolving continuum.

On a simple rectangle-shaped volume and around three patios placed off-center of the house, the kitchen, dining and living rooms appear.

Various kinds of materials – wood, translucent and transparent glass among others, provide alternating effects of opacity and obscurity, whereas transparency occurs only within the patios.

The project aims to develop new ways of looking at the relationship of architecture to environment, and of building to site. The single-folded volume appears as a means of reconsidering questions of figure-ground, no longer creating a separation between them, but one where a continuous and reversible dialogue can occur. A folding across lines helps to create uncertainty between boundaries, instead of defined boundaries of separation.

The house is not one space and one site but many spaces folded into many sites, and folding as a means of creating a blurring of inside-outside, solid-void and space-to-space thresholds.

N. ROSSETTI HOUSE

Gonzalo Sanchez Hermelo Architects
Argentina

Location: Kentucky Club de Campo, Funes, Pcia. de Santa Fe, Argentina
Design team: Gonzalo Sánchez Hermelo Architects
Site area: 20,828 SF.
Total floor area: 2,885 SF.

The house concept is based on simplicity, which is reflected both functionally and formally. Two pure volumes, a primary one and another for service, are combined using a minimal set of materials and large glass that expands the interior space creating a direct relationship with the landscape surrounding it.

For the layout of the rooms, we took full advantage of the orientation and the view the lot has towards the large eucalyptus on the main street. In addition, an extensive gallery was generated looking north where the main rooms lie.

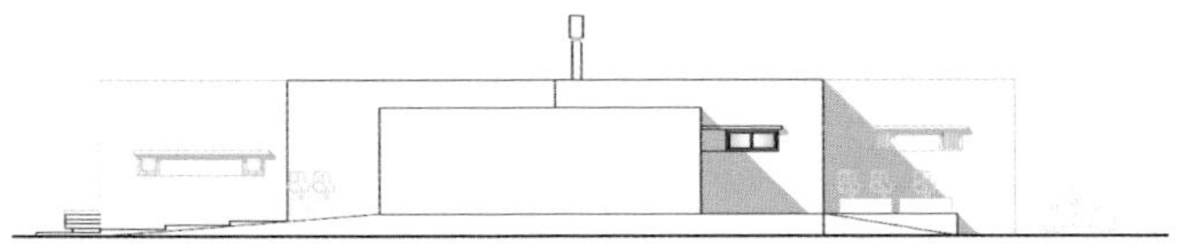

South elevation

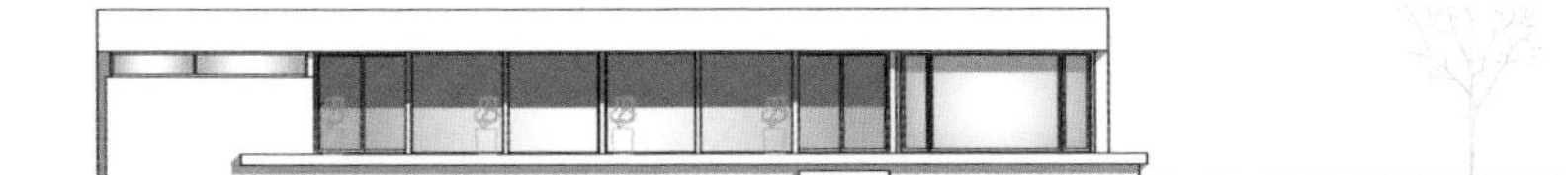

North elevation

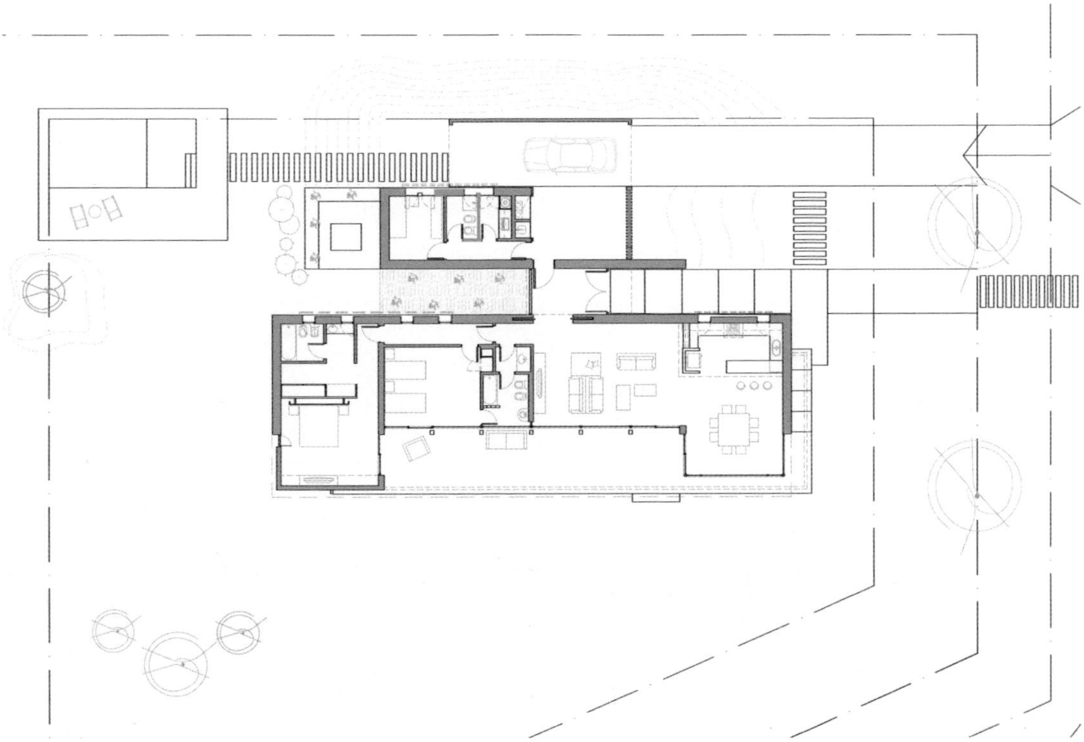

Ground floor

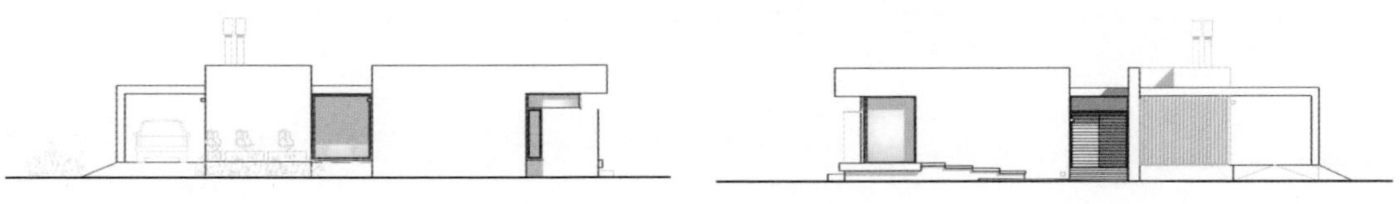

West elevation

East elevation

FISHERMAN'S HOUSE

José Cubilla & Associates
Paraguay

Date: 2010
Location: Villa Florida, Paraguay
Design team: José Cubilla & Associates
Collaborators: Mauricio Ortiz, Dahiana Núñez, Álvaro Dibernardo, Bibiana Escanciano, Luis Bellasai, Javier Juárez
Engineer: Enrique Granada
Total floor area: 2,320 SF.

A stark, well-ventilated dwelling, which happily houses temporary events, and can be shut like a trunk in the silence of absences...

The house captures the existing shade (the yvyra pyta tree), creating a central space that is typical of the area (pleasant and unifying), and presents us with a terrace overlooking the Tebicuary River.

Recycled materials (wood or formwork from the structure used for fences along the boundary lines and at the entrance, leftover cut pieces of stones from the quarry used for the white platform, or mortarless walls to promote cross-ventilation), make this house an interesting laboratory for experimenting with building materials, without sacrificing respect for traditional methods.

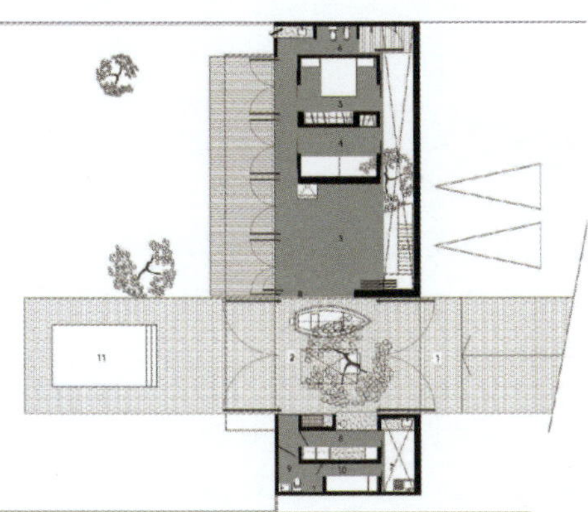

Ground floor

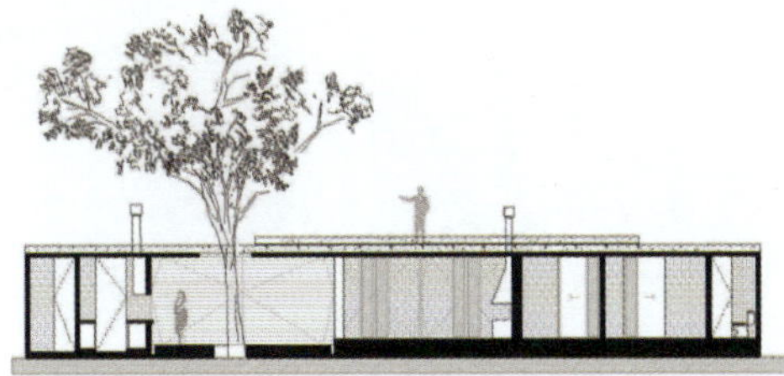

Longitudinal section

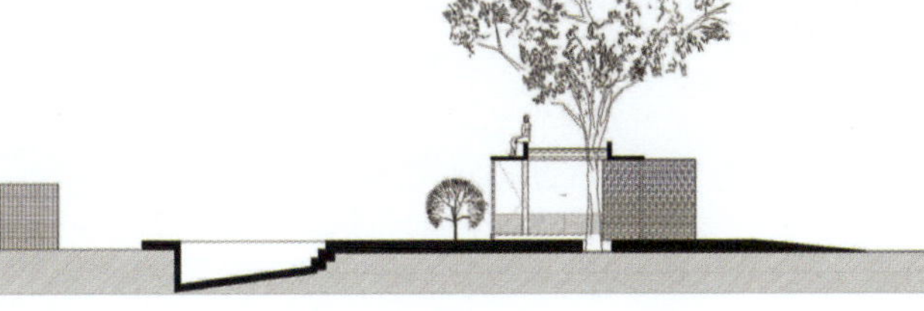

Transversal section

AMARILLO AND ITS COMPLEMENT / Buenos Aires, 2005. Argentina Series. 2010_Image specially composed for this book by G. Stahl.

SEARCHES ON LARGER SCALES

AREA, LARGE, SIZE, FOOTAGE, CORRELATION, SCOPE, SIGNIFICANCE, NUMBERS, MAGNITUDE, FRACTION, METRIC, HARMONY, IMPORTANCE, EXTENT, SMALL, PHYSICAL, DIMENSIONS, VOLUME, PROPORTION, WEIGHT, EXPANSE, QUANTITY, AMOUNT.

JUJUY REDUX

APARTMENT BUILDING IN ROSARIO

P-A-T-T-E-R-N-S + Maxi Spina Architect
Argentina

Date: 2008-2012
Location: Rosario, Argentina
Design team: PATTERNS + MSA. Principals in charge: Marcelo Spina, Georgina Huljich and Maximiliano Spina
Team Members: Rick Michod, Nathaniel Moore, Giuliana Haro, Daniele Profeta, Mike Wang
Structural engineers: Jose Orengo
Furniture: Forcen Design + Nosten
Total floor area: 13,500 SF.

The vertical apartment building, or so-called PH (which stands for the Spanish phrase "propiedad horizontal," or horizontal property in English) is perhaps the most intellectually underestimated architectural program in Argentina, an uncanny combination of both economic speculation, driven by private developers and construction companies, and the constraints of an over-subdivided urban grid that provides very narrow plots for actual interventions. A major percentage of the city has been, and continues to be, built according to a typology that celebrates homogeneity and monotony.[1]

Jujuy Redux is a mid-rise apartment building located in Rosario, Argentina. As our second commission for an apartment building in Argentina (also located aon Jujuy street) the project presented the possibility of rethinking urban housing. The project consists of 13 small, shared-floor units and a duplex organized as a cross-ventilated plan. The ground floor provides parking for 10 vehicles, and a common terrace on the 8th floor provides outdoor leisure spaces.

Occupying a corner lot, the new development aims to revitalize Rosario's traditional "Pichincha" neighborhood. Adjacent to both the historic downtown and the Parana riverfront, it enjoys generous street sizes, large amounts of vegetation and a low-density urban area with a valuable cultural heritage, making it the ideal environment for young families and students. As a result, the demand for new mid-rise interventions stands at an all-time high. Jujuy Redux proposes a subtly delineated mass, operating both at the scale of the entire volume and the scale of each apartment. This flexible duality overcomes issues that exist with many mid-rise housing typologies, such as the occurrence of fixed, scalar transformations that play either with the envelope meant as detached from the units, or with the units themselves.

A transition from mass to volume, from volume to surface, induces a visual and physical distortion at the pedestrian level. More importantly, it enables the weighty appearance of the building to sinuously dematerialize towards the corner, letting the social space par excellence of each apartment connect visually with pedestrian activity in the street below.

Shifts on Demand: Balconies

Problematically, balconies are the inevitable cultural element in mid-rise residential buildings in South America. Typologically, balconies have become the playground for formalism, often neglecting issues of spatial integration into an overall scheme or, worse, even dissociating them from social issues and human inhabitation. By contrast, the formal, spatial and material treatment of the balconies of Jujuy Redux is one of the most significant, innovative and socially performative aspects of the project.

We recognize the open cultural condition associated with balconies in apartment buildings that are not yet coded into an architectural typology. Jujuy Redux' balcony design takes inspiration from the polygonal bay window as well as from the horizon-

1. From the project description, 2003.

tal balcony. While traditional bay windows perform strictly as interior spaces, Jujuy Redux balconies perform directionally as they open up toward the corner, allowing both for exposed spaces with oblique vistas and more intimate ones, sheltered from the weather and direct views from the street.

While the project is built almost entirely of cast-in-place concrete, the interior space of the balconies is clad with grey Venetian tile. This arrangement produces a sense of contrast between the outer white concrete skin and the inner walls of the balcony, while also accentuating a sense of spatial enclosure for the outdoor living space of each apartment, enhancing its use as each inhabitant negotiates the threshold between private and public space.

Spatially ambivalent and nuanced, Jujuy Redux's balconies are conceived as highly articulated pieces of scalar diversity that incorporate openings/fenestrations, railing, direct and indirect LED lighting as well as material changes. A built-in bench provides a place for leisure activities and small gatherings, while allowing inhabitants to tailor its use according to their individual needs.

Down on the Ground: Opening the Corner
At ground level, concrete cross braces receive the diagonal deviations produced by the balconies, creating a double-height urban corner free of columns. This cantilevered corner gives way to an inconspicuous building entrance located on Jujuy Street, followed by a sequence of spaces: a gated porch and main hall linked by a two-story glazed doorway, and the elevator lobby, all clad in polished Carrara marble.

High Above: Conquering the Roof
The formal sequence of diagonal deviations intensifies at the roof level, where the building tapers to accommodate a set of mechanical spaces, a corner duplex, a common terrace with a solarium and semi-covered areas for barbecuing – all of which enjoy attractive views of downtown and the riverfront. Visually, the building opens up and lightens its contorted mass as it rises in sequenced diagonal recesses to meet the city skyline.

Articulation: Whole and Holes
Following the geometry of the balcony system, triangular openings along the shell open up a series of threshold spaces to control sunlight, natural ventilation and views. Where the shell doubles up,

it becomes perforated, creating a passive solar technique which, in addition to the cross-ventilated layout of the apartments, helps to produce an effective natural cooling system. Similarly, the chamfered corner and main entry are punctured, albeit in a larger number, allowing the building porch to receive filtered morning light while offering passers-by voyeuristic peeks into the building.

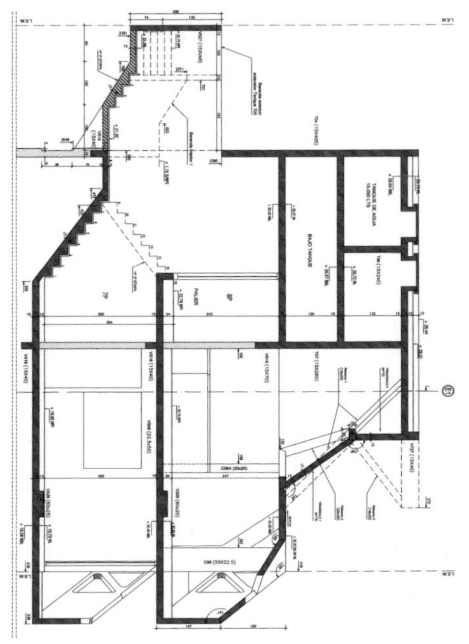

In and Out of Material: White Concrete

White walls have traditionally been associated with the stripping away of details and ornamentation, often resulting in a stale materiality, like the overt whitewash found in many nineteenth-century buildings. Alternatively, Jujuy Redux explores a different kind of whiteness: one that privileges overall plasticity over local materiality and engages in high or low contrast to address depth and flatness, subtle white to off-white.

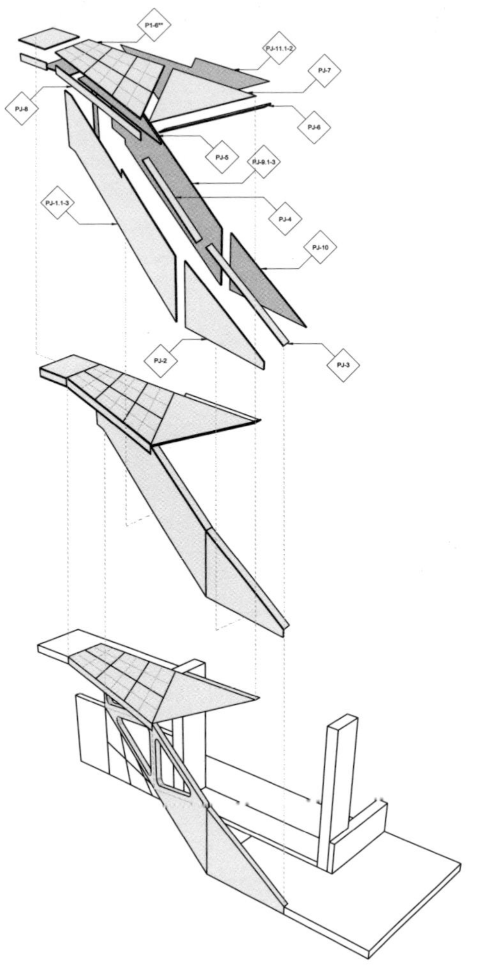

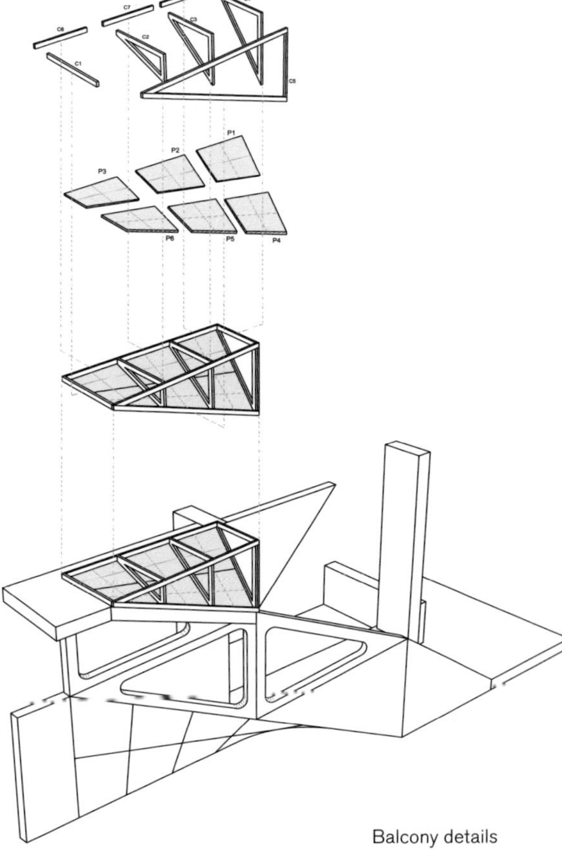

Balcony details

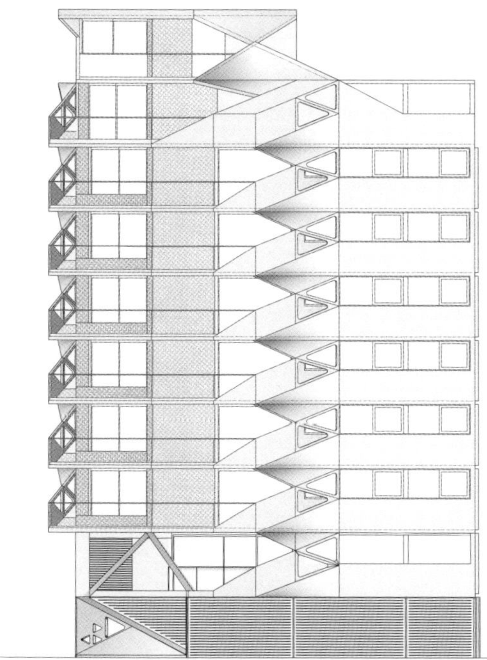

East elevation

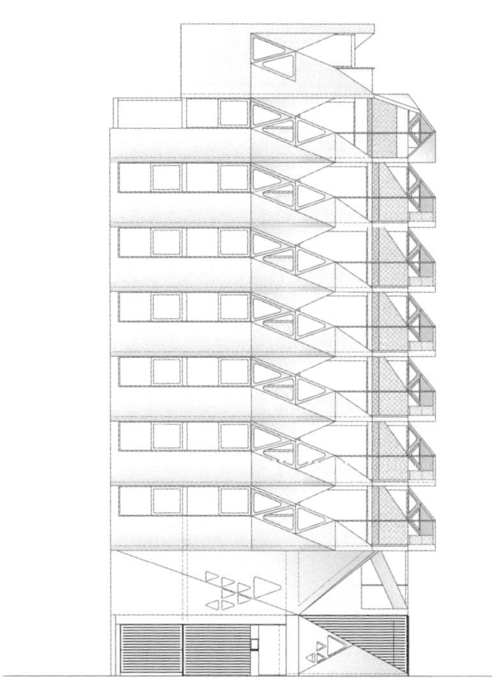

South elevation

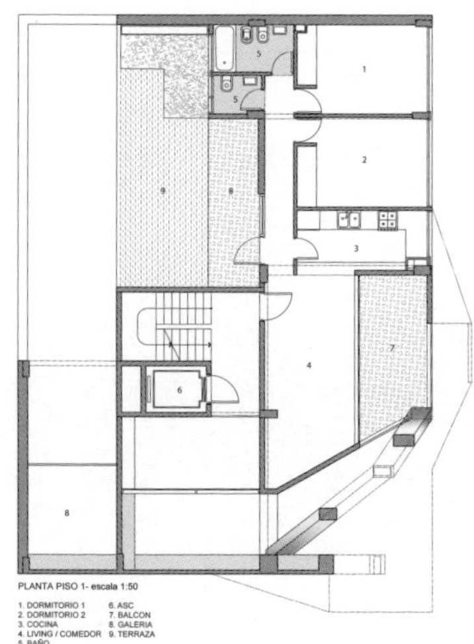

Floor plan level 1

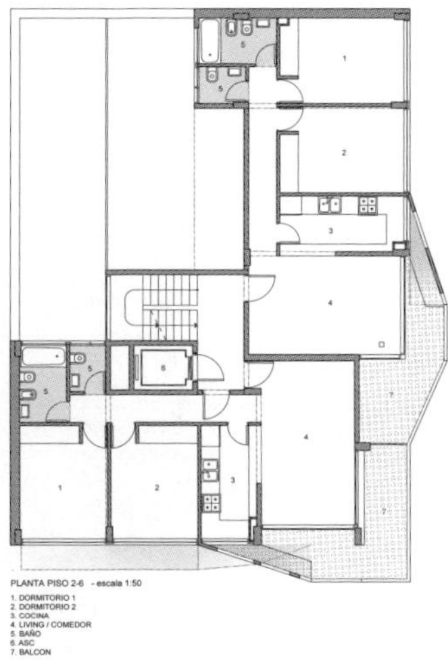

Floor plan levels 2-6

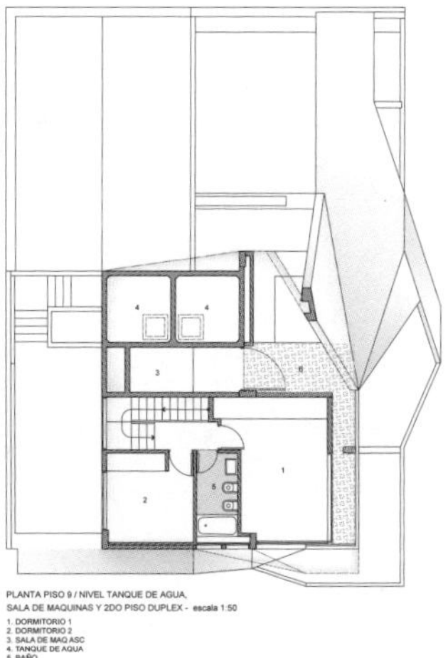

Floor plan level 9

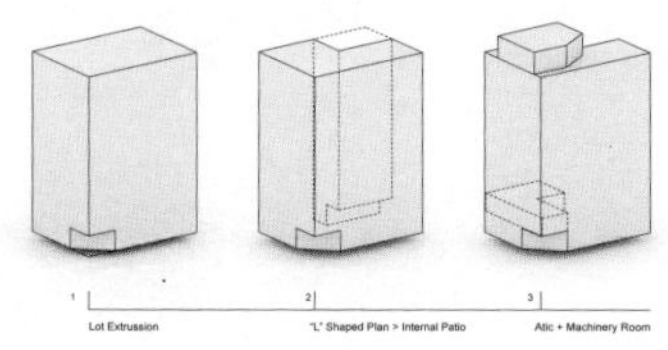

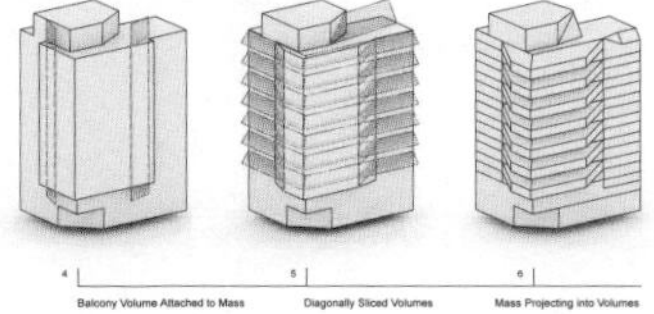

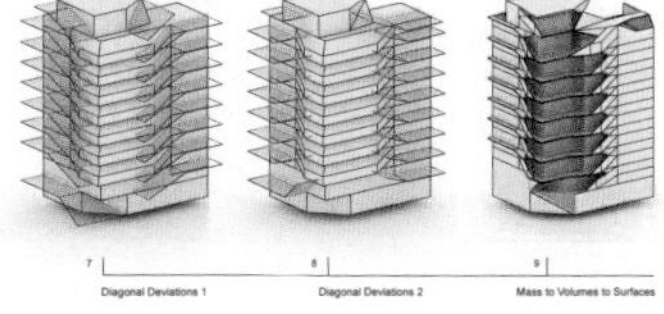

Mass evolution

CLAY
APARTMENT BUILDING

Dieguez Fridman Architects & Associates
Argentina

Date: 2004-2007
Location: Clay 2928, Buenos Aires, Argentina
Design team: Dieguez Fridman Architects & Associates: Tristán Dieguez, Axel Fridman, Brenda Levi, María Carranza, Odile L'Hardy
Structural engineering: Sebastián Berdichevsky
Lighting consultant: Pablo Pizarro
Landscape: Cora Burgin
Total floor area: 2,200 SF.

In a residential district of Buenos Aires, this housing project seeks to incorporate to its' apartments different spaces, elements and details like those of single-family houses.

The eight units are organized across two levels, with the living room as a double-height space that connects them. Both the main bedroom and the living room have wide terraces in front of them, one overlooking the other, closed by glass sunshades that reduce solar gain and transform the façade into an intermediate space between the interior and the exterior: an outdoor space protected from the wind and rain, and from the views from the sidewalk.

The units are organized in such a way that they all have cross ventilation. The circulation area, stairs and patio are in the middle of the units, which are divided into two sets of four apartments. All public circulations are outdoors, stressing the apartment's characteristics as "little houses". Cars and people enter by the same place: a low platform with a wooden floor, which serves as parking at night and as playground during the day.

The interior frosted glass divisions let the light pass from one room to the other and generate reflections and the play of shadows of the kind usually more frequent in shops. The play of shadows are also in composition with the solar shadings and the exterior and patio glass façades, which all constitute a series of veils that create different types of light during the day.
During the 20th century, some of the biggest housing building projects in the city have proposed reflections or experiments concerning different problems, some related to houses and ways of living, and others more related to architecture's relationship with nature, constructive systems, or climate. This project aims to go beyond the imposed regulations' limitations and the need to maximize economic profits that these initiatives have nowadays, trying to regain this aim for experimentation.

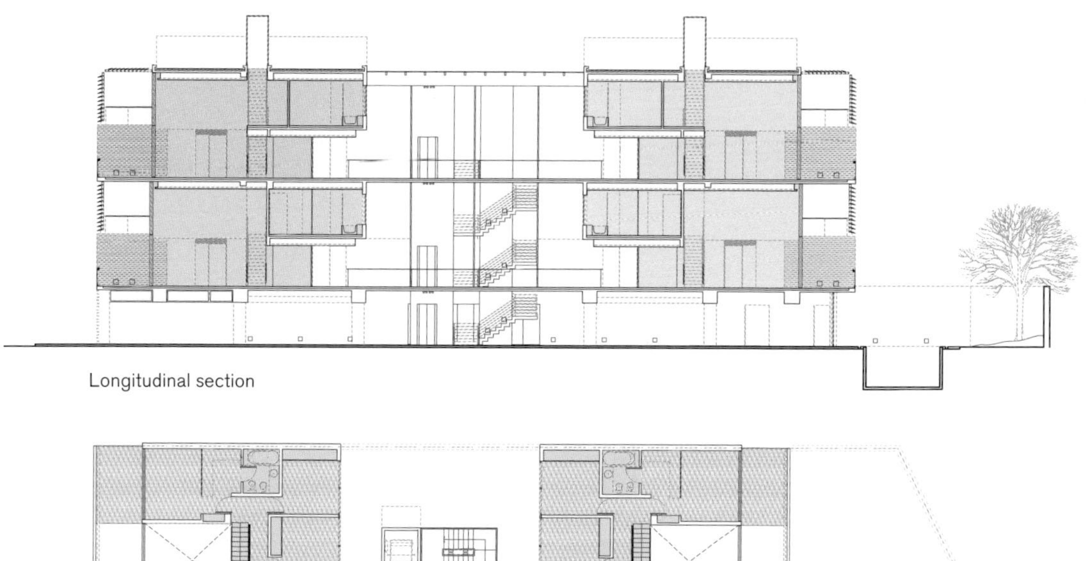
Longitudinal section

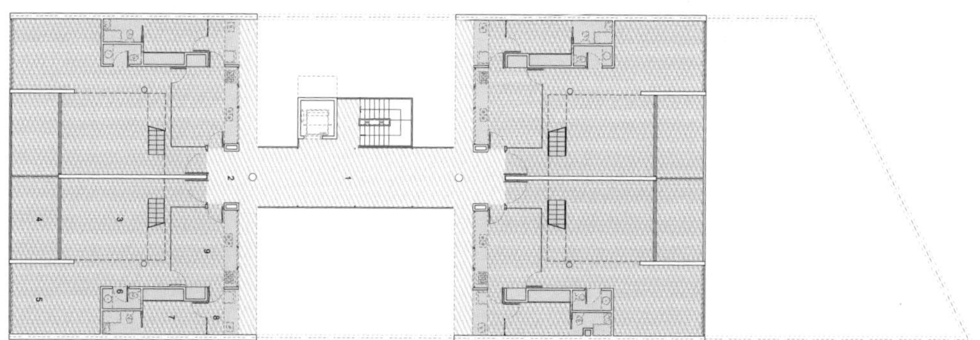
Floor plan level 2 and 4

Floor plan level 1 and 3

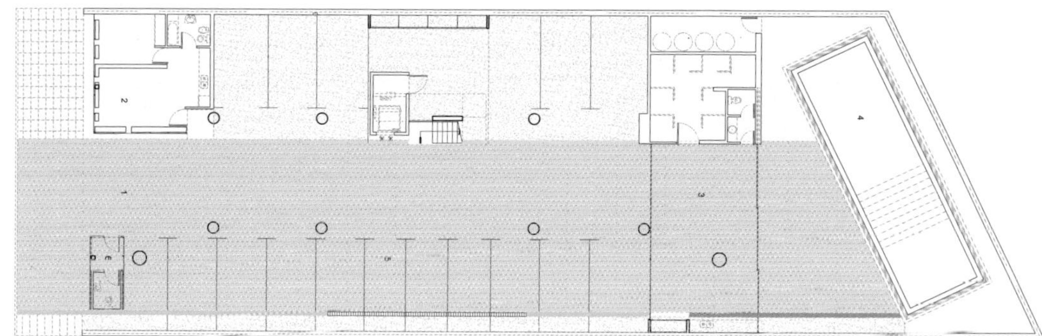
Ground floor

RODAS
BIKE SHOWROOM

Gerardo Caballero - Maite Fernández Architects
Argentina

Date: 2009-2010
Location: Rosario, Argentina
Project team: Principals: Gerardo Caballero and Maite Fernández
Collaborators: Sebastián Sanchez and Juan Fonseca
Structural engineer and construction: Sergio Monge
Total floor area: 717 SF.

Caballero consciously weakens his presence as an "architect that expresses himself through his work." In each of his works there is one implied notion, which is that the architectural project or design is not a vehicle for an architect to express himself, but rather a vehicle for the place and architecture to express themselves. To prove this, nothing more eloquent than his sketches, which are never preconceived formal images but rather the intimate expression of thought maps coming to life. Though in Caballero's work there is no interest in exhibitionism, it is also true that its strangeness makes it impossible to overlook. According to Walter Benjamin, architecture is experienced collectively in a state of "absent-mindedness", by its everyday use and sensory perception. Even though Caballero's work seems to reflect Benjamin's idea, an attentive and lengthy look at his work will find infinite meanings and discoveries. Caballero's work is basically discrete and sensual; if analyzed, it produces great intellectual happiness[1].

1. Extracted from "Gerardo Caballero's Town Dwellings," by Diego Arraigada, in Summa+ no. 80 Special edition: Casas (Houses) Donn S.A., Buenos Aires, Argentina, June 2006.

The project is about creating a visual relationship between the observer and the objects. Pursuing that, the bikes are exhibited in an elevated window, which allows for maximum visibility from the avenue. The building turns itself into a kind of billboard, which defines a space meant for exhibition, clearly differentiated from its context.

The construction concept consists of a metallic structure isolated from the party walls, which was carried to the place and assembled at the construction site. It has an exterior skin of white corrugated sheet-metal skin, and the whole interior space is covered in drywall. The ceiling is made of a refracting tensed fabric, which allows for indirect artificial lighting without any lamps visible in it.

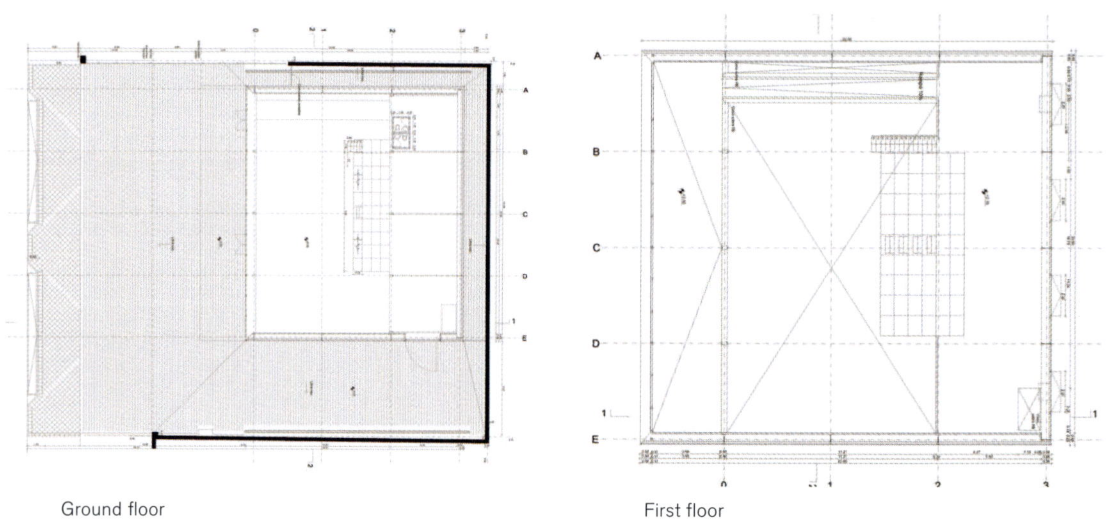

Ground floor

First floor

Elevations in relation with the street

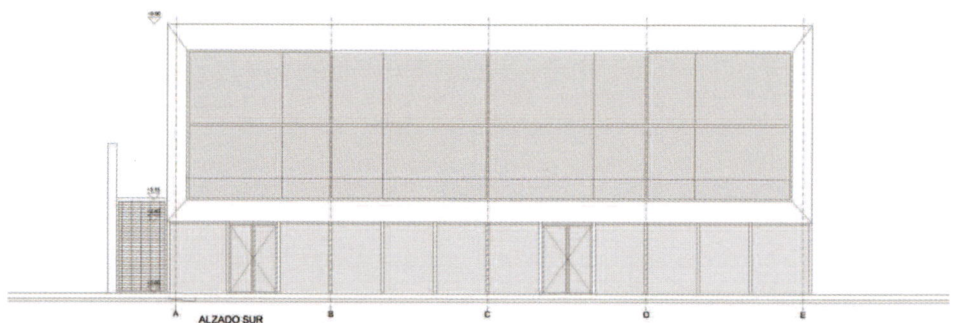

South elevation

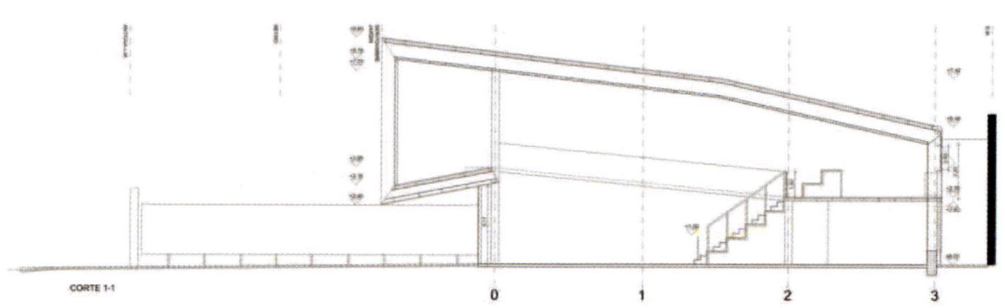

Transversal section

SHEDS AND SIGNBOARDS

Juan Manuel Rois[1]

While traveling on the roads through the Argentinean pampas, a subtle hypnotic game traps one looking out of the car window. Half asleep by the car noise, our mind escapes with our gaze, toward the horizon. Suddenly, we start noticing that everything moves at different speeds. The road posts disappear in a blurry foreground while we try to concentrate on the trees, clustered in groups, close and far away.

Some trees go faster than others. Something weird is going on here. We start concentrating on an almost immobile point, straight ahead, where sky and earth meet. For an instant we believe that the car is navigating an infinite circumference surrounding this central point. In the pampas, there is no perspective, only depth. The abstract game of movement of planes played by the trees is what gives us a sense of distances in this horizontal vertigo. In counterpoint, some white points create inner tensions in this game: houses, silos, sheds.

For the one driving, everything is different. An infinite central perspective develops at high speed. Trees either move parallel to the road creating zones of velocities, or perpendicular, creating territorial walls to cross. The lines of the road meet at a distance; a bend in the road entertains us; a shortening of the horizon brought about by a slight topographic move creates suspense for what is yet to come, now unseen. What comes is more of the same; we know that already. In this cinematic game, rhythmic punctuations regularly appear: bridges, exits, posts, signs and boards.
A hundred kilometers north of Rosario, on route 34, San Genaro going north, a signboard of great dimension sticks out on the road. In its interior, big farm machinery is exhibited. This is a signboard with a big interior space, or a shed with a big public screen. This is a hybrid that brings together the best of both typologies: the visibility of the sign and the utilitarian space of the shed. With a simple and precise geometric operation, the rectangular plan of the shed opens up in diagonal toward the road and its perspective deformation intensifies the visual cone, multiplying the visual impact of the artifact.

The "Farm Dealership" project by Gerardo Caballero is the sublimation of the Venturian[2] proposal of the decorated shed. In Robert Venturi's theory, the sign deals graphically with architectural signification, while the utilitarian structure of the shed deals with the programmatic requirements. Fortunately, the project on Route 34 reclaims for architecture the work that Venturi delegated to the sign: Gerardo Caballero interiorized the sign and transformed it as interior space.

The metallic structure, covered with galvanized sheet, is of a material simplicity that hides a geometric sophistication of great precision. The game of perspective intensification is achieved by a simple formal operation and with exquisite control of proportions: a diagonal from one of the vertices of the rectangle extends beyond it for exactly half of its longitude and returns to the rectangle in orthogonal fashion, defining in this way a frame parallel to the road of 3:1 proportion. By defining space in depth, the frame toward the road assumes its advertising function with a radical efficiency, better than any sign on the side of our roads. The farm machinery exhibited rotates in all its glory while we drive at a distance in front of it.

The sheet-metal corrugation in vertical fashion gathers shades of blue. The Farm Dealership approaches us on the road like a knife cutting the open sky of the pampas. It is an object against the horizon that we finally reach. The triangular canopy at the main entrance reminds us of the formal game and the building rotation towards the road. Inside, the ceiling created by the single pitch roof transforms the diagonal in a spatial effect and once again intensifies the perspective game: from this monumental interior space, we gaze again on a newly distant framed horizon.

1 Extracted from "Sheds and Signboards," by Juan Manuel Rois, architect and an assistant professor at the University of Illinois at Chicago – Summa+ no. 114 (Metal) Donn S.A., Buenos Aires, Argentina, April 2011.

2 J.M.Rois' reference to Robert Charles Venturi, Jr. (born June 25, 1925 in Philadelphia), an American architect, founding principal of the firm Venturi, Scott Brown and Associates, and one of the major figures in 20th century architecture. Together with his wife and partner, Denise Scott Brown, he helped to shape the way that architects, planners and students experience and think about architecture and the American built environment.

BROWN BUILDING

Gerardo Caballero - Maite Fernández Architects
Argentina

Date: 2005
Location: Brown 2909, Rosario, Argentina
Project team: Principals: Gerardo Caballero, Maite Fernández architects. Orlando Alloatti, Gonzalo Carbajo
Collaborators: Gerardo Bordi, Maria Eva Contesti; Juan Fonseca, Mariana Suso
Engineering: José Ramón Orengo
Developer: Horgen Construcciones
Construction company: Proas S.R.L.
Total floor area: 14,000 SF.

The project is located in the northern area of the city of Rosario, which has recently attracted interest owing to a series of public and private interventions that have endowed it with new leisure spaces and services.

The site, 14 x 19 meters in size, is situated at the northeast corner of a typical urban block, without much obvious appeal, apart from its potential to create visual links to the river and the islands found within view.

This inspired the idea of developing the stories like viewing cones in order to make this relationship more eloquent from the interior of the apartments, framing the landscape on the horizon.

This is a two-tower residential building, consisting of 9 units each, 700 square feet respectively. The last floor houses a swimming pool and a small gymnasium.

The concrete frame is made up of flat slabs and a series of perimeter walls lined with bricks on both sides. The result is a 36-cm-thick exposed brick wall. These walls, folded like screens, are the most significant element of the project and functionally organize the whole building.

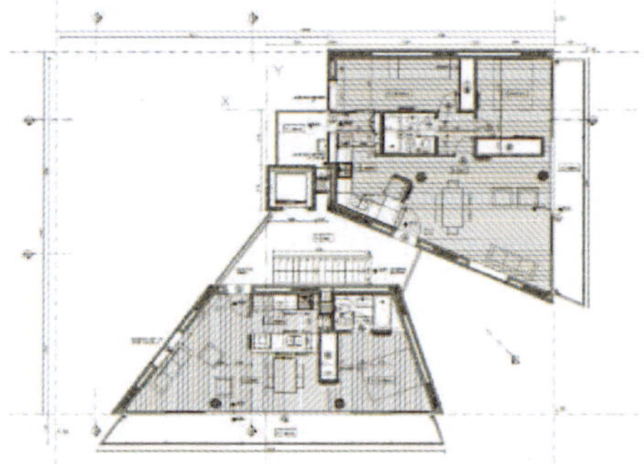

Type floor

VENDIDO
VENDIDO

SINGULAR_The Kavanagh Building and Companions. Designed by local architects Sánchez, Lagos, De la Torre in 1934.
The Kavanagh building in Buenos Aires was the highest reinforced concrete structure in the world at the time and the tallest building in South America for many years. 2010_ Image specially composed for this book by María de Brea Dulcich.

OFFICE BUILDING

Vila Sebastián Architects VSA
Argentina

Date: 2003
Location: Buenos Aires, Argentina
Design team: VSA-Vila Sebastián Architects: Marcelo Vila, Adrián Sebastián & Asociates

Austerity

In this line of thought, the notion of austerity is not associated with the false construction of an image created before the process that links it to the reproduction of an image associated to lack of resources, but on the contrary, to summarize several actions in a single action.

Austerity will always be a very conscious issue. The reference to that value will be present in the constitution of the project.

There is no deliberate pursuit of poverty in our view of austerity; on the contrary, we divest from excess or gesture so we can concentrate on the essential, on the spiritual. We want to highlight the concept of austerity as a positive value and not as the absence of things or resources, but as their possibility. What we seek to define is absolutely opposed to the notion of minimalism as an artificial operation of scarcity based on a vast range of resources.

Simultaneously in all this intellectual process the notion of material as a possibility of the project appears strongly: its structural condition and constructive results in the physical sense of the work. The result of these thoughts expressed us the essential conditions of creating beauty as the result of the conceptual synthesis of this process – the matrix that gets across the work, beyond its particular condition of site, material and opinion.

COURTHOUSE

Vila Sebastián Architects VSA, Argentina
Cristian Boza D. & Jose Luis Macchi R., Chile

Date: 2005
Location: Santiago de Chile, Chile
Design team: In Argentina: SA-Vila Sebastián Architects: Marcelo Vila, Adrián Sebastián. In Chile: Cristian Boza D. & Jose Luis Macchi R.

Regional

As social beings we choose to build and transform reality from a particular place, and architecture is a tool from which we, as intellectuals, contribute in the construction of a common knowledge that, in our speciality, we call "architectural culture". We have a moral duty that commits us to our place and time: to understand the location from where we think is really important to explain what we create.

Architecture is the space where the physical construction of a cultural process materializes. Working over the coherence of thought and project gives a meaning to our making. When we talk about thought, we talk about a critical lecture of the world in which we were born and when we talk about project, we mean the consequences of that thought, with our inherent tools.

We should allow a trend of thought and coherence to get across the architectural work and make, also the reverse path. In consequence, architecture is a tool of opinion. The ideology must be built into the thought mechanism so that it will finally translate in the materialization of work.

TWO PARKS

Vila Sebastián Architects VSA, Argentina
Irene Joselevich, Graciela Novoa,
Alfredo Garay, Néstor Magariños, Argentina

Date: Micaela Bastidas Park, 2003.
Mujeres Argentinas Park, 2006.
Location: Of both, Capital Federal, Buenos Aires, Argentina
Design team: In Argentina: SA-Vila Sebastián Architects: Marcelo Vila, Adrian Sebastián, Irene Joselevich, Graciela Novoa, Alfredo Garay, Néstor Magariños
Total surface area: 914,935 SF.

Contemporary

The compromise in which we engage when thinking of architecture should assume its temporary condition; the place of thought is made from a specific time: contemporary time.
In this sense, the modern movement, which was conceptually complete, expressed notions of unity. Postmodernism unfolded the phenomenon of integrity to recover the value of history but producing, simultaneously, a break in the relationship between signifier and signified. Moreover, the contemporary world produces, once more, a split in terms of image and meaning that expresses itself as the phenomenon of generic architectures.

We must assume this state of world culture can find expression in a simultaneous manifest system; all the recent phenomena of "signature" architectures could be read in this way. Our time does not reflect the absence of manifests, but the fall of the grandiloquent universal stories that the Modern movement used to tell.

In this context, we believe that the way to generate new paradigms is to stand in the place where we are, always moving its boundaries.

Beyond the frame of global uncertainty, we have the cultural and social commitment of building; from our view point this means new logics of understanding. We should move these boundaries toward new frontiers. We live in a time in which our ethical responsibility is to build new certainties. Our culture provides us with many tools so as to ride on external uncertainties.

MICHELET 50

APARTMENT BUILDING

Dellekamp Architects
Mexico

Date: 2010
Location: Anzures – Mexico City, Mexico
Design team: Dellekamp Architects, Derek Dellekamp
Project leader: Ignacio Méndez
Collaborators: Aisha Ballesteros, Jachen Schleich and Pedro Sánchez
Construction manager: Gabriela Saldaña

A collaborative design process that synthesizes externalities and existing conditions to create singular architectural environments with distinct atmospheric conditions characterizes Dellekamp Arquitectos' work. Our projects emphasize the integrity of the built product, emerge from a specific sense of place, and are based on a multidisciplinary approach of continuous learning and research.

Situated at the center of Mexico City, the project for Michelet, an apartment building, creates an urban retreat by connecting interior and exterior spaces through a network of green zones that permeate the building. These living interventions interact with the structure to determine the organization of the façade, the location of interior programs and the availability of green space.

To give the building a human scale that is missing from its dense surroundings, organic elements divide the building into three blocks, each with a differing apartment typology. By setting the building back from the street, we were able to make a green zone that buffers the apartments from the dense neighborhood. The vegetation growing in this zone intrudes into the building at three points where vines crawl up the façade and up to the roof. These areas, which are evident from the service quarters, directly improve the quality of interior spaces. Each apartment façade also occupies an entire block, allowing for an unimpeded connection between the inside and outside. The geometric composition of the glass façade contrasts the organic elements separating each block, calling attention to the integration of the vines within the apartment program. This continuous interplay between the inorganic and the organic ties the project together into a cohesive whole.

As we were developing this project, the Mexican artist Jeronimo Hagerman installed one of his artworks at the Sala de Siqueiros Museum in Mexico City using vining plants that perfectly matched the ones we imagined for the green walls. With kind permission from the artist, we were able to replant the vines in this project after the exhibition was over.

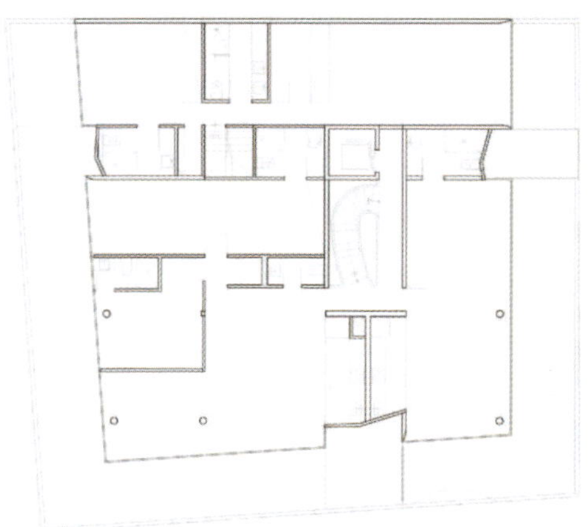

General floor

Ground floor

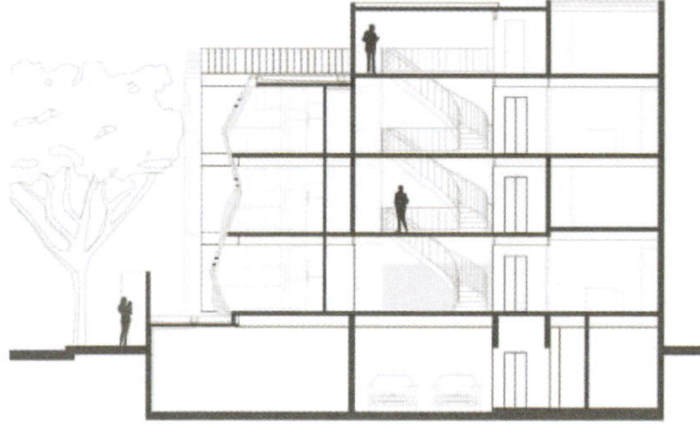

Section

Scheme floor

29

DOOR OPEN-DOOR CLOSED. From Series: Trip to South America, 2004 / Visit to Rafael Iglesia Studio in Rosario. 2010_Both images specially composed for this book by I. Bracher.

TO OPERATE AND TO ACT

Giancarlo Mazzanti

Architecture is formed and acts, in the first place, from material organization and special materials, which is what composes its physical construction and, in the second place, for what it produces, what it is able to induce in human conduct and behaviors; these two values, when they do interact, they define and allow to build architectures based on exchanges that are diverse and, many times, in contradiction with the place or parts of the program. What that we are looking for is for these two material conditions and interrelations to act together to promote new forms of behavior and organizations with adaptive intelligence open to change.

We believe that the value of architecture is not based only on itself, but in whatever it produces, in its performative capacities; that is why an architecture that is defined by what it does and not by its substance interests us; we are interested in inducing actions, effects, events, ambiences. This allows us to develop forms, patterns or open material organizations which perform in a direct way as instruments that induce the construction of social actions between users, not as a simple efficiency of function but as propitiator of new daily relations – an architecture able to provoke new behaviors and relationships, encouraging people to behave mentally and physically in ways that would have been thought impossible before.

It exists also a stress interest to understand architecture as a material practice; we act upon matter and space to transform reality, to relate with our environment, generate agreements, open operational building systems. Projects are instruments that allow social and ambient exchanges, unfinished and undetermined architectures – a practice that operates in and between the material world. We aim to find organization models and their behavior to induce new different and contradictory actions, not just based upon the idea of functional efficiency but also from organizations that are capable of stimulating or facilitating new and different activities in the same time and space.

Projects presented in this book don't pretend to be finished and closed architectures. On the contrary, we look forward to the construction of an architecture based upon open and adaptive configurations; composed by modules, bands or patrons of association that generates dispositions; able to adapt to the many different situations, be they topographic, ambientalist, urban or programmatic. This generates buildings able to grow, change and adapt according to particular or temporal circumstances, a strategy that admits changes, incidents and interchangeability, thought more as a method than as a permanent form and that exists only in virtue of its capacity for change. Open projects with order ideas based on disposition and its adaptive intelligence.

Background Image: The construction is composed of a repeatable modular polyhedron, supported by a tubular metal frame.

BOSQUE DE LA ESPERANZA

Giancarlo Mazzanti
Colombia

Date: 2010-2011
Location: Bogotá, Colombia
Design team: Giancarlo Mazzanti, Juan Manuel Gil, Lorena Gonzaléz, Jonathan Hernandéz, Liv Johana Zea, Charline Lalanne
Structural engineering: Nicolás Parra
Construction supervision: ARQ-Consultoría
Landscape design: Mazzanti arquitectos
Client: Fundación Pies Descalzos
Total floor area: 7,535 FS

Bosque de la Esperanza (Hope Forest) is a sports center designed by Giancarlo Mazzanti on the outskirts of Bogotá, where the community can practice and engage in several sports and take part in various recreational and academic activities that help foster a cooperative community. This project was made possible thanks to the foundation Pies Descalzos, founded by the Colombian superstar Shakira and the Spanish NGO Ayuda en Acción.

This Project is located in the municipally of Soacha, Altos de Cazucá. This lies in a very depressed area that lacks public infrastructure. This area is known for its security problems and it has become the shelter of thousands of people who have been displaced from their home towns due to recent conflict.

Mazzanti came to the project with the belief that architecture's value lies in what it can produce. Mazzanti is interested in producing actions, change and relationships which in turn help generate shapes, patterns or open organizations that act in the construction of social actions. Hope Forest is what Mazzanti calls an open project, a project made out of modules that have the potential to grow and adapt to different situations. It consists of a canopy where modules can be added depending on the circumstances.

The Sports Center consists of a 1,744 m2 horizontal surface and a 700 m2 dome of spatial structure, which "evokes a bunch of trees as a symbol of nature, union and hope in the area of Altos de Cazuca". The dimensions of the canopy are approximately 22.7m x 30.8m, with a perimeter of 138.2 m.

Each of the modules is a polyhedron of 12 surfaces: a dodecahedron. These are custom-fabricated and iterate numerous times to form the canopy. The structural canopy functions as a beam plane, supported over the two axes of the columns. The materials used were expanded mesh, round metal pipe and translucent tile.

GERARDO MOLINA SCHOOL

Giancarlo Mazzanti
Colombia

Date: 2004-2008
Location: Bogotá, Colombia
Design team: Giancarlo Mazzanti
Collaborators: Andrés Sarmiento, Juan Manuel Gil, Gina Amado, María Constanza Saade, Carlos Melo, Alberto Aranda, Ana María González, Jorge Gómez, Manuel Mendoza, Edgar Mazo

More than an isolated school, the aim is to develop an urban project that encourages new sectorial centralities with the facilities that are already being used by the school such as the library, the auditorium, the cafeteria, the support rooms for neighborhood activities.

As the project will be winding and turning, it will be opening to the city, leaving space for small squares and exterior parks for public use, leaving behind the bars and walls that stereotyped educational institutions as closed spaces.

The conformation of small squares and green spaces with trees direct on the surrounding streets, accompanied by the auction modules, will redefine direct accesses. The borders of the institution produce the closures; the school will not have bars or walls.

The project is raised as a modular system which is capable of adapting itself to the most diverse situations, whether they are topographical, urban or the result of a program. It is based on a regulated series of procedures and ordered actions (protocols) and on the construction of a chain grouping system skilled for intertwining and acting depending on the place, the amount of sunlight, the topography and the events (adaptive system).

The model develops a normative offer which seeks to establish a few rules of operation directed to achieving two objectives. The first one (spacial-classrooms) tries to promote the spatial ideal relations between the parts and the place: views, privacy, sunlight, communication, etc.

The construction of the model is based on the combination of rotated models. The latter is a unique piece system capable of developing a more complex and adaptive organized structure than the sum of the parts. The grouping system is raised as a chain construction in which each module is related with the ones next to it and element chains are produced while configuring ships that generate, at the same time, spaces where unexpected and surprising diagonals and vacuums are produced, enriching the school tour and usage.

The grouping system also allows for the conformation of courts, streets, subsectors, gardens and tree isolations in the exterior space.

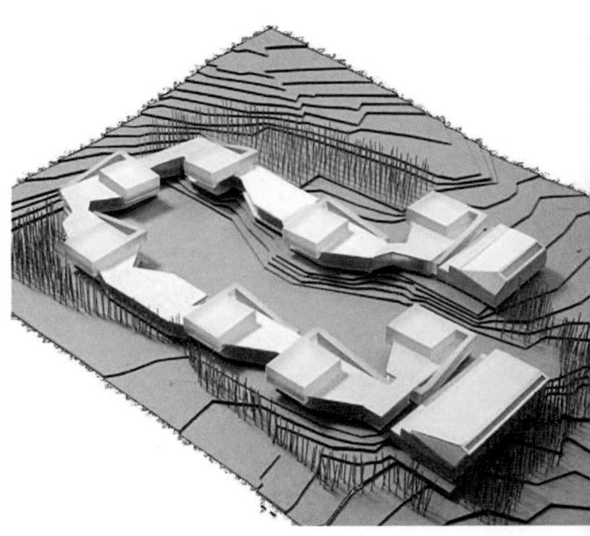

EL PORVENIR

SOCIAL KINDERGARDEN

Giancarlo Mazzanti
Colombia

Date: 2009
Location: Bosa, Bogotá, Colombia
Design team: Giancarlo Mazzanti
Collaborators: Fredy Pantoja, Susana Somoza, Ricardo Silva, Andrés Sarmiento, Juliana Angarita, Rocio Lamprea, Jairo Ovalle, Andrés Morales, María Alejandra Perez, Felipe Castro, Beatriz Robayo, Ramón Morales
Model: Jaime Borbón
Construction company: Unión temporal MAO-PZO
Engineering: Nicolás Parra
Client: Secretaria de Integración Social
Total floor area: 22,600 SF.

The project is planned as an adaptable system to the most diverse situations, like topographical, urban or the program. Grouping of tape and modules, it can mix an act according to the site, the solar radiation, topography and the events, and in a regulated procedure and ordered actions series; system rules to follow to be implemented.

It seeks to build a model based on the combination of recognizable units (the tape and public use modules), with the possibility of the production of a unique pieces system that can develop a more complex organizational structure and adaptive than the sum of the parts.

What is inside the tape belongs to children (classrooms); it is colorful, infantile, and there are defined sub-spaces for small groups. It is introverted and private. Outside of the tape are grouped the uses that can be public (administration, kitchen, etc.); it is outgoing and toward the city, for meetings of large groups.

The tape which defines the edges of the project (public-private, adult-child), and produces the adaptation to different types of lands and lots is an element able to assume the differences; it is the system organizer.

The rotated modules (classrooms for children), are planed like a chain construction; each module is related to the next, generating spaces in which diagonal sides and holes occur, which enrich the journey and the uses of school. Forming yards, streets, sub-spaces in the gardens and isolates wooded in the inside space, ideal for meetings of child groups. Use public modules (adults) are planed and act around the tape, turning around and adapting to the possible types of lots, allow itself to be used without entering the circle (tape) of the children, making them open spaces. It defines the accesses.

The public building must not only fulfill its role as urban equipment, but as a collective element that dignifies the living; therefore it must play a role beyond their specialty, it must create a social space, educational and dignity of life.

Different ways of implementing the building were studied; finally it was decided to develop an implementation to build a clear front, defined and generous toward the city which in turn will maximize the function. The capacity of optimizing these functional infrastructures leads to degeneration into a landscaped green areas and fun for the sector, compacting the program it was looked to make the largest possible amount of public space.

The project plans the composition of the place through the manipulation of base level as a

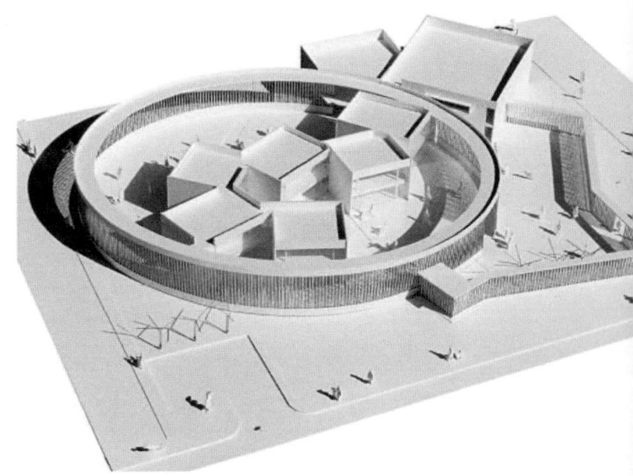

unifying element of the urban piece, a platform that rises from 0.00 level to operate the pool, because the area has serious problems of water table as it is filled. This image is presented as an artificial topography capable of promoting events that congested the location of new activities, enriching the city with a new centrality.

The architectural design is planned, positioned and dimensioned based on its relevance and ability to enhance as much empty space in the block. In this sense, its design allows for complete autonomy; it is also an excuse to become a trigger project for a process of reorganization of the sector where it is located. The building is planned as a container of curtain walling (lattice metal) mounted on a base as a balcony, which is located in the four programs, like boxes inside the container, each one with a different skin type, whether or stacking program differentiating each thematic box. Its façade is metal laser cut designs alluding to the four programs. It can only generate an access to four different entrances to buildings (boxes), making each one independent.

The project proposes the restructuring of the place through the manipulation of base level as a unifying element of the urban piece, with an artificial topography capable of promoting events. The platform as a base that unifies the three buildings and four programs.

Interstitium, a contemporary axiom, a hole making the heavy volume get lightness, and floating off the ground slightly. It produces cracks that communicate all three of these buildings to an integrated system.
The container, it has a skin (metal lattice), which unifies the image and produces a public building with character, the skin that covers let light and water pass, like a wrap in a paper bag. The great mass specified the architectural object – strong, heavy, noticeable in its entirety, dual, translucent and solid, monumental, contemporary, nature and artifice. Its materiality associated with the transmission of light.

The building envelope and the amount involved, (container and contents) at the same time are covered by a skin or large envelope of alabaster that protects them, hides them, nuances them or vanishes them depending on the use.

The building is designed as a great symbolic unit, but within their areas are specialized and are characterized in a particular way, whose skins are inspired by nature and contents of didactic speech and describes an experimental way for user: the pool is in silkscreen; glass and wood in the training space; the theater is plating of flagstone very low price; the hearing and the station in white foil type Metcol.

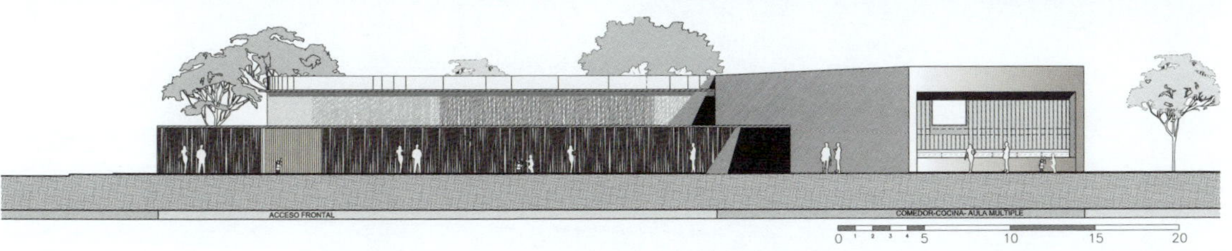

TIMAYIUI KINDERGARTEN

Giancarlo Mazzanti
Colombia

Date: 2011
Location: Santa Marta, Colombia
Design team: Giancarlo Mazzanti, Susana Somoza, Andrés Sarmiento, Néstor Gualteros, Óscar Cano, Lucia Largo
Structural Engineer: Nicolas Parva

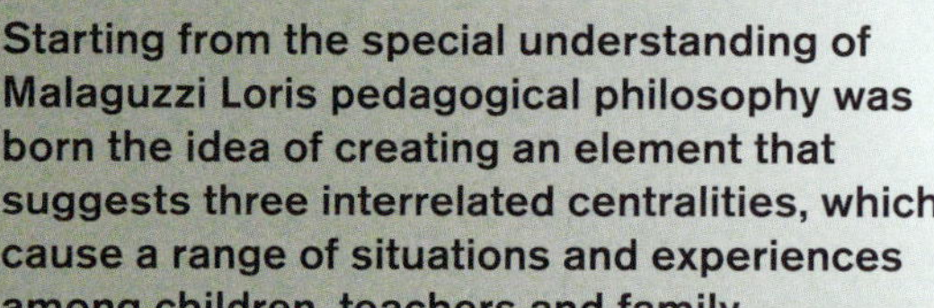

Starting from the special understanding of Malaguzzi Loris pedagogical philosophy was born the idea of creating an element that suggests three interrelated centralities, which cause a range of situations and experiences among children, teachers and family.

Moreover, in pragmatic terms there is a need to generate progressive growth for future linkage of more children to the center; the idea is to employ a modular system based on the three centers, which can be added, depending on the needs and expansion possibilities.

A chain system is created, based on a module type and following the morphology of the site, that holds the architectural program requirements and spatially. Therefore creating meeting places for the free entertainment that involves learning.

The module type is characterized as a flexible and neutral space that allows for the development of multiple activities within it. It relates with the nearest external surroundings (indoor and outdoor yard) allowing for a close relationship among all children and teachers.

acceso principal
cancha multiple
alameda peatonal

INVEMAR BUILDING
COMPETITION

Giancarlo Mazzanti
Colombia

Design team: Giancarlo Mazzanti and Andrés Sarmiento
Collaborators: Juan Manuel Gil, Susana Sumoza, Lorena Gonzales, Santiago Ramos, María Elena Garcés, Felipe Cuellar, Luis Alejandro Carvajal, Stephany Zapata, Néstor Gualteros
Renders: Taller 301

The project involves the construction of a complex that occupies the site, allowing for the emergence of thematic spaces inside. This organization leaves one outer piece edge toward the city, generating open public spaces for the community such as an event plaza towards the sea and a public park on the edge. The screen usually appears on specific projects that leave a broad green space without control.

The site is proposed as a major botanical garden that relates to green corridors through urban areas, mountain ecosystems and sea border; in this way it develops an ecological restoration of native species of tropical dry forest now in danger of extinction. That is why the project raises the occupation of the lot for a ring system containing collections and educational eco systems.

The project takes the form of a coral (Montastrea cavernosa), not as metaphor but as the same order structure that has an organizational intelligence. This allows the project to act and grow like the coral (hard limestone systems), which are composed of polyps that are independent structures (organisms that live inside limestone structures) and that sum constructs what we call coral reefs, which are home to many marine organisms.

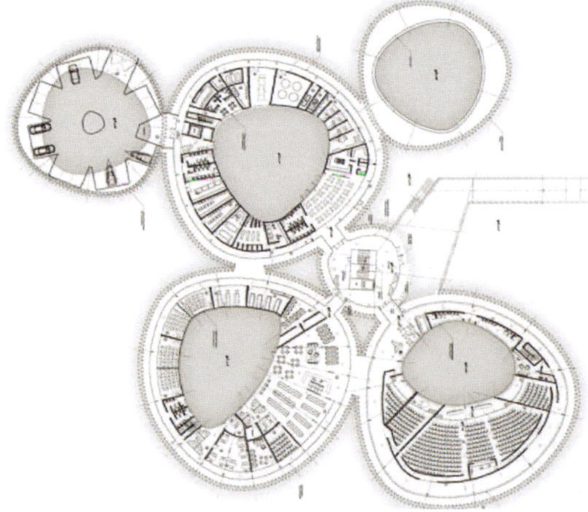

PUERTA DE ORO
CONVENTION CENTER
COMPETITION

Giancarlo Mazzanti + Daniel Bonilla
Colombia

Architects: Andres Sarmiento, Juan Felipe Herrera, Jorge Gómez, Juliana Sperotto
Collaborators: Julio Velez, Aixa Navas, Luis Carvajal, Mauricio Mendez,
Graphic design: Santiago Ramos
Render: Taller 301

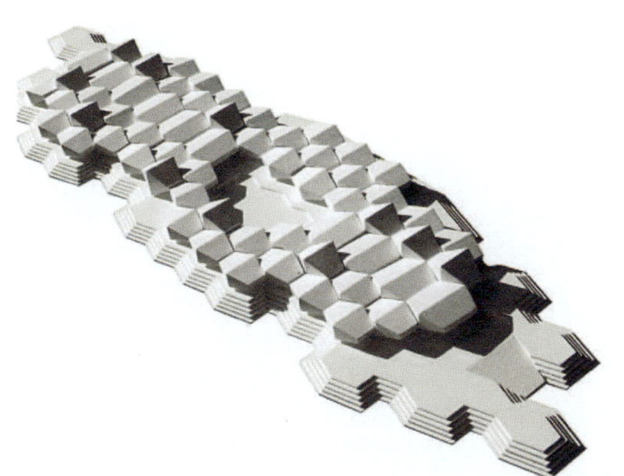

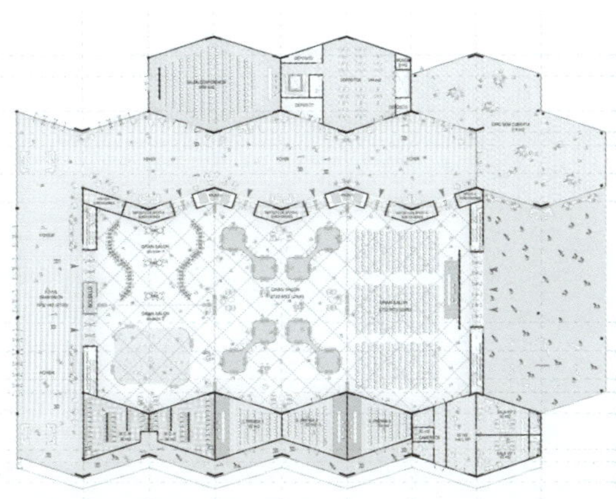

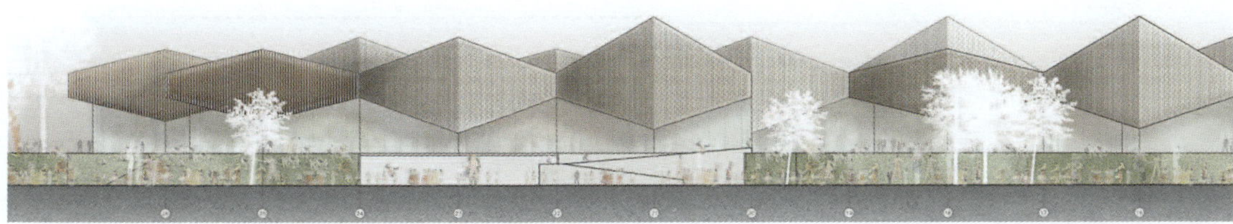

2010_Collage specially composed for this book by K. Klinger.

BOGOTÁ. "Big and Tall: The desire for identity today may be read through physical aspirations to tower over the mountains. Meanwhile, real gems of Bogotá already exist in the fine textures of its evolutions yesterday. Tomorrow will be an interesting moment in time to witness the dialogue between regional Bogotá and global Bogotá."

COLISEUM FOR THE SOUTH AMERICAN GAMES

Giancarlo Mazzanti + Felipe Mesa
Colombia

Date: 2008-2010
Location: Medellín, Colombia
Design team: Giancarlo Mazzanti, Felipe Mesa
Collaborators: Andrés Sarmiento, Jairo Ovalle, Luz Rocio Lamprea, Fredy Pantoja, Carlos Bueno, Ana Prado, Carlos Acero and Jaime Borbón
Soil Engineering: Solingral
Structural Engineer: Nicolás Parra and Daniel Lozano
Plumbing engineer: Jorge Granados
Electrical Engineering: EBINGEL
Bioclimatic study: Jorge Ramírez
Lighting Design: ISOLUX
Area: 306,940 SF.

The project has been designed as a new geography for the interior of the elongated Aburrá Valley, midway between Cerro Nutibara and Cerro El Volador. It is a building that seems to be another mountain in the city; from the remote or from the top has an abstract image geographic and festive; from the inside, the movement of the steel structure allows the filtered sunlight to get inside the space, which is the suitable condition for holding sporting events.

The outdoor public space and sporting venues are in a continuous space, thanks to a large deck built through extensive stripes out, perpendicular to the direction of the positioning of the main buildings. Each of the four sporting venues operates independently, but in terms of urban space they behave as one large continent built with public open spaces, semi-covered public spaces, and indoor sports.

Each of the four scenarios can be understood as a separate building, connected with another on an urban scale. The three new scenarios can also be understood as a single large building, related to the existing Ivan de Bedout Coliseum. The four coliseums can be understood as a great place to set both the buildings and public space.

1. The skeleton of the project is the pattern. Here the structure is an organization system or the understanding of vitality. It means that the relation the project proposes is its skeleton.
2. The skeleton of the project is made of the symmetry of the structure and the muscles. Here the structure is the way in which the limit or physiognomy of the project is equivalent to the skeleton. The skeleton is on the outside or the epidermis and vice versa; it is an expression of architecture. Architecture is qualified by the structure.
3. The skeleton of the project is the structure. Columns, bases, beams, roofs. Stripes, canals. Interior space.

The intellectual structure of this project matches the supporting structure. In the architecture of this project, the intentions that support work, the final network that will eventually use the subject, and the structure or skeleton of the building all coincide. The contrary: a containing architecture, of supposed flexible interior that hides the structure on the perimeter. This doesn't have anything to do with the skeleton because it would not be occupied as a skeleton but as a void. The skeleton that we have analyzed doesn't construct empty spaces.

The mixture of these three orders or ways of understanding the skeleton propose a pattern for growth and variation of the project that expand its status. They make it more as a vital and beating form than a stable form.

In the interior of the sceneries the image of the skeleton seems raw when the trusses are exposed; they are no longer melted down with the skin but directly with the structure. The force lines lose a little vigor due to its swelling and the perception of a hat becomes more evident. Even the industrial image. The project melts public space with the interior activities because the structure avoids finishing (stopping) at the swelling. The skeleton of this project is a real structure...

POETIC STRUCTURES OBSERVED

CONCRETE, EXPRESSIVE, SYMBOLIC, SENSITIVE, VISIBLE, COMPOSITION, SYSTEMS, ELEGANT, ANATOMY, METRICAL, LYRICAL, FINE, IMAGINATIVE, TANGIBLE, BEAUTIFUL, PHYSICAL, CONFIGURATIONS, SUBSTANTIAL, GENUINE, ARRANGE, PALPABLE.

DE LA CRUZ HOUSE

Rafael Iglesia
Rosario, Argentina

Date: 2007
Location: Rosario, Argentina
Architecture: Rafael Iglesia
Design team: Pedro Farías, Pedro Aybar, architects
Structural consultant: Ing. Bianchi
Site area: 4,850 SF.
Total floor area: 2,485 SF.

When composing this text I noticed that I said almost the same words explaining our building in Mitre Street, with its emphasis on stone. The same thing happened when I wrote about the clinic built with stainless steel. All these works display the same concepts; they say more or less the same thing in different architectural languages.

There is not much to say about the house's brief. It responds to the needs of the owner and that can be read in the plans. The free covered area on the ground floor, limited only on the sides, acts as a traditional *galleria*. This space melts into the back garden, with a more domestic courtyard in the front of the house.

Bedrooms on the second floor face the street; however, the relationship with public space is restricted for privacy as well as for safety reasons. Simple piling holds the ground floor structure together; it gains stability with the weight of the floor on top of it. For added safety, a tension element is included in the light wall that defines the kitchen space.

Gravity forces, therefore, do not reach the ground by the shortest route as is customary. Loads here are distributed asymmetrically. This makes gravity almost a Baroque feature. I have always been wary of the structure in Mies' pavilion, with columns disposed symmetrically. The Modern Movement sought asymmetry, denying the value that Classical architecture gave to symmetrical dispositions.

The outside wall is made of bricks, simply piled, one on top of another and backed on the inside by a thin R.C. wall that provides binding. The soil on which the house stands was very weakly structured. That forced us to sink deep piles along the whole perimeter. Therefore, we decided to build only two deep R.C. walls and cantilever the second floor on them.

Over the street, a large door of mirror-polished stainless steel almost vanishes by reflecting the environment. There are no other openings, neither doors nor windows to compose a façade. Thus we avoid the banal, "didactic" façade surface, where different openings express a variety of room uses.

The silent language of the house says nothing, or perhaps it says more than words. As declared by the Chilean architect Alejandro Aravena in his book The Place of Architecture when, referring to a house by Oswald Mathias Ungers, he says that it is "an architecture without attributes", perhaps this house has other attributes, but it does not reveal its identity or what goes on in the inside.

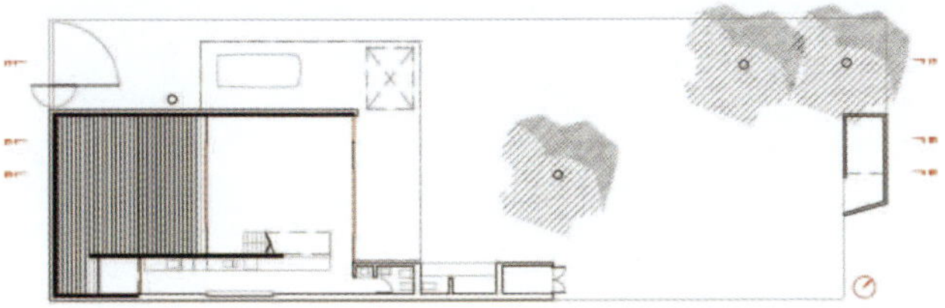

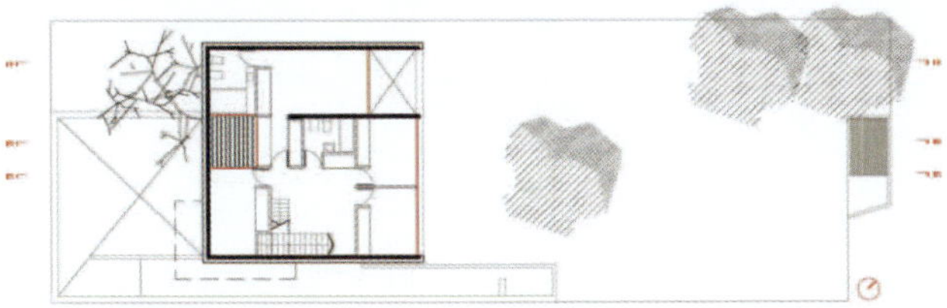

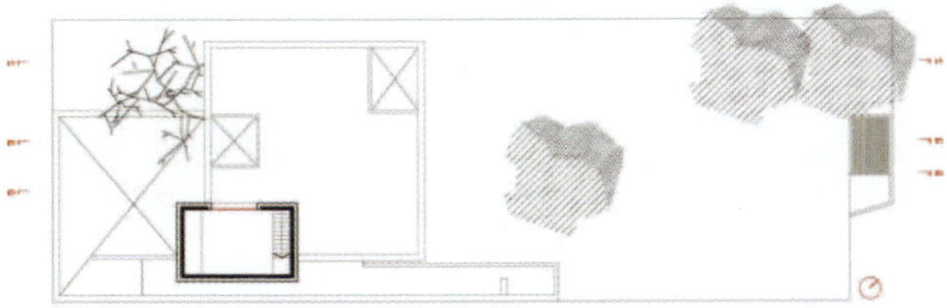

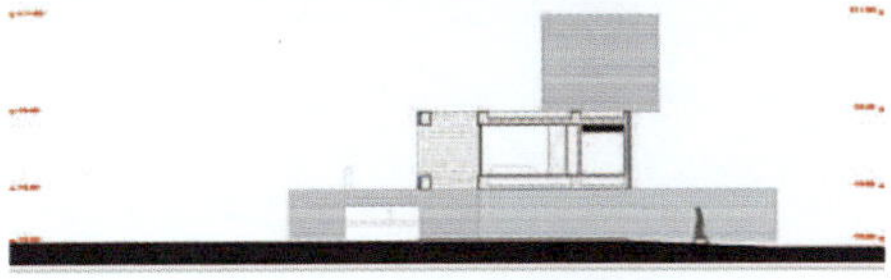

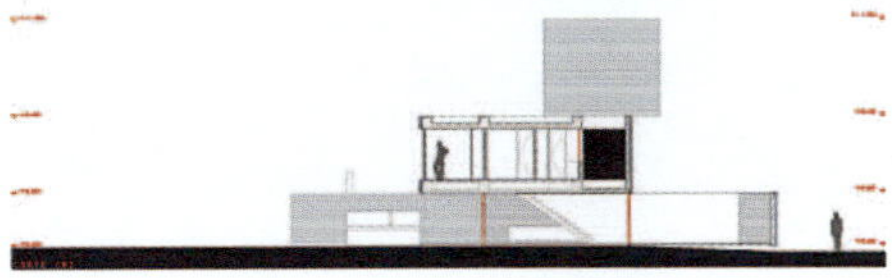

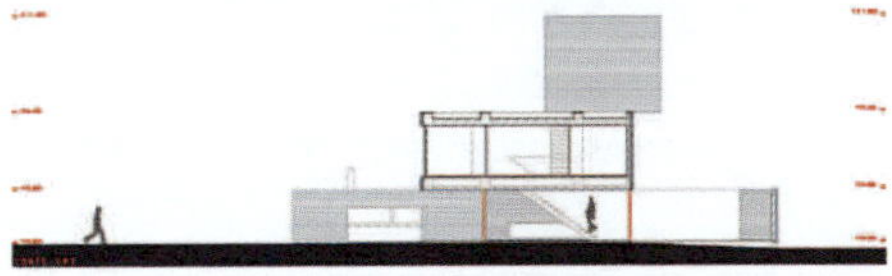

MARABAJO
FOUR HOUSES

Nicolás Campodonico
Uruguay

Date: 2005
Location: La Pedrera, Rocha, Uruguay
Design: Nicolás Campodonico
Site area: 10,000 SF.
Total floor area: 4,150 SF.

The project is located in La Pedrera, a small seashore town in Rocha, Uruguay. These four aggregated houses work with local themes, especially materials and forms of life, in order to elaborate them in relation to site conditions.

The lot is part of the old town, the first blocks on the ocean front. Good orientation, the natural slope of the terrain and the ocean views will coincide with an imaginary diagonal line cutting across the block. This is the principal argument for the majority of design decisions, either for looking directly at the ocean or for hiding it to generate times and paths for rediscovering it. The initial strategy consisted of elevating the living room and locating the sleeping area underneath, taking advantage of the natural slope. With this decision, all the social areas of the house have clear views over the bay, and the dormitories relate to more intimate courtyards.

A series of operations stress the visuals towards the sea: An eleven-degree rotation of the house with respect to the street, the diagonal of the windowpanes, the tension of the concrete cantilever and the roof slope. The articulation of courtyards, walls and staircases gives the project an image of solidity. This image changes as we walk through the house. When we arrive at the terrace, and the open air, we are confronted with the sea below as the culmination of our path.

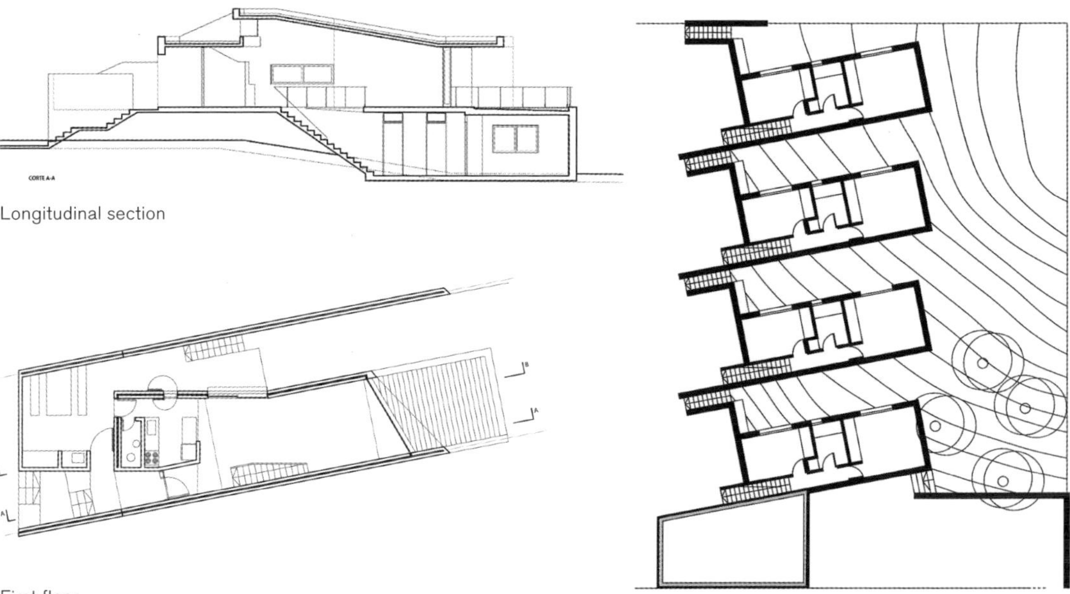

Longitudinal section

First floor

A PILGRIMAGE TO ATLANTIDA

Craig W. Hartman
San Francisco, USA

My journey to physically experience the work of Eladio Dieste began on a Saturday in June 2007, in a chilly pre-dawn Buenos Aires fog with professor Ana de Brea, a friend Viviana Espósito, and my wife, the architect Jan O'Brien. What we expected to be a two hour ferry trip across the Río de la Plata to Montevideo, Uruguay, and a short drive to Atlántida, turned into six hours, most of which were spent on the lower deck of the motionless ferry, waiting for the fog to lift.

The goal was to personally experience Eladio Dieste's early masterwork, Cristo Obrero Church in Atlántida. I confess that, like many US architects I had been unaware of Dieste's work. Oddly, it seems that cultural awareness in the Americas travels latitudinally, with North and South America connecting most powerfully with Europe and Asia, rather than longitudinally with one another. As a result, the wealth of great architecture in South America from the last three centuries is only superficially known to many of us in North America.

I had become aware of Dieste's work only two years earlier, ironically in Taipei, while serving on a design jury with Aaron Betsky, Fumihiko Maki, Kurt Forster and Stanford Anderson. As part of the proceedings, we were each asked to make a public presentation of our work. Anderson, then Chair of the Department of Architecture at MIT, presented the research that had formed the basis of his new book about the work of the Uruguayan architect and engineer. The presentation was memorable and, for me, Dieste's work had an immediate and profound resonance.

For Dieste, whose practice was comprised of agrarian and industrial structures and, improbably, two extraordinary churches – entirely within Uruguay, architecture and structure were truly inseparable. His architecture was a search for dynamic form in which the forces of nature were resolved through the shaping of space. His architectural language was based entirely upon the most modest of materials – primarily locally cast brick – but was assembled using an innovative pre-stressed technology not yet common, even in countries with access to the most advanced construction technologies. To build these structures, Dieste would often recruit farmers.

The roof structures and the spaces he created are beautiful in their fluidity. But what especially resonated with me in Anderson's Taipei lecture images was Dieste's poetic use of light. In some cases slivers of light separate horizontal and vertical planes, creating an unexpected lightness in a material vocabulary historically associated with weight. In other instances light deeply rakes walls or softly dissipates to shadow as it bathes curving vaults, enhancing the sense of fluid space. When I returned to the US, I bought a copy of Anderson's book and promised myself I would find a way to personally experience Dieste's spaces.

The opportunity to make a pilgrimage to Uruguay came sooner than expected, with an invitation from professor Ana de Brea to lecture in Buenos Aires and be a critic for Ball State University College of Architecture and Planning students who were doing a summer design

workshop at Palermo University in the same city. At my suggestion, Ana expressed delight about adding a trip to Atlántida to the overall agenda and, soon enough, we found ourselves on the fog-delayed ferry in the Buenos Aires harbor.

With the four-hour delay, we were worried about getting to Atlántida before sundown and, as the shadows lengthened, our four-cylinder rental car reached terminal velocity. We eventually came to a stop in front of Cristo Obrero in a cloud of dust – literally. The church's setting on the outer edge of Atlántida remains modest, sparsely settled with one story structures with many unpaved streets, a vivid reminder of the primitive conditions within which it was constructed 60 years earlier.

Although we had arrived early enough to experience the light in the nave, to our dismay the church was locked. Ana and Viviana went in search of the priest and came back shortly with a parish sister, brandishing the keys, who turned the church over to us for the rest of the afternoon.

My first impression of Cristo Obrero Church was not unlike my arrival at the chapel of Notre Dame du Haut in Ronchamp as a hitchhiking college student 30 years earlier. Having studied both in advance through books, drawings and photographs, I thought I knew them intimately and understood their scale. But I had mythologized and inflated both buildings. Cristo Obrero and Ronchamp were both physically much smaller, yet much more powerful emotively than I imagined.

The first thing one becomes aware of when approaching Cristo Obrero Church is not monumentality, but rather modesty and extraordinary integrity. Although it does not literally appropriate any of the historic forms of the Catholic Church, it is instantly recognizable as a sacred space and it is uniquely of its physical and cultural place. The architectural form is unlike anything before or since, yet it possesses a timeless quality of being that is derived from its natural fluid forms and the utter simplicity of its materials. The structure balances gravitational forces through the strategic placement in space and the singular use of one of humankind's most ancient materials – brick, brought together with Dieste's intuitive understanding of the potential of induced stress in achieving new levels of performance from primitive unit masonry.

The entire structure, its shell form roof, its undulating, canted walls, and its bell tower are all constructed of exposed, locally cast brick used in innovative ways that resist forces through shape, not mass. Per Stanford Andersen: The structural action can be read in the section of the building and approximates the shape of the bending moment diagram for the structure. The junction between the wall and the roof is a most lucid exposition of Dieste's desire to resist through form.[1] The reductive use of a single material (brick) and the innovation in its deployment is stunning. Dieste used this minimal palette in almost every imaginable way, from the church's structurally shaped enclosing envelope to the spiraling cantilevered steps within the bell tower.

The promise of the church, conveyed in the images I saw in Taipei, was more than fulfilled when finally standing within the nave in Atlántida. It was clear

1. Stanford Anderson, on *Eladio Dieste: Innovation in Structural Art*. New York: Princeton Architectural Press, 2004.

that Dieste's deployment of material and form was focused not on the object but rather upon the space contained. The fluid volume contained within Cristo Obrero's nave feels as though it is pressed into its shape – as if the exterior form were a mold and the interior void was revealed through a lost wax technique. The interior is the precise reciprocal of the exterior form.

The most striking quality was the poetic use of mysterious light with the sanctuary, ennobling the humble brick from which it was constructed. The deep waves formed by the sinusoidal east and west walls are softly lit by mysterious points of light. It isn't until one advances to the altar and turns back to face the entry that the source of illumination is revealed to be small fenestrations Dieste has cut into the south face of each "wave", allowing rays of light to strike the surface of the adjacent wave.

Light is also used to clarify the church's structural properties. One example is the separation of the main east and west structural walls from the non-bearing north and south walls that are inserted into the overall volume. A continuous sliver of light around the entire perimeter of these walls separates them from the load-bearing sinusoidal walls, communicating their non-bearing status. The visual weight of the south entry wall is further reduced by the introduction of non-load bearing panels, tipped in plan, each in the opposite orientation of its neighbor. These panels redirect the powerful exterior south light, bathing the interior panel faces in raking light.

Beyond the tectonic and spatial innovations, there are also ideas related to Catholic liturgy as interpreted in Dieste's architecture that I found intriguing. I had made my pilgrimage to Atlántida just as the Cathedral of Christ the Light in Oakland, California, which I had designed, was nearing to completion. I had spent seven years observing and discussing sacred space with scholars of the Catholic faith. Some ideas that were perhaps radical when Dieste designed Cristo Obrero Church in 1950 are now accepted as common practice. One is the idea of a non-hierarchical gathering of

The Church of Christ Obrero, Atlántida, Uruguay, was entrusted to the engineer Eladio Dieste in 1952.

the clergy and worshipers around the altar as a single community, as distinguished from the linear basilica form in which Gothic cathedrals were built. This was a concept that was under discussion in Catholicism and was formally adopted as part of the 1962 Vatican II reforms in the Catholic liturgy. But at Cristo Obrero, the most dramatic liturgical interpretation is the placement of the baptismal font underground. It is a particularly powerful gesture, descending into the darkness, arriving at a top-lit space for absolution and then ascending directly into the sanctuary. In the end, this was for me an affirming and inspiring pilgrimage. It affirmed again the inseparable relationship between form, structure and material in any work of architecture that aspires to meaning and critical authenticity. For any architect who is inspired by these qualities, it is worth the trip to Atlántida.

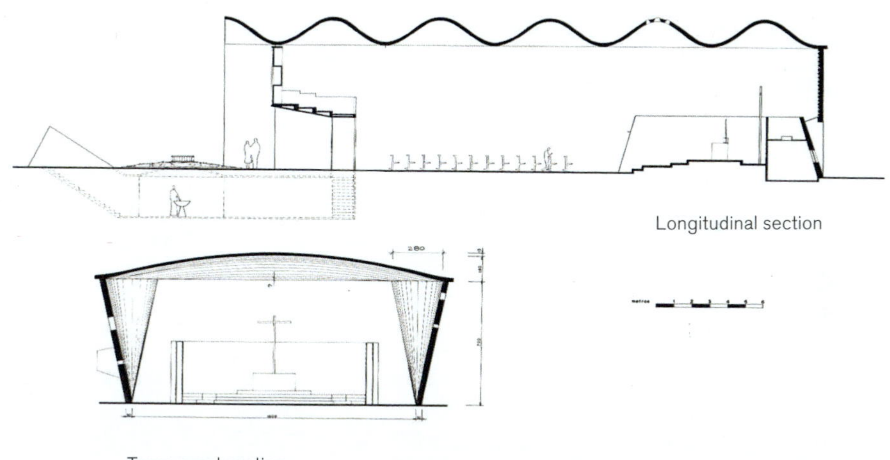

Longitudinal section

Transversal section

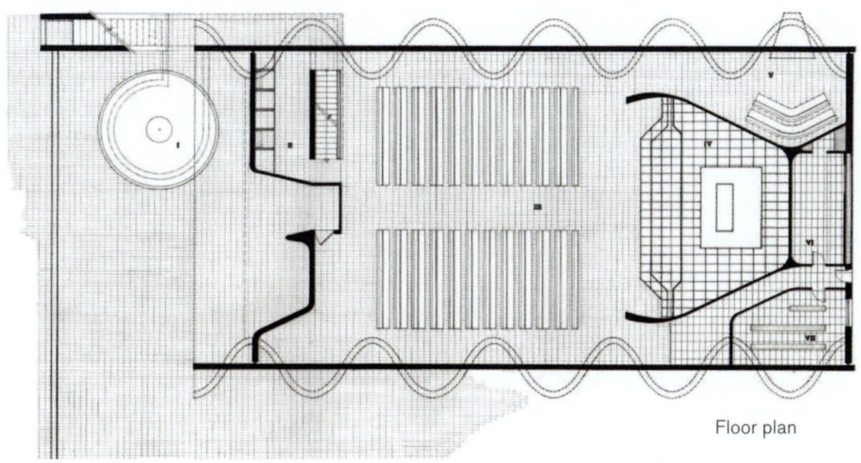

Floor plan

Series: Trip to South America, 2004.
2010_Image specially composed for this book by I. Bracher.

R. ANTOÑIZ HOUSE

Marcelo Villafañe
Argentina

Date: 2005
Location: Fisherton Golf Club, Rosario, Argentina
Design team: Marcelo Villafañe
Colaborators: Laura Rois, Eleonora Flores, and Juan Romanos
Engineer: Gonzalo Garibay
Construction company: Architect G. Picarelli

Between Density and Lightness

The R. Antoniz house is located on a corner plot in a residential district to the west of Rosario, on the site of a former golf club. It is an L-shaped house, shaded by tall eucalyptus trees, with flat roofs and a large mass of exposed brickwork. Nestled amid the surrounding trees, both floors have a concrete structure and double-layer brick walls.

The concept is linked to the visual route and oblique lines of sight, despite the house's orthogonal design. Its rich material quality comes from a fundamental robustness; the character of the project strikes a balance between density and lightness. In spatial terms, the circulation creates several vanishing points as an inviting and entertaining way of connecting the interior and exterior, giving the spaces a pleasantly irregular feel. The work was thorough and hard, always taking into account the needs, requirements and perceptions of the client, which were responsible for modifying the project. The proposal was closely tied to visitor circulations and oblique visuals, despite the orthogonal order of the house. The materials had their rich moments: dense and calm, intermittent.

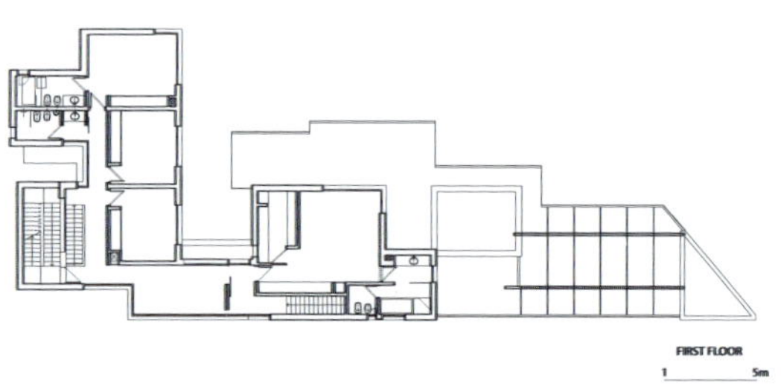

TENSION AND RELEASE

Diego Petrate
La Plata, Argentina

Jorge Luis Borges, in his 1932 book Discussion, quotes the historian Edward Gibbon, observing that in the Koran – the Arab book par excellence – there is no mention of camels. Borges used this as a proof that the book was written by an Arab, in this particular case Muhammad. Should it have been written by a foreigner, a tourist or an Arab nationalist, camels would have probably appeared on every page. But, for Muhammad, like for any other local person, camels were part of their reality, very much like air itself, and he did not mention them.

Following this idea, we could say that South American architects are defined as South American not for the presence of local color or folklore in their work, but by the way elements are arranged syntactically. The house we are presenting here is made of bricks, local bricks – handmade, imperfect, unaligned – each of a different size and ecologically incorrect, since they are produced with topsoil. And they do provide local color, but we will not discuss the choice of materials, simply because it was not ours; the owners suggested it to us. What we did then was to use them in two ways simultaneously.

First, as a material; they are the basic cells that provide rhythm and geometric order. The evenly placed units create the matrix that define possibilities in space. This is a customized Cartesian grid with two modules in each direction: X and Y. Modules A and B; A for joints and B for the material itself.

Secondly, as a concept the bricks are used in a metaphorical sense; larger blocks are created for each of the programmatic elements of the house: living areas, bedrooms, studio, service rooms, outdoor dining, and so on. Relating these different cuboids in three-dimensional space generates the massing of the house. They are arranged with a number of mechanisms, but avoiding the idea of a catalog. They are spaced apart, collided, piled, imbricated, fused and stretched until they almost touch. In other words, we can say that using bricks as a material and a concept, gave us simultaneously a regime of order and a regime of liberation, which produces a constant friction between stable and unstable, tension and release; and it is this balance between order and chaos that we find fascinating.

Vstas of the Arditti-Wynne House, City Bell, Argentina.

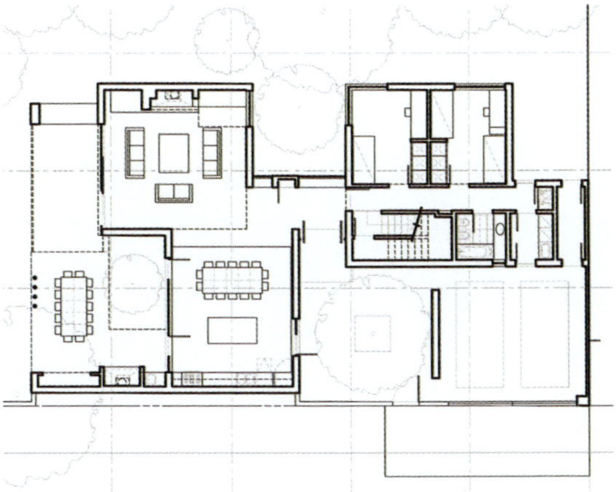

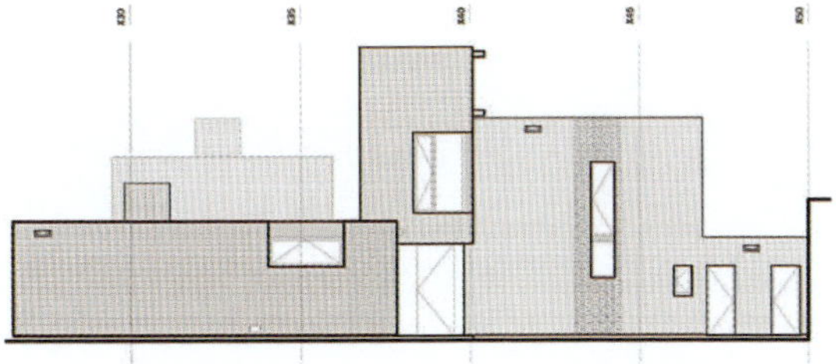

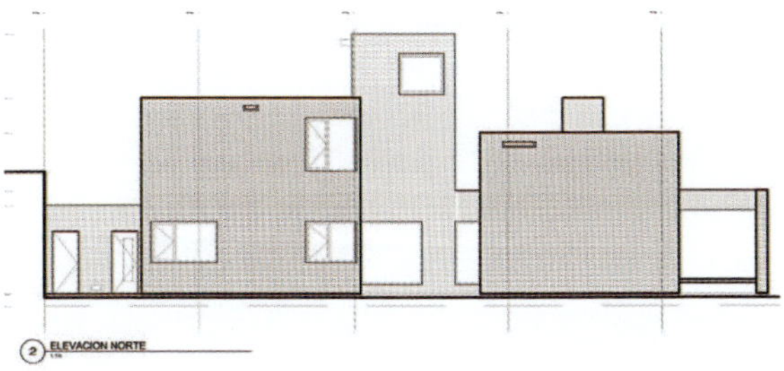

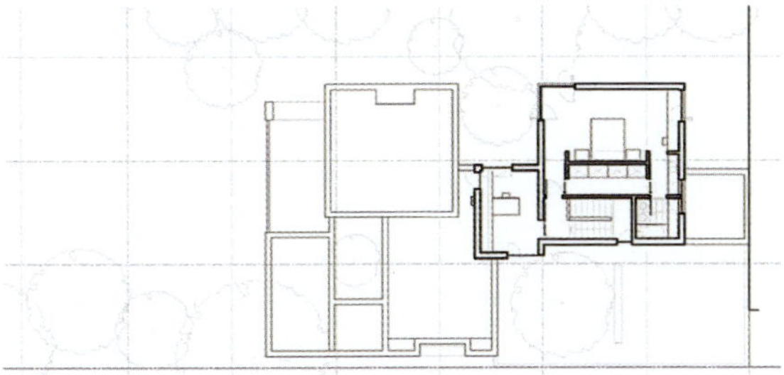

ELEVACION NORTE

SYNOPSIS ON BRICKS

Néstor Bottino
New York, USA

Midway through my undergraduate studies in architecture I made a journey to Argentina where I had lived until the age of seven. I had returned to Argentina frequently but this was the first trip since starting at university. I saw the country and its way of building in a new light. My simple observation of Argentine construction methods during that trip had an important impact on a number of buildings designed and built over the next thirty-five years. Following are some notes on this process.

1976, Province of Buenos Aires
Common construction in Argentina and much of Latin America is radically different from building methods in the United States. Instead of stick-frame and steel-frame construction, a preponderance of Argentine construction consists of poured-in-place concrete frameworks infilled with hollow clay block; ladrillo hueco or hollow brick. The entire assembly is covered with stucco. The most intriguing element of this assembly is the block infill. Unlike the finished buildings, which are achromatic and largely devoid of texture and ornament, the underlying block walls are a vibrant terracotta earth color, are highly textured, and show the hand of the masons who laid the blocks. Is it possible to make buildings that retain the richness of infill block walls? Instead of being hidden behind whitewashed stucco, can the clay wall be an expressive architectural element? The closest examples I have found are Eladio Dieste's constructions in brick, but in his work brick is used to create continuous walls with minimal texture. (Images 1/2/3)

1982, University of Texas-Austin
Traditional Texas buildings have decorative brick fronts, but their side and back walls are constructed of fired-clay block, similar to the hollow brick of Latin America. This is an interesting coincidence, given that Texas was historically the northern reaches of Hispanic America. At a brick showroom, I find an elongated hexagonal clay piece used for underground drainage channels. The texture and orange-red color remind me of the Argentine hollow brick. The hexagonal pieces are made in a small, almost-forgotten plant of beehive kilns in the town of D'Hanis, west of San Antonio. On a trip to D'Hanis I see piles of discarded clay shapes and wonder if these shapes could be used in making contemporary architecture. (Image 4)

1990, New York, New York / Dayton, Ohio
Hardy Holzman Pfeiffer Associates, the New York firm where I've been working since 1985, receives the commission to design a synagogue for a congregation in Dayton, Ohio. On a trip to Dayton, one of the firm partners and I see several old clay block buildings made of yellow clay. The initial design we develop for Temple Israel proposes a front wall constructed entirely of Ohio red sandstone.

The cost of the sandstone exceeds the project budget, so we begin developing alternative designs. One option is to construct the synagogue of textured block, similar to the hollow brick I had seen fifteen years earlier in Argentina. We make phone calls to the D'Hanis plant in Texas and visit a small beehive kiln clay plant in Uhrichsville, Ohio. A variety of clay shapes pile up in our New York office and a new design for the synagogue construction starts to take shape. The resulting 200-foot-long front wall is faced in horizontal bands of clay shapes: long-ribbed block for the base and stacked hexagonal clay shapes for the middle courses. For the top third of the wall, D'Hanis agrees to split standard vent blocks in half

1. Typical Hollow Brick Construction; Province of Buenos Aires

2. Hollow Brick

3. Typical Hollow Brick Detail; Province of Buenos Aires

4. D'Hanis Plant; D'Hanis, Texas

to create a field of vertical half-round shapes. The synagogue's sanctuary is square in plan with a pentagonal heavy timber frame that defines the central seating area. The timber roof framing needs to bear on the perimeter wall of the sanctuary so we construct a double wythe clay block wall. Thick load-bearing block with lightly scratched faces form the inboard structural wall, exposed inside the sanctuary. The outer wythe of shaped clay block clads the sanctuary's exterior.

The walls of the synagogue have the rich color, texture, and shaping we hoped to achieve. The clay block is a main component of Temple Israel's architectural design and the building's most identifiable characteristic. (Images 5/6/7/8)

1995 New York, New York, Fort Worth, Texas
At the Walsh Performing Arts Center at Texas Christian University, we construct the exterior of the complex's studio theater in rich materials that contrast with the standard yellow brick used in other campus buildings and in the main portion of the performing arts center. The terracotta clay shapes closely match the color of Texas red granite. The granite forms a solid base for the theater, with square and hexagonal clay block stacked above it to give the shape a strong vertical characteristic. In contrast to Temple Israel, the clay block at TCU highlights one of several building shapes and creates a folded surface rather than the more textured and varying walls of the synagogue. In the strong sunlight the full height folds in the clay surface define deep shadows that create large-scale versions of the texture on the Argentine hollow brick. (Images 9/10/11/12)

2002 New York, New York/ Corpus Christi, Texas

The concert hall Hardy Holzman Pfeiffer Associates is asked to design at the local university has a site constricted by underground utility lines. The footprint of the auditorium space occupies almost the entire site. To increase the available site area and to solve the common problem of mechanical noise intrusion in acoustically sensitive spaces, we decide to build a stand-alone three-story-high mechanical building on the other

5. Clay Shapes: Temple Israel; Dayton, Ohio

6. Exterior; Dayton, Ohio

7. Exterior Detail; Temple Israel; Dayton, Ohio

8. Sanctuary Interior; Temple Israel; Dayton, Ohio

side of the buried utility lines. Connection to the upper floors supplies the concert hall with conditioned air and minimizes the connection of the mechanical building to the acoustically sensitive space. To maximize the acoustical separation of the mechanical building, we construct it entirely of thick structural clay block. D'Hanis produces a custom ziz-zag-faced block for the project that creates texture and shadow in the strong South Texas sun. The same ziz-zag shaping is used for the elongated brick that clads portions of the concert hall. The shaped clay is the common uniting element between the building components. The strong Hispanic influence in South Texas makes the use of clay shapes an appropriate material for this project. The terracotta material of roofing tiles and hidden wall construction of Latin America is now a central architectural element of the Texas A&M-Corpus Christi Performing Arts Center, one of the city's most prominent public buildings. (Image 13)

2011 Province of Buenos Aires

On the highway between La Plata and Buenos Aires, four identical multi-story residential buildings are under construction. They are in various states of completion. The least complete structure has all its clay hollow brick infill but no finish. The last building in the group is entirely finished in stucco. The stucco-clad building is almost entirely devoid of character.

There is no indication of how it was built, what it was built with, and who the masons that constructed it were. In the adjoining buildings, the color and texture of the construction material disappears as the stucco is spread over the walls. Over the last twenty years I have been part of a practice that has designed and built projects in the United States, highlighting a building material ubiquitous in Latin American construction but often hidden from view. It is a material more often seen in the partially finished constructions of

9. Exterior; Walsh Center for the Performing Arts; Texas Christian University; Fort Worth, Texas

10. Interior; Walsh Center for the Performing Arts; Texas Christian University; Fort Worth, Texas

11. Exterior Detail; Walsh Center for the Performing Arts; Texas Christian University; Fort Worth, Texas

12. Wall Detail; Walsh Center for the Performing Arts; Texas Christian University; Fort Worth, Texas

low-income neighborhoods, but which is covered with stucco in finished buildings. Our projects have focused on revealing the strong characteristics of the hollow clay brick. An important result of these efforts has been to support and foster small clay plants in Texas, Ohio, and California, many of which still use beehive kilns.

We have strived to preserve the operations that can supply the most varied, quirky, and economical clay shapes that have become an important component of many of the buildings we design. We have incorporated a common Latin American building material I saw thirty-five years ago into architecture rich in color, shape, and texture.

13. Exterior; Texas A&M University-Corpus Christi Performing Arts Center; Corpus Christi, Texas

DOWNTOWN NEVER ENDING STORY / La Boca, Buenos Aires.
2010_Image specially composed for this book by M. de Brea Dulcich.

LG

PARAMETERS

Daniel Bonilla
Medellin, Colombia

Poor urban planning, the rapid and overflowing migration to the cities, the commercial surge of real-estate promoters, a generalized conservative attitude and overly conservative academies have been a scene of confrontation for architects in Colombia. But for the last decade, concern for dignifying the city and creating equity through public works and public space has grown due to various reasons, but especially as a result of the presence of political leaders, such as some mayors who have sought more humane and inclusive cities. Additionally, a national law that requires the realization of open competitions for public architecture or urban projects, based on merit and transparency, has fostered high-quality public works and highly significant transformations.

Within this framework, Colombian architects have had the good fortune to contribute significantly to the construction of the city through public works, around which architectural and urban achievements concentrate.

Framed within these parameters our office has attempted to build its own particular vision of architecture by focusing on defined positions:

–Proportion between mass and voids – "The Civility of the Project." Every place, lot or terrain has the potential to contribute to the urban fabric and communal space, so that the void is more relevant than the filled spaces.

–The dissolution of limits: It is intended to dilute the sharp difference between internal and external, public and private.

–Maximizing flexibility: Aiming for an architecture that can change its size and usage conditions.

–Speculations on the theme of the skin and working with textures: Looking for the possibility that skins can determine the relationships between internal and external as a resource, without always resorting to the conventional window opening. Exploring the textures of skins is especially valued, and therefore new issues appear, such as repetition, sequence, framing, weaving and so on.

–Structuring sequences and premeditated thresholds: The conditions of sequence, steps and thresholds are used to enrich the sensory experience of space.

–Simplification of shapes: Generally using prismatic basic solutions, as opposed to the excessive and Baroque style of existing architecture.

–Study and experimentation with different materials: Although mostly working with few materials for each project, it is particularly attractive and important to evaluate the diversity of materials and the infinite potential of their interpretation and use.

–Merging architectural detail and industrial detail: In a field where the construction-associated industry is focused on standardization, it is important to contribute with research and development through each project.

–Composition based on the construction of duality: The relation of dependency in architecture is unlimited. The project cannot be seen as something abstract and, therefore, depends on dualities: there is light if it is not dark; there is no void space without filled space; there is no cold if there is no heat.

Bogotá Chamber of Commerce, Chapinero's Headquarters.

Omegablock Classrooms Building, Anglo Colombian School.
Exterior general view.

Omegablock Classroom Building, Anglo Colombian School.
Inner courtyard.

Los Nogales School Chapel. General view with open doors.

Los Nogales School Chapel. General view with closed doors.

North Point complex entrance hall. General view. Skin texture exploration.

North Point complex entrance hall. Interior view. Merging architectural detail and industrial detail.

International Convention Center Medellín. General view. Urban landscape design.

Julio Mario Santodomingo Building, Los Andes University. Courtyard collage. Skin-texture exploration.

Julio Mario Santodomingo Building, Los Andes University. Interior view. Skin-texture exploration.

Julio Mario Santodomingo Building, Los Andes University. Wood Inner courtyard skin detail.

BUYERS_ La Boca, Buenos Aires.
2010_Image especially composed for this book by M. de Brea Dulcich.

tex

TOPICS UNDER CONSIDERATION

**TO REFLECT ON,
TO CONCENTRATE, TO THINK
ABOUT, DREAM ABOUT,
ARGUMENTS, FANTASIZE ABOUT,
KEYNOTES, CALL TO MIND,
ANTICIPATION, QUESTIONS,
RESPONSIBILITIES, POINTS,
BE OF THE VIEW, RECOLLECT,
CONCERNS, SUBJECT MATTER,
OBSERVATION, THEMES.**

DOES A CONTEMPORARY LATIN AMERICAN ARCHITECTURE EXIST?

Ana Fernández
Barcelona, Spain + Groningen, Holland

Does a Contemporary Latin American Architecture Exist?

This personal reflection aims to put to the test the existence of an architecture that can be classified as Latin American. It is a very delicate matter to include under this concept the work of so many Latin-American architects who strove, and still strive, to find their own identity in the face of external influences and the marked tendency towards globalization.

If we analyze our geographical territory, Latin America extends from Tierra del Fuego to the United States in North America, an enormous area in which an endless array of landscapes flow one into another. The immense north-south extension of this continent, traversed by a large number of latitude lines with their corresponding climates, produces a logical dispersion expressed in the widely varying manners of inhabiting the territory. In spite of this gigantic spread of variables, there is one thing that acts as a connecting thread for this vast spectrum, and that is the common language that relates us all.

If we probe into history a little, we find first the pre-Hispanic cultures, the great indigenous powers that developed in certain regions of our continent. However, there are also zones where none of these cultures left any trace. Where they did, they bequeathed to us our ancestral inheritance with their legends, ceremonies and ruins.

After the empires came the Conquest, and later the continent's independence from its subjection to Spanish colonialism. By this time, mixture and intermingling had become our fundamental and firmly rooted characteristic. The cross-pollination of ethnic groups, traditions and knowledge was inevitable. The European colonists and the native populations mixed their bloods in the typical Latin-American phenomenon of crossbreeding, in some areas more than others. By the start of the 20th century, we find that half of the population of the city of Buenos Aires was foreign-born. And so, given this situation of eclecticism, how can we achieve one single form of architecture that will identify us? Extreme heterogeneity was our starting point as a society, and architecture as a social discipline will also manifest this characteristic.

Can we have, then, a Latin-American discourse taking this plurality as its base?

Personally, I firmly believe in the search for what is proper and inherent to us, but in Latin America this will only be possible on a limited scale. I have more confidence in finding an identity by regions, and I believe it is possible to interweave tradition with modernity to achieve architecture adapted to the zone. There is still a lot more work to do to raise our awareness of our heritage and integrate it as a modern element in our designs. The puzzling interest that induced us to look to Europe or the United States should be set aside, and we should rectify our course with the aim of becoming, finally, ourselves.

Not allowing oneself to be influenced is an arduous task, and I personally attempt to look to the place for the answers to questions concerning, especially, the implantation and materialization of projects, which the "genius loci" will decide. Whether I am designing in Europe or in Latin America, my work will respond to local particularities, geography, climate, fauna, vegetation, the cultural expressions and other characteristics of the society in question. As the social theme is intimately linked to our discipline, I choose to work with a multidisciplinary creative team in which architects, along with sociologists, urban planning professionals and historians, tackle the issues together from the very first moment of generation of each project. The place will dictate the identity of the new elements to be inserted there.

Consequently, I conclude that we would do better to subdivide this generalized "Latin-American architecture" into a series of local architectures in which projects will be committed to their location and history, will have a modern language marked by its immediate surroundings – whether they are urban or rural – and will be projects of their time.

1. Project of urban insertion in a non-structured neighborhood, 68 public housing units and a residence for senior citizens with disabilities. Hengelo, Holland. **2**. Renovation Goethe Institut, educational establishment for German language in Barcelona. **3**. Temporary restaurant building in the port area in Barcelona, Spain. **4**. Reinforcement of the perimeter of the old town by means of the insertion of a residential-commercial complex, which includes the renovation and conversion of a former convent into a hotel, its chapel being a historical monument. Ootmarsum, Holland. **5**. Project selected in an urban planning and landscaping competition for a group of detached houses. The idea of rural character assimilates the age-old agricultural typologies of the region and promotes an ambience equivalent to the traditional atmosphere, recalling and reinterpreting the former setting. Enschede, Holland. **6**. Urban planning/architectural competition for apartments and offices beside the Ij River. The project will define the new artificial horizon for this part of the city of Amsterdam, Holland. **7**. Competition for an archaeological museum. The largest part of the program is located underground, in keeping with the primary state of the archaeological pieces. This helps to reduce the visual impact of the building in the setting of the nature park where the museum will be located and also intensifies the visitor's sensation of immersion into the archaeological world. Mallorca, Spain.

CONSTRUCTING INTERPRETATIONS

Alejandro Stöberl
Buenos Aires, Argentina

When we get to the issue of thinking about architecture as an expression that comes from us as individuals, embedded in a given context, and immersed in a social reality that is typical of the region in which we live, it is quite difficult to understand the genesis of the design process that eventually leads to the built work. Is this subjective, or substantially rooted in the tradition of the region where things are carried out? Or maybe since, nowadays, globalization is an irreversible fact, that makes it extremely complex to distinguish the location of any work without the necessary data?

There are several moments in architectural history in which the relationship building/location was questioned. There are two examples that seemed to carry this to an end, and both in the same place: the Museum of Modern Art in New York. The first case was in 1932, where the term Modern Style was established and quickly spread throughout the planet. This reform broke with hundreds of years of understanding architecture as rules of composition and led to a new way of understanding our profession. That moment is when the internationalization of architecture began, reaching its climax with Rational Functionalism in the 1950s. Almost at the end of the 20th century, in 1995, the Light Construction exhibition again tried to rediscover the simple, transparent, almost meaningless works, most of which had no identity – works that could be built almost anywhere in the world.

A series of economic, social and technological advances changed lifestyles worldwide – in particular, the acceleration of communications produced by computer technology – which led directly to the phenomenon of globalization. An economic reality that wiped out borders and ideologies in all fields, causing a great homogeneity and a great cultural mix, where regional identity is overshadowed by a global character. The idea of living in a terrestrial paradise anywhere in the world is the result of massive production and its consequences: the exchange of goods and products, today, is also taken to the point of exchanging buildings, architects, or even urban solutions. This new architecture resulting from globalization, promoting international uniformity and somehow leaving aside the context, probably means that form is not related to function anymore. A building can be anything and could be located anywhere.

The concept of distinctiveness understood as the continuation of the same things in time is a necessity of all human existence, but in many ways it is starting to fade. Although all these facts are strong, we believe they cannot lead us to an architecture that is completely uprooted.

Reading once again the text by Gilles Deleuze, "Spinoza and the Problem of Expression", helps us to understand this old dilemma, also raised by many other philosophers, all of them trying to deconstruct the dichotomy of form / content, explaining that an action does not necessarily take the form of local identity. In fact, it expresses a universal aspect without rejecting its uniqueness, in a clear attempt to set apart the uniqueness of the universal. Architecture does not seem to be defined by distinctive traditions, ways of building, typical morphologies or local materials. Spinoza argued that whenever we speak of a potential expressing itself in actions, we must distinguish three terms : that which "expresses itself ", that "which expresses" and that "which is expressed." Expression always involves the three terms, then it forces us to think of form and content together.

Forest building, Buenos Aires, Argentina, 2012.
Marcelo Del Torto and Alejandro Stöberl Architects.

The architects of a region express their thoughts through their work. Those architects' projects are the essence and the substance of the region where they belong. There is a point here: it is not about the forms, the materials or the programs. It is about the way those architects reflect on architecture, the way they interpret it, and understand it at a particular moment and circumstances. We believe that, as architects, we must be able to read those circumstances in order to make the best architecture we can. In our office we understand architecture as the best way of interpreting our clients' desires, as well as valuing the invisible aspects of the site, the economic context, and the social moment. We look at all these concerns as layers, and what we build is just the superposition of all of them.

A DETAILED LOGBOOK BY A PERPLEXED ARCHITECT

Claudio Ferrari
Buenos Aires, Argentina

ONE

The vertiginous century has begun, and we have already come to the proliferation of images, saturation, and hyper information. We are the latest generation of pencils, the mutants who survive producing architecture without computers. Our present time seems to separate us more than a century from what we have learned. It marks us in history with a dynamic that makes it impossible for us to locate ourselves in the present. It seems that everything is and everything has been at the same time.

We find it impossible to categorize contemporary architecture, at the same time that the *ism* is no longer satisfied with defining current lines of thinking and appears as some convergent affinity group. We are immersed in a large bazaar where everything seems possible; where things are validated in the present tense ipso-facto, by merely existing. Only for being new do they arouse interest and entity; novelty produces instincts that are attracted by instants of time, in spasms, and fall into oblivion as soon as they are born.

TWO

Buenos Aires, May 2002.

The country is economically bankrupt. We no longer have a currency or a government. We are much better because we are no longer as affluent as we thought we were; we are much poorer. But the Lord said that the Kingdom of Heaven is for the poor. We have returned to glass bottles. I have even seen a street milkman. I understand that you're upset, but isn't it a good idea to get rid of plastic?

There is a paucity of food. People are thinner and serious, very serious and concerned. How nice it is not to see happy people; how ugly happy people are!. Ladies return to get their original 1950s and 60s clothes out of their wardrobes, because they cannot use the new clothing which is a repeat of the 1950s and 60s. So they look fashionable, but with period dress. How much better and more beautiful original clothes are!

People walk more; it is healthier, and there are fewer carbon emissions. Fuel is scarce and expensive. Levels of cholesterol have decreased; people get together and talk… there is nothing else to do. There are no jobs so friends like "Cholo," who we call "May the First"[1] are exempt from prosecution.

IT IS ENOUGH TO CONVINCE PEOPLE THAT WHAT THEY DO ENTERTAINS THEM.

Everything is free: theater, cinemas, museums, shows, and even concerts. Mainstream politicians who are still elected are unwilling to kill the middle class. Who would vote for them? Imagine, on Wednesday we could see *Tristan und Isolde* with Daniel Baremboin for free at 2p.m. at the Teatro Colon. When we were back outside, there was a warm July sunlight. At this time of day, the Finnish and Swedish pay fortunes for a bit of Sun on the Costa Brava.

All immigrants who came in the 1990s are gone: Bolivian, Peruvian, Paraguayan, Romanian, Russian, only the Chinese who supply food to

1 May 1st is Labor Day in Argentina, and also in many South American countries. May 1st is a common nickname used for someone who is not very passionate about working.

Naranjas [Oranges] and the Spirit of Aldo Rossi in a Grocery Store. Montevideo, 2009.

thousands of supermarkets scattered throughout the country have stayed. The exchange rate no longer favors them. Don't forget that a peso [Argentinean currency] was worth a dollar less than a year ago. There is barter. Projects and work are exchanged for food or living animals. In the absence of supplies we are again drawing by hand, back to the pencil. This is the best of all worlds! If only we could build with bricks again…

It has now been fifty years since the death of Evita Peron. There are many people who think that we should get her out of her tomb. (Repetition of phenomena generates feelings and impressions; these produce a mutation in the process of knowledge; the emergence of concept). The concept does not reflect the external aspects of things or isolated experience; it captures the essence of things. Knowledge graduates from feeling to thinking. To reach progressive understanding of the inner contradictions of things and phenomena to the explanation of laws, man does not know a thing without approaching it, without practicing the circumstances of the thing. (But the thing does not end there; it is only half of the way. It does not stop at rational knowledge. It is not only to be able to explain. The essential clue is to use objective knowledge to effectively transform the world).

THREE

A poem to Buenos Aires

Buenos Aires is featured photos of horizontal density.

Buenos Aires is a city pressed against the edge.

There is a provocative resistance of the city in the edge product of the laws of the Indies.

The tight edge is made of water; the soft edge is the Pampa desert.

The city grows up without limits; it is bulimic.

The originating fires in Garay´s fort during Buenos Aires' foundation are now repeated in the area where the ecologic reserve stands.

Pampa in the Quechua language means "flat country"; this is the Argentinean totem, the idea of a territory defined by the sublime immensity.

The national landscape is the myth of dimension without limits; from Domingo Sarmiento to Jorge Luis Borges, this myth has been sustained.

Civilization and barbarism remove the (Indian) desert and populate the city (civitas).

Borges talks of Buenos Aires as a city between two deserts: the pampas and the river.

Horizontal vertigo, horizontal density.

Buenos Aires was built on top of the desert, the pampas and invisible rivers.

The extreme size, the immensity, is what defines our landscape.

Frame and fabric regulate the urban form and give scale to this form of emptiness.

Suburbia and periphery form a great spot of oil on an apocalyptic demographic scale.

Unhappy with the city, there is a return to the countryside.

New closed cities are created with their own logic.

We are as chess players losing games against a computer.

To define the city is exhausting, an infinite mantle which absorbs everything, even the catastrophes.

It is impossible to set rules.

We can work on the fragment.

In a line of tension between nature and artifice, in the margins, we can be marginal.

Fabric carpet indiscriminate parcels out, first the lot, afterwards the infrastructure versus the vertical city.

The old destiny suggested by Sarmiento has finally come true: barbarism is flat, and civilization is vertical.

The "beautiful city" is dreamed as a series of private neighborhoods; it is only a territorial kidnapping of entrepreneurs.

Panamericana Avenue is a corridor of death, full of road accidents.

The interstices are pockets of misery as a latent threat.

It is a fair of vanities, the house as an ideal advertisement, concentrated economic power, reactionary inequality.

Security. *To be saved is the new paradigm.* What does it mean?

The problems of architecture are not the flat roof, concrete or brick anymore, but the logic of the market.

Capitalism destroys spaces looking for new places for reproduction.

Social inequity forms two types of private neighborhoods: the "country" and the "shanty town." But Buenos Aires is generating another alternative: private square blocks, a tower on a walled city block.

New generations with fear of contact with others, fear of confrontation.

Interaction occurs "online," a sterile communication.

Privatization of public space.

Future of plugged-in cities, hyper-connected, with parasite security, separated from the rest. It provides security, certainty… urbanism is not determined.

There is no order. It is uncertainty, accumulation of processes, layers; it is not stable.

Diluted borders.

There is no dogma, no more totems.

The Nietzschean logic has prevailed with the will of power.

We cannot be solemn; we are contributors [not makers] resisting in pessimism.

The bad gulp has to be endured and forgiveness granted to everyone.

We no longer have control of anything.

FOUR

In architectural production, more than in any other disciplines, it is difficult to assess the contemporary validity of buildings. Unless there is a complex network of data and interpretations that allow us to understand where and how such a thing or another have been made; and that generally seem to come in a package of the same origin. To the extent that buildings could be set more as results or consequences of marketing strategies than ideas. At this point, the confusion between image and idea is commonplace. Architecture today is an image first and foremost. Then we design how to build it. It is not the result of an internal process that creates habitable space for people. (No image can foresee the project, considering the project as a tool for thinking, not as a support for media.)

This can lead to a classification of the product-buildings, usually associated with commercial operations and worked out under marketing rules. This last mode, the more widespread and accepted by far, though not the only one, embraces all kinds of superficially designed buildings, adapted to the logic of consumption – Frenchified, modernist, regionalist, folk or simply fashion buildings – likening (architecture) to the ephemeral rules of dressing, hence the importance of the skin more than other abstract aspects like structure or the materiality itself. These modalities have put the field of engineering in the place of the waste of what actually is desired: the image. Today, a kitchen blender has more constructive experimentation than housing. Modern architecture has been an actual revolution in this regard: not only is the idea of classical composition transformed, but it also emphasized the plastic value of materials, the possibility of exploring the space through its construction, and the ability to deal with all kinds of programs integrally within the project.

FIVE

Architecture opposes resistance and in this resistance lays its intelligence and its particularity. It is not a design on paper, or a painting, or a slogan. It is serious, heavy [big] and laborious. It is performed with scarce, often non-renewable, goods and requires a great productive force, which often has served the development of peoples, not only in economic terms but also in the most virtuous aspects of their culture. We keep on producing images fighting against the ropes like boxers on the verge of succumbing, losing our identity, forming legions of animators and "3D-modelers" at the mercy of consultants who will know how to give life to the dreams of a real estate developer.

Based on the Loos[2] definition, "An architect is a builder who speaks Latin" cheers to the anachronistic, to the builders with art and craft and to all those who praise the creation of universal spaces form people, here on Earth as in Heaven.

SIX

Pending issues

Expressionism improvised

I call this architectural school line of thought a born native to these savage pampas where you can be haughtily ignorant; that is the worst aspect of any Argentinean native said *Don Borges*.

Antiseptic landscape

These are the urban ideals, which create photographic images where no visual disturbance could draw us out of our clean dream. Today we would like that only if our urban life were ideal. Who is this miserable person lying on the sidewalk? Why doesn't the municipality collect the trash in the streets?

Public spaces

The urban dynamics are based on the general meddling, expulsions and phobias; that is the vision of a trained observer. I'm not naïve. I have already been corrupted.

Picturesque

To go from the *Luncheon on the grass* by Manet to the *Cumbia rhythm of the shantytown on the southern Buenos Aires waterfront* without anesthesia is celebratory. Otherwise, we would be in reactionary models flowing into the events of Paris in November 2006, modern ghettos, and those of '45 will seem like a fairy tale.

Useless speed

Transport, circulations, connectivity, communication, optical fiber, satellite, cellphones, bands, waves, networks, ether, Chat, Facebook, Twitter, Internet City, but I cannot see you. I cannot touch you, and that soft warmness of your body is no longer captured by my aureole.

2 Author reference to Adolf Franz Karl Viktor Maria Loos (December 10, 1870 – August 23, 1933) was an Austro-Hungarian architect. He was influential in European Modern architecture, and in his essay "Ornament and Crime" he repudiated the florid style of the Vienna Secession, the Austrian version of Art Nouveau. In this and many other essays he contributed to the elaboration of a body of theory and criticism of Modernism in architecture. [extracted from Wikipedia the Free Encyclopedia]

THE NEW GENERATION = COLLABORATIVE WORK

SuperSudaca
Network of countries

In an almost stubborn way Supersudaca refuses to believe that the only space left for architects in Latin America is to build villas for rich people (though it does not discard that option altogether!). Its main driving motto has been to connect the usually disconnected Latin American architectural arena with projects directly related to the public perception such as recreation spaces, public spaces, installations, etc. in various locations such as Caracas, Lima, Tokyo, Talca, Buenos Aires.

Supersudaca continuously uses the workshop format with students from various universities worldwide to launch campaigns for such projects.

Besides direct actions, Supersudaca has two ongoing (award winning) research projects: one related to experimental social housing in Lima (Y PREVI?); and another about the impacts of tourism in the Caribbean. Both of them should end in a book at the end of this year.

More recently, Supersudaca also started to practice architectural ideas directly and won the international competition of 'vanguard' social housing in Ceuta, Spain with 170 houses.
Supersudaca has received various kinds of funding and grants, above all from Dutch foundations such as The Prince Claus Funds and the Stimulering Funds for Architecture.

Series of images of different projects by Supersudaca as collaborative work

MEDELLIN MUSEUM OF MODERN ART / First Prize in The International Ideas Contest for the MAMM extension. Medellin, Colombia. 2010_Project by Supersudaca.

INTIMATE PUBLIC SPACES. PLACES TO BE ONESELF IN THE CROWD

Julio Arroyo
Santa Fe, Argentina

Michel de Certeau explains that men and women in big cities must apply creative tactics in order to survive in such a constrictive milieu.[1] Why is it necessary to survive in cities? Supposedly cities are places where people wish to live. The city, specially big ones, is a paradox: at the same time it offers people all kinds of material and symbolical exchanges, but it pushes inhabitants to look for psychological and physical enclosure in a reduced sphere of privacy.

The extremes of publicness and privacy incite the tension between the individual – the ordinary man or woman – and the others, those whom the individual has to deal with in everyday public life. By doing so, the individual becomes part of a collective subjectivity. The collective construction of public life in Latin American cities, characterized by unequal social conditions, is always dramatic. These lines try to rehearse places which belong to the public realm (institutions), but nevertheless enable people to find a little bit of privacy just by moving aside the fluxes.

To be fully immersed in the fluxes of Sao Paulo, Mexico City or Buenos Aires leads to a moment when such places are needed. Sometimes the individual has to look for those places, other times he or she gets caught by them. These places are not refuges because the city can't be understood as a threat, even if it is hard to live in. It is better to think of them as existential places, where it is possible to recover one's own subjectivity so as to balance the overwhelming experience of city life.

The following examples focus attention on 5 relatively small places in different cities recently visited by the author. They are important from a personal point of view but, at the same time, they point out one of the roles architecture might still play in our cities: to produce singular places where individuals may vividly experience what it means to be one in the crowd.

This is a powerful encounter of the most important forces a man/woman can experience: the mineral tectonic of the land and the circle as the perfect form of human reason. There, the flux of space and time is stopped to get people to feel the elemental energies that give meaning to life.

We must not misunderstand this patio seeing only an empty space, because it is full of terrible memories (this was the inner patio of the city's ancient penitentiary). Recently, the prison was transformed into an Art Center, and bad memories gave up their place by means of rediscovering the force of architectural materiality. Colored walls and modulated pavements bring up a metaphysical space that sublimates the negative memories into hopeful and libertarian actions.

Sculpture Space, University City Cultural Area, Universidad Nacional de México (UNAM), Mexico.

1 Michel de Certeau (1990). *La invención de lo cotidiano. I- Artes de hacer.* México DF: Universidad Iberoamericana, 1996.

Main Patio at Centro de la Artes, San Luis Potosí, Mexico, 2009.

SESC Pompeia, Sao Paulo, Lina Bo Bardi.

Ateneo bookshop, former Gran Splendid Theater, Buenos Aires.

Patios del Rectorado. Universidad Nacional del Litoral, Santa Fe, Argentina. Santa Fe.

Theaters used to be one of the places for the self-representation of the bourgeois urban society that built up its class identity looking toward the European capitals of the XX century. Now, bookshelves are in the place where the audience used to sit and customers are on the stage, leisurely drinking a coffee or a beer. In spite of the increasing virtualization of the world, the concrete presence of the book still evokes human communication, minds opening, the desire for knowledge, and dreams. It is a good place to put aside the vulgarity of consumerism and prosaic life.

An industrial city, a working class neighborhood, a vacant industrial building. Social commitment, civic institutions and a clever architect contribute to generating a social center. A large number of commerce and service sector employees and plain citizens are admitted to enjoy the cultural and sporting facilities. Here opportunities are widely open to everybody. When people of all ages fill the spaces, in a very calm and pleasurable atmosphere, the concept of equality is strongly aroused and the old warehouses host a communitarian life.

Santa Fe is the city where the author of these lines lives, teaches and practices as an architect. The peaceful patios of the President Building at the UNL, with their palm trees and well-scaled architecture, are very inspiring places. Here birds are even more boisterous than the noisy streets of the surroundings.

AUTHENTICITY OR DEATH*

Mauro Bianucci
Barcelona, Spain & New York, United States.

1. Identity

The very title of this book opens up the question of Identity.
Is there anything that can be called "Latin American Architecture" today?
And if so, what would make architecture "Latin American"?
Before dwelling into this, we might also want to ask: Why would we care about local identities when the world is global, connected, networked, instantaneous...?

2. Global / Local

Identities emerge through contrasts. 'Local' identities do not exist in isolation. In our globalized world, whether by physical or technological means, distances between different 'local' identities have been shortened.

Globalization, in its ubiquity, has the potential of flattening out the differences that make each identity 'local'.

Architecture is not immune to this phenomenon.

Even though we do not need to keep local identities in "suspended animation" (a kind of extreme preservation that is often based on fear of change) the existence and maintenance of the 'local' is vital.

The relationship and exchange between the 'local' and the 'global', the dialogue between different cultures, and the embrace of those differences constitute a path for cultural growth and social understanding. From a personal point of view, this path ultimately leads to a better world.

At the same time, globalization provides the opportunity to enrich local identities in a unique way. For this reason, architecture should not reject or oppose global flows. Instead "...these global flows can be absorbed and regenerated through the filter of local cultures..." (Stefano Boeri). This new filter with which to see contemporary architecture becomes a requirement for any relevant work today.

3. Authenticity

So, how do we define a Latin American identity in the globalized world?

I can only write about Argentina, since I do not have any first-hand experience of other countries in Latin America.

In my view, the clue to creating, sustaining and evolving an identity is authenticity.

By authentic I do not mean the opposite of fake, but instead the embrace, consideration and processing of all contextual dimensions (local *and* global) surrounding any creative production.
In Latin America's architecture (as in other places) the opposite of this authenticity is regularly manifested in the attempt to replicate other architectures and 'force' them into the Latin American context. This phenomenon obviously grows exponentially with the speed and accessibility of information.

4. Translations

This authenticity is more commonly found in disciplines outside architecture.

*The title *Autenticidad o Muerte* is a play on words of the famous *Patria o Muerte* quote attributed to Ernesto "Che" Guevara (roughly translated as "Homeland or Death"). Without intending to refer to actual death, *Autenticidad o Muerte* is meant as a way to describe that the only thing to be had is authenticity. Without it, there is nothing.

Take an example from contemporary Argentinean fashion: *Tramando*. Its production is intrinsically Argentinean yet maintains a dialogue with the international stage by simultaneously feeding from it, while also making a unique contribution to it.

Several other examples can be taken from the Latin American art world: from Ernesto Neto in Brazil to Doris Salcedo in Colombia, from Gabriel Orozco in Mexico to the Mondongo group in Argentina. Even though none of these artists would claim that their work is a traditional example of their native country (and most of them live abroad), their work is deeply pervaded by their local identity.

This kind of authenticity is what strengthens Latin America's identity and provides it with the uniqueness needed to have a lasting and evolving dialogue on the international stage.

5. The role of critique

What these artists have in common is their willingness to take a stance. They expose themselves and open up to discussion, dialogue, and critique. It is through this taking of positions that identity is defined.

To continue moving forward we need to escape critique in its current 'descriptive' form, and allow contributions and dialogue to nurture a solid body of serious critical thinking. This is essential to any form of relevant cultural and architectural production.

Sources and further reading: Kenneth Frampton, *Modern Architecture: A Critical History* (Thames and Hudson, 1980). José Pablo Feinmann, *La Filosofía y el Barro de la Historia* (Planeta, 2008). Paul Virilio, *El Cibermundo, la Política de lo Peor* (Catedra, 1997).
Stefano Boeri, *The Eye of the Needle of Local Space – Manifesto for a New Idea of Localism* (Abitare, 2010).

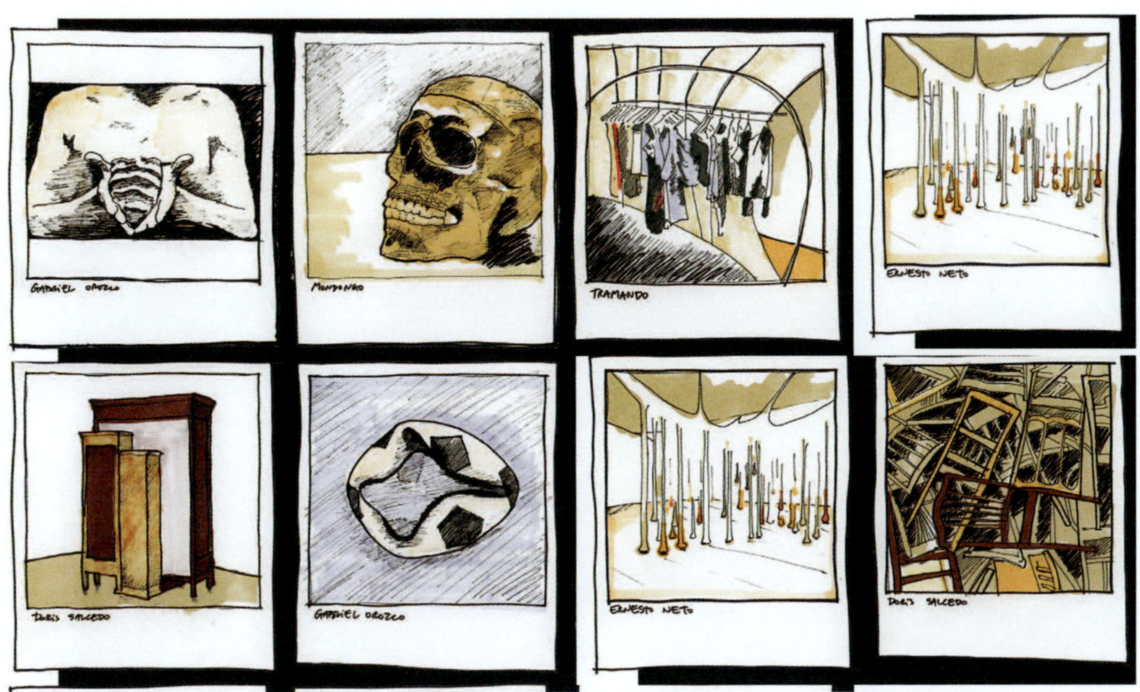

Collection of study sketches done by the author of different artwork pieces by the artists mentioned in the essay. From the author's point of view, each of them expresses an authentic Latin American dimension.

SUBJECTIVE RATIONALISMS

Sergio Forster
Buenos Aires, Argentina & La Paz, Bolivia

This essay is part of the research on the relationship between design plans and informal settlements. Precisely the work pays attention to the street markets in the city of La Paz, Bolivia, central example of a situation that occurs all over Latin America.

The natural condition of a practice cannot be separated from its surroundings. It is obvious that a structure of thought, a project or an action cannot survive if it is not adapted or negotiated with the environment.

This negotiation is not the cause of the project development, but the information and components on which the project must rely.

A creative production necessarily takes place in a time and space where the given elements relate with one another and which will be referred to as information.

For a production to evolve and develop, it is necessary to subject it to some kind of operation, to a work capacity that will allow it to transform into increasingly consistent successive layers since they hold both simple and complex relations between the components.

At this point we can see, although adding complexity to the problem, that some operations are cohesive and will thus give consistency to the production, while others are dispersive and will tend to lessen consistency of the product in process.

We seek to make rational, subjective operations that produce relations, which can yield/allow the recognition of material and work systems.

We work with complex systems capable of relating to their own evolution and with new external bonds until the internal-external duality is dismantled. We position and require them not to be unique, absolute and true systems, but to force the exploitation of their mutual capacities. Evolving work is capable of transforming and being transformed in accordance with new rational, successive subjective networks.

In this way operative mechanics, using and prioritizing coherences and cohesions, can engage a kind of detachment of concepts, prefigurations or prejudices and lead to the possible appearance of unexpected components that might be hidden by concept reduction.

Promoting free production environments where the task is the project itself, allows for non-discontinuous evolution with unforeseen results.

It is about producing a project through successive coherent operations in the process. The design architect does not decide on a solution to the problem beforehand but he rather conducts the process while doing, discovering tendencies and making decisions in a specific productive field with precise and definite connections.

Some aspects of diagrammatical techniques allow us to withhold solutions, ideas or interests temporarily and in many cases detect false problems in the manner Bergson presents them.

The interpretations of what is mobile are in many cases marked by the effect they produce, by the transformations in the structure and the layout of the substance they affect.

The concept reduces the qualities of the object to its abstract properties but it could also be described by enumerating the *n* dimensions that compose it, using no conceptual reduction. Description will provide a more productive reality if we consider its qualities and components with the capacity to participate in new relationships or connections within the work system.

Intuitive recognition is imprecise in itself. It is formed of concepts or notions that make up a preconceived subjectivity.

In this sense, the design process does not passively adapt to external conditions and to its demands, nor does it necessarily impose its own logic; rather it is an increasingly complex structure that makes the most of all those conditions it encounters. It is an evolutionary structure that uses all the problems it encounters for its own benefit and for that of its environment, actualizing them in a new way, actively reacting and solving the problem.

Mercado Rodriguez, one of the oldest markets in the city of La Paz.

Itinerant market in La Paz, Bolivia.

ESTAR FUERA DE LA MODA (BEING OUT OF FASHION)

Wes Janz
Indianapolis, USA

In the hills outside Chihuahua, Mexico, a sporadic residential landscape built of recovered wood and plastic pallets, doors, corrugated metal, plastic sheeting, wood flats, cable spools, blankets, signs, and box springs. A home grows in a leftover space.

A household bound with wood pallets, planks and scraps; corrugated sheets and panel remnants in Buenos Aires, Argentina. All rough, all reclaimed, all local. Here, in La Boca, it is a big landscape of small architectures, waste materials, and promising lives.

The Valle de Urraca neighborhood of Panama City, Panama. Emilia Sanchez – a precarista (someone living precariously) – builds a permanent house adjacent to her "meanwhile house," or *la casa mientras tanto*, constructed of reclaimed wood and corrugated metal sheets purchased at Cerro Patacon, the city's main dump.

Fashion? In Chihuahua, Buenos Aires, and Panama City?

Maybe fashion (conventional definition) as "style in clothing, hair, and personal appearance" if you consider found outfits, self-done haircuts, and no hot water as "fashion." Yes, possibly fashion as "a business, as creating, promoting, or studying the latest styles" if you're talking about entrepreneurial activities at the town dump, of cardboard scavengers in pre-dawn hours, or Joe Snow, the informal garbage hauler in my neighborhood.

Being "out of fashion" is of interest because it is a way of life for so many people:

– One in six billion people on the planet are slum residents, pavement dwellers or squatters,

– The majority of the planet's population growth in our shared foreseeable future will be among the poorest people, and

– According to Robert Neuwirth in his 2005 book Shadow Cities, squatters "mix more concrete than any developer. They lay more bricks than any government... Squatters are the largest builders of housing in the world—and they are creating the cities of tomorrow."

Here, I like the verb "to fashion" (conventional definitions) as in: "to shape or form something, to adapt something, to make something suitable." Now, for me, to fashion is to learn how shape is given to a life lived under difficult circumstances; to understand how another person adapts herself and her children to a life that must be lived closely, efficiently, and sustainably (she has no choice); or to know how to make something suitable from what many would consider less than nothing.

To place human beings at the center of our architectural work. To strive for a humane architecture. To be of use to young people who seek meaningful work, who themselves want to be of use, who want to learn.

These are the intentions that rouse me to action, first as a citizen, then as an architect.

Estar fuera de moda is what inspires me these days.

Neighborhood, Chihuahua, Mexico.

Pallet House, La Boca, Buenos Aires, Argentina.

Emilia's Meanwhile House, Panama City, Panama.

Family living, Buenos Aires, Argentina.

Man, bus shelter, Buenos Aires, Argentina.

Heidelberg, Detroit, Michigan, USA.

Informal, East St. Louis, Illinois, USA.

Abandoned houses, Gary, Indiana, USA.

WORKERS AROUND THE TABLE / Original Painting, 100 cm x 70 cm . Acrylic on paper drawing.
2010_Painted especially for this book by Roberto Frangella.

PRAÇA DES CRIANÇAS

Santiago Cirugeda
Rio de Janeiro, Brazil & Seville, Spain

The technical and design solutions for the project executed in the Vital Brazil neighborhood were presented with a symbolic and functional idea of filling a wasted space. The excuse was perfect and again, architecture works as a binding force to gather similar interests and generate a working team that will be able to continue with projects in this cooperative line. The designs were made by brainstorming ideas and evaluating the level of difficulty in their construction, access to materials, functionality and a pleasing image. The decision making and data collection for the development of the project were done in a short time including participation and suggestions from several children who helped, in a democratic way, by voting and selecting the name for the plaza. They were instructed to choose a name that had a collective meaning for the children in Vita Brazil and a name that would keep its meaning over time. The demolition, cleaning, the platform for the bleachers and benches, the murals, the fence to keep balls from getting lost, the wooden swing used by the kids, all helped set the foundation for building a space, especially a human space, that will have to be improved and maintained. During the work, a pipe was broken in the plaza which was cause for celebration and fun for the kids. These kinds of accidents have happened to the residents while building their neighborhood, fomenting a sense of positivity and camaraderie, which is the fundamental basis for tackling construction in a common space.

People like Magrau, Carlos, Luana and others have also been very important to the procees. I have mentioned them because, after this experience, they started a collective effort called Enxame, which we maintain a relationship with and we help when we can. Again, it is an example that all experiences in collective building generate new groups, who develop a strong working link as well as friendship.

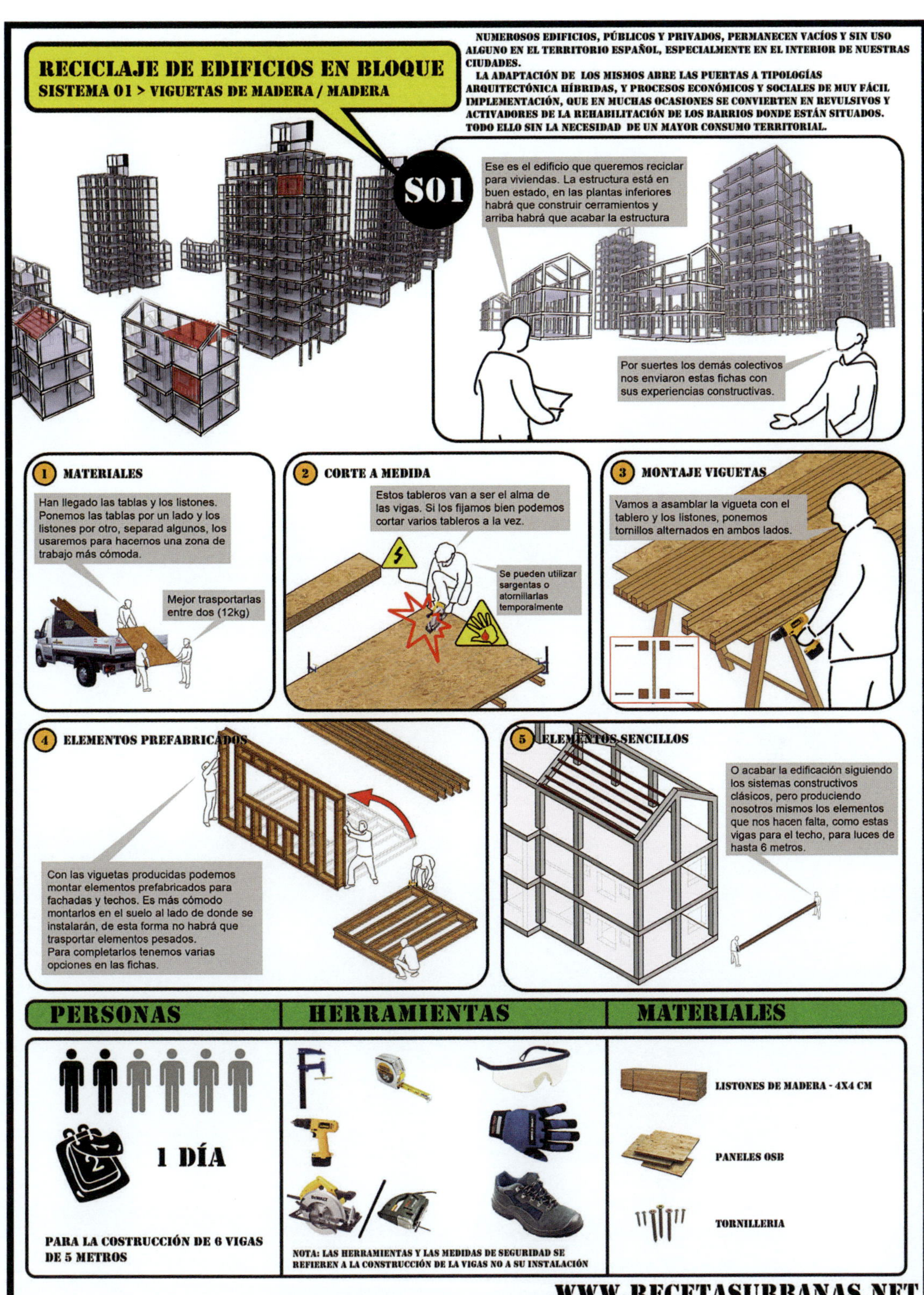

RECICLAJE DE EDIFICIOS EN BLOQUE
SISTEMA 01 > VIGUETAS DE MADERA / MADERA
NUMEROSOS EDIFICIOS, PÚBLICOS Y PRIVADOS, PERMANECEN VACÍOS Y SIN USO ALGUNO EN EL TERRITORIO ESPAÑOL, ESPECIALMENTE EN EL INTERIOR DE NUESTRAS CIUDADES.
LA ADAPTACIÓN DE LOS MISMOS ABRE LAS PUERTAS A TIPOLOGÍAS ARQUITECTÓNICA HÍBRIDAS, Y PROCESOS ECONÓMICOS Y SOCIALES DE MUY FÁCIL IMPLEMENTACIÓN, QUE EN MUCHAS OCASIONES SE CONVIERTEN EN REVULSIVOS Y ACTIVADORES DE LA REHABILITACIÓN DE LOS BARRIOS DONDE ESTÁN SITUADOS. TODO ELLO SIN LA NECESIDAD DE UN MAYOR CONSUMO TERRITORIAL.
S01
Ese es el edificio que queremos reciclar para viviendas. La estructura está en buen estado, en las plantas inferiores habrá que construir cerramientos y arriba habrá que acabar la estructura
Por suertes los demás colectivos nos enviaron estas fichas con sus experiencias constructivas.
1 MATERIALES
Han llegado las tablas y los listones. Ponemos las tablas por un lado y los listones por otro, separad algunos, los usaremos para hacernos una zona de trabajo más cómoda.
Mejor trasportarlas entre dos (12kg)
2 CORTE A MEDIDA
Estos tableros van a ser el alma de las vigas. Si los fijamos bien podemos cortar varios tableros a la vez.
Se pueden utilizar sargentas o atornillarlas temporalmente
3 MONTAJE VIGUETAS
Vamos a asamblar la vigueta con el tablero y los listones, ponemos tornillos alternados en ambos lados.
4 ELEMENTOS PREFABRICADOS
Con las viguetas producidas podemos montar elementos prefabricados para fachadas y techos. Es más cómodo montarlos en el suelo al lado de donde se instalarán, de esta forma no habrá que trasportar elementos pesados.
Para completarlos tenemos varias opciones en las fichas.
5 ELEMENTOS SENCILLOS
O acabar la edificación siguiendo los sistemas constructivos clásicos, pero produciendo nosotros mismos los elementos que nos hacen falta, como estas vigas para el techo, para luces de hasta 6 metros.
PERSONAS
HERRAMIENTAS
MATERIALES
1 DÍA
PARA LA COSTRUCCIÓN DE 6 VIGAS DE 5 METROS
NOTA: LAS HERRAMIENTAS Y LAS MEDIDAS DE SEGURIDAD SE REFIEREN A LA CONSTRUCCIÓN DE LA VIGAS NO A SU INSTALACIÓN
LISTONES DE MADERA - 4X4 CM
PANELES OSB
TORNILLERIA
WWW.RECETASURBANAS.NET

A PERCEPTION OF TERRITORY

Martha Kohen
Montevideo, Uruguay & Florida, United States

Project: Memorial in Remembrance of Disappeared Detained Citizens (2003)
Location: Montevideo, Uruguay
Authors: Architects Martha Kohen and Ruben Otero
Landscape architect: Rafael Dodera
Visual artist: Mario Sagradini
Collaborators: Pablo Frontini and Diego Lopez de Haro
Consultants: Engineer Ricardo Hosftadter (lighting); Magnone Pollio (structural engineers); Medina and Possamay (building contractors)

A Perception of Territory [*A critical perspective on the materialization of an architectural concept, inserted in the Latin American environment*]

The Memorial project inserts itself in a Latin American way of thinking and making architecture. The principal components of this specificity can be derived from my personal experience with professional work elsewhere, in Europe, Asia, and the USA.

The importance given to the public realm and, in particular, public space is widespread in Latin America. This can be seen in the project's placement resulting from a Municipal strategy focused on locating significant public works in deprived neighborhoods, thus democratizing and dignifying the periphery.

The thought processes in Latin American architecture are decisively participatory. In this case, participation occurred in multiple superimposed layers, starting from a vast and representative National Committee – in charge of framing the political boundaries of the Memorial – followed by a public competition that brought together more than 200 professionals, and then a public exhibition, with panel discussions.

Participation extended to the implementation process. This was a hands-on construction process, with ONGs from the community called on to provide actual manual help in uncovering the underlying bedrock, before the construction documents were finalized. And the funding for the project was obtained by public subscription, involving a great number of people in fundraising efforts, both at home, and among the Uruguayan diaspora.

Thinking and making are interlocked and go hand-in-hand in Latin America. Thinking is not complete without the input of the making processes, and very vividly so in the case of this project. The process is adaptive; it involves artisan work with many degrees of craftsmanship including manual modifications of the landscape. The input of the construction industry was limited to very specific interventions involving technology-dense pieces.

Latin American architecture is firmly grounded in the site – intimately combined with it, without the fear that we perceive in other cultures of creating a permanent scar on the virgin territory. The territory in our continent, in spite of the gigantic imprint of the colonial and the modern periods, is still the domain of the indigenous and the sacred; the colonial, to a large extent has absorbed the indigenous. This project is not only grounded in its new-found territory, it is the territory and has become sacred as a consequence of its content and meaning.

Latin America has traditionally been a realm of scarce resources, and this has fostered inventiveness, as much as many of the traits are associated with sustainability. The architecture of Latin America is naturally sustainable, a veritable arte povera, careful with its resources, the provenance of its materials, the use of human resources, and mindful of maintenance and upkeep concerns. It differentiates itself strongly from the carelessness with which the developed world utilizes space, energy, materials and land. In the case of the Memorial, materials – the most engaging ones – were strictly local, as were the human resources needed for the construction, achieving expression using the minimum amount of resources.

Finally, Latin American architects usually work with an enhanced sensibility for social concerns and address ideas of solidarity and social justice, many of which originate in their university education, traditionally engaged in social issues.

The combinations of qualities that lend an identity to this project include a very strong and expressive materiality, building on the contrast of natural and technological materials. Form has a high component of the unforeseeable and, incorporating the unforeseen, the random and the adventurous create the final form. Form is derived from the interface of man and nature, and determined by human perception and use. The Memorial is a harmonic symbolic structure open to penetration, passage and congregation; human actions such as walking, standing, sitting, playing, observing, and meditating lead to the natural appropriation of the place and help to shape the various meanings that affect the place in the eye of the actor-spectator. The evolving nature of the exposed stone sensitive to degradation, the growth of the flora, the views through the crystals into the wooden areas, and the acoustic qualities are all factors that help in this process of public appropriation. At the same time, the Memorial is far away from traffic noise so that it can nurture itself with the sounds of the wind and the songs of birds, the play of light in the trees and the naked anatomy of the bedrock. All these elements anchor the work to the essential values that it is meant to convey.

Bird's-eye view, the bedrock and the green spaces.

Internal Corridor

i_DENTITY / Who Are You Latin America?
2010_Collage composed especially for this book by M. de Brea Dulcich.

who are you?
atinoamerica

THE OBJECT OF DESIGN AND ITS CONNECTION TO ARCHITECTURAL SPACE

Ricardo Blanco
Buenos Aires, Argentina.

The title of this article describes a hypothesis that needs to be confirmed.

It is always a good idea to define the words that establish the essential elements of a written article; in this case, when we refer to *architectural space*, we know what we are talking about, but it is important to define *design* and *art*.

Design, what is called industrial design, is the discipline that creates and develops objects that establish a connection between human beings and their environment; these objects are considered *utilitarian items.*

By *art* we mean the manifestation of society and its moment in time, and this manifestation is reflected in works of art that take their strength from their classic shape, such as paintings, engravings, sculptures, etc., and also, from present expressions, such as performance, virtuality, land art, body art, etc.

The hypothesis today is that utilitarian items, in the architectural space of every day life, can be seen and valued as art items.

The objects of use, once designed, become an important aesthetic manifestation.

The key lies in the way users perceive these objects, i.e. if we consider every single daily action as a succession of stages, performance, rationality, experience and objects, we access a different universe that allows us to live aesthetic experiences.

The participation of the item in architectural space has to be seen from the point of view of the user. Architectural space is also part of the architecture in lowercase letters: architecture that shelters everyday life, a life full of objects, objects that sometimes are design items (since some objects have been designed, others have not; they are only objects of use or daily objects). This is why we speak of designed objects.

This influence is interesting from an aesthetic perspective, since we assume that the vision and usefulness of the object in architectural space generates an influence of aesthetic contemplation in the user that has not yet been given its due dimension.

We perceive that the aesthetic appreciation of a utilitarian item, for the user, is a situation that goes beyond his/her sensibility, since he/she is not merely a user of the object. We also believe that this stage of going beyond the mere use or functionality of an item in order to appreciate its formal and symbolic qualities constitutes the first step toward valuing the abstraction of what constitutes an architectural space.

Trying to reflect on this unquestionable relationship between art and design, what can be better than to look at everyday life in order to see how both interact?

M. Heidegger, in "Paths in the Forest", establishes a sequence: the thing; the useful thing; the work. He calls plants and stones things; he calls useful the thing that is used and serves, and works refers to the art piece.

But, even though design is concerned with utilitarian items, we think that not every utilitarian item can be considered a design piece, nor every painted piece can be considered an art piece.

In order to perceive design items as art items, we must first define design items.

Utilitarian objects are considered "design items" if they are:

Techno productive: *well* manufactured, with the appropriate materials.

Functional, correctly designed for the function and use they have been designed for, and they perform well.

And, on the aesthetic-formal level, they need to have formal quality and to consciously participate in some defined aesthetic orientation.

These values are extremely generic, but there is another factor that cannot be minimized: one, the fact that the objects are made by a designer, a conscious author, who knows he is making a design, i.e. the design of objects is the design activity in which an author designs a utilitarian object with aesthetic values (when we consider the author, we subscribe to Danto's concept of aura in art). That is how we can consider the objects of design to be a category within the works of art, since that object provides us with an aesthetic experience.

This is the point from which we can start to analyze how objects of art are presented in everyday life and in architectural space. An object can be considered a design because of several reasons:

A utilitarian object can be acknowledged as an art piece that actively participates in our lives and spaces from three different perspectives:

The first one, through its *concrete use.* The service they provide and how they perform it can determine whether this object offers an aesthetic enrichment or not.

Second, based on *perception.* Its manipulation (manual perception) and its image (visual perception) can also provide aesthetic enrichment. A utilitarian object can be visually appreciated as a work of art, even though we are well aware that it is a utilitarian object. We know that it is necessary to resort to the beauty of the object, and we should accept that even though beauty is one of the variables, it is not the only important thing in art, and it is considerably overvalued.

Finally, appreciating it as *design*, i.e., an element that has been vindicated as a paradigm of the design universe, whether historically or as a design by a renowned author, in which case it pertains to an aesthetic category of its own.

It is important not to forget that the intention is to make clear how it is possible to have an aesthetic experience every day, and it is not necessary to go to a museum, since it is possible to have it in our daily architectural space when we use designed objects.

In order to be able to evaluate the condition of the object, it is necessary to establish the scenery where that object is – home, work, urban. There are three possible architectural spaces where we can recognize the object of design as an element that can generate a positive aesthetic experience, that can act – as Uribe said – as an "aesthetic resounder".

At *home,* the possibility of feeling this experience is conditioned upon the moment and place where the object is presented. For example, if we consider setting the table for an important dinner, we can distinguish the following steps:

Setting:

Plates, cups, cutlery, bottles. Everything responds to a criterion of harmonic distribution between shapes and colors, sizes and positions.

As performance:

How dinner guests use the objects becomes a "happening", with characters, main stars and chorus, with a choreography of the elements, "music" (table sounds), etc.;

Finally, the stage of untidying, of disordering this initial scenery that leads to another stage, in which chaos is what becomes relevant.

We can continue with another stage, the rationalistic and systemic activity of doing the dishes, and the subsequent organization by family, type, material, etc. and whether objects are put away or not.

Furniture in general, is normally evaluated from the aesthetic perspective rather than its function, and also from the standpoint of symbolism. Furniture completely represents life and the social status of the user; *they constitute objects with memory and opinion.* On the other hand, furniture qualifies rooms. A room with no furniture can be assessed from a certain perspective, for example: because of its living space, when it is full of furniture, this assessment changes and turns into an aesthetic (not utilitarian) assessment, in which the symbolic can be an essential element.

As regards work, utilitarian objects (such as tools, machinery, etc.) participate in a space that might be considered of community use (a factory) or private use (a workshop). It is here that the utilitarian objects are assessed, when they are purchased to fulfill a need; the main force in this assessment is its usefulness, or the technical aspect, and an efficient use increases the assessment incorporating aesthetics, while an inefficient use eliminates this assessment.

In *urban space,* nobody can deny the visual influence of automobiles. The automobile concept is the most repetitive in the urban stage and we see it static, moving, speeding, opening, shutting, in line, with mixed colors, defining trends, etc.

When these useful objects are shown at exhibitions or in the media, their assessment is initially led by their aesthetics (beauty); there are no "ugly" utilitarian objects.

These descriptive stages let us consider certain concepts as leading to the assessment of everyday objects: first *order.* We have already seen that, when we refer to a table, when you prepare it, the relationship between objects makes it possible to assess them as regards style/taste. We can imagine a table set before the dinner starts and then after the event. This last scene is disorganized and chaotic, negative when compared to the first one; we can also think about the performance during dinner.

This situation can be considered as leading certain proposals (Alejandro Ruiz in Milan, for Alessi) (Figure 1), where a series of "*little animals*" was created for the scenery-table and they were actually personalized saltshakers. There are also saltshakers with wheels so as to be able to pass them without raising them off the table (the myth is respected).

The way an object is presented is crucial.

It is interesting here to mention Alessi's (the Italian producer) recommendation, when he advises his designers to propose vertically-shaped utilitarian table objects, with a stronger presence, so, after being used, instead of being placed in a drawer or cupboard, they are placed in a glass cabinet to be shown as works of art. (E.g. P. Starck's juicer) (Figures 2, 3).

Design has taken certain concepts from art, and art has taken certain conditions from design.

We can consider the multiple designs from the 1960s as a rupture with the aura of non-reproducibility, so dear to art. (Figure 4)

On the other hand, engravings are done in numbered series, because they are reproducible. Design has taken up this concept for certain key pieces.

So, the paradigms have been changing and adapting, and, as a consequence, the need for manifestation in art and design are constantly getting closer. There are, however, areas of design and art that still keep their own paradigms:

Originality, long valued in art, today, is not a value in design.

The concept of beauty in design still validates a work or piece.

What design has not accepted yet is horror; there has not been a Damian Hirst with his formaldehyde shark in design.

But art uses utilitarian objects (Duchamp) to shake its own foundations.

Walter Benjamin, in his famous article on the reproducibility of art (1936), deals with the conditions that arose in art as a consequence of the influence of photography, due to its ability to be reproduced. It is surprising that he did not deal with utilitarian objects, considering that the article was written in Germany, where, the Bauhaus had just been dissolved in 1933.

We think that the reason he does not deal with utilitarian objects is that Walter Benjamin considered the Bauhaus a factory or workshop of individual pieces and, at the time, that was the concept of art (actually, it was the concept in most designed objects).

Even though a photograph, with its negative, constitutes a reproducible element, it can be different from another photograph, since it can be manipulated in the process of developing the film. In the process of product design, when there is a cast – the essential element for reproduction, there is no room for modifications.

But the concept of mass reproducibility has been the concern of many designers; Enzo Mari, and specially Gaetano Pesce (Figure 5) managed to differentiate objects with molds for high production, thus making the pieces unique, as art desires.

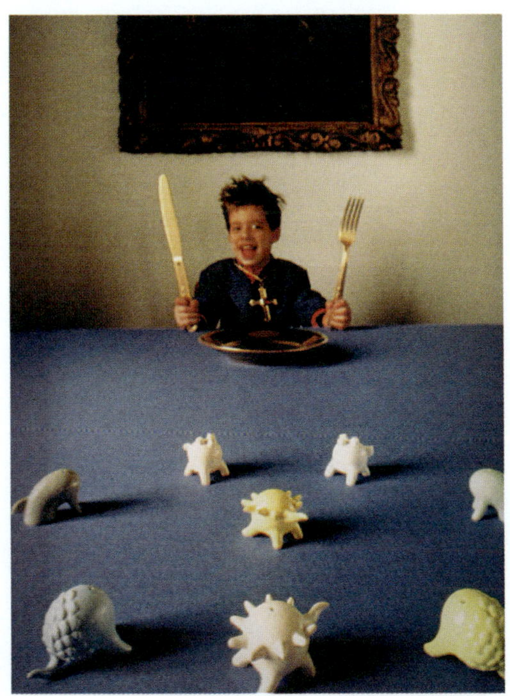

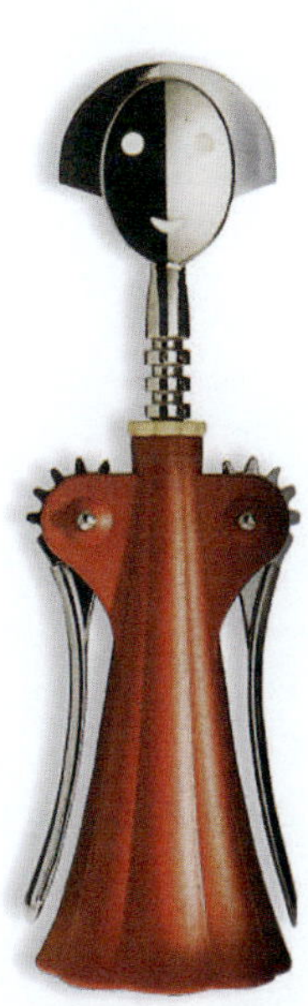

1. GLIUNNIMI - Alejandro Ruiz. Small personal salt shakers, each person uses their own and the table is full of little beings.
2. STARCK - Alessi. The famous Starck juicer, with its functional flaws, has come to be a fetish of contemporary design.
Maybe it is the vertical position that helped his success in the collective imagination.
3. ALESSI CORKSCREW - Alejandro Mendini. As ANNA G's corkscrew, by Alessi, its anthropomorphic features make it difficult to forget.
4. PRECIOUS OBJETS - Alessi. In 1972, Alessi made pieces by sculptors of the stature of Pietro Cosagra, Gio Pomodoro, shaped according to the designs of many artists.

Now, these thoughts are all referred to the connections between utilitarian objects and art pieces, but not between the acts of the makers, whether artists or designers.

That means that the relationship between art and design can also be considered from the perspective of the maker; since, in the case of the artist the piece is thought of directly and, in the case of the designer, it is subject to the process of execution, whether by a cast or the work of a craftsman. This close collaboration between the designer and the craftsman also exists between the artist and the helper or aide; sometimes it is a craftsman who actually makes the piece.

At present, in artists' workshops (Murakami, Koons) there are countless numbers of helpers who execute an artist's piece, whether by reproducing it, or because of its size or complexity. Sculptors send digital files to the cutters to do their job, and so on and so forth. Thus, we want to make it clear that, if in art, the manual work of the artist constituted a paradigm, today it is not considered essential, and the production of a work of art is similar to that of an object of design, whose massiveness does not constitute an excluding value. Today, the production of a unique personalized piece is possible thanks to modern manufacturing processes and the socio-cultural importance of design.

But, in essence, this matter of art and design can be simplified with the saying (almost a truism) by Mario Bellini: *"A design is anything we recognize as design, and a work of art is what is considered a work of art."*

Summing it up, we can define design as the art of turning a utilitarian object into a beautiful object.

The environment of the design of industry-generated products used in architecture has many dimensions, one being functional technique. The elements are made to answer needs. Bathroom faucets allow us to get water; a door allows control of privacy and safety, etc. These elements have been planned according to the old aphorism: *"Form follows function"*. It means that if we further the action performed by the objects in order to better interact with the environment, a shape will manifest itself and, in turn, it will shape the environment, the habitat, etc.

Another line of product design is based on the criteria that determine space, a room, etc. and will lend character to it; furniture, for example, has stylistic formal characterizations that resort to its articulation with the architectural space, but it has developed in such a way that it has accessed the instance of meaning and symbolism, therefore acquiring an identity of its own (Figure 5).

There is furniture that responds to a certain style, others to a line, others to a system, others to a certain nationality, so, the universe of these objects becomes something detached from architecture and it is not an element that adds value to it.

There is a more modern variation that looks for the creation of objects that interact with the architecture, based on new scenes and social trends, whether urban or habitat, and conditioned by the actions or performances of the users.

5. SANSONE - Gaetano Pesce. The table is manufactured in a cast or mold, to be filled with the necessary quantity of resin. In this case, using less resin the cast is not entirely filled, i.e., a system of serial production is used in order to obtain unique pieces.

6. ASTACÁ - Copa Italia - FADU, Buenos Aires. A system of artificial "reeds" used to define space, with possible variations.

7. TUM – Only Planet, Buenos Aires. Element to generate music in cycles, with the fortuitous participation of the urban man.

8. AIRPANEL - Copa Italia - FADU, Buenos Aires. The panel is manufactured in punched metal allowing for the flow of hot or cold air, softly or strongly, not only regulating the temperature of the room but also – when it takes air in – making possible to hang papers or fabrics to change the visual aspect of the room.

As regards this way of thinking about objects within a habitat, it is worth mentioning experiences connected to the design of new space elements referred to architecture. One was the *"household mutations"* experiment, organized by the University of Reggio Emilia, Italy, within the "*Copa Italia"* competition (Figure 8). The second was the Nokia workshops organized as part of "*Only Planet"* (Figure 7), held for the Industrial Design Course in the Architecture, Design and Urbanism department at UBA University.

The idea of "Household mutations" was to generate objects which made it possible to change architecture without affecting it. Five projects were developed around the idea that architecture is connected with space and with the body of the user.

One referred to a concrete object, a panel, which also functioned as a wall, and air was expelled or taken in; it could be conditioned, changing the speed, and the wall also was used to fix light elements or fabric that constantly changed the space.

Another was a "descender," an articulated arm used to go down between floors, and to move around the space in different directions, not only up and down like a normal elevator or in diagonal, like stairs; all according to the intention of the user.

The third one was a fabric tunnel with air that affected the body when entering the house, getting rid of everyday stress.

There was also a series of vertical lineal individual pieces, resembling reeds, of different lengths that could be organized so as to obtain virtually limited spaces, which could be permanently modified (Figure 6).

Finally, there was an imaginary proposal, as if "from the reverse". If a lamp lightens when it is dark, why not have a lamp that darkens when there is light? The same way there are lamps that emit light, there could be lamps with directed shadows making it possible to create areas of shade in architecture and to establish areas blocked only by the shadow, or that could be used to "dramatize" the space.

The experience of Nokia in the Only Planet workshop made it possible to develop products related to architecture. Architecture is considered the future scenery in which digital technology will play an important role. The conjunction of scenery and social trends, in this case, the participation of different people, made it possible to imagine new products that modified architecture considered as a place to live, according to different times and eras.

UTOPIAS

Horacio Torcello
Buenos Aires, Argentina (At the Venice Biennial 2014)

"Utopia is on the horizon. I take two steps, it moves two steps away and the horizon runs ten steps further on. So, what's the use of Utopia? Just that; it makes you walk."
Eduardo Galeano

The roots of the term Utopia are Greek, and its meaning should be understood by following a two-way etymological path: the one established by the literal translation u-topia (no-place), but also the one suggested by the homophone eu-topia (good place). Its use to designate a plan, project, doctrine or optimistic system that appears to be unrealizable at the moment of its formulation is attributed to the dictionary of the Real Academia Española and becomes more general with the publication in 1516 of the work *On the Best State of a Republic and on the New Island of Utopia* by Sir Thomas More. Although the idea of the geometrically perfect and politically organized city already appears in Plato's *Republic*, besides being a work of political philosophy More's book – together with certain contemporaries like *Gargantua* by Rabelais, *Città del Sole* by Tomaso Campanella and *The New Atlantis* by Francis Bacon – serves as a starting point for urbanism to consolidate, strengthen or induce the social virtues which, in the opinion of each author, are the fundamental virtues required to achieve a happy, perfected society. A reality that does not exist but one which is considered ideal and, to a certain extent, essential.

Utopias, therefore, are presented as an alternative to the living conditions of that particular moment, the promise of a profound improvement, not designed to solve specific problems but to transform society as a whole, bearing implicitly the disconformity with the present and the desire for radical change.

The social critique directed by the intellectuals at the beginning of the 19th century, in the form of writings and projects for the city, could be thought of as the third great stage of urban utopias. Nevertheless, although these cities are presented as places of happiness in response to a crisis situation (the anarchic aspects of the Industrial Revolution and the exploitation of the workers), their realization is not considered by its authors; more than generating an ideal, they seek to plan a new model of society that will restore order and harmony to the turbulent society of the industrial revolution.

From that point of view, utopia is not the result of a delirious imagination; on the contrary, it is the fruit of a creative mind that seeks in unreality the transformation of a reality it considers to be decadent. In these cases, the utopian architect is a great connoisseur of his world, of his environment and of his history.

Utopia *is projected towards an ideal, unreal, abstract world but does so from a position that is critical of the real, concrete world.*

The 20th Century

In the first half of the 20th century the architecture of utopia followed very diverse experimental paths ranging from Le Corbusier and the avant gardes, who proposed to fuse art and daily life with an approach to nature, to the Japanese Metabolists with their theoretical studies of "cellular agglomerations" which they put into practice by means of the assembly of "modular units."

At a time when the world was experiencing a series of financial crises, anguish and political instability, Le Corbusier visited Argentina, where the liberal class continued with the frenchification of architectural forms, at a very eclectic moment when historicism was a strong presence. With the aid of architects Kurchan and Ferrari Hardoy, in 1938 he designed a Master Plan for Buenos Aires, born out of the need to modernize the existing city.

Images extracted from the Argentinean catalog "Ideal/Real/Ideale/Reale," national participation at the 14th International Exhibit of Architecture – Venice Biennial of Architecture 2014

In his plan, Le Corbusier applied the new technical and infrastructural systems for the conception of a new image of the city anchored in its past. He foresaw urban reorganization based on a concentration of structures according to the prevailing theories of functionalist rationalism, to appropriate the natural (and disorganized) forces of progress and channel them through organized planning, conceiving a city that would respond to a new form of life based on new technologies, standardization and flexibility.

Although the Master Plan was never applied, and remained more as a utopian project than one that could actually be constructed, the concepts employed to give form to multifunctional infrastructure networks and systems were the work of Kurchan, Ferrari Hardoy and Bonet who, together with others, formed the Grupo Austral.

The Group took its inspiration from the ideas of Le Corbusier and introduced the novelty of articulating the modern architecture of their projects as a germ for the future city, and as the particular manifestation of a broader conception of the city, based on humanist ideas and made to the scale of man. Their proposal sought to make nature accessible to the great masses of population, creating high-rise buildings in the middle of green zones and, with that, recover the harmony the once existed between beings, nature and objects, basically through a very pure and avant-garde aesthetic, which moved away from nationalist positions to try and bring to the country ideas of modernity, through utopias that, at the time, seemed to have the power to change the world.

This objective was also a constant in the work of Amancio Williams, who back in the 40s, in his *Proyecto de Viviendas en el Espacio* and in *Conjunto de Blocs*, revealed his intention to place homes in their appropriate natural environment, not only in response to architectural needs but to needs that are profoundly human, such as health, natural life and recreation. His desire to preserve natural spaces led him to talk about a compact architecture in elevation, occupying minimum surface areas and maintaining rural environments very close to urban ones.

On the other hand, following the path of the Metabolists, we arrive at the second half of the century. Richard Buckminster Fuller's *Dome over Manhattan* project is a creative delirium that speaks to us about the need for radical proposals to solve the problem of environmental quality. In this same line, the "Plug-in City" of the Archigram group, the "Superarchitecture" of the Archizoom group or the "Spatial City" of Yona Friedman represent the dream of creating enormous environments that are urban, modular, mobile, mutating and adaptable to changes, which stimulate creativity from the aesthetic of pop culture and which boast all the services a city needs.

Faith in industrial, economic and technological development and the sensation of durability of fossil fuels underlie the ideal of these utopias characterized by the aspirations of a form of life in which speed, connectivity, flexibility, automation, unlimited verticality, the conquest of land, air and water are part of daily business.

Here mention should be made, for example, of the Hydrospatial City project by Gyula Kosice. Borrowing from the scientific theories that claim that nuclear fusion would allow water to be transformed into clean fuel, Kosice designs a city that also seeks to change the habits of its inhabitants, proposing new activities for its spaces.

The proliferation of this kind of project for specific spaces that represents the triumph of modern technical rationality, but which is on occasion unnecessary or unrealizable, together with the abuse of certain political forces that drove them on while leaning on utopian bases to develop authoritarian and totalitarian systems, was the pretext for post-modernity to condemn utopias, dismissing them as vestiges of a time of ideological impositions and unitarian visions.

Anti-utopias, in which modern forms of alienation and domination take shape: the histories of industrial spaces (from Ledoux to Ford and Taylor or to the modern Kanban system) or of the prison and concentration universes (studied by Foucault and Sofsky respectively), or the vision of the Soviet constructivists, have made way for those spaces that Marc Augé defined as "non-places" and which, faced with the idea of stability traditionally linked to the very concept of space, appear as the framework for uncontrolled circulations in the new world of networks.

To that should be added the emergence of numerous "artificial paradises" which, from vacation enclaves to theme parks, integrate and domesticate the discourse of utopia in the mercantile circuits of advanced capitalism.

Utopia in the 21st century

Despite the apparent death of utopia with post-modernism, the failings of the present demand new projects for society, in which solutions can be found not only to the non-sustainable city but to the process of urbanization, to the forms of spatial mobility and even to the instruments of contemporary urbanism.

This is so because the abandonment of utopias has not proven to be a path towards truly plural proposals and has made way, on the other hand, for another kind of totalitarianism.

Ortega and Gasset said that in Argentina utopias are not necessary because the Argentines "*live from their illusions as if they were real.*"

But what is true is that, in the environment of world recession and uncertainty that surrounds us, we are probably experiencing the most important opportunity for change in the last century.

So utopias reemerge as tools for analyzing reality and postulate alternatives for understanding the present and imagining the future.

As Pascaline Guillier has claimed, every project is essentially utopian or ideal until the last phase of its construction. The execution of the project marks the end of utopia, which is then transformed into a program and maintains in man the hope of a better world, thus becoming a source of new utopias.

Utopias are a connection with new realities: they are ideas that travel through the universe...only a few impact on our planet...

They represent the synchronicity of the present with an as yet inexistent space.

OPERA PUBLICA AND MICRO-TERRITORIAL EXTIMACY IN LATIN AMERICA

Claudio Vekstein
Argentina

1. Morpho-political construction

Opera Publica is originally the Latin name used for public works in ancient Rome, the construction or urban engineering projects and infrastructure carried out by the State in the name/ on behalf of the community, which can no longer provide works for itself due to a shift of territorial scale and the political scope of the interventions. Generically, these works include civic or recreational space, basic community health facilities, education or justice services, as well as the collective urban habitat and territorial infrastructure of lands, roads, dams or canals. While in a heterogeneous complex of increasing urbanity and social emergency, today in Latin America, Opera Publica builds localized technical and social armatures for sustained political understanding through adaptive design tools to drive public interest challenges and socio-political demands towards the natural and built collective construction.

Within this shift, it is necessary to study the transferring process of technical responsibilities from the community to the State, and how this operates passing along with it the imaginary and symbolic universe associated with the construction of everyone's works. The technical labor promotes, on the one hand, the obsequencial resolution of problems following a lined, internal, autonomous logic, an evolutionary development to the case of advanced and experimental attempts, tending to the progressive domain of the disciplinary materials. On the other hand, the public practice demands from the collaborative, heteronomous and participatory efforts and brings into the equation the inexorable relationship to life: the further articulation between the domain of the disciplinary materials and the relationship to life is what we used to call craft or "oficio", where Opera Publica acts as "the art" of the public project.

The first purpose is revisiting and colliding together the internal development of the architectural, urban and environmental design disciplines and their immanent procedures of the project transcending them along the external decisional logic and mechanisms of immediate political action and vital implementation of great ideas to serve the common good. Opera Publica serves then as a strategic, organizational endeavor functioning on the multiple scales of the greater territorial project, from architectural to urban design, from ecological landscape to environmental and infrastructural planning. It provides tactical and political sustenance for public space in the city, conjugating public policy and formal idiosyncrasy while contributing to the coexistence of our communities and the advance of the collective urban habitat.

This public coalition propels responsible civic engagement and effective action on initiatives of environmental and social impact, articulating new opportunities for the future sustainable development of communities, cities and territories, with disciplinary confidence thus forming new, useful and thoughtful knowledge for transformative realization. This reciprocated transformation of the physical and social work pertaining to the territory with the research and reflective practice of the project acts as an integrative function of the public service responsibility. Through this integration, it is possible to reconstitute the morphological-architectural with the ecological-environmental, the economic and political with the social and cultural, the territorial landscape with the urban, and to foster a cultured vision with the local and vernacular imagery.

It is compulsory to respond in a transformative, certain and versatile manner with the properly attuned disciplinary tools to the dynamic emerging challenges, engendering precise and specific solutions for the collective enhancement of the habitat, as well as ensuring the inclusivity of public space, to actively intervening in ordering the urban sprawl, equitable regional planning, the management of environmental control and the consolidation of the social community bond. Along the established principles and newer interactive research procedures applied to the project, these initiatives devise and merge indirect models of collective collaboration, facilitation, exchange, negotiation or a more direct participatory inclusion.

Focusing on specifically tailoring the project knowledge to secure the particular interest and character of the community's micro-intimate territoriality, its spatial manifestation and public demonstration, Public Operators can undertake complex collaborations, through public, non-governmental, community, municipal or political organizations, along with developing entities and private/public funding and financing to meet and transcend specific needs throughout the territory. These complicated enterprises of morpho-aesthetical and highly political involvedness, along the vital interaction between social actors and interactive/participatory decision-making processes and mechanisms, demand a new and adapted project operatory. This tool manages the micro internal conflicts extending into future problems or ongoing resolutions over time. Through the project's clued-up mechanics, Opera Publica expands the self-sufficient discourse to the concrete and comprehensive, far-reaching opportunities and benefits for a real sense of accessibility and spatial coexistence of all citizens in the community.

2. Micro-territorial articulation

Opera Publica shoulders the territorial perspective from social geo-semantics, meaning the sum of a sense of place whose definition is validated by a community: the territory as a socio-ecological system assembling society and the environment it inhabits. Activating the territory both in its vertical relationships (between society and the physical environment and their characteristics, economic organization, political, demographic, physical and built environment affecting society, etc.) and horizontal relationships (between the various and diverse micro-territories that comprise it), Opera Publica reaches the proximity principle needed to develop design refinement, specificity and fine-grained vicinity. It facilitates exhaustive, intimate depiction preventing the fine detail being smoothed over, averaged out and replaced with a lower-resolution coarse-grained model due to abstract, systematic or political purposes.

The sociological difficulty for depicting the inhabitants of popular neighborhoods, arising from the existence of a multiplicity of particular situations, as well as the typical planning outlook has often considered territories or neighborhood areas as a uniform whole. Therefore, notions such as exclusion, inclusion, integration etc. could result as fallacious or useless for the purposes of thorough knowledge and resulting operational strategies, since it subsumes the diversity of situations and trajectories of populations leveling their environmental conditions and struggles. Opera Publica enters the situation with expectations of finding multiple idiosyncrasies and consequently deploying simultaneous actions on multidirectional developments, making it possible to reveal different forms of micro-intimate segregation, allowing for the emergence and activation of focused, hyper--articulating tactics.

The lower the territorial observation scale, the greater the difference between social, cultural behaviors and finer the grain of spatial, environmental conditions inhabiting the area. Focusing the inquiry shifts the tools from statistical facts to revealing very rich sociological mechanisms of public interaction, diverse ways of living within communities, mixed inhabitation patterns and self-organization strategies, spatial and material appropriation and vast local imaginary, turning generic public opinion measuring polls into vital public interest action programs. The proximity enables mapping the micro-territories through describing their specific characters and identities along their ongoing processes, transforming quantitative and ciphered/stochastic fields into qualitative, embodied cosmoses.

These micro-procedural and ethno-methodological differential progressions inform and shape the project's innermost materials and engrained techniques, nurturing hyper-articulation and challenging typification.

The micro-territorial perspective provides a shift in observational and operational position, a new theoretical point of sight and action, linking the exposed and public with the most intimate minutiae and intricacies; it does trespass through private zones into the innermost without necessarily carrying a "subjective camera", since the same bare object still remains "out there" while uncovered. Micro-territoriality makes the public object intimate, revealing the existence of multiple, intense societal inner performances, giving visibility to distinct collective flows that are not necessarily outward protagonists of their respective quarters because they do not restrict their actions to institutionalized participatory spaces.

3. Intimate-extimacy architecture

The public/intimate breach turns into a bridge; it is not reducible to a dialectical synthesis since they do not act as opposites but work as a continuous description (differing from the conventional public/private antagonism). Slavoj Žižek describes Psycho, Alfred Hitchcock's masterpiece as an opportunity for bridging the parallax gap through "the staging of an architectural antagonism: is Norman not split between the two houses, the modern horizontal motel and the vertical Gothic mother's house, forever running between the two, never finding a proper place of his own? In this sense, the *unheimlich* character of the film's end means that, in his full identification with the mother, he finally found his *heim*, his home. In modernist works like Psycho, this split is still visible, while the main goal of today's postmodern architecture is to obfuscate it. (...) Directly combining the old mother's house and the flat modern motel into a new hybrid entity, there would have been no need for Norman to kill his victims, since he would have been relieved of the unbearable tension that compels him to run between the two places".[1]

Opera Publica realizes this dramatic traversing of the public/intimate breach, as a critical short circuiting between the two apparently distant aspects, where the closeness, intimate convolution of the "opera" joins the "public" openness, finally revealing the Real – the primordial object, the mysterious something of an ordinary object, where the sublime dimension shines through it. "One of the most effective critical procedures to cross wires that do not usually touch: (...) which brings to light its "unthought," its disavowed presuppositions and consequences. (...) Lacanian psychoanalysis is a privileged instrument of such an approach, whose purpose is to illuminate a standard text or ideological formation, making it readable in a totally new way. (...) The point is, rather, to make him or her aware of another – disturbing – side of something he or she knew all the time".[2]

Extimacy, the term coined by Jacques Lacan *extimité*[3] from the term *intimité* (a superlative of the Latin positive adjective *intra* or within, its comparative interior or deeper than, and superlative *intimus* or deepest of all, innermost) in the same manner that it is not the contrary of intimacy, it problematizes the apparent oppositions between inner and outer, between container and content. As Jacques-Alain Miller proposes: "It is necessary in order to escape the common ravings about a psychism supposedly located in a bipartition between interior and exterior. (...) The exterior is present in the interior. The most interior – this is how the dictionary defines "intimate" (*l'intime*) – has, in the analytic experience, a quality of exteriority. (...) This is why Lacan invented the term *extimité*. It should be observed that the term "interior" is a comparative that comes to us from Latin and of which *intimus* is the superlative. There, there is an effort on the part of the language to reach the deepest point in the interior".[4]

At the inner-outer surpassed deadlock, internal and external architectural worlds have no more consequential meaning for the micro-territorial extimacy of Opera Publica, revealing its public intimacy. Losing their contrast, they become reversible: the extime refers now to the innermost, the intimate, which is found on the outside – as the culture determining the subject, referring to a topology that vacillates between interior and exterior. Architectural extimacy being very intimate and familiar becomes radically strange; her being intimate turns into the most distant and unlocalized, the familiar unknown. The extimacy marks the traumatic passage for the subject from the plenitude of the Real to the de-centered universe of the Symbolic; for Lacan, the inner-center of the

1. Žižek, Slavoj. 2009. Architectural Parallax – Spandrels and Other Phenomena of Class Struggle at http://www.lacan.com/essays/?page_id=218.

2. Žižek, Slavoj. 2006. The Parallax View. Short Circuits. Cambridge, MA: MIT Press.
3. Lacan, Jacques. 1986. Le seminaire, Livre VII: L'éthique de la psychanalyse, Paris: Seuil, chap. VI.
4. Miller, Jacques-Alain. 2008. Extimity. Universalism versus globalization. Text established by Elisabeth Doisneau and translated by Françoise Massardier-Kenney, in *The Symptom 9*.

subject is out, it is ex-centric. The subject remains nostalgic for what has been lost and seeks reunification; a subject who is an object outside of itself. The Other is "something strange to me, although it is in my heart."

Opera Publica and its architecture undertake the shock of the Other in the intense, overwhelming Real with a bare Latin American self ("magical realism", "the marvelous real", and so on). It does not seek a new sterile modern synthesis or an idiosyncratic architectural local dialect, but growing its own twinkled short-circuiting construction, as a hyper-articulate expression of micro-territories, inside-out reveries entwining structures, stories, landscapes, and people.

Montessori School, City of Lujan, Buenos Aires Province, Argentina (2013-14)

Arch. Design: Claudio Vekstein and Marcelo Barreiro. Assistants: Dolores Cremonini, Carolina Telo, Florencia Spina, Gabriel Tyszberowicz, Ricardo Bodini, Maria Yoma, Haotian Xu, Susan Franco. Landscape Design: Lucia Schiappapietra and Teresa Rozados. Structural Design: Pedro Gea.

Memorial Space for the 100th Anniversary of the Alcorta's Revolt (Grito de Alcorta), Alcorta Town, Santa Fe, Argentina (2012-14)

Arch. Design: Claudio Vekstein for the Special Projects Unit of the Public Works and Housing Ministry, Government of Santa Fe Province. Assistants: Carolina Telo, Mariana Pons, Pedro Magnasco, Mercedes Peralta, Martin Flugelman, Santiago Tolosa, Stephen Wanderer, Susan Franco, Alisha Rompre, Pamela Galan, Maca Cerquera, Hernán Landolfo. Structural Design: Tomás del Carril and Javier Fazio. Landscape Design: Lucia Schi appapietra and Teresa Rozados, Elena Rocchi. Assistants: Cecilia Chiesa, Clara Miguens. Client: Agrarian Federation of Argentina, Town of Alcorta, Government of Santa Fe Province, Argentine Federal Government.

UNTITLED / Buenos Aires. 2008_Jason S. Johnson.

A HUMANIST VISION

Noemi Blager
England

"Lina Bo Bardi: Together"[1]
Curator: Noemi Blager
Art Installation: Madelon Vriesendorp
Film Intallation: Tapio Snellman

Noemí Blager talks to writer Clare Farrow about how she discovered the work of Lina Bo Bardi[1], and how she curated an exhibition with the aim of bringing the sensory experience of Bo Bardi's architecture to life, as a piece of theatre that focuses on the relationship between people and place, communicating the architect's thinking and essential humanity. Her inclusive, observational eye, her dismantling of hierarchies, her willingness to look outside the boundaries of architecture, and her conviction that nothing should be wasted, make Bo Bardi hugely relevant to contemporary audiences.

The conversation took place in the Victoria & Albert Museum in London, on the 7th November 2014.

Clare Farrow: What first attracted you to the work of Lina Bo Bardi?
Noemí Blager: My first encounter with Lina's work was in 2006, when I drove past the Museu de Arte de São Paulo (MASP) on Avenue Paulista. The avenue is all tall buildings and skyscrapers, but suddenly you see MASP and everything changes: the experience is like an urban pause. Everything is vertical, but MASP is completely horizontal. It is lifted from the ground, generating a public space underneath like a seductive, generous invitation. So this prompted me to find out more.

Was your next step to visit the Glass House?
It wasn't as automatic as that. Before I visited the Glass House, I stayed with a set designer in Rio. She started getting down books and magazines from her shelves, to show me Lina's set design and graphic design.
So you realized that she was more than just an architect?
Yes, she was an amazing set designer, and an activist. The director of SESC São Paulo has described her as 'a cultural agitator'. Architecture for her was not just about making buildings. She also used writing and publishing as a tool, and a form of teaching. This began when she became an architect, when the war started, and she moved from Rome to Milan. She wrote about the fact that there was no construction in Italy, only destruction. In the last years of the war, she also travelled with a photographer, making newspaper contributions about the state of Italian cities.

Did this make her aware of the social implications of architecture?
Yes. She lived at a very special moment, when the Modern Movement was calling for radical change. She fundamentally understood the social dimension of architecture. She was also a very sensitive person. Her father was a painter and manufactured toys.

So she had an artistic childhood.
Definitely. She was also a very keen observer. She observed people and life, not only buildings and art. She was interested in how people interact, and the relationship between people and place. She didn't look at things with preconceived ideas, but with a very strong sensitivity. So when she went to Brazil she observed with this innate interest and sensitivity and the freshness of an outsider. Lina could value things that the Brazilian people did not value. It was as if she put a mirror up to the Brazilian people, to show them their own things, but with her eyes; and to help them value what they did not even see. She observed a lot of richness and intelligence, in how the craftsmen and people with very low incomes could make the most of very limited resources, with ingenious designs.

1. Lina Bo Bardi, née Achillina Bo (December 5, 1914, *Rome, Italy* – March 20, 1992, *São Paulo*) was an *Italian*-born *Brazilian Modernist architect*. A prolific architect and designer, Lina Bo Bardi devoted her working life, most of it spent in Brazil, to promoting the social and cultural potential of architecture and design. She was also famed for her furniture and jewellery designs.

Was she also observing with a socialist eye, a political eye?
I would say that she observed with a humanist eye, a social eye. She was a political person with strong social values, and she used her skills to try to achieve improvements for people, especially those who are less privileged. She could see a different kind of wealth. She valued the capacity that those people with limited resources showed in terms of their wealth of ideas.

Did she see with a Modernist eye too?
I would say that she was a Modernist in terms of the Modern Movement's social values, but after her first period in Brazil, from 1946 to 1958, she did not continue with its formal language. She took and absorbed with her modern eye, and her openness, all those cultural elements that she could freely see in Brazil, and delivered work that embraced the Modernist social values, but with a free language that responded to the local culture. I think there are two words that define her approach: respect and generosity.

How did her move to Salvador change her?
The north of Brazil has a much more rooted culture, and this influenced her work. The buildings that she designed in São Paulo were airborne, horizontal volumes, lifted from the ground. But after her move to Salvador in 1958, all her architecture is rooted in the ground. She also did the refurbishment of the Solar do Unhão in that period, converting it into the Museum of Modern Art of Salvador. During her five years in Salvador she realized that Brazil is a blend of Portuguese and African cultures and she observed and learned from traditional craftsmanship. She was immediately asked to do an exhibition of Brazilian popular art, which she did in the foyer of the Teatro Castro Alves. There she used all the leftovers from old set designs to set up the exhibition. So she was recycling when it was not a word that was used much in architecture. For her, throwing away materials was a sin, and this belief became very strong in Salvador because she saw that poor people do not throw anything away. She observed how people used old oil-cans as sugar containers, or put oil into old light bulbs to turn them into lamps. Today, the world is also poorer in resources and we have to think with the same mentality. Lina observed and applied this approach. So the staircase that she built in Solar do Unhão, which spirals in wood, doesn't have a single nail. She learned this by observing how people in Salvador made wheels for ox carts. She was a free thinker and chose her own sources of learning.

Had she curated exhibitions in São Paulo?
Yes, exhibitions of art in the first years. Her husband was an art collector and dealer. When they arrived in Brazil in 1946, they were on their way to Argentina, but they met the Brazilian journalist and entrepreneur Assis Chateaubriand, who said that he wanted to open a museum of modern art, and this is how MASP happened. But before MASP was built, they put on exhibitions in Chateaubriand's newspaper buildings. Many years later, when SESC Pompéia was built, she organized many exhibitions there, including one of Brazilian toys.

Were there many foreigners in Brazil at that time?
Yes, in Salvador in particular. There were many disillusioned Europeans there after the war, into music, art and photography, and she became an important part of this group. In South America, a person is not valued until they have done something abroad, and when someone comes from abroad they are looked up to. Lina hated the word 'folklore' because she thought it was a patronizing, demeaning word. She felt that craftsmen should be considered as highly as educated people. In Salvador there was a celebration of that; it was very contagious. Those were her happiest years. I feel that she was always looking for something, and she found it there. Before that it was just theory. In Salvador, she found the source of a new architecture and design language.

Was she idealistic?
Totally. But realistic too. It's a difficult combination. But there are architects now who are now looking to Lina's approach. In fact, it was a wonderful coincidence that I discovered her at the moment when her work became so relevant.

The exhibition focuses on SESC Pompéia. What makes this project so important?
This is her most mature project, and one that embodies the most important values of her work. The site, which was a community center, was already functioning in the original, industrial factory building. When Lina arrived, her first observations were children playing football, and older people playing cards and dominoes. She observed an experience of happiness there, so she didn't want to change this atmosphere; she wanted to enhance it, to build around it, to add things to it. Her drawings

always had lots of written notes on them too, like the script of a play. I remember before, we talked about how Jorge Luis Borges said that literature exists only when there is a reader. In the same way, architecture should be the background that helps to generate life. Lina's architecture is only complete when people are experiencing and using it.

So she brought new dimensions to SESC Pompéia, like a theatre, and a canteen that plays many roles (a concert hall, a dance hall), like an actor in a play. Her architecture is like theatre, and is about how can you get more life experience into a building.

Did this emphasis on life and theatre determine your exhibition structure?
Yes. There should be joy and pleasure in experiencing architecture. But how do you communicate an approach that is about life experience? This cannot be done by showing drawings and models. Also, her goal was not the aesthetic result, but the atmosphere and life that the building generated. I wanted to communicate the experience of being in her places, and SESC Pompéia encapsulates her values. If you enjoy the experience first, you can learn more afterwards. To use a music analogy: as an architect, when I observe drawings, I see in three dimensions; or when I see a model, I don't perceive it in miniature, but as something that surrounds me. But a person who is not an architect sees something completely different. So with music, I enjoy the experience, but I can't play or read music; when I look at a score I don't hear music, as musicians or composers do. So I didn't want to do an exhibition for architects only, but for everybody. I wanted to communicate through the senses. The exhibition is about what her work feels like.

So it is a creative response to her work?
Absolutely. The people involved —Madelon Vriesendorp, Tapio Snellman, Assemble— used the experience to penetrate the world of Lina Bo Bardi, and learn through doing. I think Madelon, the artist, has so many things in common with Lina: she is a humanist, extremely playful and generous. She is a collector as well: of toys, anything she likes.
For example, if she finds something that has a flaw, she prefers it, because it has the presence of humanity. There is a total connection with Lina. When I went to SESC for the first time,
I wanted to find the means to transfer that experience, and I realized that the only way would be through film installation. Tapio captured the human rhythms and textures of the building.

Was the end result as you imagined?
I curated without giving directives, so there was no preconceived image. It was an open process and we were all equal. Everyone put creativity into the process. I was the articulator, the link. Madelon suggested that we go to Brazil together, to bring back objects, and involve the hands of the Brazilian people. Some of the objects we found in flea markets, some were made in workshops that Madelon conducted in Brazil, and some she made herself, using recycled cardboard. She chose things that caught her eye, lots of different Exus, a kind of traditional deity in the north of Brazil, reflecting the mix of African and Portuguese traditions. The objects that she created herself are playful expressions of these. When we went to the Glass House, we were shown the objects in Lina's cupboards: little Exus, traditional toys, funny little objects that she found in markets, even seashells. There were no hierarchies in the way she displayed things. She mixed everything, including leftovers from set designs. To her, a De Chirico painting or a Modernist design was no more valuable than a craft object; what mattered was the humanity that she saw in something.

How was the Instituto Lina Bo e P.M. Bardi in São Paulo involved in the exhibition process?
There was so little written about Lina. But the Instituto connected me to people who had known or worked with her. They also gave me access to the archives in the Glass House, and that's where I saw the Bowl Chair for the first time. Lina was married to a man who politically was very unwelcome. He was a supporter of Modernism, but he had friends in Italy who were Fascists, so this had a very negative impact on the way in which the architectural scene in Brazil received them. Oscar Niemeyer was a communist, after all. But I think that Lina did a lot more in social terms than Niemeyer. Pietro Maria Bardi was both a hindrance for Lina and an enabler, because it was he who Chateaubriand asked to create a museum of modern art, and that is how Lina became the architect.

The Bowl Chair plays an important role in the exhibition.
Yes, it represents much of what Lina was about. She cared about what is essential. It was a totally new idea, because the chair is made of two independent objects: a base, which is a circle with four

legs, and a shell that is the chair, which you can separate, and put into different positions. So again, as with her architecture, what completes the chair is the person. I was told that she was thinking of doing it for the museum, so it would be stackable. She also designed it to be customized, with different finishes and fabrics, to suit the person. It was on the cover of an American magazine, but was never manufactured. I think it was too advanced for her time. It's such a unique and clever object, so I wanted to bring it to life, and that's how Arper became involved.

Was it difficult to balance the design's integrity with new materials and technology?
There is a prototype in Brazil, and a very simple, geometric drawing by Lina. There were also watercolors, showing how it could be customized and the bowls stacked. But there weren't details of the internal structure. Arper used a contemporary plastic, which works better for the design. I think that is completely in the spirit of Bo Bardi.

Is it important that she was a woman?
She was not a feminist. She wanted to be an equal, but without making a point about it. However, I think there are things about being a woman that are important in her work. Her projects were almost like her children, and she never had children. What I would say is that she was a connector. Her work was like a seductive invitation, making you want to know more.

Drawing courtesy of Madelon Vriesendorp

A LOOK AT LABORATORIES

EXPLORATORY, ATELIER, TRIAL, STUDIO DISCUSSION, TERRITORY (OF QUESTIONS), EVALUATE, LABOR, PROCESS, EXAMINATION, CHECKING RESULTS, EXPERIENCES, TEST SITE, RETRYING, WORKSHOP, EVIDENCES, INVESTIGATE, SEMINAR, ACADEMIA, SCREENING, ANALYSIS.

Creative Credo

GrupoSP
Brasil

We are convinced that the construction of spaces for everyone can (and should) be engendered by collective actions, which are essential for the expansion of our specific knowledge. Unfortunately, in today's world it has become inconceivable that a project should be a collective venture. That a project doesn't necessarily have an author or a single source but that it belongs to us all has become an outdated idea. Mondrian stated that the artist is essentially the continuation of a past and, that being so, the artist then complements the previous work. If we believe in this idea then there is no dilemma or problem. However, invariably, today the opposite is true because, in the end, it comes down to market forces that seek hegemony. Nevertheless, we emphasize the idea of a project done by everyone.

Our office is the result of the association of architects who graduated at different moments and who came together in 2002 to develop competition entries and projects.

We don't believe that we are architects of different generations, because we don't believe exactly in generations. We all belong to one single genealogy: of our time.

gruposp is not intended to be a traditional office: a hard core that is closed off; rather it is intended as a flexible organization that admits collaborations and partnerships as the work develops. It is a space open to the participation of other architects and other professionals interested in discussing the production of living spaces and spaces of the city. We believe that there are no more architectural offices. There are architects. We build mobility with these floating associations and maintain a small structure that allows us to choose the jobs that interest us.

In recent years gruposp has been dedicated to working on architectural competitions, projects for NGOs and public institutions, while incorporating everyday activities into participation in research and teaching.

We believe strongly in the importance of architectural competitions as a means of architectural debate and the possibility of employability. Competitions also give us the perspective of realizing a project without so many restrictions or interference, which is so common nowadays. We also believe that the exercise of the profession with the prospect of its discussion and publication seems to be possible only in the academic environment. In school, we can test hypotheses that are often hard to articulate in the daily life of an architectural office. It is only within academia that we can articulate temporal dimensions and extrapolate the contingencies of concrete and objective demands and conducting trials and speculations that undoubtedly will contribute to building better spaces.

One idea that brings together architects in Sao Paulo is the construction of voids. The city we live in is marked by a dense occupation that shuts out the perception of its original topography as well as its few unoccupied spaces. This is especially the case for those spaces defined and configured by the original site, by geographical phenomena. One of the challenges for "paulista" architects in this century is to insist on the construction of "voidness" as a way to open clearings and enable new dimensions and spaces for living in our city.

What characterizes, therefore, our professional organization is our continuous openness to affiliate with different architects, with different forms of acting and thinking. In this way, opening new perspectives and possibilities.

We do an architecture of the possible, based on where we are and how we could be. We believe that what you do is an action which brings together the cultural output of our country, our language and our way of life as a single expression. This expression goes into everything we do; it is integrated into our homes and our planet, the earth that always welcomes us. Sometimes we don't know how to reciprocate our existence intelligently.

To be an architect is to be a builder of culture; it is to be a builder of both the world we know and the world we do not yet know.

QUEROSENE HOUSE

Morro do Querosene

The fact that a large portion of land lies three meters below street level and the typical conformation of this urban batch 10X40 meters allowed for a large open space that is straightforward and transparent. This space is defined on one side by the north face structure, a parallel free wall which houses a library containing 7,500 volumes and, on the other side, by a parallel block, an all closed space – a block with three stories that contains all the services, equipment and dormitories.

To access this block concrete stairs positioned parallel to the south limit of the bath; to access the wall of books metal platforms connected to the service block placed in an interleaved manner.

The design takes advantage of the difference between the street level and the lower level of the plot by positioning the living room in this lower level, which ensures the required privacy and maintains the view of the distant landscape through the void. This simple home adopts simple constructive solutions, reducing the actions required for its achievement. The structure of the volume is resumed to masonry walls and reinforced concrete. Installations are apparent and performed without interference. After that, the finishes are simple: monolithic concrete flooring and white Portuguese stone. The walls without finishes are ready as built. A single exception: the wall with books is finished with time and history.

Location: São Paulo, Brazil, 2008
Design team: grupoSP. Alvaro Puntoni, João Sodré and Jonathan Davies
Structural design: Eduardo Duprat
Building services engineer: Ramoska + Castellani
Construction: Roberto Growald
Total floor area: 4,844 SF.
Plot area: 3,875 SF.

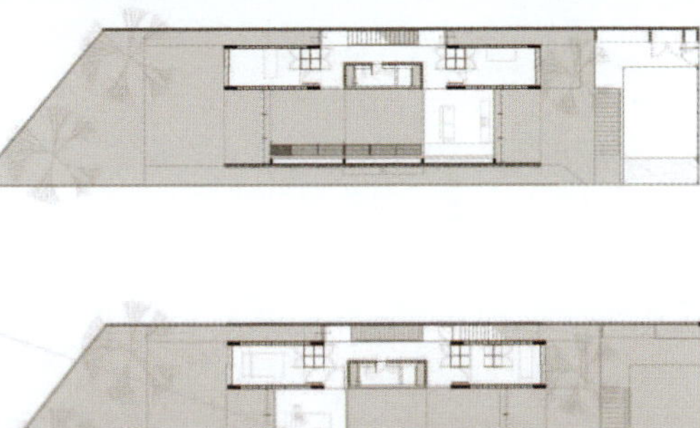

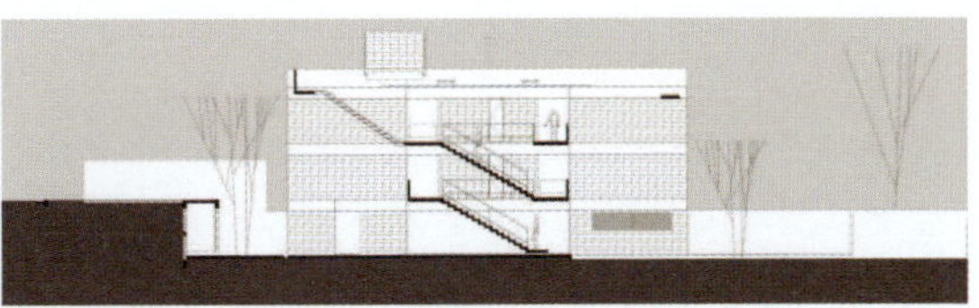

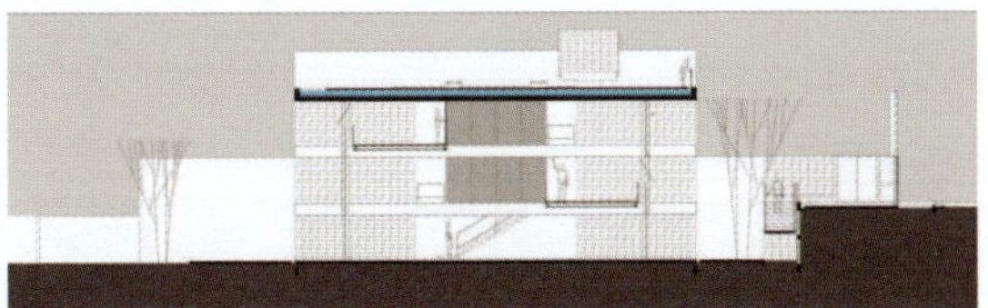

The geometry and the clear plan simultaneously with the construction of this "nebulous haze, almost an idea," a unit between the first scratches and the first reasons. Technique: graphite and ink on paper with digital postproduction. Chancery Annex Project . 2010_Padrevecchi/ SAVA, Argentina.

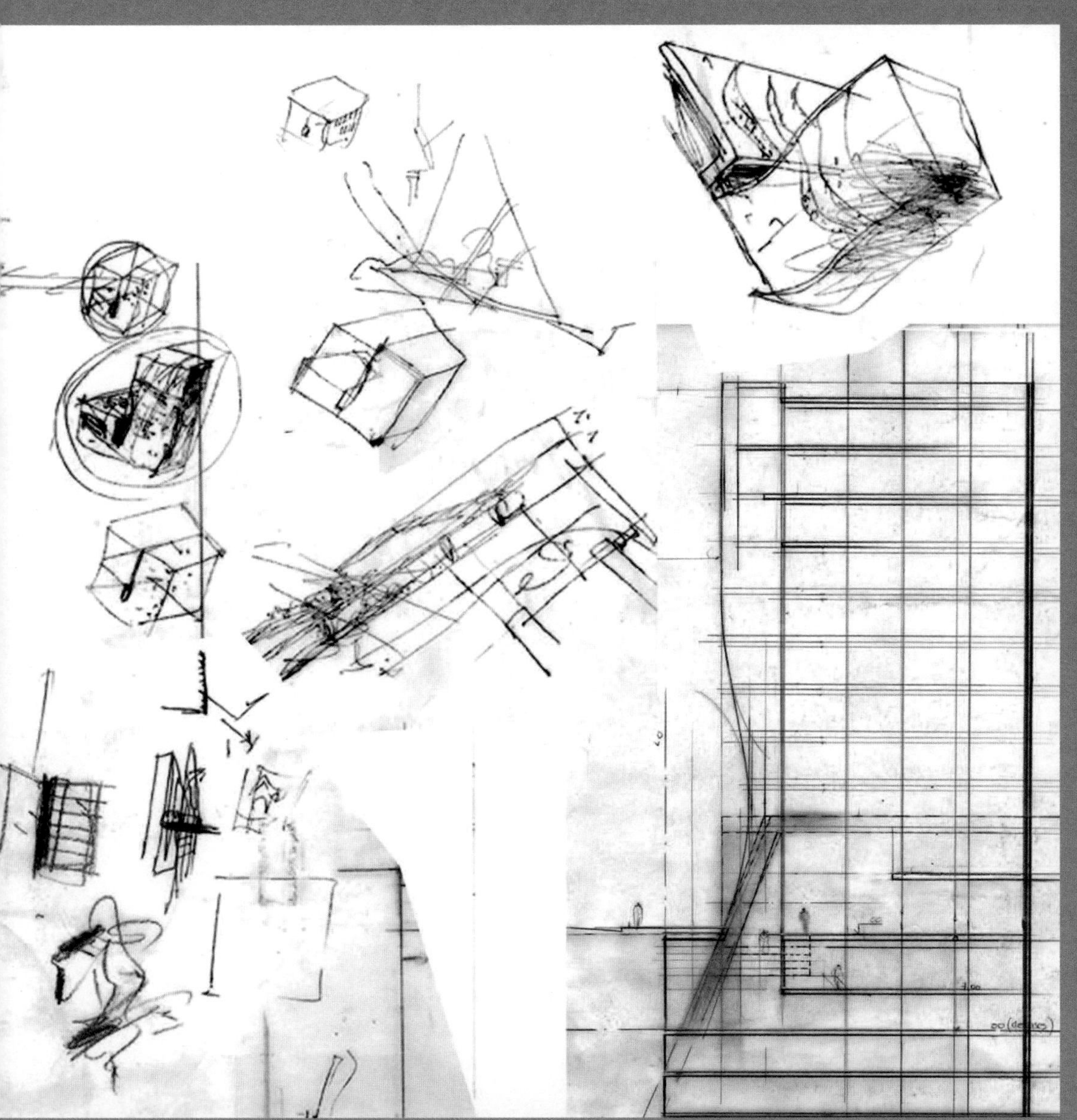

Transforming a City

Camilo Restrepo + Miguel Mesa + Luis Callejas
Colombia

We were commissioned to design Medellín Mayor's Office exhibition for the 50th BID assembly. They asked us to represent the recent transformation of the city under several requirements: to make an itinerant open air show, resistant to sun, rain and lateral winds of 150km/h. It shouldn't weigh more than 400 kg per m2 as it was to be placed over the main room of the Convention Center. They asked for a typical museum hall, a neutral container that would not compete with the works exhibited and that would be readily recognizable. The show had to include ten video monitors, supply networks and receive six thousand people in three days – after which the it would be open to the general public.

In addition, we had to follow a script that covered from the development of the urban area of Medellín to the mafia violence. From the subway to the social urbanism of Sergio Fajardo and future plans. The pavilion had to be up and running in just 40 days, including installation. We proposed a pavilion that would not aim at representing the city change but at constituting a new and singular space for it. We wanted to inscribe our project in the frame of some of our keen interests about contemporary culture: performativity, recycling, fast undertakes and the match between the natural and the artificial. To this purpose we thought of an industrial object we believed materially suitable and gave it a chance. Distributing the script in ten water tanks of 10,000 liters capacity each.

Making holes in the tanks with a cutter machine we could turn them into capsules and receive the public inside. The tanks endured weather, had low weight, resisted the strong wind, had malleable interiors, protected the screens and served to support graphic information. During the day, the sun rays would dim when hitting the tank surfaces providing homogeneous light, but temperature was an issue to solve –as it could rise a lot in the afternoon– and night illumination as well. On one part we chose to cover the tanks with vegetation and installed humidifier systems; on the other, we opted for an illumination system based on LED tubes attached to the cover.

Temporary exhibition, 2008-2009
Location: Main Square of Medellín, Colombia
Design team: Camilo Restrepo, Miguel Mesa, Luis Callejas (Paisajes Emergentes)
Collaborators: Federico Mesa, Santiago Cadavid & Farid Maya (architects) & Juan David Díez (graphic designer)
Construction and installation: Juan Camilo Muñoz, Marco S.A. Laszlo Yurko, Ecoluz (Illumination), Andrés Ospina (Landscape consulting)
Total floor area: 4.305 SF.

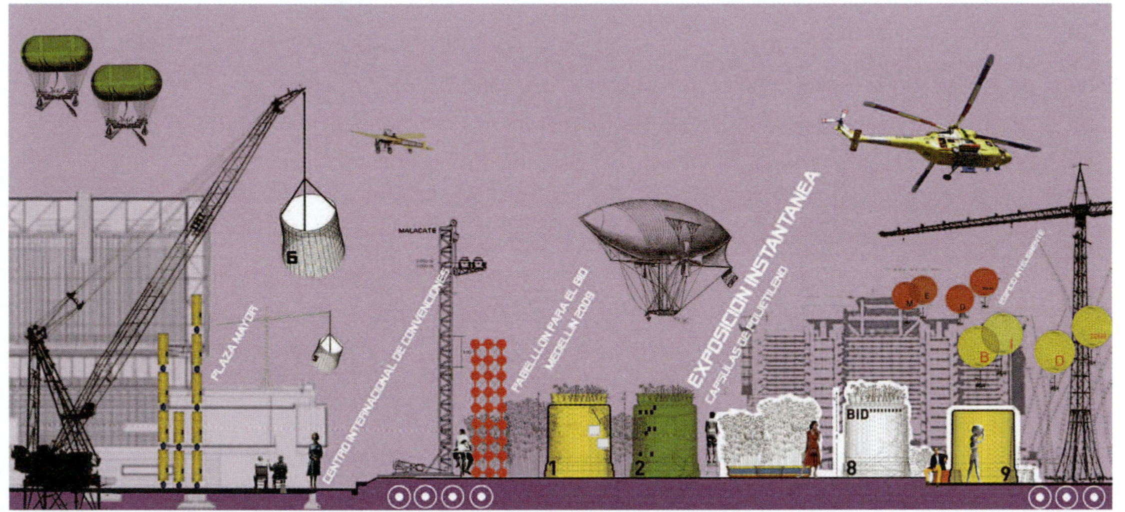

Perspective

General view

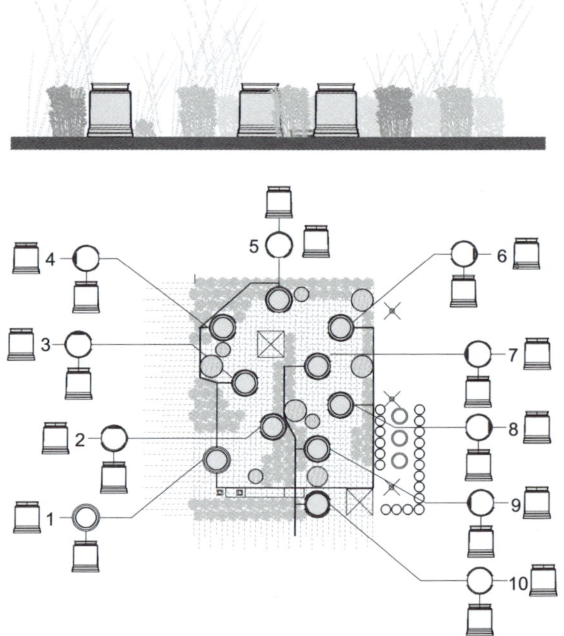

5
4
6
3
7
2
8
1
9
10

Exposición

ORCHIDEORAMA

EXHIBITION FACILITIES

plan:b + JPRCR Architects
Colombia

Architecture and organisms

The Construction of an Orchideorama should touch on the relation between architecture and living organisms. It should not make any distinction between natural and artificial; on the contrary, it should accept them as a unity that allows architecture to be conceived as a material, spatial, environmental organization that is deeply related to the processes of life.

Two scales of the organic

The organic is understood on two different scales, and each of them allows us to understand different aspects of the project:
Micro scale: A scale that holds the principles of material organization, defines geometrical patterns; it is nature living structures configuration.

Visual - external scale: It allows us to relate phenomenologically and environmentally to the world, and perceive, notice the world.

The "organic" as material organization

The microscale of the organic, such as its capacity to be organized in precise laws of geometry patterns (Direct example: Honeycomb structure), allows us to build a single module (we call it Flower – tree, which means a flower form figure with the size and properties of a tree), that when it becomes systematically repeated, it allows us to define growing properties, its evolution and its adaptability. Its geometry.

The "organic" as environmental phenomena

The big scale of biomorphic structures, and in this case specifically: Flowers or/and trees allows us to define perception as a situation where visitors can feel the extension of a forest, a shadow garden. On the other hand it allows us to display a set of technical facilities such as collecting water and to structure the modules as hollow trunks.

Doing architecture like sowing flowers

We propose the Orchideorama to be built like sowing flowers: One flower – tree grows, and just beside it, another will appear, until the complete system of Flower – tree structures are defined. They can grow or be sown where possible, adapting its system structure to the field where it is intended or needed.

An Orchideorama is not a storage facility structure

Industrial architecture is not the response to develop an Orchideorama. The Orchideorama is composed of 10 Flower – tree structures, that can be built individually, and allow the system grow or respond to any uncertainties, such as budget, unexpected events during construction or political decisions.

Three species of Flower - Tree structures. Lively Patios

The Flower - tree structure has three different contents according to is location and its definitions. Each Flower - tree is "hollow" in the center and each of them configures a small hexagonal patio.
The patios have three different characteristics:
1. Flower- tree - Light (Small temporary gardens).
2. Flower - tree - plants (Orchids, exotic and tropical flowers).
3. Flower - tree - animals (Bird feeding facilities - butterfly breeding place).

Orchideorama (Orchid exhibition facilities), 2006
Location: Medellin, Colombia
Design team: Felipe Mesa + Alejandro Bernal (plan:b Architects) & Camilo Restrepo + J. Paul Restrepo (JPRCR Architects).
Collaborators: Viviana Peña, Catalina Patiño, Carolina Gutiérrez, Lina Gil, Jorge Buitrago
Structural engineering: Germán Serrate
Construction supervision: Ménsula S.A.
Total floor area: 42,000 SF.

Aerial View

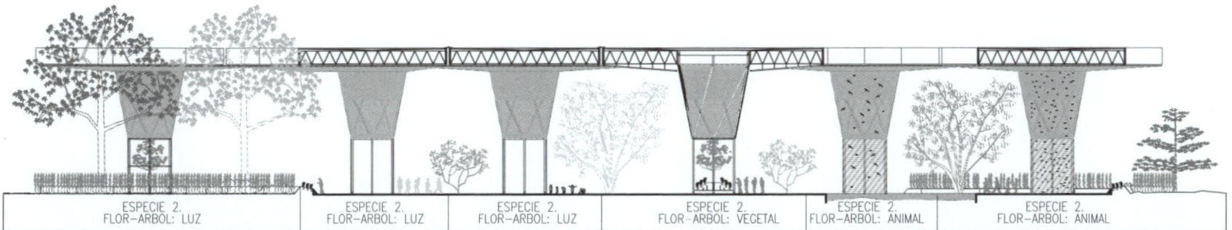

Section

CALLE 76
BOLIVAR
CALLE 77
CARRERA 51
CARABOBO
CARRERA 52

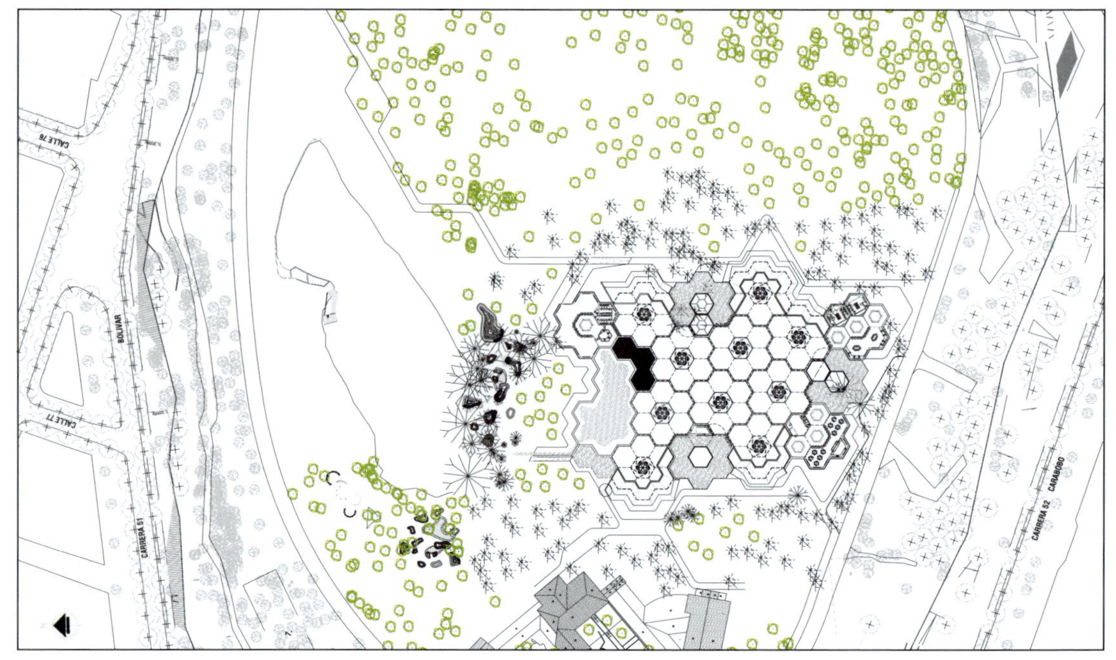

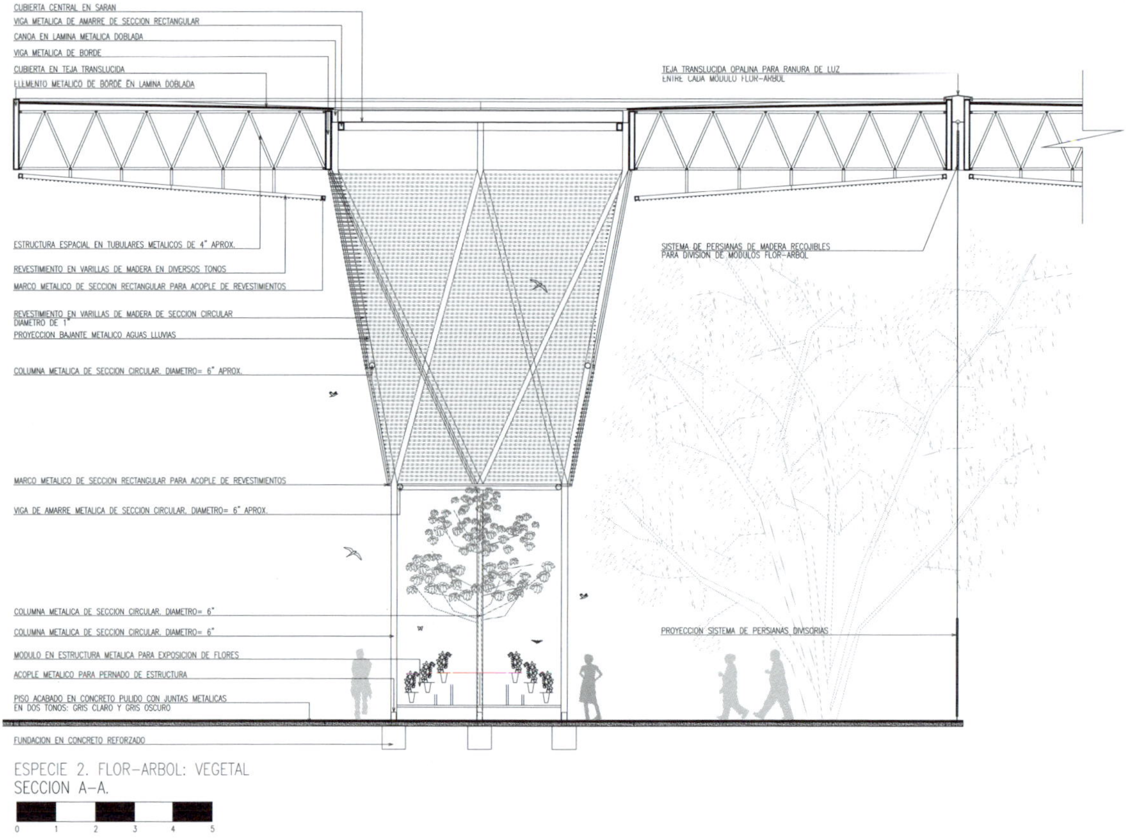

CUBIERTA CENTRAL EN SARAN
VIGA METALICA DE AMARRE DE SECCION RECTANGULAR
CANOA EN LAMINA METALICA DOBLADA
VIGA METALICA DE BORDE
CUBIERTA EN TEJA TRANSLUCIDA
ELEMENTO METALICO DE BORDE EN LAMINA DOBLADA
TEJA TRANSLUCIDA OPALINA PARA RANURA DE LUZ
ENTRE CADA MODULO FLOR-ARBOL
ESTRUCTURA ESPACIAL EN TUBULARES METALICOS DE 4" APROX.
REVESTIMIENTO EN VARILLAS DE MADERA EN DIVERSOS TONOS
MARCO METALICO DE SECCION RECTANGULAR PARA ACOPLE DE REVESTIMIENTOS
SISTEMA DE PERSIANAS DE MADERA RECOJIBLES
PARA DIVISION DE MODULOS FLOR-ARBOL
REVESTIMIENTO EN VARILLAS DE MADERA DE SECCION CIRCULAR
DIAMETRO DE 1"
PROYECCION BAJANTE METALICO AGUAS LLUVIAS
COLUMNA METALICA DE SECCION CIRCULAR. DIAMETRO= 6" APROX.
MARCO METALICO DE SECCION RECTANGULAR PARA ACOPLE DE REVESTIMIENTOS
VIGA DE AMARRE METALICA DE SECCION CIRCULAR. DIAMETRO= 6" APROX.
COLUMNA METALICA DE SECCION CIRCULAR. DIAMETRO= 6"
COLUMNA METALICA DE SECCION CIRCULAR. DIAMETRO= 6"
MODULO EN ESTRUCTURA METALICA PARA EXPOSICION DE FLORES
ACOPLE METALICO PARA PERNADO DE ESTRUCTURA
PROYECCION SISTEMA DE PERSIANAS DIVISORIAS
PISO ACABADO EN CONCRETO PULIDO CON JUNTAS METALICAS
EN DOS TONOS: GRIS CLARO Y GRIS OSCURO
FUNDACION EN CONCRETO REFORZADO
ESPECIE 2. FLOR-ARBOL: VEGETAL
SECCION A-A.
0 1 2 3 4 5

Section of the flower tree

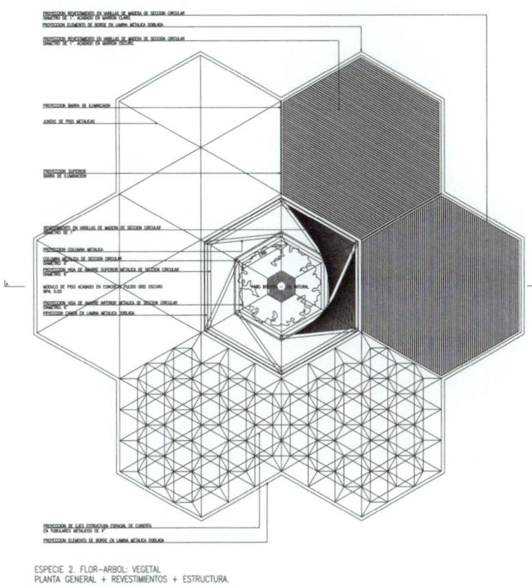

Flower tree structure

SAN CRISTOBAL LIBRARY

Camilo Restrepo + Tres Arquitectura + Masif/Camilo Ramírez
Colombia

Date: 2009
Project: San Cristobal Public Library
Location: Corregimiento San Cristóbal, Medellín,Colombia
Design team: Camilo Restrepo O., Tres Arquitectura, Masif, Camilo Ramírez Architects
Collaborators: Hugo Herrera, Santiago Cadavid, Michael Carmona, Andrés Osorio, Carlos Andrés Serna (all architecture students)
Area: 40,000 SF.

San Cristobal district and its community are reluctant to abandon their rural customs to become an urban society. Our proposal puts forward a third option detached from those two original patterns, that is, a "rurban" state – a suitable way to sustainably deal between city and country.
The project as reality redefinition: We believe our action on the site should consolidate San Cristobal as an exchange and transition territory.

Organization structure

The project displays a series of bands of various widths intermingling urban situations and landscape conditions. In each groove a twofold property activates creating an exchange space:
Skill 1. Passive and practical: the space is used for storage and parking while providing a rest area.
Skill 2. Participative and productive: space is collectively produced providing benefits and income.
Skill 3. Informative and educational: space spreads information and conveniently formalizes it for users.
Skill 4. Landscape ecosystem: it's an exchange network.
Skill 5. Porous spaces: the project is a sponge where urban life can abide and improve.

Planting purposes

Deconstructing the notion of natural resource. Promoting relationship of humans with environment. Giving things a voice. Implementing constant elaboration principles. Guaranteeing diversity. Constructing facilities and transferring technologies. Working with closed cycles.
Enhancing reciprocity between social and organic entities.

Harvest of actions

-Closed Cycle: The project aims at self-sustainability energetically speaking: the library becomes the organic garbage collector of the neighborhood.

-From the planting garden to the woods: Each 18 moths, a planting garden disappears to become a native tree wood. Within twelve years the whole plot would be reforested.

-School-plots: Public space: becomes a way to teach new agriculture practices.

- Alcoves and Nests: Both animals and people can abide in the façade.

- Democratic Agro-labels: Each plot has a neon sign with the name of the plantation.

- Food Market Indicator: The façade of the building has an LED board connected to the local distribution marketplace displaying the current prices in the city.

- Info-traffic: The library is the first public building one can see when entering or leaving the city through the Pan-American route. Providing traffic information is critical here.

- WiFi Garden: The country is an open classroom.

Therefore, little technological bushes provide free Internet access.

-Blog Plot: Each plot has a blog. Students publish their experiences.

-Info-cabin cloud: The cabin has meteorology sensors; this way the planters can have permanent weather reports.

[Other] Five Points in Architecture

Ana Rascovsky
Buenos Aires, Argentina.

5 points in architecture

Local
I'm interested in architectures that research the potentials of the native in an innovative manner.
It's not always easy to find what that is when one is immersed in his field. So I think important to experiment in various disciplines to see things from another point of view.

LA
I think many Latin American architectures are interesting ,without being ironic or cynical. Their strength derives from purity.

specificity
In each work I search for the core of the matter, so each work is like a tailored suit, designed with a very specific goal.

start
Material has always been an inspiration for me. I'm seduced by the characteristics of a material, and I imagine new functions to use that quality.

Urban
Surroundings precede architecture. Constructions are just one more piece in the context, but have the potential to modify it. I try to use that chance for good purposes

NIDO

Mobil, 2007
Architect: Ana Rascovsky, Irene Joselevich, Billy Gutraic

The nest is an exaggeration of a wicker basket. Tigre, Buenos Aires province, is characterized by its craftsmanship in wicker, but always in baskets, strollers, briefcases. I wanted to use that know-how, and do the same on the scale of "architecture."
The irony is that no one dared to challenge Mimbrero to do something so great.

VILELA BUILDING

Buenos Aires, Argentina, 2007-2008
Architect: Ana Rascovsky, Irene Joselevich, Billy Gutraich
Collaborator: Fernanda Torres, Architect

Vilela building is formed by a glass box surrounded by a vegetation veil. The buffer zone resulting between both structures holds several functions. The glass box allows full vision of the surroundings, A metallic frame holds the vegetation. In 40% of the apartments the size of its gardens is bigger than half of the inner surface.

BAÑO HIAWATHA

Location: Río Capitán, Tigre, Buenos Aires, Argentina, 2004
Architect: Ana Rascovsky

The work is a glass box, inserted into a wooden box It's a bathroom added to a wooden house from 1907, surrounded by a deep forest on a floodplain. The bathroom is a place to be almost inside the forest.

SPA VILLA SOPHIA

Location: José Ignacio, Uruguay, 2005
Design team: Ana Rascovsky, Irene Joselevich, Florencia Moralejo

This spa is part of a landscape design done in Jose Ignacio, Uruguay. It is built entirely with Bamboo brought from Salta, Argentina. The Spa is a path around a pond through spaces with varied programs: gym, massage room, jacuzzi, sauna, fountain and labyrinth. The bamboo walls create intimacy gradients, making the visit a discovery.

Scratches and reasons in construction of synthesis and identity. Technique: intuitive parameterization 3d, over graphite and ink on paper with digital postproduction. Chancery Annex Project. 2010_Padrevecchi/ SAVA, Argentina.

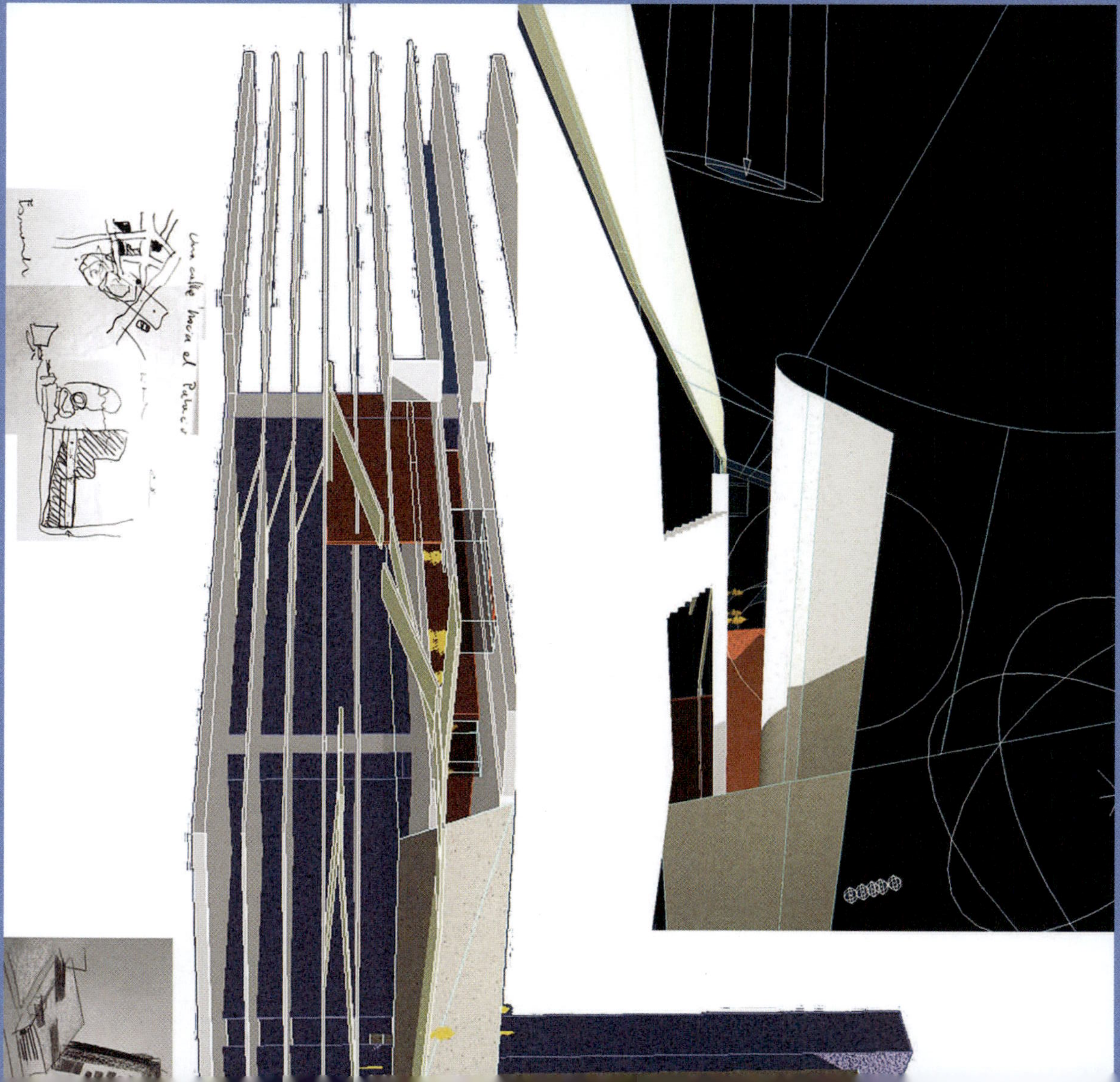

String Installations

Collaborative conversation

26.26.26.25 + Ana de Brea
USA & Argentina

Boceto | Espacios, translated literally as "Space Sketch" is a series of architecture installations in galleries throughout Buenos Aires and California created by the architects and designers Jerome Daksiewicz, Adam Janusz, Wes Janz and Devin McConkey. The group of designers referred to nebulously as 26262625 continually questions the role of architect, global-citizenship, commercial-centric design, and traditional notions of beauty. Their architectural work nearly always operates with extremely limited budgets, using them as opportunities to uniquely explore materials and practices. Projects have been built or proposed with steel sheets, tree branches, window screen, rejected limestone blocks, found objects and industrial cabling – most using the material in no-waste construction methods.

In 2003 in collaboration with Argentine architect and professor Ana de Brea they coordinated a gallery installation at Buenos Aires University, School of Architecture, Design, and Urbanism. The designers found, built or repurposed construction kits (a suitcase fabricated from recycled cardboard and found luggage pieces) bringing with them the entirety of construction materials. Working again with very low cost material – only a few dollars worth of string – the installations explore found conditions of the galleries; each network is informed only by existing connection points, interior objects and spatial patterns intuited by the designers.

String itself has two inherent forms, catenary arcs when hanging from two structured points or as straight lines when maintained in tension. The Boceto | Espacios installations are formed in complete tension; the construction method a dialogue between its string members as one piece is put into tension, the web reacts; strings relax, and then get pulled back into tension. Each line communicates with the next, keeping the nebular structure in tensile form.

The series of two dimensional line-work is expanded to fill each gallery with varying degrees of complexity, opacity and void – exploring each gallery's perceived notions of negative space | positive object, movement/ flow and the viewer's place among them. Each process begins with a point – the connection to the existing space. The installation can only take form from these connection points found among the space; in this way it enters lightly, lives temporarily and leaves without marked notice. These points becoming lines, generated from first thoughts of the space and directly communicating with the initial existing connection point, the dialogue then becoming an object.

Note: The same year, the experience was also conducted in Rosario, Argentina, at different locations (interior and exterior spaces). The opportunity motivated a series of formal talks and group design discussions at the School of Architecture, Rosario University, which attracted a wide audience of professional and students, as well as invited panelists such as Rafael Iglesia, Fernando Fritz, Marcelo Villafañe, among others.

boceto / espacio
moduladores
* ana de brea
* wes janz*
[1 al 11 de julio de 2003]
FADU

T-Fabs

Experimental Academic Studios

Fabrication Workshops are an instance for development and applied academic research that allows students to confront the industry's severity and tangible difficulties in design and construction.

TIUNA EL FUERTE CULTURAL PARK

Model of Sustainable Micro-Urbanism & Multipurpose Open Room

Alejandro Haiek Coll (Lab.Pro.Fab)
Venezuela

The Tiuna El Fuerte cultural park was created based on a system for academic and recreational production to provide services in arts, crafts and communication. It is located at the heart of the El Valle parish, well-known as one of the most important artistic communities in Caracas. Every day, more than 500 children and adolescents pass through its doors for cultural and artistic training; its sustainable architecture platform is based on the application of alternative technologies for construction, control and energy management.

The proposal stems from a persistent problem of public space in the Capital District, since the city of Caracas has less than 5 m^2 of green space and recreational areas per inhabitant, and only 0.26 m^2 per person in the Libertador municipality (location of the project). These are alarming figures that indicate a minimal distribution of parks, squares and recreational space for its approximately 2,103,404 inhabitants.

The idea of the project focuses on transforming and reprogramming interstitial or indeterminate spaces in the city, turning them into cultural parks as models or options for public space in the city on the scale of microdevelopments.
The park uses the strategies of recycling, reconditioning and reprogramming unused industrial containers, transforming them into flexible modular elements with the possibility of progressive growth. They are organized and arranged in multiple combinatorial patterns, which helps provide support for the different training activities offered in the space. In this vein, the project employs pre-assembled systems based on low-cost elements. Their sustainability revitalize the surroundings, while minimizing maintenance and making it easier in the medium and long term.

The plot will ultimately formalize a 9,977 m^2 socially productive ecological park, where there used to be an abandoned parking lot, including a series of open-air auditoriums made up of five built volumes. In between, there are additional spaces for training workshops, classrooms, cafeterias, social services and sports facilities; all with street lighting, street furniture and landscaping. The Tiuna El Fuerte cultural park aims to consolidate a model for sustainable microdevelopments with complementary mixed-use programs, promoting comprehensive social development.

Project: Tiuna El Fuerte Parque Cultural, Model for Sustainable Microdevelopment. Location: El Valle, Caracas, Venezuela. Design team: Alejandro Haiek Coll (LAB.PRO.FAB) and Alfredo Albañez, Ana María Brito, Arch., César Castillo, Arch., María Alejandra Bausson, Dis., Sebastián Miranda, Silvia Colmenares.

Collaborators: Eleanna Cadalso Vera, Michelle Sánchez De León Brajkovich, Yasnaia Reyes Coll, Lorena Sánchez De León Brajkovich, Alessandro De Berardinis, Aldo Guguielmetti, Álvaro Requena, Bahirmary Ramos, Gabriela Joa, Gabriela Reni, Grecia Silva, Lleana Pita, Laura Sabal, María Valentina Hernández, Micaela Lepori, María Fernanda Prieto, Melicia Planchart, Nicolás Garín, Nicolás Pappaterra, Rafael Machado, Sebastián Miranda, Silvana Rodríguez, Sara Vicenzi, Odette Valente, Xavier Apotheker.

Engineers: Esteban Tenreiro, Tomás Borras, Carlos Bezanquen.

Total floor area: Park 63,065 SF. Project: 107,391 SF.

Reuse and reconceptualization of abandoned devices of affluent society to incorporate inactive devices and deteriorated lots. Occupation of non-regulated territories. Redefinition of the city's cultural circuits.

Permeable auditorium complex, with five naves that develop complementary spaces for educational workshops.

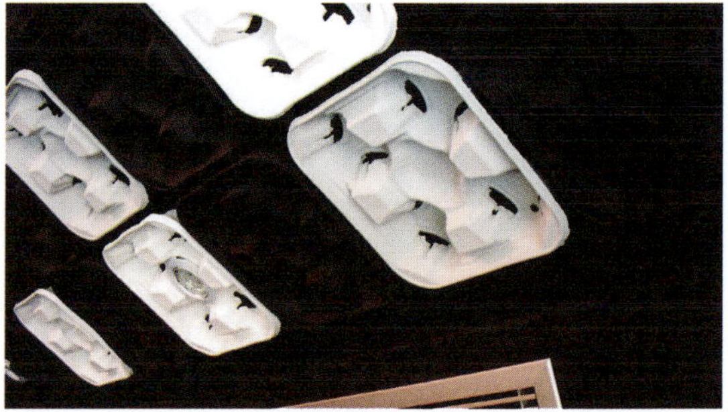

Autonomous elements that can be assembled in situ and can be manufactured from serial processes of industrial production and recycling.

Multipurpose meeting contexts. Urban scenes: dynamics of social exchange. The city is a ruled space that starts in the streets.

Conversion of urban waste. Redefinition of urban lands, new cartographies. Recovery of inactive landscapes: empty spaces.

Environment and scenery dimension of the occupied territory. Urban lands as multiple programmatic corridors. Refoundation of the city from cultural occupation.

Cultural programs inserted in the urban mesh from road infrastructure interventions. Cultural programs inserted in the urban mesh road infrastructure as a cultural platform.

REPLICANT SURFACES

Alejandro Haiek Coll (Lab.Pro.Fab)
Venezuela

In recent years there has been an increasing imbalance and mismatch between demand and supply when it comes to materials and components used in the construction industry. This has resulted in unstable construction processes in terms of time and cost.

The goal of all Intelligent Manufacturing systems or techniques centers on their capacity to produce parts with different levels of complexity and different scales in an industrialized fashion. In other words, through systematized mass production.

Manuel Gausa points to the increasing importance in contemporary architecture of tactical prefabrication, based on the use of structural and technical components that are combined into a complex yet compact system.

There is a clear tendency toward versatility in today's building systems, which reappear as a replacement for the built volume. The walls made from twinned elements are now supplanted by operative multi-layered skins that combine enclosure, technical systems and structural elements. Traditional systems work with limits as perforated systems; a logic that is based on wet walls, reinforced mainly by heavy and massive components, which then need to be perforated in order to create spatial continuities. These ineffective and fixed limits do not have the capacity to resolve the concurrence between technical systems and the line of enclosure. They regularly have to be torn down when the building systems fail or when it comes time to make technical and material updates.

This proposal deals with design and manufacturing methodologies from a thorough reexamination, reformulation and reprogramming of constituent elements (structure, skin envelope, technical systems); exploring the digital field and industry for techniques, mechanisms, instruments, tools, procedures and operations to the world of production can contribute to the design disciplines (architecture, industrial design, graphic and multimedia design).

Project: Fabrication workshop 07/Skin, Surface, Structure.
Location: Caracas, Venezuela.
Institution: Simón Bolívar University, Departament of Architectural Design and Fine Arts, Vertical workshop 8+9+10.
Academic Team: Invited professor architect Alejandro Haiek Coll. (Lab.Pro. Fab) Director of LAB.PRO.FAB (Design and Fabrication Laboratory).
Academic assistant: architect Carlos Ferrer.
Academic collaborators: architect Luis Emilio Pacheco (Design Department Chair), architect Franco Mucucci (architecture coordinator).
Technical assistants Lab.Pro.Fab: Designer Eleanna Cadalso Vera (art director), architect Michelle Sánchez de León Brajkovich (project coordinator), Lorena Sánchez de León Brajkovich (editorial unit), architect César Castillo, and Silvia Colmenares.
Keloide: Sebastián Miranda
Structures: Engineer Esteban Tenreiro
Logistics: architect Sven Methling. (CIPAC) / architect Ricardo Bombim (CIPAC)
Institutional support: Laboratory – E – USB – Metallurgy. Eng. Antonio Desanti (Technical Activities Coordinator, Laboratory E), Eng. Jesús Rodríguez (Department Head: Metallurgical Processes, Laboratorio E).
Students: Santiago Rizo, Gonzalo Romer, Daniela Cavaliere, Patricia Rey, Amanda Alvarez, Ana María Brito, Ana Patricia Corona, Mónica Fuentes, Guedez Desiree, Giacomo Allocca, María Fernanda Arias, Adriana Feuerberg, Jose Angel Perez, Claudio Cenedese, Alejandra Alonso, Alanna Kleiner, Rebeca Novoa, Denise Preschel, Jose Antonio García, Mariandreina Baasch, Cruz Criollo, Michel Piñango, Hariadna Piñate, Irene Rueda.
Photographs: Mariandreina Baasch, Ana María Brito, Eleanna Cadalso , Enmanuel Cardozo, Adriana Feuerberg, Alejandro Haiek , Sven Methling, Patricia Rey, Michelle Sánchez de león , Eduardo Sauce.
Sponsors: CAPEV / Montajes Amacuro C.A. / Industrias y Comercios de Venezuela C.A. / Uniteca C.A. / 8d2 Arq. group C.A. / Distorbera C.A. / Faveca C.A. / Hydraulic Hose & Couplings C.A. / Promotora Keller C.A. / Forestadores del Este C.A.
Acknowledgments: Ariel Guzmán (Maestro de Obras) - Fermín Machado (Mano de Obra)

Fabrication of a multipurpose open classroom. It involved the design and application of four different integrated constructive components, the handling of industrial materials and tools, as well as fabrication processes, assembly procedures, packing, installation, maintenance, dismantling, refurbishing and recycling.

This workshop incorporates not only the study of components, but also their implementation, maintenance and dismantling, their transport and stocking modes, based on their format or morphology and the role each of the units plays in the building.

Pavement made by using recycled PVC pipes, donated by the construction industry through social responsibility programs. This pavement has an atomized surface that lets it adapt to the topography. The installation process consists of the incorporation of a structural iron bar, inserted as the framework that anchors to the ground. Then it solidifies with pigmented surface concrete.

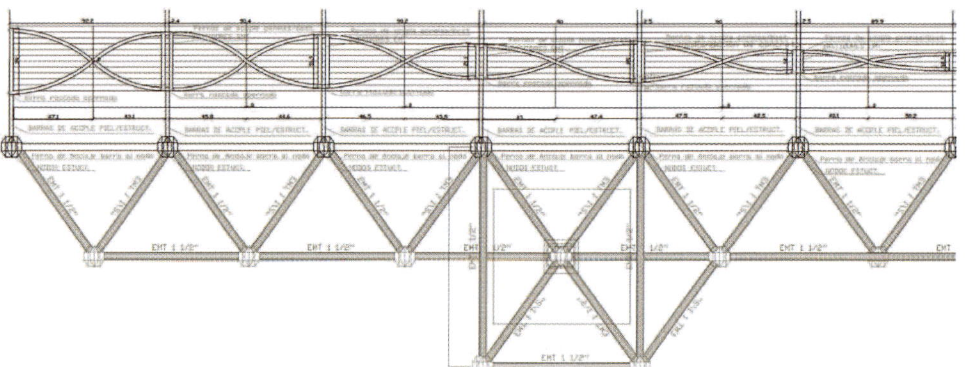

Braided and regulated surfaces. Panels made of flexible plastic corrugated hoses, braided in piping frames of ½" electricity. These panels are mounted in suspension over the three-dimensional structural mesh.

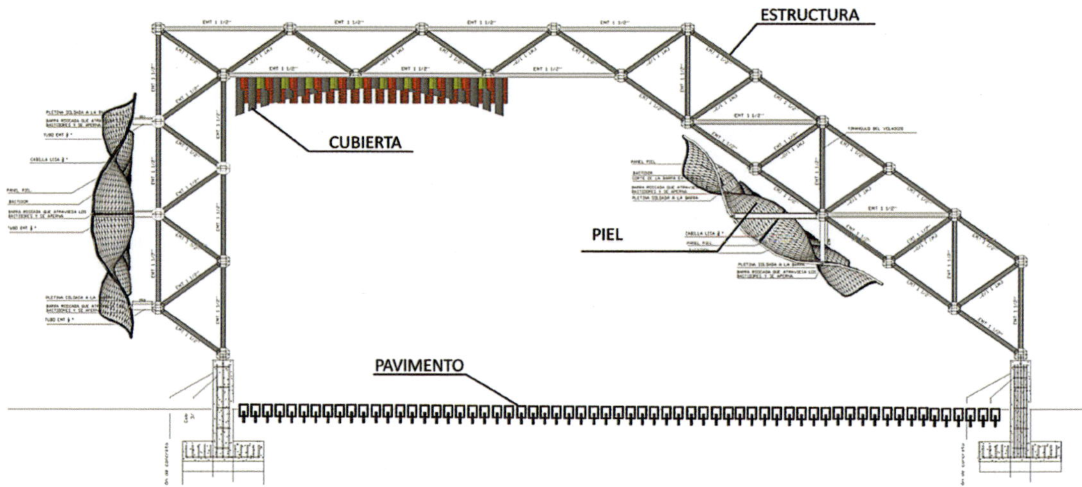

They are centered in the concrete construction of an object in a contoured scale in terms of economy and instruments, which extends to all project phases: design, fabrication, preassembly, dismantling, packing, transport and installation. This is true from the foundations to the closing elements.

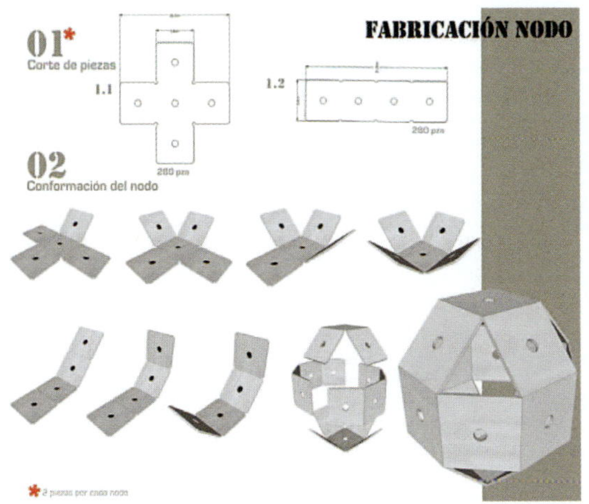

Nodal system for three-dimensional mesh configuration. Eighteen entry nodes that allow for the incorporation of threaded bars in multiple directions.

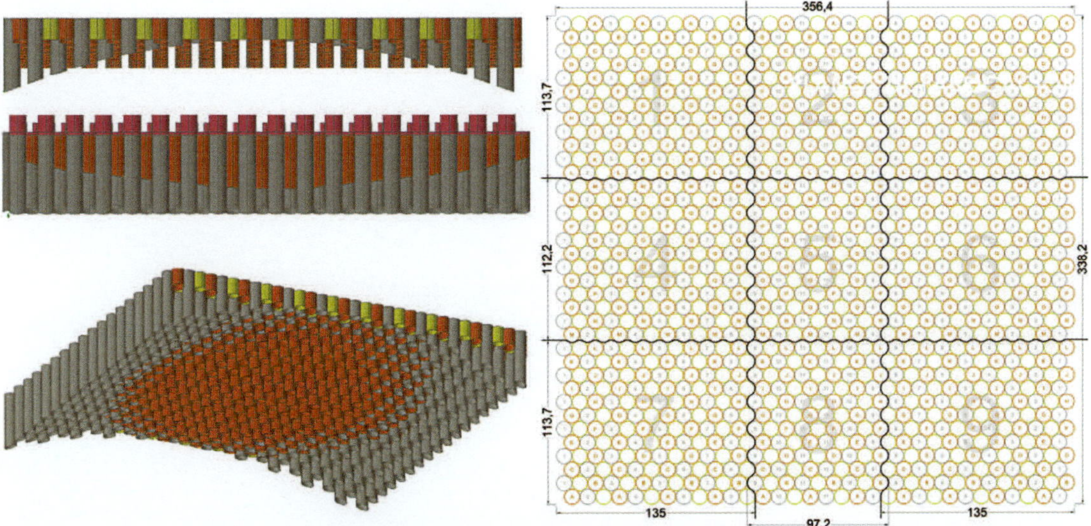

Semipermeable cover made with PVC pipe cuts and supported by sanitary piping elbows.

These workshops have allowed to increase competitiveness and innovation levels in the field of construction materials, rethinking the continent's construction efficiency and speed, having in mind the expansion of the local construction market and industry offer and the endorsement of a critical awareness focused on product performance and life-span.

YESTERDAY & TODAY (1). Series: Trip to South America, 2004.
2010_Image especially composed for this book by Isaac Bracher.

A Physical and Social Change

Blinder Janches Architects
Buenos Aires, Argentina

The large influx of people towards cities leads to transitional urban enclaves that become semi-permanent living environments for the urban poor.

The residents themselves mostly build these informal settlements on empty and undesirable lands, the so-called marginal areas. These informal settlements are not integrated in the formal city; they do not conform to zoning laws and lack urban services. The inhabitants are excluded from the urban society and economy, and have no social status. New informal settlements seem to grow faster than existing ones are upgraded and included into the formal city. Despite policy interventions, informal settlements have become semi-permanent living environments for the urban poor.

If societies do not prepare their cities for new arrivals, do not link their new homes to water or sanitation infrastructures, contamination of the urban region will become inevitable and will negatively affect the environmental sustainability of much larger areas. Furthermore, economic competition between global cities will be lost by societies that criminalize poverty and negate inequality.

This social inequity creates dangerous relationship between integrated and marginalized groups, with consequences that are difficult to revert regarding environmental aspects as well as marginality and insecurity. This social unfolding has produced asymmetrical growth in the city, which is evident in the *shantytownization* of central and peripheral areas and likewise through the widespread urban fragmentation with ever-strengthening barriers that fracture the physical and social cohesion of the city.

The institutional, economic, and social crisis of 2001-2003 in Argentina marked a point of inflection for the urban issue of exclusion, modifying the aims of municipal plans concerning impoverished areas of the city. The effect of the crisis on all social strata led not only to a widespread awareness of marginality as an issue but also to an understanding of the high level of interdependence between marginalized and integrated populations, and of the permanent character of marginalized people, who up to that moment were always considered as residents of provisory spaces.

The permanent character of these communities requires a special type of urban project that is not only focused on physical and infrastructural approaches, but also is centered on creating places that can be symbolically appropriated by their dwellers. It is through the strengthening of existing socio-cultural interactions and the identification of community through difference, both internal and with the neighboring context, that a process of urban integration will be viable.

The aim is then to define an urban design strategy for the integration of those settlements, which enables them to become neighborhoods with their own identity and socio-cultural significance. The complexity of this reality makes it important to establish a rational process to analyze the context and to define a diagnosis for each particular situation of each particular location. The premises that guide this project thus entail the identification of the pre-existing urban and social conditions in the place to be intervened. The socialization networks, the systems of daily life, and the cultural significations of the community in the *Villa de emergencia* are therefore key parameters, working as a starting point for the project, and also as a finishing line.

The project formulates strategies that fulfil the needs of an area in a clear open system. The flexibility that characterizes this openness condition in the urban design is what allows the transformation process to provide equal access to all the urban resources and opportunities available, facilitating coexistence of the diverse groups and individuals. Although the slum problem is rooted in deficiencies emerging from social and economic structural conditions, for us there are nonetheless in these settlements creative strategies for everyday life that constitute, even if in a precarious way, physical structures of positive social relationships. It is therefore important to see these strategies as strengths of the slum population, and use them as key elements in the urban design.

The identification of these existing habits and routines enables us to determine the general system of associations, tensions, contradictions, and balances in the settlement to be surveyed, as a result of which a possible process of urban evolution and transformation can be suggested. The aim of this work is to think and design alternative forms of public space in order to influence some of the social, urban and environmental problems that define the values of the urban context.

Images of Plaza Vicente Lopez (Vicente Lopez Square), Villa Tranquila neighborhood, Avellaneda, Province of Buenos Aires

Gabriela Mistral Cultural Center

Cristián Fernández Eyzaguirre + Lateral Architecture
Chile

A PART IN A PLAY

Gabriela Mistral Cultural Center
(former Diego Portales building)

When we work with an existing structure we cannot avoid making a continuous reading of the elements and the background of the original built work. We like to think that this riddle can be solved, in the words of Pierre Bourdieu, as a sense of play and it does not depend necessarily on the designers but on the passage of time and wear, and on the social agents involved. We believe that this fact alone deserves to be unveiled, and, in this case, maybe it was our only premise upon design.

We think restoring the Diego Portales building is a gift. We saw it as a challenge, but also as an opportunity of working with all this historical burden that, in our opinion, could not be wasted on short-term political desires – especially an atavistic declaration of a "clean slate" by the architect on duty.

Historical Context

This building, like no other, has been an important actor in our recent history, characterized by an ideological and political polarization and by social division. It was built as a symbol of the new man during the government of president Salvador Allende and, after the coup, it became the seat of government for General Pinochet's regime, embodying the center of power.

In the last three decades, the building has been surrounded by railings, closed and guarded according to the government's security requirements and then by the Ministry of Defense during four administrations. For this reason the building has not been regarded as a beloved object and it has a kind of bipolar biography.

The original structure was designed and built in record time. As a strategy, a large deck of colossal dimensions was conceived by the architects and subsequently installed underneath the premises defined by the regulations during the construction of the building.

From the beginning the urban impact caused was deep since a large building, on one side, is perched on the sidewalk of the main avenue and, on the other side, it invades a residential zone with little French-style buildings.

On March 5, 2006 a fire broke out in the easten sector of the building completely destroying the Great Hall used for plenary sessions, with a capacity of 2,000 people. This led the government to make a decision regarding its future, and an international architecture competition was announced.

Urban proposal

From an urban viewpoint, this piece of city has not been connected for many years. Our design strategy was to determine its role in the city. The building adapted itself to an urban design that, in our view, re-establishes the connection of the place with its context making it the exact opposite of what is today.

Our proposal, from a technical and expressive perspective, is simple since it adopts the architectural ideas and qualities of the original project, which is interpreted in a contemporary way for the construction of a new group of premises.

Four main ideas stood out but we fused them into a single concept of transparency: the openness towards the city and its urban relation by setting a large deck and loose volumes underneath; the new public spaces; the opening of the building to the community by including a community program; legitimizing the project by incorporating as many social agents as possible to give shape to a new benchmark for the city. This proposal seeks to segment this large urban outline into three small-scale buildings, articulating a set of new public spaces.

We chose to reveal and display part of the varied life inside the building to the exterior and somehow show the activities and their protagonists, sharing them with the passers-by. A building used for cultural and artistic activities should always have different degrees of transparency, being shared not only with direct users but also with the community in general.

The different degrees of transparency are displayed through a façade system that gradually goes from the wide open and transparent to the totally opaque and closed. It displays the halls for performing arts as boxes or containers in which music, dance and theater are performed.

The premises and building layout

Viewed horizontally, the building layout is based on three main volumes containing the three major areas of the project. These are, from west to east in the same order as the buildings are set out: The Documentation Center for the Performing Arts and Music (Library); Training Room for Performing Arts and Music (Rehearsal Rooms, Museums and Exhibition Halls) and the Great Concert Hall (Theater for 2,000 people).

On the level of the public space, these three buildings are separated and can be totally encircled by pedestrians and make the most of the project, but in the lower levels they are all connected to form one single building. The spaces between them have been transformed into covered squares that are the main public spaces and invite the passers-by to occupy a building that merges into the city.

Viewed vertically, the premises are connected through triple height halls in which we have an overview of the project and find our bearing in each building. These halls are connected directly to each one of the squares, acting as an extension of them.

Design and materials

All the main materials making up the building were found in the original structure and it is worth mentioning five of them in particular: weathering steel (Corten steel), exposed reinforced concrete, glass, steel and timber.

Weathering steel is the perfect link between past, present and future. This fine material is a far cry from pre-painted solutions and imitations. It is present in the original structure and now we try to take it to the extreme in the new building by using it as a coating for facades, ceilings and concrete.

This material has also been used in its varied forms such as perforated, smooth, folded and standard. Its quality over time still amazes us. Only one type of concrete has been used in the project, both in the interior and for the exterior squares, and strips of weathering steel have been placed randomly on top of it.

Restoration and relocation of Unctad III Art Collection

Many artists were convened for the original UNCTAD III project to create pieces of art especially made for the building. Many of these works were already integrated into the architecture of the building, such as the vitraux by Juan Bernal Ponce and the works of Nemesio Antunez and Felix Maruenda.

In this way, fourteen pieces of art available in the original building have been integrated harmoniously into the new project. From our point of view it would be ideal to retrieve the majority of the pieces from the UNCTAD III art collection and add them to the fourteen pieces retrieved. We total 25 works of art retrieved; this is a 60% of the total collection. Works by the same artists could replace the thirteen remaining pieces.

It is obvious that this course of action seems suitable given the UNCTAD III Collection has a high patrimonial and artistic value and it will require additional efforts by all parties involved.

Stagecraft and acoustics

Each room was treated independently, seeking out acoustic comfort according to each activity. Generally, the acoustic solution consists in a double inner layer separated from the structure, depending on the position and function in each room, so that they comply with spreading, reflecting and absorbing functions. Each case went through a design proposed in coordination with the acoustic engineer. The building also has a staging system that is unique in the country, including all the elements and equipment necessary for a proper performance.

Project: Gabriela Mistral Cultural Center (former UNCTAD III building/former Diego Portales building).
Location: Av. Libertador Bernardo O'higgins 277, Santiago de Chile, Chile.
2008-2013.
Studios: Cristián Fernández Arquitectos + Lateral Architecture.
Architects: Cristián Fernández Eyzaguirre + Christian Yutronic V. + Sebastián Baraona R.
Assistant architects: Marcelo Fernández, Carlos Ulloa, Hernán Vergara H., Loreto Figueroa A., Nicolás Olate Vásquez, Natalia Le-Bert, Nicolás Carbone, Juan Pablo Aguilera, Rodrigo Herrera, Eduardo Cid, Sebastián Bravo, Sebastián Medina, Ximena Conejeros, Irene Escobar, Ricardo Álvarez, Sebastián Bórquez, Rodrigo Carrión.
Technical unit: Verónica Serrano (National Director of Architecture)
Public Works Ministry: Eliseo Huencho Morales (Regional Director of Architecture), Patricio Montedónico (Director of Project), Lorena Parra (Inspector of Design), Margarita Cordaro (Inspector of Design), Elizabeth Barros (Architecture Office), Ximena Peirano (Building Inspector).
Structural engineering: Luis Soler P & Asociados.
Total floor area: 440,000 SF.

Congestion_Digital photo , Buenos Aires, Argentina
2007_Image especially composed for this book by Matt DeLoughery

Aerolineas Plus
110
VARILUX Crizal
PRODUCTOS
Kodak
4305 6446
TAXI
11321
GCBA

The Flexible Grid

Casas de la Esperanza

Simon Bussiere + Quilian Riano
La Prusia, Nicaragua & Muncie and New York, USA
Colombia

La Prusia is a growing informal settlement centered along a four-kilometer-long dirt road that connects the city of Granada with Lake Apoyo, both among the top tourist attractions in Nicaragua. This neighborhood does not share the benefits of the tourist industry and has fallen into levels of extreme poverty. For many years the nonprofit Casas de la Esperanza has been helping the inhabitants by building homes, teaching children, and providing technical training to the local adult population. As part of their mission, the organization approached Harvard University's Graduate School of Design in 2008 to propose a housing community design studio for eighty families. It included a multidisciplinary team of design students led by Teddy Cruz and assisted by Andrew Sturm. They traveled to La Prusia to learn about community needs; information gathered from the community, volunteers, city officials, and others was key in the design of the housing. An international community service fellowship was awarded to a strategic group of graduate degree candidates who visited again to develop and test a series of integrated prototypes within the master plan. It is a collaboration between DSGN AGNC's Quilian Riano, Estudio Teddy Cruz, Simon Bussiere (assistant professor of Landscape Architecture at Ball State University) and support from the PARC foundation.

An elastic framework

Two major issues complicated the design of the master plan: a lack of reliable information about the site; and the eventual social adaptations that would follow implementation and as conditions improved over time. We knew that topographic conditions and the location of trees would be key to the design, yet such information was difficult to obtain. It was equally problematic to make assumptions about factors of shifting social exchange and interaction among members of the community itself. This complexity was seen as an opportunity to challenge the hard-lined 20th Century site-planning paradigm, that sometimes dictates even the most minute details of a community, and instead embrace informality as a design attitude.

The master plan starts out with one goal in mind: to preserve and utilize as many existing productive trees as possible while creating safe, productive and flexible housing clusters within their dynamic canopy. To reach this goal a set of simple principles are implemented to create a flexible urban armature, within which infrastructure and other built form can be sited according to an objective reading of existing site conditions. These principles are simple and can be applied by anyone building the houses (local inhabitants, volunteers, or a professional construction crew) without much training.

Designed adaptation is seen as strength by many in the community, who have seen a renewed energy and momentum building from the latest iterations of the framework. The "plan" is explicit in defining density through multiple-use zones, rather than sectors with single functions. We sought to maximize the potential for the function and performance of the clusters of homes and their immediate landscapes to expand and adapt over time. To do that, we allowed for the growth of two more rooms at either end of the central dwelling. We then designed a roof system that is pitched to one side, allowing for more light and air to penetrate the houses and to prompt the collection of the abundant rainwater that falls in the region. Water is collected in individual tanks, with overflow leading to cisterns and used for passive irrigation in planting areas. The landscape itself is the extension of the domestic and economic function of the dwellings. Casas de la Esperanza has built ten of these new designs and is starting the process to build another 60-70.

Directed by Teddy Cruz. Assisted by Andrew Sturm.
Full list of 2008 Harvard University GSD studio: Julia Watson, Osseo-Asare March, Juliana Silbermins, Anne Vaterlaus, Christine Canabou, Quilian Riano March, Simon Bussiere, Chris Ryan, Sara Lynch, Brian Yang, Aron Chang, Kristen Von Minden, Doug Miller.
Design team: Teddy Cruz, Simon Bussiere, Quilian Riano, Dane Carlson, César Fabela, Mark Gusmann, Nikhil Shah.

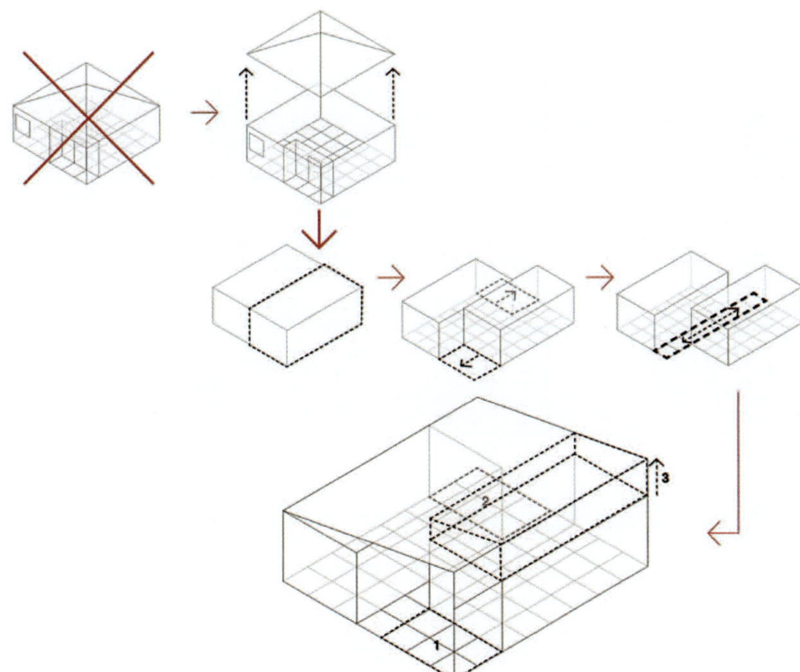

Diagram showing the changes to the houses that allow for up to three more rooms to be added to each house

The houses built around the trees that surround them and provide many functional uses.

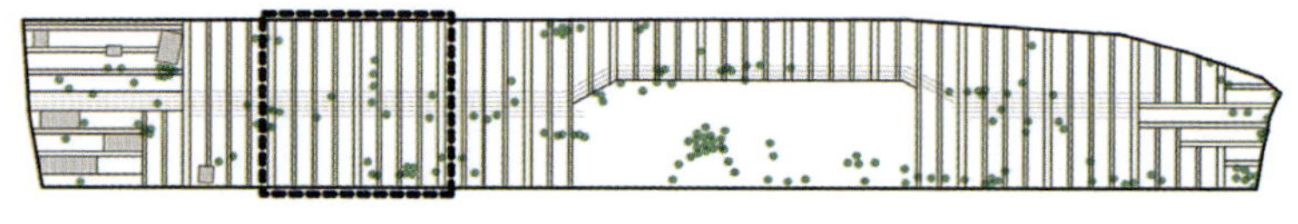

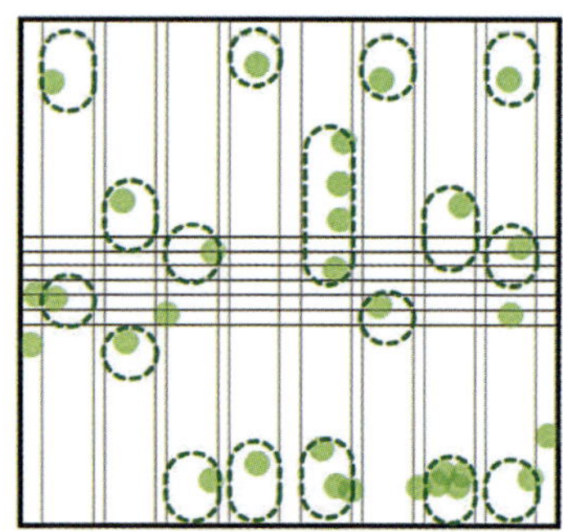

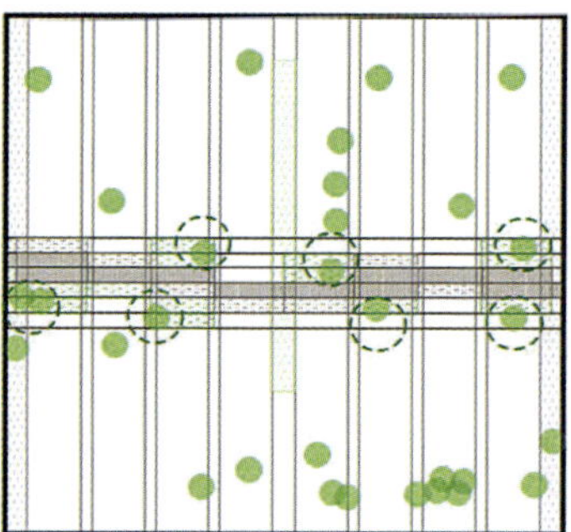

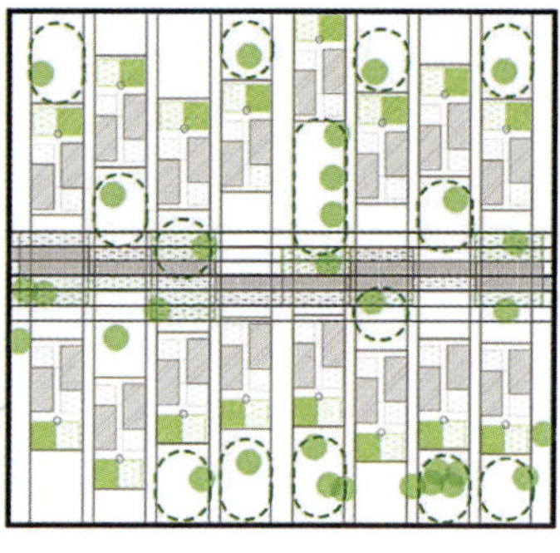

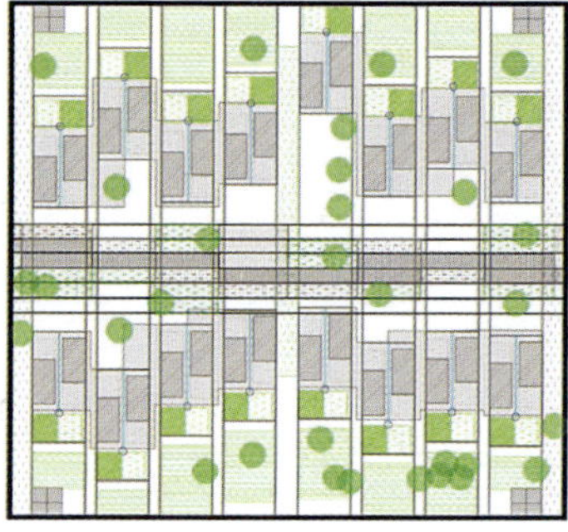

Square diagrams descriptions. Top left: First all the trees in an area are mapped, Top right: Build the road around the trees, Bottom left: Place housing around the trees, Bottom right: Complete construction of La Prusia community.

To Be Modern is no Longer Contemporary

Architecture As Urban Performance
Carlos Campos

The path we have chosen after twenty years of professional practice is today closer to the immaterial, countless, intangible aspects of architecture, rather than to the so-called permanent aspects of our discipline.
Our point of view, our field of *action-abstraction* has always been linked to the academic world, the place in which we empty our thoughts and dreams into every course. Each of the exercises developed in the different schools where I have had the privilege to work has been an experience of deep personal transformation.
Feedback is the key word, (instead of canonic).
Emergence is the key word, (instead of ideas).
Talking about some projects will be useful to illustrate this concept:

The design for the Argentine Pavilion at the XI Venice Architecture Biennale, 2008
A proto-architectural pavilion enclosed the actual architectural exhibition.
A carved-out white piece, like a carved-out white stone. Inside, bright digital images were the only source of light and color.
We used only polystyrene to build the dense sculptural cube.
The material was used under a particular condition: once the exhibition was closed, the whole piece was given back to the polystyrene producer firm, to be entirely recycled.
In the end our intervention was a transition, a sort of borrowed materiality.
Our pavilion traveled to be produced and assembled, to be recycled, but never wasted away.

Choreographies in the Sky
4th. Place at Dubai's LAGI 2010 International Competition.
This project re-articulates the connection between architecture and soil. It is composed of five hundred para-gliders, robotized wings flowing in the sky, as an artificial flock.
The project rethinks the permanence of an architectural action within its site.
Our conformation can fly, stay away from the park, elevate under the shape of a pole, or descend under the form of a wide sunshade, and also hide from the view of visitors.
The self-organized composition is sensitive to the human occupation of the park.

Argentinian icon for the Bicentennial 2010.
1st. prize International Competition. An extended hypostyle hall, reachable from water or land, shows hundreds of lights, as tiny stars. A random or geometrical constellation is ready to be activated by cell phones – by thousands of messages sent by people.
Random / Unpredictable / Composed / Self-Organized / Dynamic / Geometrical / Eventual

City of Event
Urban Performances in Architectural Education.
We trust in the opportunity a project gives us to re-establish relationships among several conditions, like chance, automatic or cyclical urban events, tradition, innovation, self-organized behavior patterns, joy, and human – not necessarily rational – interactions. All these conditions affect a project: transforming, conforming and defining it.

Many *fields of action-abstraction* are activated at the same time, even in a simple event in the contemporary city. We believe no field can become extremely dominant over the others.
To project something is to look for the integration of all these fields, adding something new into the world at the end of this process. Something *new*, always open to interpretation.

XI Biennale di Venezia 2008. Argentine Pavilion. Carlos Campos Yamila Zynda Alub Architects.

4th. Place. LAGI International Competition Dubai 2010. Choreographies in the Sky. Carlos Campos Yamila Zynda Aiub Architect.

1st. Prize. International Competition. Icon for Buenos Aires 2010 Carlos Campos Yamila Zynda Aiub Architects. 2008.

City of event. Homage to the homage to the square. Studio Campos 2007.

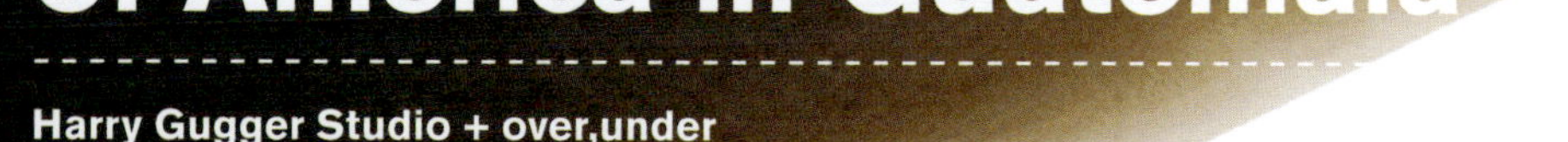

Art and Culture Maya Museum of America in Guatemala

Harry Gugger Studio + over,under
Basel, Switzerland & Boston, USA.

The Museo Maya de América in Guatemala City will become a leading venue for the public to view objects, artifacts, artworks, textiles, and information on the history and culture of the Maya civilization.

Sponsored by Fundación Museo Maya de América, the institution is among the most ambitious cultural projects in the region, aiming to create a museum that celebrates and carefully explains Maya culture.

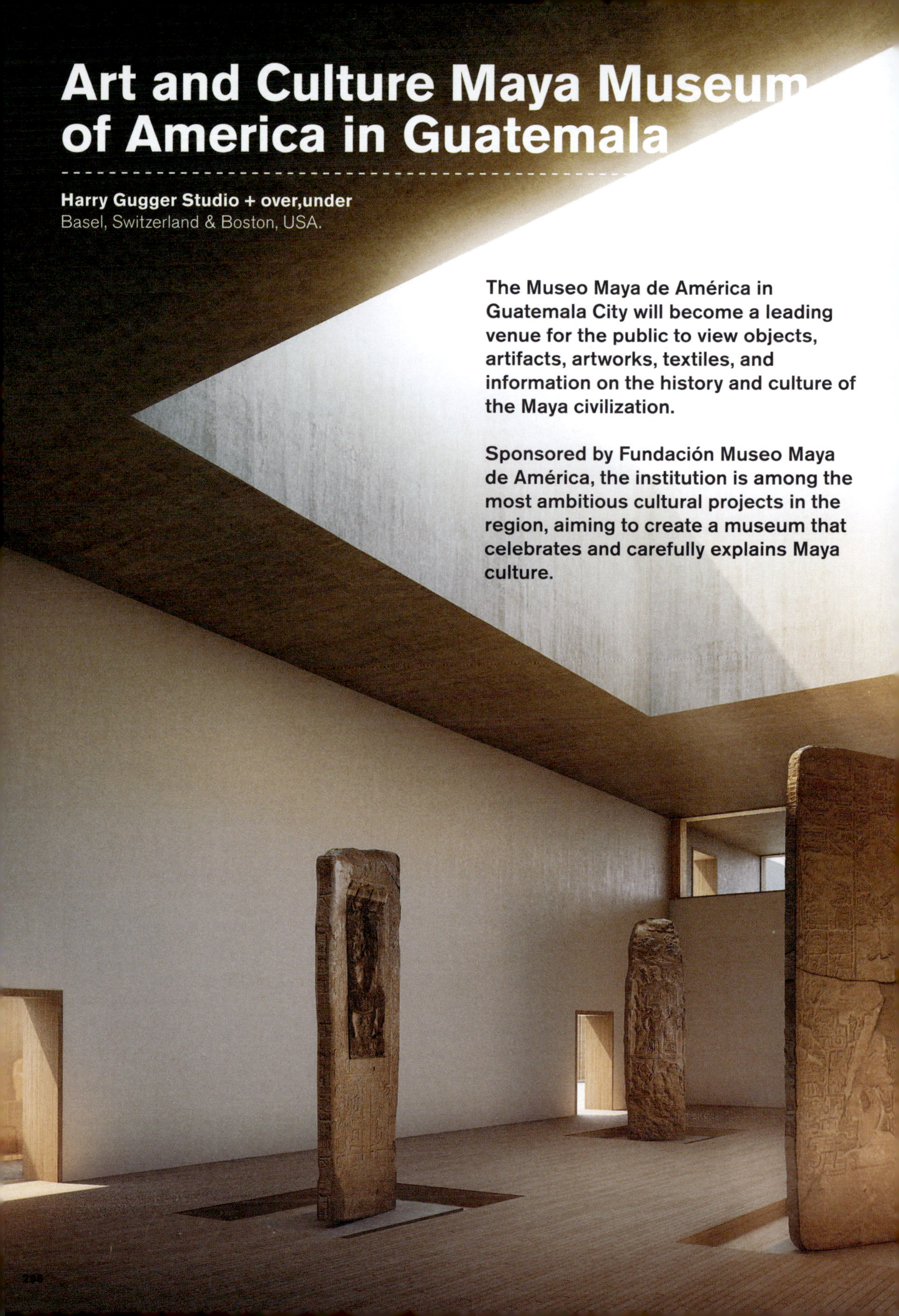

Sited at a prominent location on the northern edge of La Aurora Park, the museum will be immediately visible when exiting Guatemala City's international airport. It will become the capstone to a series of museums, including the Children's Museum and the Museum of Contemporary Art. This cultural nexus – located in what is expected to become the largest recreational open space in the city – will provide a new destination for tourists and residents alike.

The Museo Maya de América's striking design will contribute to that effort, drawing inspiration from the language of traditional Maya temple architecture interpreted through a contemporary expression of elements.

The museum appears as a monolithic box perched atop blocks of stone, as if floating above the ground. On closer inspection, a pattern of staggered stone screens is punctuated by over-scaled loggias that draw light into the building and offer glimpses inside. The building presents this large, abstract form to the surrounding city.

Organized for maximum public interaction with the site, the ground is given almost entirely to open space.

The galleries reside within the floating box, connected to the lower levels by stairs that climb their way around a central courtyard. This court evokes the cenote, a type of natural sinkhole characteristic of the Yucatan and held sacred by the Maya. Open to the sky and lushly planted, the eight-story cenote functions as the heart of the museum, its displays, and its activities. It forms an orientation point within the museum and extends down to the parking levels below ground, providing an interesting route into the museum and a special place to display underworld-related artifacts.

The building takes advantage of Guatemala's temperate climate by naturally ventilating all but a small number of spaces that require artificial conditioning. The exhibition floors are organized in a checkerboard of galleries and circulation areas. The walls of the circulation spaces are lined with glass cases to place the collection of artifacts – normally in storage – on display. The landscaped roof is returned to the general public as an accessible civic space, containing a restaurant, outdoor galleries, gardens, and viewing terraces.

The large surface of the roof will be used to collect rainwater and filter it through the cenote in a manner recalling traditional Maya practices of channeling water.

Project: Museo Maya de América. 2012–2017.
Location: Guatemala City, Guatemala.
Design team: Harry Gugger Studio Ltd. (Basel) and over,under (Boston), Architect of Record, Seis Arquitectos (Guatemala City).
Total floor area: 645,834 SF.
Visualizations: Neoscape, © Courtesy of Harry Gugger Studio and over,under.

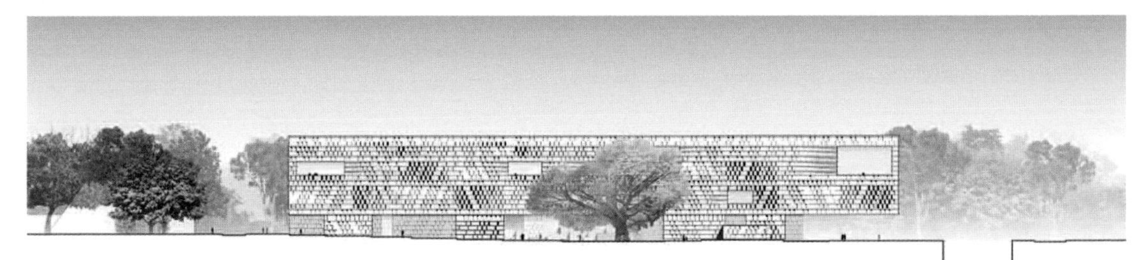

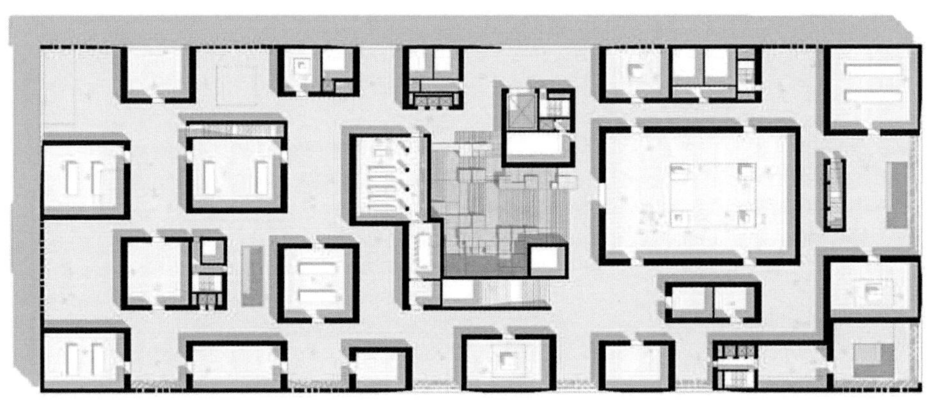

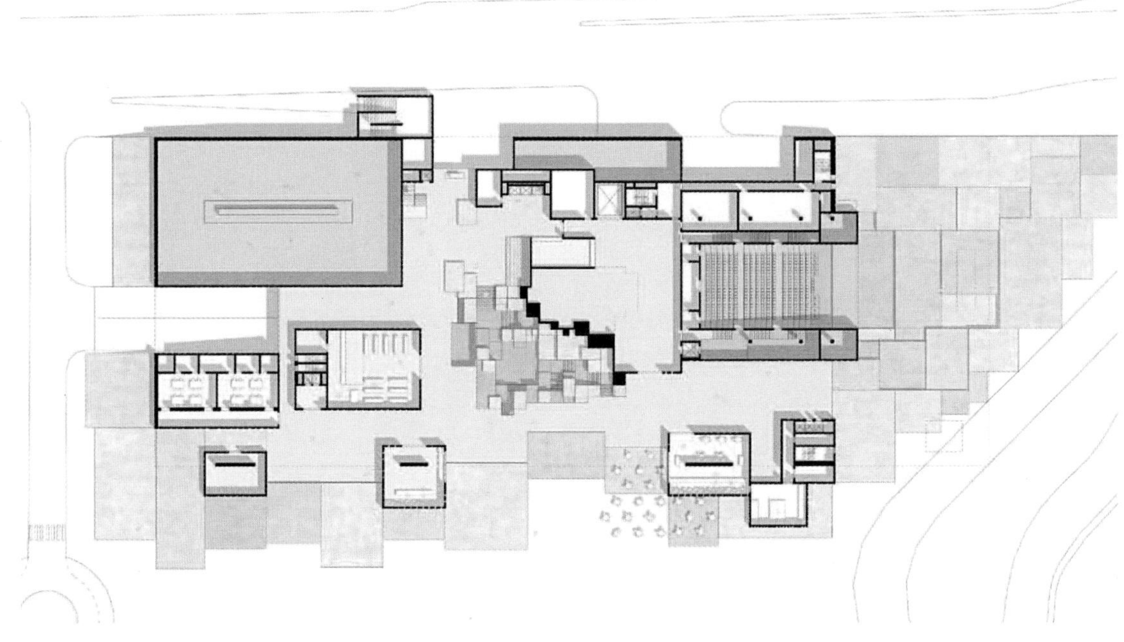

Las Americas Virtual Design Studio

Antonieta Angulo (Ongoing, international studio-exchange)
USA & South American Universities

The Las Americas Virtual Design Studio (LAVDS) is a collaborative teaching and learning experience in which a number of studios in different universities from the United States and the Latin American region make the commitment of working as a virtual studio. They all contemplate the same design subject and share the development of resulting projects through the Internet. The students work within their studios as usual, under the direction of their local instructors. At the same time, each student is assigned to an international virtual studio made up of students from different universities under the advisory of several virtual instructors. The roster of virtual instructors is made up of instructors from all the participating studios and a number of volunteer reviewers who do not have students at their particular location.

The LAVDS was created with the support of a National Science Foundation grant that funded the creation of the Las Americas Network. The Las Americas Network formerly included a few countries from Latin America, among them Mexico, Peru, Chile, and Argentina. The mission of the Las Americas Network was to organize academic activities and expand the connections between schools in the U.S. and Latin America.

Through the years, it has expanded to include more countries and several schools of architecture per country. Some current participants of the virtual design studio include: Universidad Ricardo Palma in Lima, Peru; Universidad de Mendoza in Argentina, Universidad Nacional de Tucumán in Argentina, Universidad La Salle in Mexico, Universidad de Las Américas Puebla in Mexico, Universidad del Istmo in Guatemala, Universidad de Ciudad Juárez in Mexico, and Universidad RegioMontana in Mexico. In addition, a number of large transnational design firms have contributed with professionals acting as virtual reviewers. The increasing availability of digital networks for educational and social purposes, the amount of applications that provide for sharing and cyber-meetings, as well as the necessary expertise for the implementation of virtual collaboration and participation has made the implementation of the LAVDS an annual event for almost fourteen years.

Since its inception, the LAVDS has always addressed the topic of design for hospitality, ranging from hotels for tourism and business to recreational eco-lodges. The studio has also addressed subjects that combine hospitality and specialized healthcare facilities. The sites that have been chosen for the projects over the years have been located in different geographical locations in South, Central and North America, from National Parks to urban settings in large and small cities.

India Dunes. National Lakeshore, project by the student Melissa Guerra Sánchez.
Las Americas Virtual Workshop, 2013.

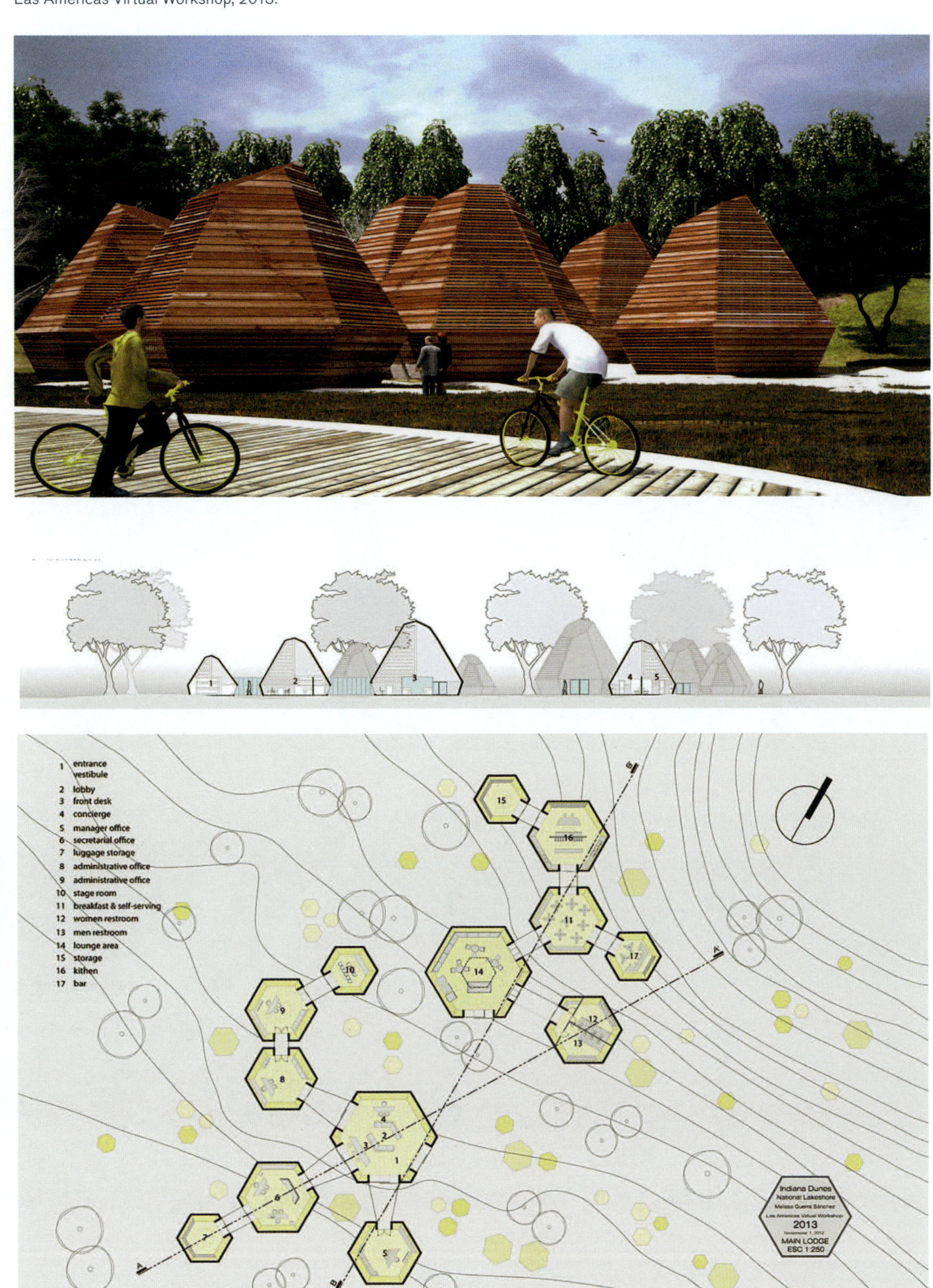

Artistic / Original photographs: Xul Solar Museum (Buenos Aires, Argentina) + Art Installation at Universidad Católica de Chile (2008).
2012_Collage especially composed for this book by Tessa Pobanz and Mishayla Binkerd.

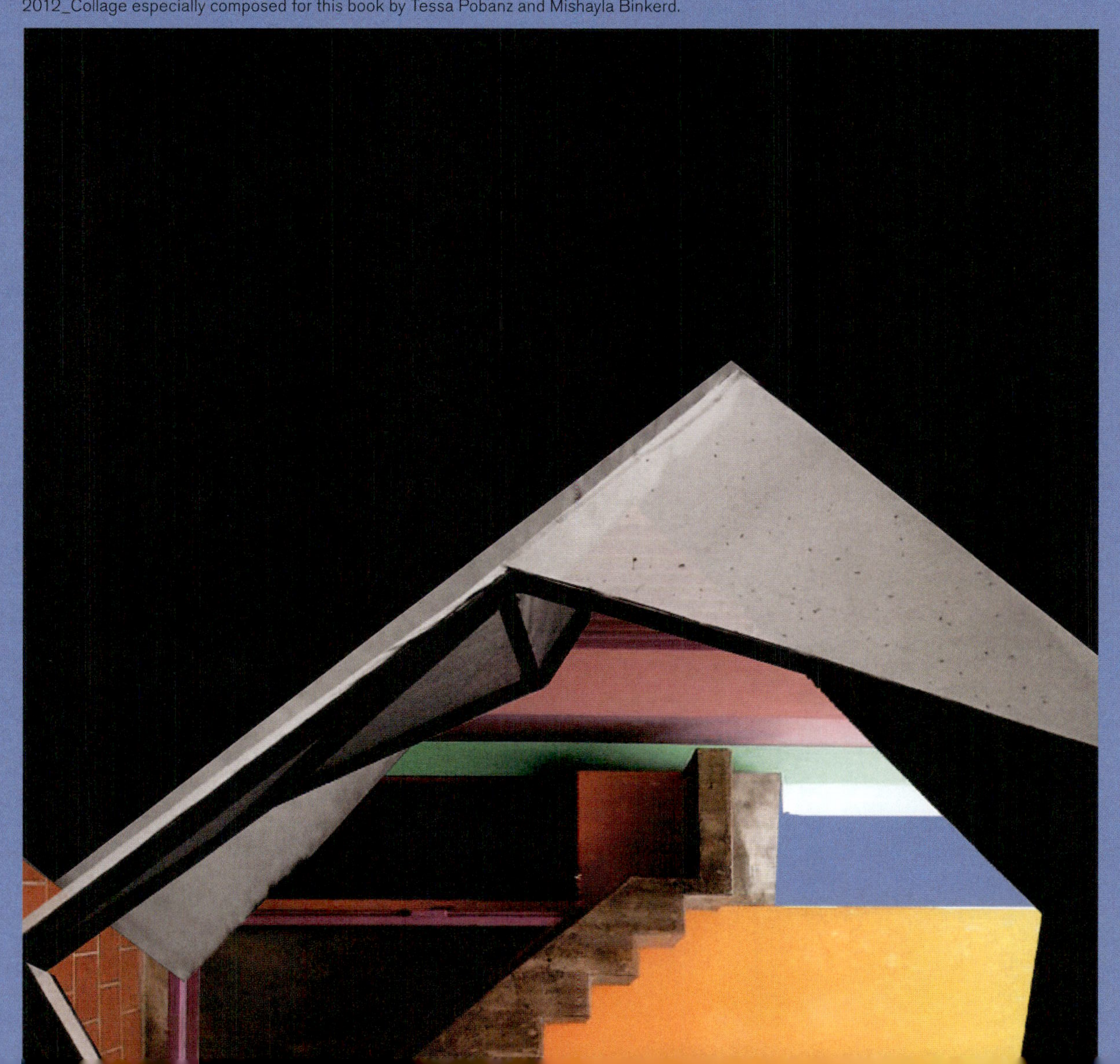

TERRAIN LANDSCAPE TOPOGRAPHY

GROUND, TERRITORY, ENVIRONMENT, SCENERY, SETTING, BACKGROUND, SITE, PANORAMA, GEOGRAPHY, SITUATION, SURROUNDINGS, CIRCUMSTANCES, PAINTING OF VIEW, STRUCTURE, RANGE OF CONCERNS, SKIN, FOCUS, POSITION, BASE, ARGUMENT, REGION.

In Another World

Rafael Iglesia
Argentina

It has been said: all those who have instituted Daedalus, the builder, as the first architect, have lied to us. His labyrinth may be everything but architecture. A construction which fades; which, in order to work, needs to be not acknowledged; a construction which conceals its form cannot be architecture.

Ariadne is an architect, who, with the sole help of a slight cord, restores the direction and composes the trajectory, establishes distances, and organizes space. Ariadne "interprets" the labyrinth, breaks it down and returns the form and the hero to us. Since Ariadne's times, the same story has more or less been repeating itself, except for the necessary change of the champions who have borne the cord. And it has been quite a long time since we please ourselves with repeating the great deeds of the last of titans: Le Corbusier.

Engrossed in the increasingly sterile repetition of this story, we did not see that the latest of the technological inventions affecting the foundations of our world was coming: Internet. With the promise of democratizing (globalizing) information, the web makes present what is absent and revolutionizes the concepts of space and time with which our reality is organized. Jorge Luis Borges dreamt for us his prefiguration and called it "The Aleph". I will quote only two phrases: "What my eyes beheld was ***simultaneous,*** but what I shall now write down will be *successive*, because language is successive." And later on: "The Aleph's diameter was probably little more than an inch, but the cosmic space was there, actual and undiminished." The quotation sets a difference of perception and distribution between image and discourse that may help us to interpret another relationship: reality, the environment, is *simultaneous*; architecture is successive. It is an order, possessing hierarchies, it has been so until today. This is the reason why we have been going from one place to another according to a discipline, which orders the different privacies through visibilities and the rationalization of circulation. But things are changing.

Maybe the approaching state of thought shall be *simultaneous* (like the visual record, which is totalizing, understanding, deeper) and shall replace successive and linear thought, subject to the language template. If we follow this supposition, it is likely that in the near future our challenge will consist of understanding that it will no longer be possible to consider places inhabited by man as areas where time and space are uniform and absolute but as series of times and spaces, in an increasing and vertiginous web containing them – divergent, convergent and parallel at once.

Rather sooner than later, Internet is transforming all areas, turning distance into a new barbarism. New conducts appear, new ways of becoming related are show, new worlds, ultimately: another ecology.

It will be necessary to see if we are able to accommodate what is to come. Very soon, architecture must be measured against what it does not know and, to do so, it will have to be not current; i.e., it will have to be done as it is no longer practiced, and subjunctive, as it is not yet done. Only in this way will we be more or less reasonably able to provide answers not only to the present but also to the future seed living in it. Please excuse me for going back to Borges but he is, in my opinion, the best Argentinean architect. For instance, when he states: "The Word, when it was made flesh, passed from ubiquity into space, from eternity into history, from blessedness without limit to mutation and flesh". Internet follows the inverse way: it recovers ubiquity, eternity and blessedness without limit for its virtual universe and it discards history (tradition) and flesh (matter). As a result of this reversal, many of man's activities no longer need to substantivize themselves in places and be verbalized.

The time has come to question our times of *in*-formation, to see how we formalize spaces without the need for placing walls, bars, and barriers – obstacles which new technologies have rendered obsolete. It is also necessary to rethink the relationship between public, semi-public and private spaces, overcoming the old Renaissance look. In this way, we will be able to face the globalized world that sets up great inequalities. To ask ourselves what the spatial answer will be to allow the different social strata to share the same area is, definitely, to ask what the future city will be like.

And while we try to escape from the paradigm of the successive, today more than ever, it must be urgently accepted that what is needed are words, not facts. It is fundamental to retake the construction of the great stories – since it is from *discourse* that we will find the *course* itself; it is essential to wonder by means of the word, even if there is less and less to be said, and to get rid of the oppressive historical archetypes which are still worshipped.

Maybe in these times, geography is more important than history since it is orientation that we need. Facing the unknown, experience – essentially historiographical – yields the way to experimentation, which, assimilating itself to geography, gets deep into new territories. To experiment is to move forward, toward the future; experience is the opposite: to look backward, toward the past. The sooner we understand that many years of human evolution find their closure today, the earlier we will be able to deal with this new environment and help it produce its best fruits for everyone.

We may try an overcoming synthesis and be, at once, Daedalus and Ariadne. The mythical trade of building labyrinths must be retaken, because in labyrinths two neighboring points can be very near or inevitably far away, and balls of thread must be given out so that everyone can build their way. Or, as a certain American writer used to say, so that everybody can "make a slit onto the open and windy chaos". Awaiting this chaos, we will finally settle down in other times, other spaces, in another world.

Meeting Rafael Iglesia in his office with a group of students, Rosario 2005.

HOUSE IN THE COUNTRYSIDE

Nicolás Campodonico
Argentina

Date: 1998
Project: House in the Countryside
Location: La Playosa, Córdoba, Argentina
Architect: Nicolas Campodonico
Site area: 20,000 SF
Built area: 750 SF

The house is located in the east of Córdoba province, just where the *Pampas plains* end. It is designed to be lived in permanently, but with high space flexibility at the same time.

The site combines two opposite situations: the 'monte' (an uncultivated rural area, covered with trees and bushes), with its buildings and inhabitants; and the open countryside. The house is placed between these two conditions, becoming a transition and combining both spatial experiences in its interior spaces.

The house is articulated between eucalyptus, olives and silver berry trees that are essential components of the project. Walls and volumes define different levels of permeability, as well as open patios that work as a link between the house and the *monte*.

From the inside, perspectives of the patios are alternated with views of the open countryside, with the horizon line as the only reference. A line that is sometimes thick and heavy and sometimes ethereal, diaphanous, subtle.

AYUTUN HUE HOUSE

Roberto Busnelli + Roberto Amette
Argentina

Date: 2003
Project: Ayutun Hue House [guest house]
Location: Bariloche, Río Negro, Argentina
Design team: Roberto R. Busnelli, Roberto Amette
Project team: María Elena Cuppollo, Martín Nicolini, Patricio Beltrán
Consultants: Arrieta & Arrieta Construcciones, Vidriería Moreno, San Carlos de Bariloche, Vivero Lenga
Area: 1,800 SF

Architecture is the effort of the material toward being, an effort to make visible what is not: thoughts. A thought, in the same way as a feeling, belongs to the world of undetermined things, a world whose form has not been shaped yet. There is no architecture without reliance on the material.[1]

Our work intends to open a space for reflection on the material condition of our projects. For that purpose, an academic experience and some professional research work will help us to think over new alternatives in the dilemma of how to materialize our ideas.

Technique and technology have developed so much that they are hardly restrictive. In this sense, if almost anything is possible, should anything that is built be considered architecture? To find the answer to this question, we have to focus on the very essence of architecture – that quality of architecture that makes it what it is; that which builds in contrast to that which destroys. That specific condition we call *constructability*: the constructive character. It implies that whatever we design may be intended to be built or manufactured with our means or in the fantasy of a utopian future; or it may belong to an irretrievable past.[2]

Materiality is the essence of the project; it is born and develops with it, it imposes its physical properties and technical conditions, and all these have an impact on the geometrical order, on the structural description and on the unshakable relationship between form and space.

All prior projects are part of the last project. Anything seen, heard, touched, imagined or built is incorporated or finally reappears. Any new line contains in itself all the previous lines. Each new configuration will hardly be glimpsed in the fragility of the ephemeral moment, before being transformed again in the following layer. An operation that is in a chain of transformations that began long before. This accumulation of experiences is not necessarily related to the passage of time but with the intensity, deepness and continuity of its study and exploration. In the words of Alvaro Siza,[3]

"… reality is made of super positions, transformations and recoveries…".[4]

In the guesthouse built in the Argentinean *Patagonia* the limits of the construction become confused with nature, where the escarpment becomes the slab, and the slope becomes the stair that ends in a courtyard, with its access perfectly established by the architecture and the slope. The structure is entirely in concrete with four steel columns that create a special interior atmosphere; it seems like the slab is flying through the lake. This entire transparent box is interrupted only by four opaque pieces of wood, which are the sole opening windows of the house. The house frames the view of the lake and the mountains; the view is increased by memories or reflections of a larger site. The architecture is intimately linked to the experience of the place.

1. Mansilla, Luis Moreno, "Sobre la Confianza en la Materia." Escritos Circenses, Editorial GG, Barcelona, 2005.
2. Campos, Carlos. "Antes de la idea," Bisman Ediciones, Buenos Aires, 2008.
3. Álvaro Siza, a Portuguese architect, born 25 June 1933 in *Matosinhos*, a small coastal town near Porto. He graduated in architecture in 1955 from the former *School of Fine Arts* at the *University of Porto*, the current FAUP - *Faculdade de Arquitectura* da *Universidade do Porto*. Siza Vieira taught at the school from 1966 to 1969, returning in 1976. He has been a visiting professor at the *Graduate School of Design, Harvard University*; the *University of Pennsylvania*; *Los Andes University of Bogota*; and the École *Polytechnique Fédérale de Lausanne*. Siza's work is often described as "poetic modernism." [*From Wikipedia, the free encyclopedia*].
4. "Il Procedimento Iniziale," Alvaro Siza, *Lotus Internacional*, no. 22, Milano, 1979, p. 49.

Panoramic view from outside

Exterior views

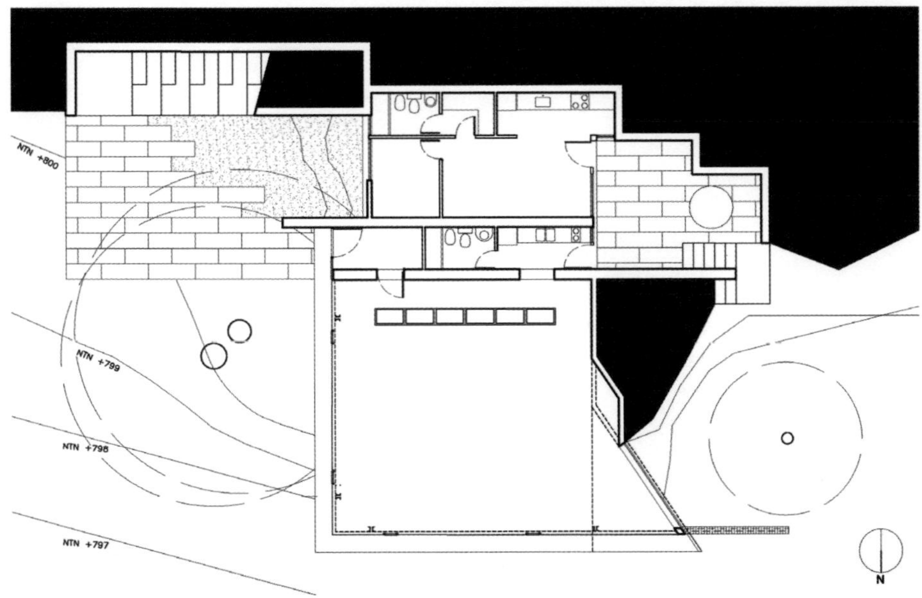

Ground floor

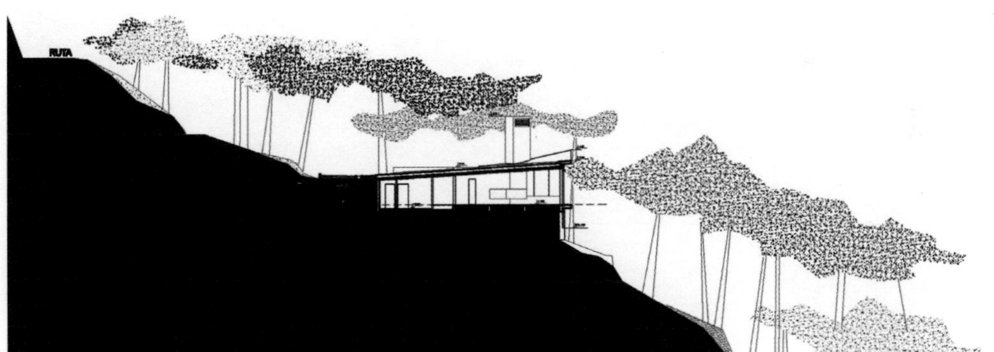

Cross section

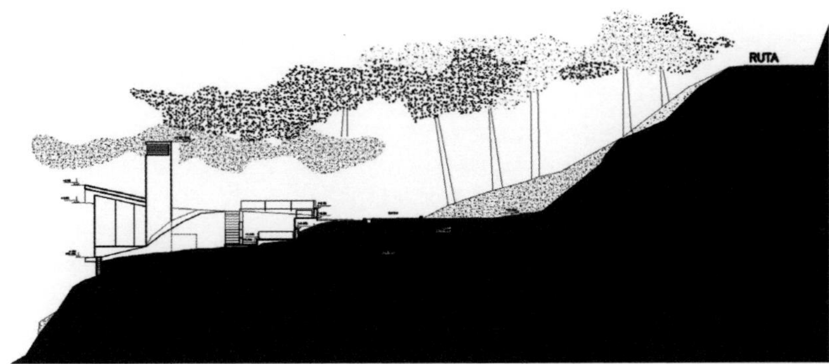

Elevation

PORCIUNCULA DE LA MILAGROSA CHAPEL

Daniel Bonilla
Colombia

Date: 2004
Project: Porciúncula de la Milagrosa Chapel
Location: La Calera, Bogota, Colombia
Architect: Daniel Bonilla
Design Team: Daniel Bonilla, Akira Kita, Ana Lucia Cano
Constructor: Jaime Pizarro

The chapel in La Calera has a basic geometry that tries to alter the territory as little as possible. It uses natural features of the environment, the wind and the light to create an essential harmony. The chapel is designed to open to the outside to allow worshippers to gather for mass. This architectural design appeals both to small private groups and large public functions, in a country full of contrasts, making this transformation a symbol by itself.

The relationship between a still and a mobile volume represents the passage between two worlds, between the known and the unknown, the light and the darkness. As the door opens, a mystery is revealed, and has a dynamic and psychological value, not only showing us a landscape, but inviting us to pass through it.

This change of focus, scale and perspective transforms the component of the chapel; the space for the altar turns into the space for the choir, the main nave transforms into the lateral nave and the tabernacle becomes part of the landscape. To make all aforementioned things possible, the placement of the building was scrupulously studied.

The materials work on these same principles; they mimic the natural surroundings. In this way the rigid structures are static as the stones, while the mobile body made of steel, glass and wood forms an interwoven design. The reflecting pond, on one of the chapel's sides, dilutes the massive structure into the landscape, and it also accents and distorts the volume to make its density fade away.

Exterior view

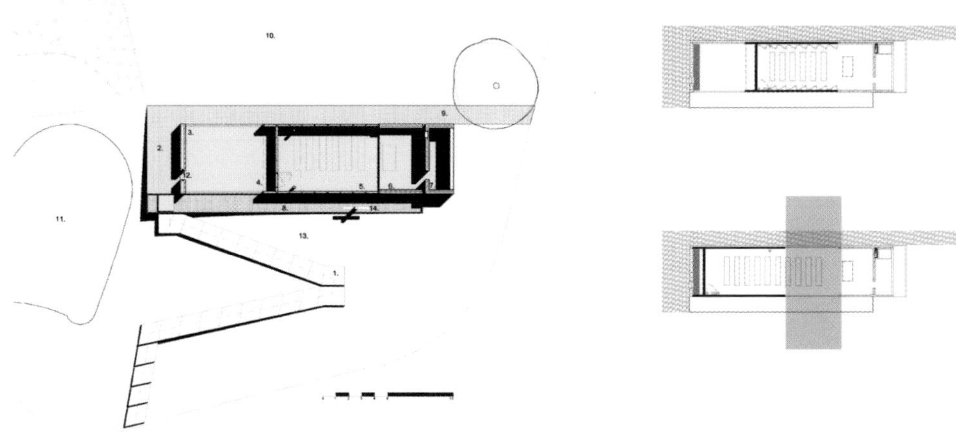

Site plan

Closed/open chapel indoor mass

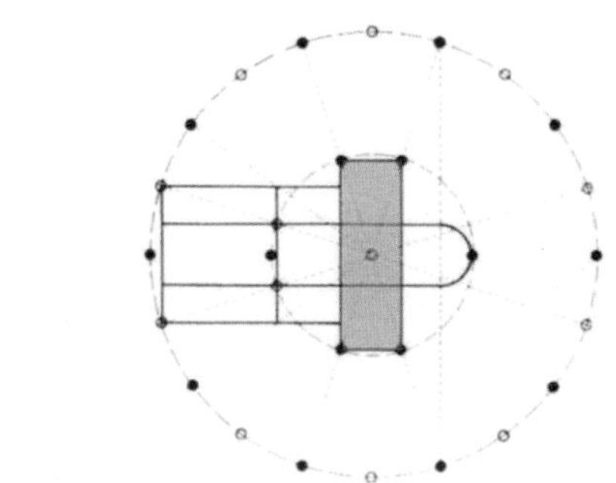

Roman basilica

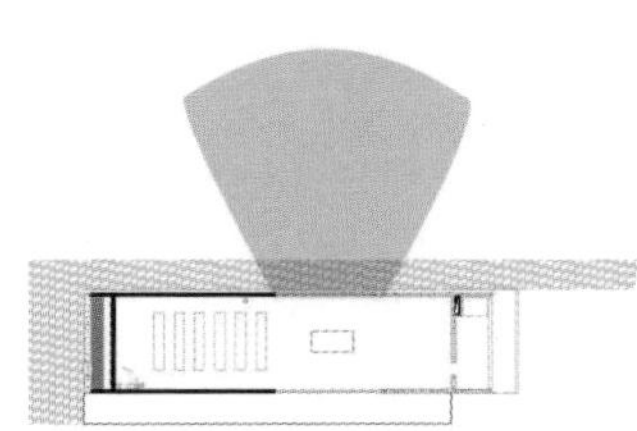

Open chapel outdoor mass

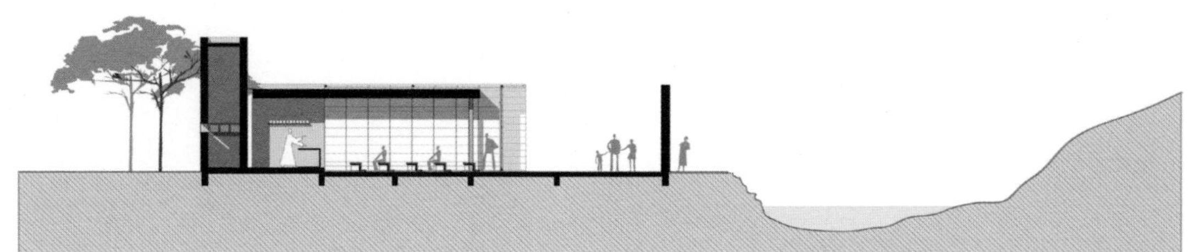

Closed chapel section

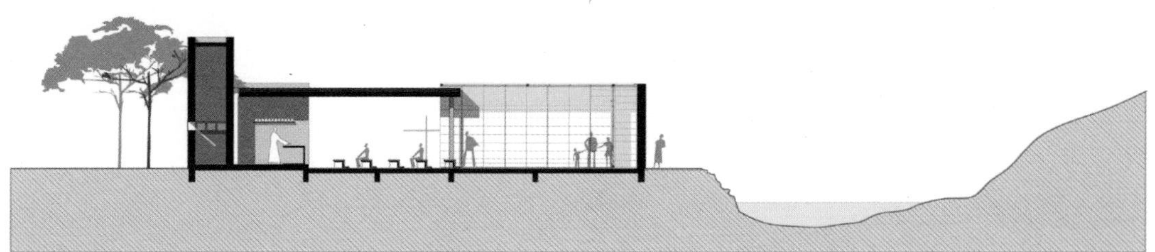

Open chapel section

General view with doors open.

Interior with doors closed and open.

EXPLORING SOUTH AMERICA. Camino del Inca – Walking toward Machu-Pichu.
Pictures of a remarkable journey from Bolivia to Peru, home to some of the most particular landscapes, and cradle of the impressive Andean Culture.
2009_ Images especially composed for this book by Nicolas de Brea Dulcich, Argentina.

CASA O

01ARQ
Chile

Date: 2009
Project: Casa O
Location: La Reserva, Huentelauquén Norte Canela, IV Región, Santiago, Chile
Architects: 01ARQ Associated Architects, Cristián Winckler, Pablo Saric andFelipe Fritz
Collaborator: Álvaro Baile
Structural engineer: Víctor Palma
Lighting: 01ARQ Associated Architects
Total floor area: 3,250 SF.

The house is located north of the city of Santiago in a suburban neighborhood called La Reserva. The triangular site has a slope that descends toward the north.

On the first floor, the house is buried creating a retaining wall to the south and west. This operation allows for locating the parking lots next to a wide ramp, which connects the street with the main entrance of the house.

A reflecting pool, two concrete walls and a window that shows the interior space articulate the entrance.

On the first floor the project intends to create maximum flexibility in the living spaces; they can make up a single space when the sliding wall that separates the kitchen from the dining room is open. During the summer the glass facades are hidden behind concrete walls, transforming the living and dining rooms into a large covered terrace that joins the outdoor pool and garden.

The kitchen opens to the south through an interior courtyard; this space organizes the service programs.

The second level contains bedrooms, bathrooms and the TV room; a skin of wood slats that is separated from the walls so the wind can pass through, optimizing climatic comfort.
This "skin" covers all four façades. The skin is folded to provide views over the valley from inside the house.

The vertical connector located in the center of the house provides access to a roof terrace. From there, you can see the valley and the Andes Mountains. This element also creates an upward airflow that allows temperatures to drop inside the house in the hot summer months.

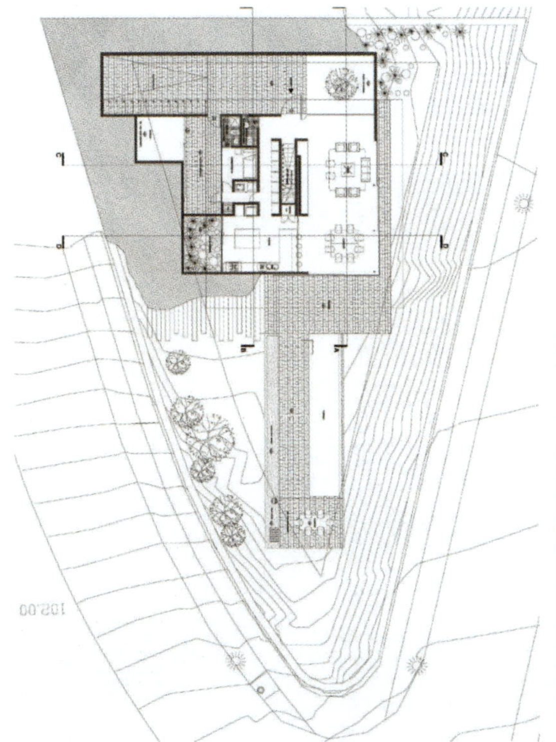

First floor

Main access

View from the pool

View from the pool

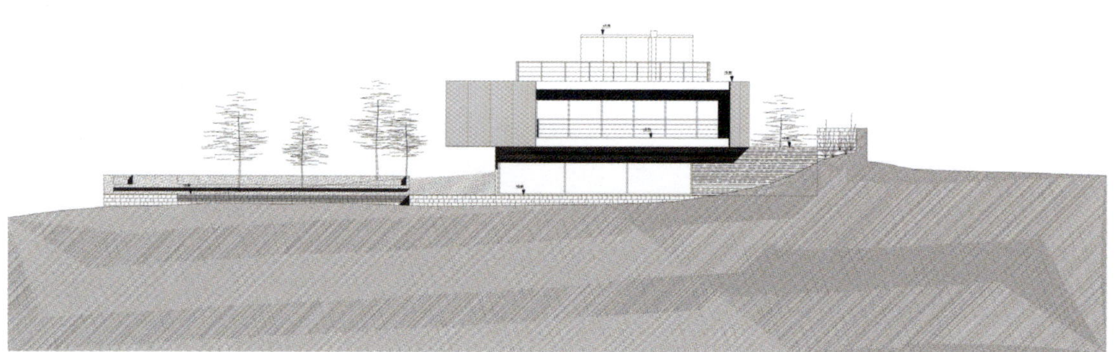

Elevation

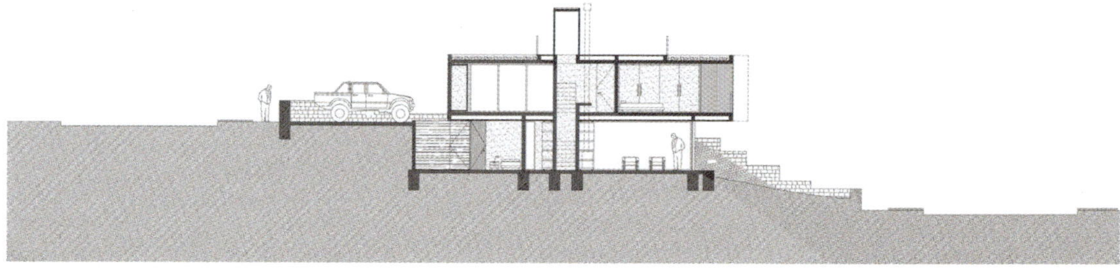

Section

CASA W

01ARQ
Chile

Date: 2008
Project: Casa W
Location: Parcela C11 Comunidad Agrícola Huentelauquén Norte Canela, IV Región, Chile
Design team: 01ARQ Associated Architects, Cristián Winckler, Pablo Saric and Felipe Fritz
Collaborators: Álvaro Baile, Miguel Ortiz, Óscar Terrazas, Simón Henríquez, Javiera Barrientos, Amalia Oats, Arturo Bustios, Rodrigo Gómez, Juan Pablo Duarte, Monserrat Buale, Mauricio Bruna, Alejandro Gandarillas
Structural engineer: Víctor Palma
Lighting: 01ARQ Associated Architects
Total floor area: 1,350 SF.

Located in Region IV, in the windy coastal town of Huentelauquén, W House develops a program that includes 3 bedrooms, 2 bathrooms, living room and terraces. The commission presented two restrictions: the first was to create spaces protected from the wind; and the second not to exceed a construction budget of 12 UF (US$ 500) per square meter.

The site of 50 meters by 100 meters is next to a rocky area where the waves break; to the north is the neighboring site and to the east is the driveway. The southern boundary is a 25-meter-high cliff, which allows, on one hand, for distant views as well as providing access to a small beach.

The house is located parallel to the sea, maximizing the view. Common areas are located to the south, taking advantage of views over the existing cliff; these consist of a large space that includes kitchen, dining and living room. By a continuous wall of pine, set vertically, the house expresses three of its four façades. This helps it to articulate different patios and isolates the interior from future constructions.

The program for these patios refers to the need to control the prevailing winds. The first patio is developed as an intermediate space for an expansion of the living room area and the second is designed to accommodate the tents of the children who can camp in safety. Between the two patios the access and the parking for two cars are located. The west façade is made up of a series of double glazed vertical windows that run on different rails so they can be grouped one over another. These allow for a complete opening of the living room and a visual connection from the interior patio to the sea.

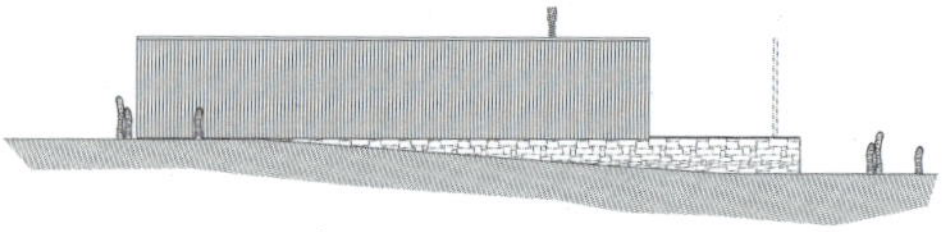

ELEVACION NORTE

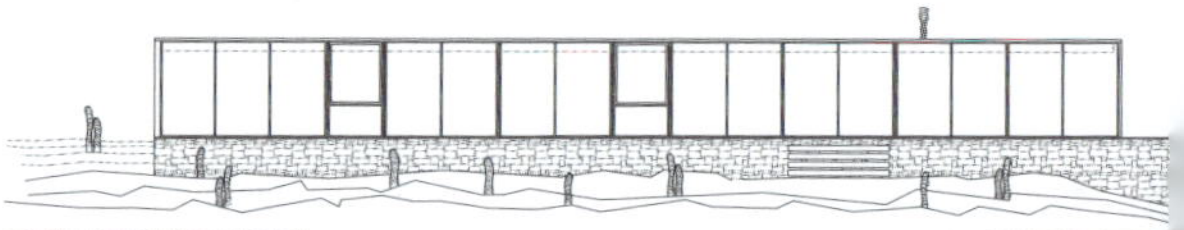

ELEVACION PONIENTE

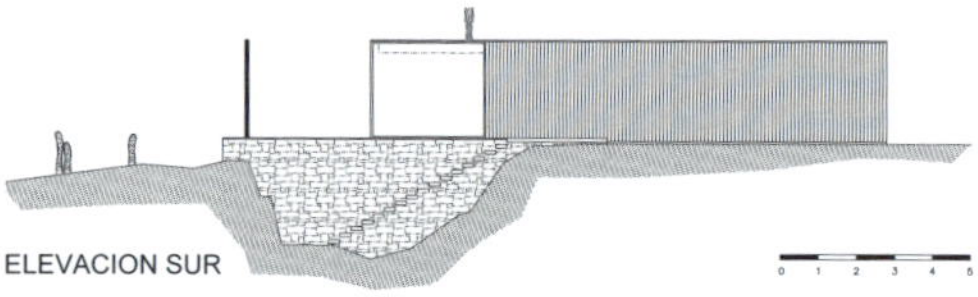

ELEVACION SUR

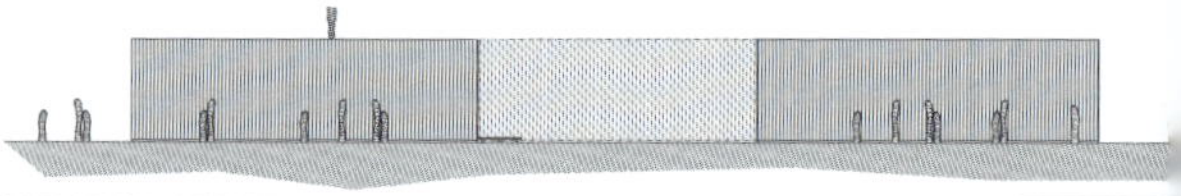

ELEVACION ORIENTE

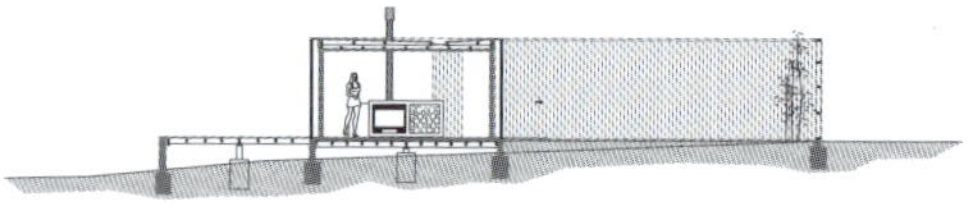

CORTE B - B

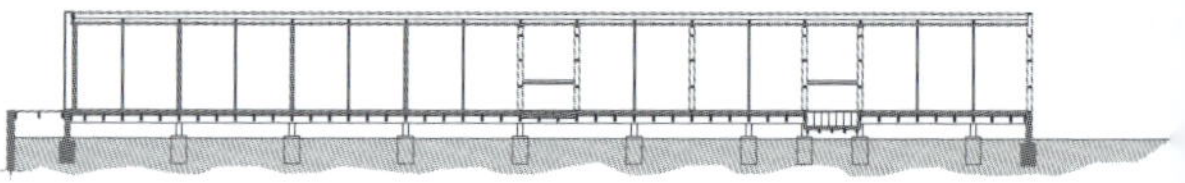

CORTE 1 - 1

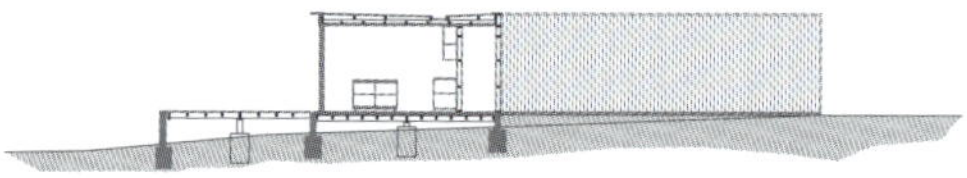

CORTE C - C

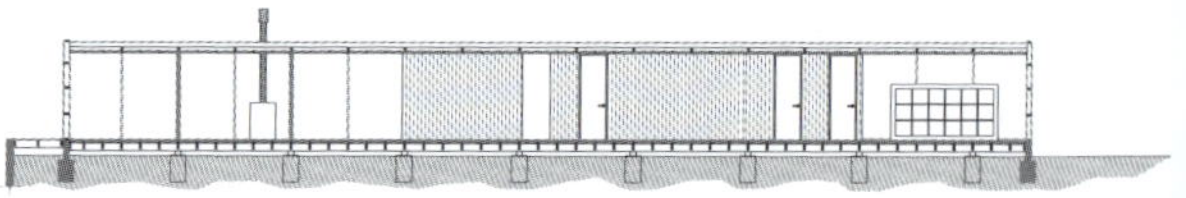

CORTE 2 - 2

Sections

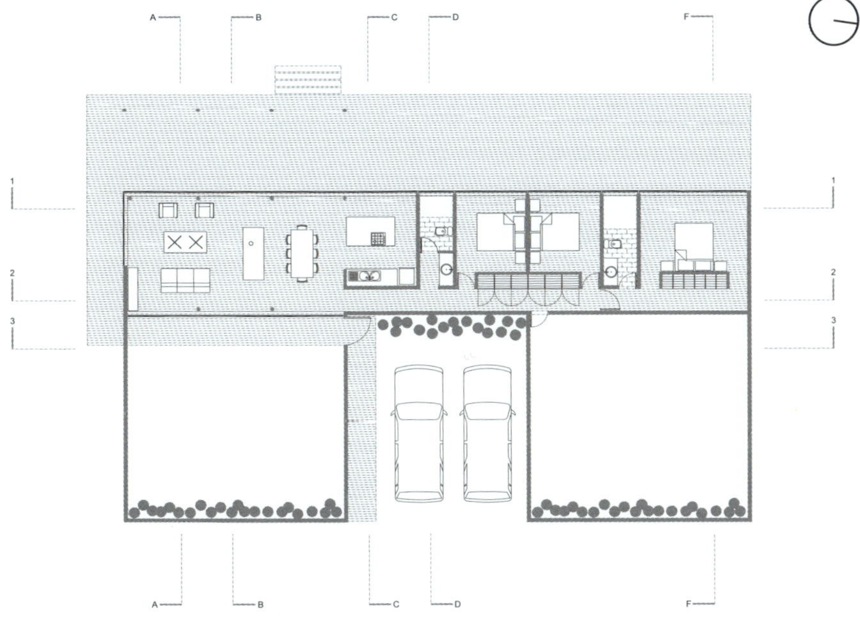

Floor plan

HOSTEL
SALTO DE PENITENTE

g+ Marcelo Gualano - Martín Gualano Architects
Uruguay

Date: 2004
Project: Hostel, Parador Salto del Penitente
Location: Lavalleja, Salto del Penitente, Uruguay
Design team: Gualano-Gualano Architects / Marcelo Gualano + Martin Gualano
Collaborators: Christian Bernhardt, Lorena Díaz, Jorge Epifanio, Ignacio de Souza.
Total floor area: 4,000 SF.

Single notes and words

When we were asked to write about the production in our office, we came up with some notes, in no particular order; just single notes. Words that cross us over and over again, which cross each other and that cross our minds.

N01_Reality

g+, is a Uruguayan architecture office that operates from Montevideo, embedded in the socio-economic and cultural reality that defines us and defines our architecture.
This scenario, from which we operate, has defined to some extent what we think, what we do, and what we can do.

We produce in various fields, from the office and from the university, both areas of creation and production, of constant learning. Two realities that are overlapped and enjoyed the same way.

We take our local reality as a restrictive framework from which to make architecture, instead of seeing it as something negative. We like to see it as an opportunity to develop architecture from these realities and, as a result, provide architecture that is adequate for these places. Austere, responsible, honest, and simple architecture.

Biennials, workshops, conferences, seminars, etc., in which we have participated, have allowed us to meet many architects from the region, with whom we are fellow travelers and from whom we have learned a lot. They give us the certainty that in these southern lands you can make good architecture, and it does not depend at all on technological development.

N02_Interests

Our office has been finding more clear interests as we have been building our projects, participating in architectural competitions, in international meetings, teaching in university workshops, and in many other relevant conditions.

This experience of making things go, this growth, helps you find a friendly territory, where similarities are discovered – whether they are spatial, formal, or functional – and they begin to define some approaches to adopt certain ways of doing things.

And certain themes that are recurrent; some architectures teach us more than others. With those architectures we understand more, we enjoy and we get excited. And we take another look and then start another visit.

N03_Synthesize

It's about finding what is just and necessary, in an effort to find a balance in the decisions to make, in determining the things that will be represented. Nothing more, nothing less.

Program Synthesis. Space Synthesis. Landscape Synthesis. We synthesize the inside and the outside. We filter the landscape data, geography, reality.

Synthesize the demands acting on a project.

We try to find the instruments, movements, devices, parts defining the project strategy, to make it powerful, clear, effective.

Synthesis is what we look for when we define how a building is positioned in the landscape, how clearly it draws a gesture, how it is generated. The project is the synthesis.

N04_Amplify

From simple starting points, specific, schematic, synthetic ones, we try to find possible expansions. Amplify decisions. The time in the buildings; the different scales; the different levels to approach a problem.

On every double click, we try to find new spatiality, new textures. As we approach, we try to find bifurcations and, when making them, discover other ones.

N05_Scales

The buildings are created from different scales. They are made to different scales and each scale has its scale. The skyline has its own. The landscape has its own. The program has its scale. The user has his scale too.

The different scales of approaching the project, pondering scales and distances, parts out of scale, the distortion of scale and the scale to scale.

A bench measures 54 meters long.
A 20x20m platform in a waterfall.
A 80x80m prism in Montevideo's port.
A 60x60m cast is a façade.
We are interested in being able to manipulate, distort and work at different scales, depending sometimes on the distance from the observer, or which scale the building designed for; or its parts.

The building responds to each scale differently, is expressed differently.

N06_Limits

The limit as an abstract concept is almost inherent in architecture; everything is a limit – each line we draw bounds, marks, defines, and divides.

We are interested in the limit as the element capable of being manipulated, softened, stressed. The dotted line, as a blurred line, is still a limit.

An inside that is a bit outside, an inside that ends outside. An 'above,' which is a platform, and a 'below' that is a shadow, that of a building.

A platform, which is a line on the horizon, a plane in the landscape. A level contour, a new place.

A building that is a dotted line, which allows going through, linking both sides; it separates parts of the program and then puts them back together.

A building that is edge, soft edge, active edge. An in-between, between the bench and the pavilion; that stresses a long space

A façade, a light skin, a porous skin, a thick haze, rare, white. It is a limit and a body, and the two of them together, say if I am around or if I am away.

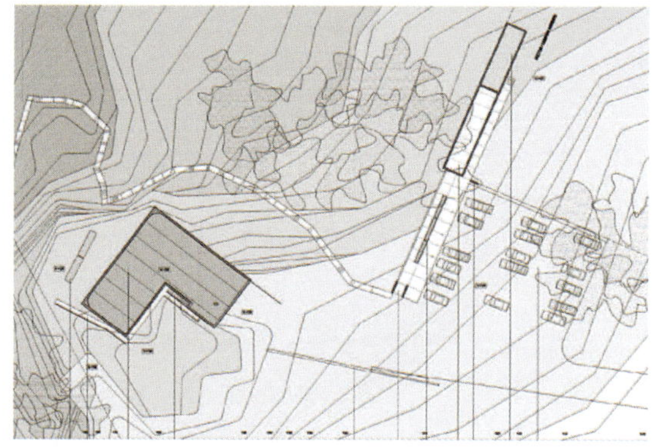

Site Plan

Schemes

The project seen from different angles

ALTOS DE SAN ANTONIO CLUB HOUSE

Dutari - Viale Architecture
Argentina

Date: 2009
Project: Altos de San Antonio Club House
Location: Av. Costanera, Villa Carlos Paz, Córdoba, Argentina.
Design team: Ian Dutari, Santiago Viale
Collaborator: Carlos Paz
Total floor area: 20,150 SF.

The structure, which resolves the program of a Club Spa, is located in the town of Carlos Paz in the Argentine Cordoba hills. Its location in the hills affects the situation that aspires to harmonize the building with views of the hills, generating a windbreak in the central platform. In section, the whole staggers the program organizing functions in relation to the heights.

The upper volume is open to the view and the lower, by using stones, reflects the stony slopes of the hills.

We propose to divide the site into two functioning sectors. The upper level: reception area, cafeteria restaurant, micro-cinema, all-purpose hall, and service area, as well as day care; and in the lower level: gym, spa, covered swimming pool and children's playrooms.

The materials chosen (concrete, natural stone, glass and aluminum) are intended to be low maintenance. The covered surface is 21,693 SF.

The program is organized using two parts: the higher level a semi-cloister opening up to the views and protected from the prevailing winds; the second part on the lower level is formed by an uninterrupted wall, backing the rest of the program adapted to the existing topography.

EL ALTO / La Paz, Bolivia.
2015_Image especially composed for this book by Ana de Brea.

HOUSE IN RIO DE JANEIRO

Angelo Bucci
Brazil

Date: 2008
Project: House
Location: Rio de Janeiro, Brazil
Design team: Angelo Bucci, principal at spbr Architects
Collaborators: Ciro Miguel, João Paulo Meirelles de Faria, Juliana Braga, Suzana Jeque,Tatiana Ozzett
Structural engineer: Jorge Zaven Kurkdjian
Landscape architect: Fernando Magalhães Chacel
Lighting design: Ricardo Heder
Site area: 45,000 SF.
Total floor area: 4,814 SF.

On Top of the Hill

Santa Teresa is a historic neighborhood that offers some great views of the city of Rio de Janeiro. The house is located on one of the highest points of Santa Teresa's hill. From the north side of the house it is possible to see the old downtown from its south side, a more panoramic view of *Pão de Açucar*[1] and the Guanabara Bay. The site starts at 100 meters above sea level at the cable car street and finishes at 125 meters at a breathtaking viewpoint of *Pão de Açucar.*

The project takes into consideration the two pre-existing levels of the pronounced topography: 120 meters and 125 meters above sea level. At the lower level, there is a linear block that leads to the bedrooms and the office. Their main glass façade opens up to the delightful garden on the east side. These two prismatic and linear volumes are opened on the east and west sides but are completely closed on the north and south sides, leaving the ground under them empty. The roof was designed to make a complementary platform on the upper plateau.

1. Reference to the "Sugar Loaf Mountain," a landmark well known in postcards of Rio de Janeiro, Brazil.

The living room is located over the higher plateau, providing a view of downtown on the north side and of the Guanabara Bay and Pão de Açucar on the south. This volume is closed on the east and west sides to avoid sun heat and to emphasize the magnificent views on the other sides. It leaves the level below completely open. Thus, there is a bare level between bedrooms and living room, which is filled by the kitchen, where, according to the traditional Brazilian culture, most people will spend their spare time. It is a spread out and blown-up construction that should become part of Rio de Janeiro's landscape.

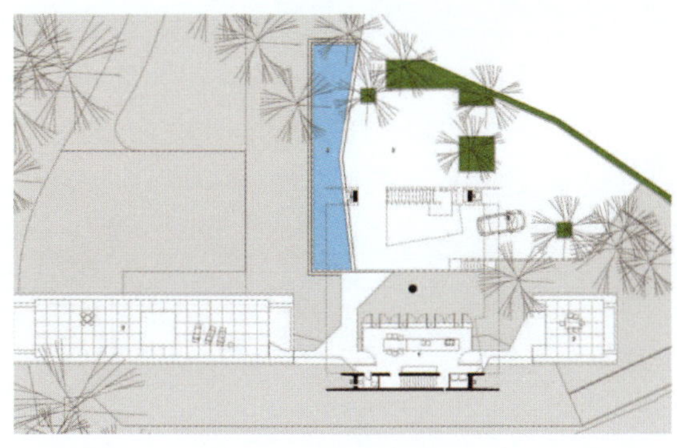

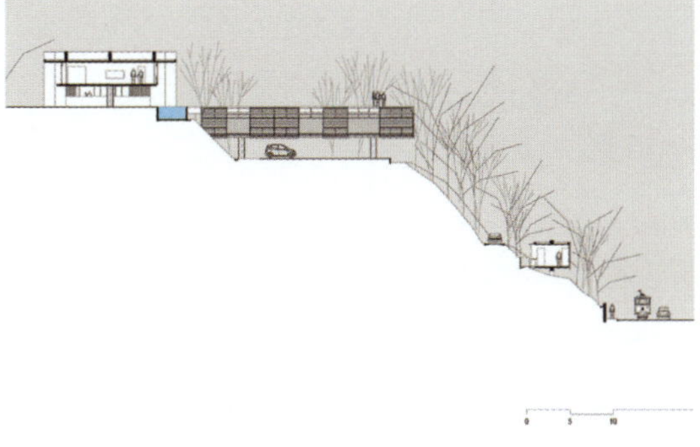

HOUSE IN ROCHA

Claudio Ferrari
Uruguay

Date: 2009
Project: House
Location: Tajamares de la Pedrera, Rocha, Uruguay
Architect: Claudio Ferrarri
Total floor area: 1,290 SF.

First of all, to think about the house involves thinking about the place, and the challenge of temporarily occupying it under the conditions imposed by the surrounding dominant and exotic nature. This is not an urban house; it is located by the beach, near La Pedrera, 145 miles away from Montevideo, in the municipality of Rocha.

The house is used primarily during the summer, taking advantage of its proximity to the sea, which is 2,000 feet away, behind a pine forest. The site is characterized by the typical Uruguayan countryside, where several plots for summerhouses were marked. The lot where the house is situated has a unique particularity: it is crossed by a small hill, covered with native trees and very old scrubs that make up an ecosystem where an important variety of species of animals and plants live. The main challenge was to inhabit the place; it was a question of finding a clearing on the hill and then drawing up the outlines. By introducing a strange and alien object, the site is redefined from its original condition. One of the challenges was not to cut the existing trees, but to include them as a part of the house.

Once the site was outlined, and I could draw a rectangle of 20 by 100 feet on the ground, the construction of the reinforced concrete volume began. The exterior envelope operates as a visual device on the interior spaces and the landscape; the outer box supports an 18'-wide slab and a basement also made of concrete, which rests in the sand of the site.

Finally, the perforated monolithic body is prisoner of the vegetation that begins to invade and reabsorb it into the hill. Time will determine the relationship between the object and nature in an unfair competition between the inert stone and the environment that surrounds it. Intentionally, this is not a home garden, but an interior space within the hill. One could argue without euphemisms that: "There is no house."

The extreme economy of means turns the object into a mere construction where the building is clipped and crossed by a clear light filtered by the trees, the sound of birds and the air from the sea. Ideally, this would be a house without windows, a stereotomic piece.

Consumption Risk | Innovative Production. Collage by Wil Marquez especially done for this publication.

In many parts of the world, the design and vision of cities has become both a contentious battlefield for change and a pathway for new forms of urbanity. Going into the next decade the business and entrepreneurship behind cities will continue to expand with a particular focus on communities – the life-blood of a city's survival. Chihuahua is the twelfth largest city in Mexico, and one of the most industrialized. Manufacturing is very important and there are nine major industrial parks and 79 maquila-manufacturing plants, which employ about 45,000 people. The city serves as an alternative destination for maquiladora operators who require quick access to the border but wish to avoid both the higher costs and higher turnover rates of employment in the immediate border area.

The Desert Workshop

Barclay & Crousse
Lima, Peru & Paris, France

As a usual thing in Latin America, the economic and political reality at that time made us leave our country as soon as we graduated from university. Once in Europe, we grasped the opportunity to acquire, through constant sketching, the visual culture that we lacked and eventually we established a professional practice based in Paris.

The upcoming new century gave us the opportunity to design, from France, three houses that were built in our home country. Without expecting it, these projects gave us both a conceptual and concrete "space of freedom" that, some years later, led us to return to Peru again.

The main advantage that we discovered by working on those projects was that Latin American architects could simultaneously work with sophisticated technology from the industrialized countries and build with a low-tech but quality craftsmanship. That specific position allowed us to propose particular solutions adapted to our environment, without submitting ourselves to the rigid, industrialized building requirements that we constantly had to follow in Europe.

The chronic economic, conceptual and material shortage that our country suffered in the past taught us how to be ingenious so as to reach our architectural objectives with few resources. In Latin America, these resources can be hi-tech or low-tech, sophisticated or basic, or even exist side by side. Those means can be used as freely as one uses a tool, rather than as an imposed necessity.

The past four years have been for us a reunion with our desert landscape. Since our return to Lima in 2006, our projects revealed something we were not expecting: the huge influence that our territory and our landscapes have on our way of thinking and making architecture. We have dedicated these years to exploring the enormous qualities and potentials of conceiving architecture for the Peruvian coastal desert. We developed an "Architectural Laboratory". Each project is nourished by the previous one and establishes new hypotheses, which are later validated or either rejected once the building is achieved and inhabited.

One of the world's most arid territories runs the length of the Peruvian coast. A long thin strip of dusty, dun-coloured desert almost at sea level, inserted between the Andes range and the Pacific Ocean, and a marine current originating from the Antarctic has a moderating effect on an otherwise very hardy climate, producing temperatures which range from 14°C minimum in winter to 29°C maximum in summer, with very little variations between day and night due to a high percentage of humidity. With these conditions, the only real constraint for inhabiting this desert is the protection from tropical sunshine, as the torrential rivers that descend from the Andes provide the possibility of water supply.

Without the need either to protect man from the outdoors or to control outside temperature, architecture acquires such freedom that it becomes a unique opportunity for spatial exploration. However, such freedom can also become a disadvantage due to the lack of criteria for determining the pertinence of the architectural *parti*. To avoid falling into this freedom's vacuum, we consider that the project's essential issues must shift from the need for shelter to the search for a necessary intimacy to inhabit this landscape. This fact becomes more evident in our works on the rural landscape.

Here, architecture has to domesticate the absolute and eternal order of the landscape without denying or betraying it.

The Peruvian desert has been inhabited since remote times, giving us the invaluable lesson of its pre-Columbian, colonial and Republican architectural tradition. Although pre-Columbian architecture and the Spanish Colonial differ in layout (the labyrinth as an archetype of the first one; and the addition of rooms around a void in the second one), their footprint on the landscape provoked certain similar solutions for the desert coast, which gave us the first strategies to approach the problem.

Every period in history attempted to occupy the maximum available area in this narrow strip between the exiguous cultivable space of the coastal valleys and the steep slopes of the Andean buttresses. Even during the colonial urban foundations, the buildings occupied the total footprint of the plot. This was not only a reflection of the Spanish urban grid, but the need to preserve the reduced inhabitable space offered by the desert. This density among the desert vastness remains, regardless of the formal differences, the uses and the customs of its inhabitants. A second factor is the formal abstraction, which resides in the use of thick opaque and geometric masses, horizontal ceilings and the almost absolute absence of details, limited only to the framing of doors and windows.

In our projects, we use these strategies as the foundation for the design. Many of the projects that we have developed since our arrival have always been inserted in small lots. We have opted for the strategy of "maximum occupation" of these areas. We imagine a preexisting prism, defined by the geometry of the plot and the maximum height allowed by regulation, from which conceptual work begins.

We embrace the project carving the prism throughout the design process, "extracting matter" that simultaneously creates and discovers the spaces within. This resembles the way in which the archeologists excavate the sand, discovering the ruins buried by time. This subtractive mode, opposite to the typical additive logic of construction, has to be consequent on all the scales of the project for it to be intelligible and thus be able to characterize the building.

Left page: Desert landscape, Cañete . Above: Desert landscape, Pucusana, Perú.

As a result of this kind of approach, the strategy to articulate the interior spaces within an enclosure arises. Such process determines the ambiguity between interior and exterior spaces, covered or uncovered, which are exacerbated to a maximum. From here, some are qualified by their relationship with the sky or with the surroundings.

Due to the strong earthquakes that often devastate the region, the necessity for a massive masonry adapts to the logic of the carved volume. The "constructive truth" of the building, as well as the use of exposed materials, had to be subordinated to that logic as well. In some cases we decided to apply a unique plaster to the entire construction, as the builders of the pre-Columbian cultures of Wari, Chancay or Chimu did. In other cases, the use of reinforced concrete with rustic forms helps merge the natural topography, architecture and landscape. In these cases, the concept of "skin" in the building disappears, and only the perception of the carved volume is left.

The use of color applied to the plaster reinforces the reading of unity of the carved prism. Using the color palettes (essentially sand and reddish ochre tones) extracted from pre-Columbian textiles and the meager chromatic remains present today in their ruins, we protect our buildings from the relentless "visual aging" produced by the omnipresent dust of the desert that settles in the walls. In the interior, the warm colors disappear, letting the freshness and calmness of white take over.

We also discovered throughout this process that it does not admit any elements external to the subtraction mode. This led us to eliminate every superfluous detail and to reduce to a minimum the range of materials. In many of our works, the difference between the concrete structure and the finished house is almost imperceptible. We reduce, purify forms and details to concentrate and clarify the spatial relationships of the building.

Without the need for shelter, architecture is liberated. The mass and transparency are arranged to give the impression of being in a bigger place. This spatial resilience modulates its properties to create defined living spaces.

The design of space based on the enclosure as a primary device for privacy and retreat is focused in several successive project strategies. In the first place, the space is delimited to be isolated. This delimitation of space is then opened to "capture" the exterior space, enhancing certain characteristics of the landscape that surrounds it. Secondly, the reciprocal connection between the isolated space and the captured space is established. The building is therefore determined as an instrument that induces a dialogue between human being, architecture and landscape, thus redefining their meanings with this action.

Working as a "Projecting Laboratory", the strategies we use are constantly sharpened through the succession of projects. Each one contributes to clarifying our project strategy, which we later apply to the next one. We still don't know the future of this open process, but it helps us define some certainties, which are fed through experimentation on the uncertainties.

Ruinas de Pachacamac, Lima.

Casa Equis. Cañete, Peru, 2003.

Casa M3 . Asia, Peru, 2008.

Museo Paracas. Paracas, Peru, 2009.

Casa M. Cañete, Peru, 2004.

Casas W. Cañete, Peru - 2009.

Lugar de la Memoria. Lima, Peru, 2010.

COVERING FOLK FACTORS

PEOPLE, INDIVIDUALS, "MEN, WOMEN AND CHILDREN", (LIVING) SOULS, INHABITANTS, RESIDENTS, POPULACE, POPULATION, RELATIVES, RELATIONS, FAMILY, NEAREST AND DEAREST, SOCIETY, TRADITIONAL, WIDESPREAD, COMMON, POPULAR, GENERAL, VERNACULAR, CONVENTIONAL, INFORMAL.

Guayaquil [reality + imagination]. Collage
2014_Taylor Henderson, foreign architecture student.

CULIACAN BOTANICAL GARDEN

Tatiana Bilbao

Mexico

Date: 2004-2014
Project: Culiacan Botanical Garden
Location: Culiacán, Sinaloa, Mexico
Master plan and architecture: Tatiana Bilbao, David Vaner, Catia Bilbao
Design team: Tatiana Bilbao S.C.
Collaborators: David Vaner, Israel Alvarez, Mariana Tello, Lina Rúelas, Sebastián Córdova, Carlos Leguizamo, Paola Toriz, Ana Yumbe, Eliza Figueroa, Julieta Sobral de Elía, Roberto Rosales.
Structural engineering: IESSA S.A. DE C.V.
Engineer Javier Ribe
Hydraulic engineering: QM Ingeniería
Engineer Jorge S. Quintana.
Lighting design: Luz en Arquitectura
Architect Kai Diederichsen
Landscape design: TOA Taller de Operaciones Ambientales
Art program and curation: Patrick Charpenel
Site area: 1,092,500 SF
Total floor area: 95,200 SF

Statement

We engage in architecture to raise human quality of life.

We work with our environment, our surrounding materials, hand labor and techniques, opening channels of communication between the various social sectors, and we detonate productive activities that enable different aesthetic experiences with strong ideas and direct definitions and intentions.

We try to understand, through our multicultural and multidisciplinary office, our world – to translate its rigid codes into architecture.

Through these strands, the office, regenerates "humanized" spaces to be aware and react to global capitalism, opening up niches for cultural and economic development.

Creating a climate of collaboration where there are various disciplinary resonances in technical areas, theoretical and artistic works which, in one way or another, believe that they affect the patterns and structures of society.

The office associates work with the theme of resonance, which matches the frequency of a given system with the frequency of an external drive, with certain information generated by another system.

As with the ethics of otherness of Levinas, the office incorporates "the other", which has not been recognized or accepted by the intellectual, political and business oligarchy, which that is on the lookout for a qualitative change and structural life.

In the end, we are building with the responsibility of understanding all that we do and we mean to do. We learn though it and we work with it.

Botanical Garden

Culiacan is a city located in the northwest of Mexico, only 80km from the Pacific Ocean and with a population of over a million inhabitants. The city has had a botanical garden for over 30 years that specializes in tropical plants and has over 750 plant varieties.

Aside from its plant variety, the garden is designed to allow visitors to enjoy different leisure activities such as sports, open-air picnics or a simple ride around to enjoy the landscape.

The Botanical Garden was conceived by its trustee's president with the intention of offering Culiacan's population a new place to learn and improve their quality of life within a contemporary cultural environment.

To achieve this goal, he decided to commission the curator Patrick Cahrpenel and 35 of the most renowned artists to insert pieces of art that can intertwine with the site, society and nature.

Taller de Operaciones Ambientales (TOA) was commissioned to reinforce and balance their botanical collection and to make one of the most important botanical gardens in the country.

Tatiana Bilbao's office was hired to develop a master plan that could integrate landscape and art, including services that could allow this new program to become a landmark within Culiacan and its visitors. Therefore, we developed a pattern that was taken by tracing the branches of a tree that belongs in the garden. Adapting the design to its surroundings, we were able to fulfill a need: a set of buildings such as cultural areas, educational facilities, laboratories, greenhouses, storage and administrative offices with public services.

Educational Facilities

Three separate buildings compose the educational compound in the Botanical Garden in Culiacan. An educational room for kids and teachers, where the kids' workshops will be held, a 100-seat auditorium for any kind of screenings and lectures, and a service building with the restroom facilities.

The complex has three of the 35 pieces of art in the garden, "New Ruins" by Tercerunquinto (2004, Mexican collective), a piece that is made out of the ruins of a building that used to be in the site but was torn down.

"Nestor O Destatuador (Zé Carioca N° 13)" by Rivane Neueschwander (1967, Belo Horizonte, Brazil), an empty comic inside the kids' room that can be filled with any story a person would like to create and a 9 screen projecting a life-like state

"Flores Rojas" from Diana Theater (1962, San Francisco, USA) inside the auditorium room.

Open Auditorium

This small open-air structure in the Botanical Garden was conceived to be the place for 70 people where a 7-minute video tour of the botanical garden will be screened to act as an introduction to the visit. This three-sided space is only covered by the shadow of the surrounding trees to give fresh open air to its users.

Art in the Architecture

a. Pablo Vargas Lugo (1968, Mexico City, Mexico). Estrella Rota [Broken star], 2007
For the bamboo area of the Botanical Garden, the Mexican artist Pablo Vargas Lugo completed one of his signature cement sculptures. Although the piece is completely fused with the landscape, Vargas Lugo tasked himself with emphasizing its artificial elements, incorporating a giant star suspended in the middle of the foliage. Curiously, this heavy mass seems to be both sustained and fragmented by the leaves and bamboo shoots.

b. Dan Graham (1942, Urbana, USA) Concave/Convex Hedge Folly, 2005
Dan Graham, one of the most outstanding conceptual artists since the 1970s, has designed a pavilion formed by three curved walls. One of the walls is shaped by a hedge of fragrant flowers and the others by double mirrors. The pavilion frames a picture of the landscape, while the glass mirrors produce a game of superimposed bodies and sparkles thanks to their refractory and translucent qualities. Since 1970, Dan Graham has worked on pieces that actively involve the spectator, transforming him or her into an essential part of the work.

c. Sofía Táboas (1968, Mexico City) Elevated Platform with Extraterrestrial Purpose, 2008- 2011
Sofía Táboas alludes ironically to certain forms of spiritual, esoteric and mystical experience that have emerged in contemporary society. To construct this piece, she took patterns from the famous geometrical crop circles that are found in many English wheat fields and whose origin is attributed to the work of extraterrestrials, constructing an elevated platform where visitors can take shelter from the elements. The structure invites spectators to enact a specific relationship with the Sinaloan sun and produces a series of enigmatic amber projections that "mutate" over the course of the day, as well as luminous circles at night.

d. Tercerunquinto (Founded in Monterrey, Mexico in 1998 = Julio Castro, 1976 + Gabriel Cázares, 1978 + Rolando Flores, 1975)
Ruinas / Nueva Arquitectura, 2011
The project by Tercerunquinto for the Botanical Garden involves design and landscape architecture, as well as certain sculptural processes. Their work consists of using the waste that was generated during the process of remodeling the garden to form mounds and put them back in their original location. The area may be used by visitors as a space for rest or recreation. It also offers the possibility of provoking reflection on the coexistence of the materials recycled from a ruin with the forms of a new architectural model.

e. Marcos Ramírez Erre (1961, Tijuana, México). Crossroads, 2003
Among other themes, Marcos Ramírez Erre's work explores the point of geopolitical and cultural encounter that is generated between different countries. With Crossroads, Ramírez Erre uses colorful arrows to indicate the direction of different cities and the distances between them and the city of Culiacán, Mexico. On the opposite side of the signs the artist includes sayings and quotes by popular figures, making reference to the respective cities and showing how people confront other cultures.

f. Teresa Margolles (1963, Culiacán, México). Untitled, 2006
Teresa Margolles is known for her polemic work linked to different processes of death. With the furnishings that she created for this garden, the artist makes reference to social grief and to the growing violence in the economic and cultural milieu of today's society and invites the visitors to reflect upon this matter.

g. Olafur Eliasson (1967, Copenhaguen, Denmark). The Flower Archway, 2005
Olafur Eliasson's work explores the relationships between science and aesthetics. For the Culiacan Botanical Garden he created The Flower Archway, a wrought metal pavilion designed from complex

and dynamic geometrical patterns inspired by nature. In this way, Eliasson takes as a point of reference the organic structure of a flower to create a piece that coexists with the garden's vegetation. The steel framework houses five different species of plants with aromatic flowers that intensify the spectator's experience as he or she passes through the pavilion.

h. Richard Long (1945, Bristol, Inglaterra) White Quartz Ellipse, 2000

Richard Long is one of the most notable representatives of land art. His work explores the concepts of place, time and locality. Much of his works consists of leaving small footprints or marks on natural landscapes, making use of rocks, dirt, clay or branches: materials he finds along the way. In White Quartz Ellipse, the artist forms an ellipse out of different-sized pieces of white quartz, which mark the landscape of the Botanical Garden without altering it in a significant way. Long's interest in integrating his work subtly into the environment reveals the possibility of a respectful interaction between man and nature.

i. Jennifer Allora, (1974, Philadelphia, USA) & Guillermo Calzadilla (1971, Habana, Cuba). Untitled, 2008

Working together since 1995, these two artists create complex associations between objects and their possible meanings. The piece found in the Botanical Garden is a sculpture of a woman's leg attached to a tree. The limb peeks out seductively, inviting the spectator to discover that, behind, is hidden a leg without a torso. The wood carving attempts to become an additional branch of the tree, or even a prosthesis on the verge of coming alive.

j. Valeska Soares (1957, Belo Horizonte, Brazil). Whimsies, 2004

Valeska Soares is a key figure in the art scene that came out of Brazil in the 1970s. To complete this architectural work – a sanctuary for contemplation. Soares cleverly incorporated a reflective pool into the landscape. At the end of a long passageway within the construction, we find a tree that shades a perfectly sculpted marble bed. The poetic force of this collection of structural elements is reinforced by the wall of fragrant plants that is raised along the perimeter.

Master plan

Culiacán Botanical Garden_Palm Garden – Pond

Aerial view

Dan Graham

Francis Alys

Allora & Calzadilla

Pablo Vargas Lugo

Marcos Ramirez Erre

Richard Long

Olafur Eliasson

Sofía Táboas

Valeska Soares

Educational area

Open auditorium

Auditorium_ section

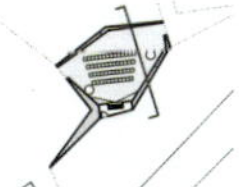

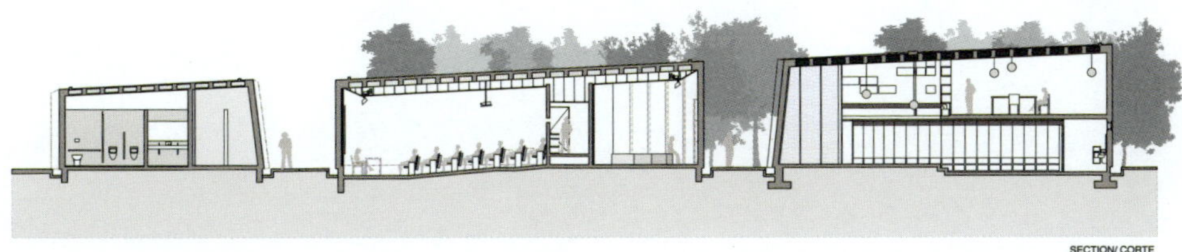

Educational area_ section

Educational space

Multipurpose room

Assembly hall

MAPPING / Participants of CAP Americano Sur, 2004 to present.
2012_ Digital image especially composed for this book by Adam Pruden and Lauren Diaz.

A total of 126 students participated in CAP Americano Sur from 2004 - 2014

NATIONAL PARKS
TWO PROJECTS

Daniel Miranda
Santiago del Estero, Argentina

CULINARY ARGUMENT

Daniel Miranda

One of my favorite pastimes is to cook for pleasure, and from time to time I read culinary literature. Some time ago I ran into "The House of Lucullus, or The Art o Eating", written in 1943 by Julio Camba. This book is an overall review of cooking manners and customs in different countries, mostly European. It is, in brief, the relation between food, flavors, condiments, kitchen practices and culture.

Reading the book, I found it is a true lesson in architecture, shaped fantastically in the paragraph I transcribe: "The true kitchen is a sedentary art, born with the first human settlements, that fished along nearby rivers, collected fruit from natural orchards, and cooked rich and pure food, until the unfortunate invention of cold storage. It was a fortunate period, when people ate but the fruit of their orchard, because, good or bad, that was, for each man, the right food, as natural and specific as maternal milk! In those days, everything was logically related, man, climate, food and landscape, and this relation was the harmony of the old world." [1]

How could this story be a lesson in architecture? Because the refrigerator is to the kitchen as technology is to architecture, where the true challenge is to think of a kitchen "enriched" by cold storage, as well as architecture "enriched" by technology, without losing the natural balance.

The skin will be the exact point of the encounter between accessible technology, resource and necessity; folds will appear just when necessary, origami will be conceptual inspiration and aesthetic non-resource. The result will be to achieve conceptual interpretation and synthesis, for each need and every place, in the complex world of the design.

Thus, architecture will be understandable and explicative, sensible and provocative, modern and with style, solid and ephemeral. Born from reflection, architecture will be able to exist without losing character and to die with dignity.

Two Projects for the Argentinean National Parks
The landscape appears as a great plain with inactive dry rivers – paleolithic channels – "aivales", alternated with forest formations. The precise location of the building is the point where the "aivales" end and the woodlands begin.

The building results from the development of the program, the interpretation of a way of building and as the answer to determinant and unfavorable conditions:
Extremely rigorous climate
Critical resource availability
Strong protection guidelines that limit the interventions in the landscape

The plan is organized along a gallery that connects closed and open programs, in a public-private sequence, characterized as an "alive circulation." In the election of the building material, wood was chosen as the natural resource par excellence.

The construction features a mixed system. Most of the work was carried out in the factory, and the final assembly was done at the site. This reduced the fieldwork carried out inside the park and offered a "clean" building system, always preferred within the *National Parks*.

1 *La Casa de Lúculo*, Julio Camba, 1943

The program is distributed in a system of volumes, placed beneath a double roof that was designed to gather rainwater and store it in a cistern as drinking water. This roofing system also provides shade, to protect the buildings from direct sun radiation, and natural ventilation in the space between both roofs.

The cistern, located beneath the building and part of the structural system of foundations, is also useful to refresh the rooms, by adding humidity with ventilation nozzles.

Following the idea that the construction process also produces environmental damage, the project intends to reduce the construction tasks carried out on the site, in addition to minimizing the visual impact of the building within the natural landscape.

As part of the message of the National Parks administration to the community, the building is architecture detached from the soil, placed upon the ground, seeking minimum invasion, respectful of the site.

The roject in Pobladores, Copo National Park, Province of Santiago del Estero
It was necessary to plan the construction of different buildings within the National Park to lodge diverse programs such as houses, sanitary facilities, an attention center, services for the tourists, headquarters, laboratories, storerooms, among others. The prototype, already tested in the National Park, consisted of the construction of double roofs as ventilation, water collector and supplier of shade. The functional volumes were built under the umbrella of this double roof. The idea was to consolidate a typical image (mark), repetitive and recognizable as the expression of the National Park.

Thus, we refer to the typical scheme of the Roman house, the "impluvium", which admitted the diversity of programs. On the other hand, the composition of the existing soil within the Park was apt to be used as ground cement in the construction.

The need to build rain tanks of a considerable size for the storage of potable water, offered us the possibility of using the soil from the excavation to build the walls.

These buildings proved to have excellent thermal behavior and the reduced cost of construction. The graphic material illustrates different moments in the execution of the work, a unique instant in the history of the landscape, of singular beauty. Besides showing a constructive process, the images express the appropriation of the natural site, in the precise moment of the transformation, which I believe deserves to be recognized in its most pure reality.

One block under construction

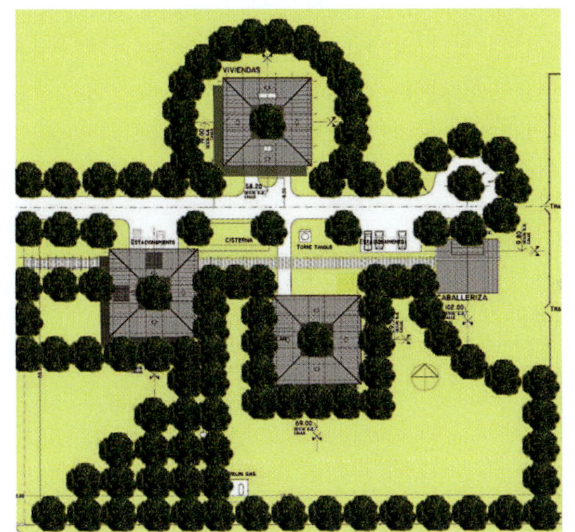
General plan

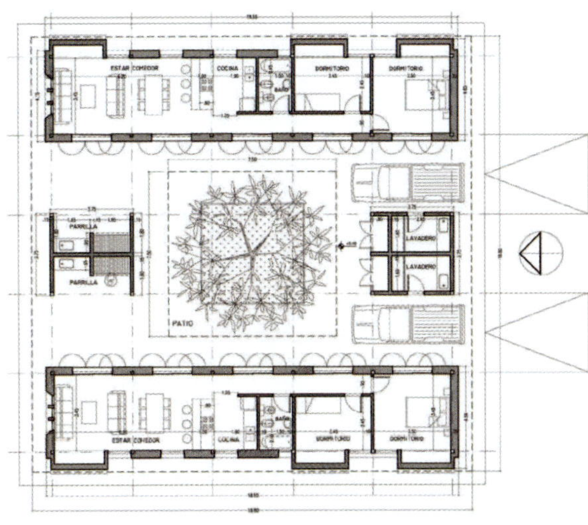
Ground floor housing block

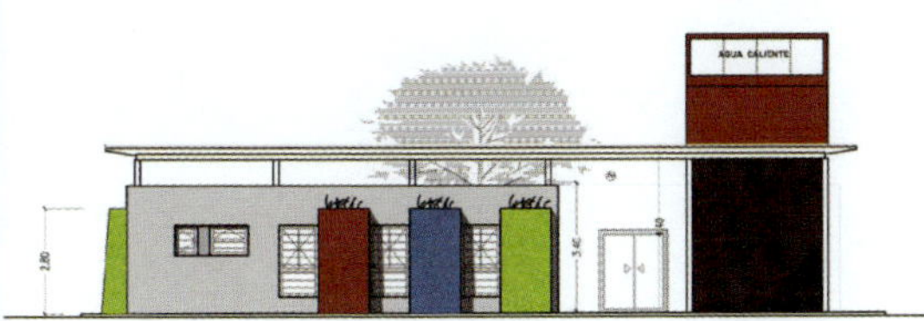

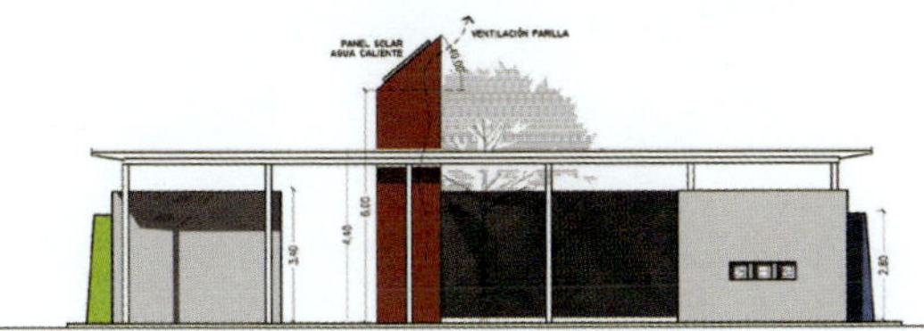

Elevations

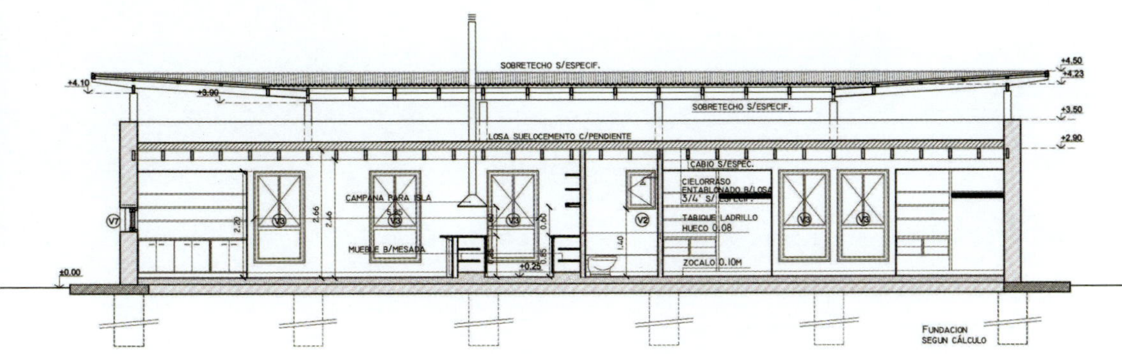

Housing block – section

PARQUE LEZAMA / Neighborhood, San Telmo, Buenos Aires, Argentina.
Photo by Marisela Echeverria.

BOEDO PUBLIC SQUARE

Castillo - Kogan Architects + Leonardo Cabral
Argentina

Date: 2008-2011
Project: Public Square,
Location: Plaza Boedo, Buenos Aires, Argentina
Design team: Castillo Kogan Architects, Paz Castillo and Carolina Kogan, Leonardo Cabral
Collaborators: Mariano Sosa, Eric Chen, Florencia Spina
Total floor area: 130,020 SF.

Mariano Boedo Plaza is located between the following streets: United States, Sanchez de Loria, Carlos Calvo, and Virrey Liniers and has a total surface area of 1.08 ha. Of the total area, 53% is allocated to green areas, trees, shrubs and climbing vines.

In the remaining 47% there is an amphitheater, children's play areas, an area for exhibitions and cultural events, a multi-purpose room, leisure areas and meeting areas. For the multi-purpose room, a section of the existing structure located on Calle Carlos Calvo was preserved and recycled.

The main purpose of the project is to generate recreational areas, which provide not only for daily recreation, but also for the development of cultural activities. That is why the project has different inclines, which structure green areas that are bounded by low walls. This organization provides for laying out spaces with different characteristics and categories, which promotes the development of neighborhood assemblies and festivals, exhibitions, meetings etc. This gives the residents of Barrio de Boedo, San Cristobal, Balvanera and Almagro a space that encourages social and cultural integration.

"EL MANGALETA"

HOUSES TO RENT

Marco Rampulla
Argentina

Date: 2012-2013
Project: Complejo "El Mangaleta" (weekend houses for rent)
Location: Calle Pavón, Lote 14, Villa Icho Cruz, Provincia de Córdoba, Argentina
Author: Marco Rampulla, architect
Structural engineering collaborators: Arch. Fernando Mattiuz, Arch. Gustavo Lozano
Costruction company: Dario Medina
Owner: Eduardo Ciaffoni
Area: 2,580 SF (3x80m^2 c/u) + swimming pool: 450 SF
Total budget: ARS $450.000
Cost m^2: ARS $1700 aprox.

On a sloping field facing the mountainous landscape there are three houses for rent with a swimming pool, which comply with the client's requirements. The buildings' locations respond to a sensible utilization of the slope and the view. The materialization of the houses consists of placing them as emerging "rocks" echoing the natural landscape of the hills, mountains and stones.

On the basis of this analogy, brick is used as a material that is in contact with the soil and that is polished from within to make the houses habitable.

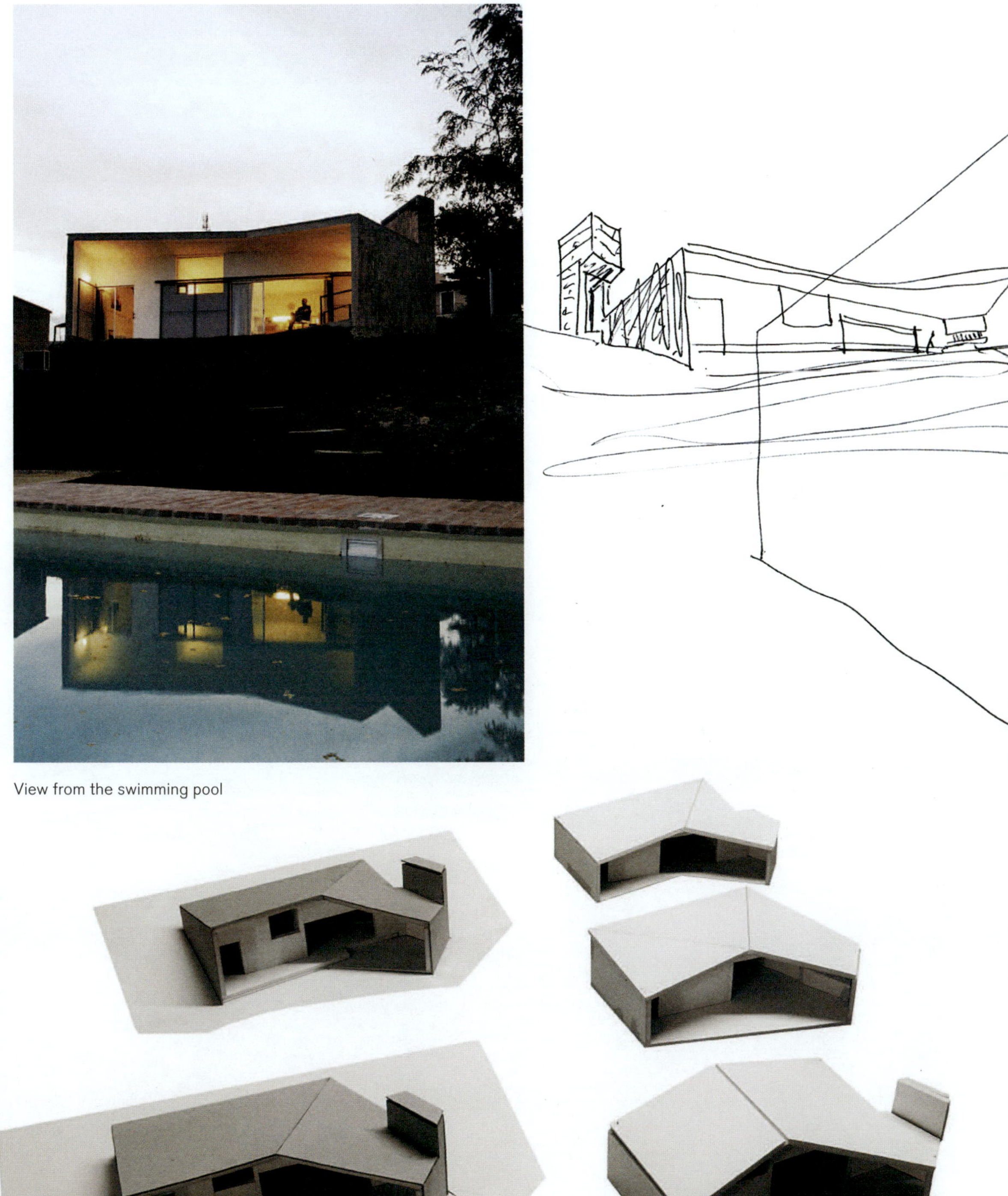

View from the swimming pool

Models

"AMORIR / A place for artistic, aesthetic and political practices".
2007-2008_The alonso+craciun collective, Uruguay.

VOLUMETRIC REASONING

(REVIEWING PHYSICAL FEATURES)

BODY, EXTENT, SUBSTANCE, FIGURE, FRAME, FORM, SKELETON, CARCASS, CIRCLE, ORGANIZATION, SOCIETY, FULLNESS, QUANTITY, PHYSIQUE, GROUP, "MAIN PART OF MUSICAL INSTRUMENT", THICKNESS, PERSON, SOMA, ANATOMY, AMOUNT, COMPANY, TORSO, STRUCTURE, ESSENTIAL, CONTENT, COMPLETE, TANGIBLE MATTER, CORE.

HE KNOWS_ [El Sabe] / Puerto Viejo, Costa Rica, 2008.
2010_ Image especially composed for this book by M. de Brea Dulcich.

Only when the last tree has been cut,
last farm sold; when all the crabs,
oysters caught; the bay poisoned.
Only then will we realize that
WE CANNOT EAT MONEY.©

AYRES STORE

Dieguez Fridman Architects & Associates
Argentina

Date: 2008
Project: Ayres Store
Location: El Salvador 466, Buenos Aires, Argentina
Client: Ayres
Authors: Dieguez Fridman Architects & Associates
Tristán Dieguez, Axel Fridman, Leonardo Buffa,
Maria Carranza, Jazmín Zang, Ana Sol Smud,
Rosario Guiraldes, Belén Gándara
Structural engineer: Sebastián Berdichevsky
Lighting consultant: Pablo Pizarro
Product design: Martin Wolfson, I'Hsiu Chen
Landscape consultant: Cora Burgin
Constructor: Javier Ferreyra Ordoñez, Sering S.A.
Total floor area: 4,000 SF.

The project seeks to reproduce in the interior of the store feelings and sensations generated by urban space: the possibility of surprises, contrasts, unexpected encounters, and changes of perspective. Just like cities are generally perceived in motion, offering multiple surprises along any route, the store changes as people move inside it. Movement is never horizontal or vertical but both at the same time. The specific functions of the – store such as exhibition areas, fitting rooms, counters or storage – are as important as the space that separates them. As happens in urban conditions, relationships between parts are more important than the parts themselves.

The initial concept is a bright white object that unfolds in curved and diagonal lines inside a dark box made out of floor, walls and roof. Materials and geometry define this play of contrasts between smooth and textured, diagonal and orthogonal. Several elements of the store move away from traditional models. The floor is not one plane, but a combination of steps and ramps. The roof is hard to identify between the folds of the ramps that become the ceiling. The fitting rooms form a labyrinth of mirrors where clothes can be seen from unusual angles, turning the experience of trying on clothes into a game that involves shoppers, clothes and space.

Through collaboration with industrial designers and lighting consultants, special elements were designed to display clothes and accessories. The zinc façade adapts to the heights of its turn-of-the-century neighbors, while introducing a new material on the urban landscape of the Palermo district; its diagonal openings are a suggestion of the space behind it and an invitation to explore it.

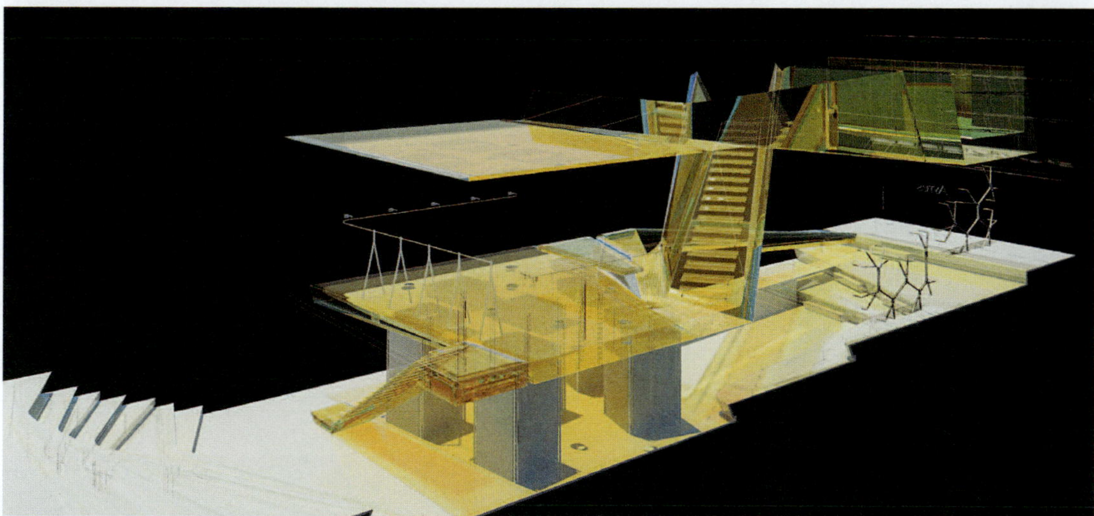

Schemes

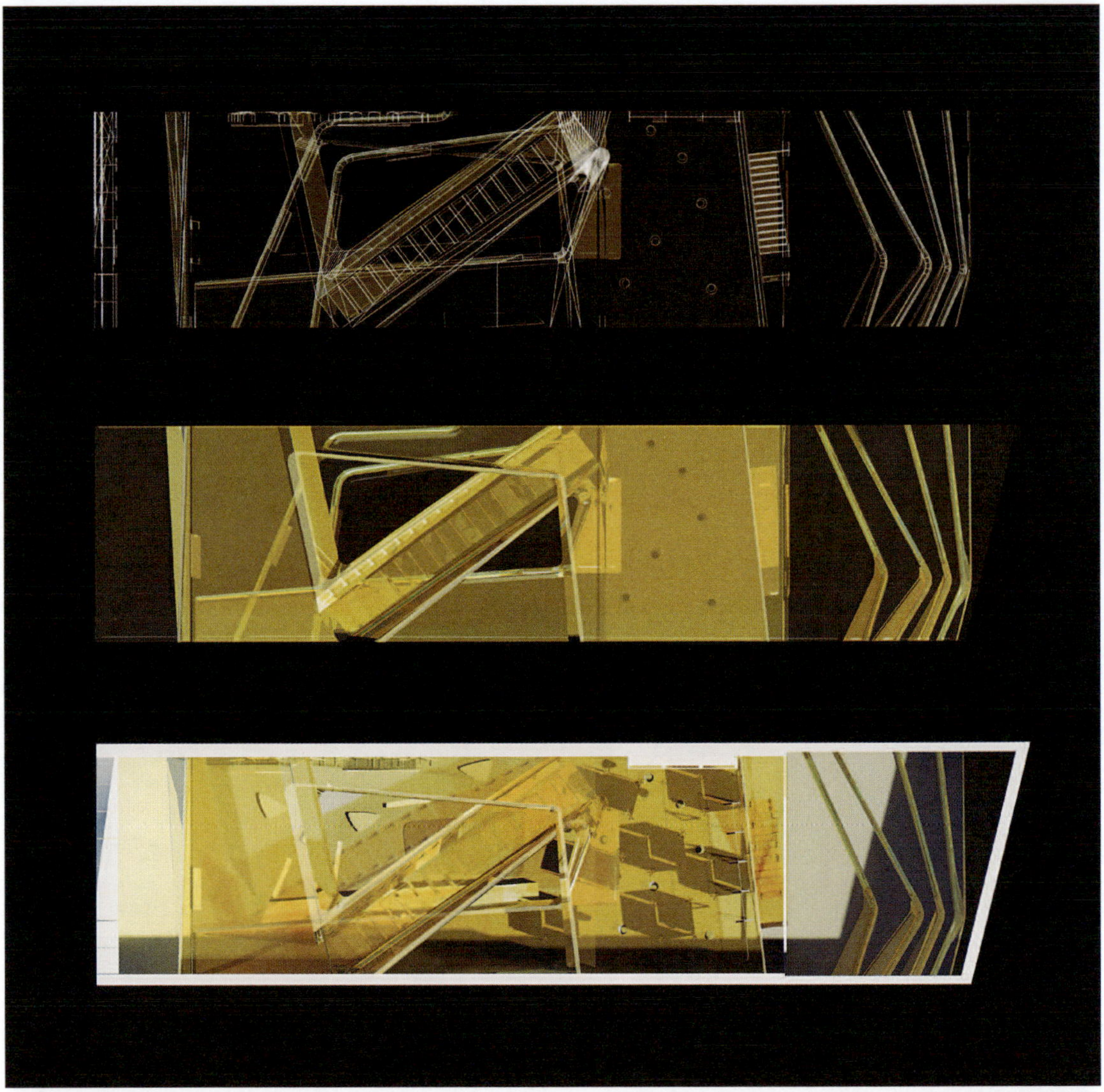

Plans

Interior details

WEAVING GEOMETRIC ANATOMIES – BUILDING ARCHITECTURAL BODIES.
Presentation at the IMA Indianapolis Museum of Art, 2007. Pecha Kucha Volume 4. Team: Erin Carpenter, Greg Josken, and Megan McCornick. 2010_Images especially composed for this book by A. de Brea.

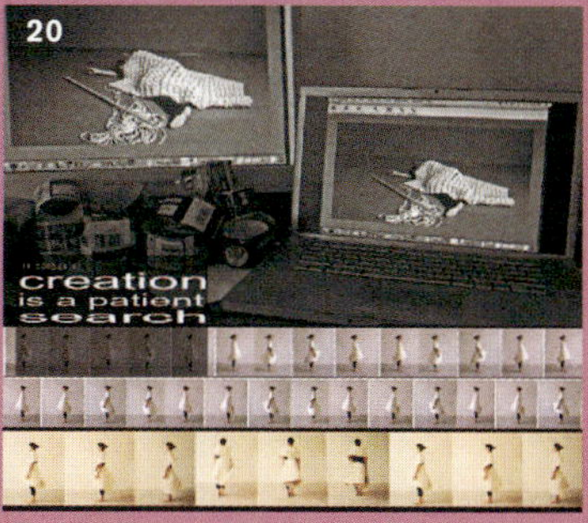

1. Fashion has not always been so unconnected from architecture; the two disciplines have a lot in common, even when they seem to express differences. Architecture is mainly permanent. Fashion is considered temporary, short-term, ephemeral, superficial.

2. Adolph Loos identified architecture with clothing. In his 1898 essay "The Principle of Dressing," Loos recognized the primacy of dress as a basic shelter, challenging architects to first engage with textiles as a method of grasping the meanings and beauty of dwelling.

3. I have been paying attention to significant thinkers related to both disciplines. I was impressed by the work done by many designers and artists. Rem Koolhaas, Frank Gehry, Zaha Hadid, Herzog and de Meuron, Hussein Chalayan, Narciso Rodriguez, Greg Lynn, Kwangho Lee, Gustav Klimt, Mark Newport, Pablo Picasso, Pascal Simon, are just part of a long list.

4. I am in the process of understanding better the matter of existence for both practices: the body. I am also interested in the relationship between weaving (a form-texture by interlacing long threads passing in one direction at the right angle) and geometry (properties of points, lines, surfaces, solids). I always draw my ideas.

5. I am interested in the value of crafting, an activity involving skill in making art pieces by hand. I believe in the making of beauty from a line to a volume, from a plane to (at least) three dimensions. I am exploring the opportunity to record my thoughts directly from making, from producing. I use no more than two needles.

6. I am interested in both protection and shelter. I am interested in the driving forces of intuition and knowledge to transform uniform two-dimensional elements into more elaborated three-dimensional forms. To get to that objective I believe it is important to experience contrasting strategies: draping, weaving, folding, pleating surfaces and materials.

7. Extreme verticality. Notion of gravity. Sensual, curvilinear forms, organic shapes. Or just the opposite. Combination of colors and textures, or solid pigments. Minimalist tendencies. Precision and flexibility. Layers, visceral layers, related to deep inward feelings rather than just to the intellect. All the senses must be involved.

8. Looking at ephemeral qualities of textures, structures, compositions, and forms. Lightness, porosity, immateriality, incorporeal, ethereal, but also tangible, clear, real, somatic, substantial, solid, essential, basic.

9. I am interested in an ongoing exploration of the structural configuration, attributes, and strong power of simple forms and not pretentious materials, but with the main intention of using them to create sophisticated and elegant design.

10. I am interested in details and function. I am interested in an individual fact or item, in the small and specific aspect of a picture and in the big part as well. I consider it important to pay attention to the practical use or purpose in design and to the relationship or expression involving one or more variables.

11. I feel motivated to investigate the physical structure of a person or an animal, including the bones, flesh, and organs. It is appealing to me to analyze and interpret methodically and in detail the proportions, dimensions, and scale of each part of these bodies.

12. Interdisciplinary work. Singers from the American band CocoRosie – sisters Blanca and Sierra Casady – last month in their first visit to Buenos Aires, Argentina, performing with Orilo Blandini – principal of DOMA design, in the traditional Margarita Xirgu theater and wearing some of my knitted work.

13. My most recent work: the two rug-filters and the practical contact with them and the observation of facts and events during a three-hour exploration with three studio students along the White River in Muncie, Indiana. Here you see the two rug/filters as two solid organic stones on the grass, but also their permeable and cellular texture and organization.

14. The translucent aspect of the rug-filters, allowing light to pass through. The structural condition of being permeable. The meaning of a membrane, the notion of an organism. It could be a window, a wall, a screen. It could be a layer or skin of various kinds.

15. The aspect of the rug/filter of also being an organic membrane. A living matter physiologically related to a bodily organ or organs. Here on the grass along the White River.

16. The rug/filters as outdoor installations. The notion of composition. The line and space created by physical nature and the organic aspect of the membranes.

17. The observation of conceptual understanding of scale, the notion of dimension, the meaning of creating physical and invisible space. The idea of freeing architecture from assumptions/presumptions of any kind. There are no formulas but formulations.

18. The playful role of the rugs/filters. The notion of a colorful physical element that can be part of the natural landscape. The intuitive intention of creating a stop sign on the ground for the people that walk or run along the river. A change of direction. A meeting point.

19. A vertical configuration of a circular two-dimensional element. The observation of light and view as well as of use. Contextualizing color and texture, being aware of the faculty by which the body perceives an external stimulus.

20. Both fashion and architecture are grounded in the human body and theories of space, volume, and movement. Each works as protection or filter between the body and the territory. Both disciplines can convey personal, social, and cultural identity.

126 HOUSE

Fernando Fritz - Eric Fritz
Argentina

Date: 2011
Project: 126 House
Location: Nordelta, Tigre, Argentina
Authors: Fernando Fritz & Eric Fritz Architects
Total floor area: 3,000 SF.

The 126 House is a single-family house project that aims to step towards structural experimentation. The design of the structure consists of two building frames and two main beams, where part of the upper floor is hanged allowing for a span between columns of 11 meters. As a result, the entire ground floor is column-free and dynamic.

Front view

Back view

Entrance

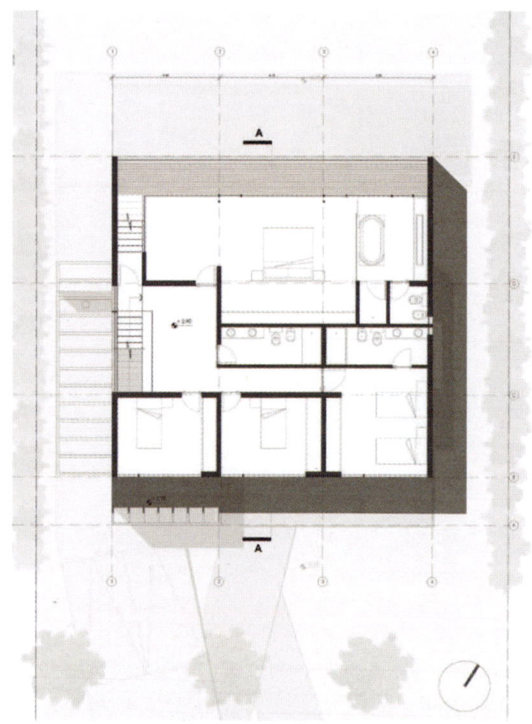

First floor

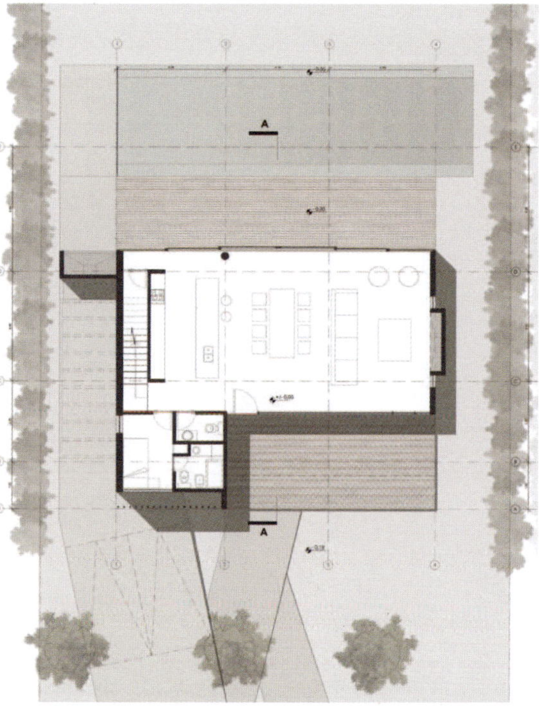

Main floor

South façade

North façade

Swimming pool perspective

Soma and Space:
A SKIN DILEMMA

Andrea Saltzman
Argentina

A didactic road implies taking a stand on how we see the world.

In the academic universe, the basic paradigm for the development of knowledge comes from science. This model is based on certainty, demonstrability, objectivity and rationality. This concept has conditioned all areas of knowledge, as well as how we rationalize, conceive and teach our discipline.

As a result, intuitive knowledge, poetic vision, perception, use of the body as a vital element in learning, has to a certain point been disqualified.

Philosophical rationalism reconstructs the world on the basis of its own categories, dissociating itself from the world we live in. "Our world" is accessible from our senses; the world of science – the "real world" – is only accessible by intelligence. According to the French anthropologist, David Le Breton, it's because of this perception that "Man's sensibility and imagination is seen as a source of confusion. From here onwards, reason imposes an abstract truth opposed to sensory evidences. To access the truth we have to set aside the knowledge provided by our body and imagination."
Thus, the duality between body and mind is radically established. At the same time, the body is dissociated from our worldly experience.

This is a difficult legacy for a design discipline.

How can we envisage space and body with this paradigm in mind?

I started questioning myself when I had to translate my formation in the field of architecture to that of apparel design. Garments present us with a particular issue: the dress, as its name implies, is born from a relationship. The dress "dresses" and, at the same time, "modifies" the body giving form to the surrounding spatiality.

In contrast with architecture, this element has no proper structure. It's through the body that it achieves form. A dress without a body can fulfill other missions, but loses its essence.

As the social beings we are, we recognize ourselves by our dressed bodies.
A garment's main attraction is its capacity to mediate. In spite of its proximity to the anatomy, it gives rise to extremely complex spatial relationships, giving expression to what the world perceives.

What's public and what's private is present in minimal dimensions. Also what's inside and outside, as well as what we feel and transmit. An indissoluble relationship is established between body and context.

We cannot design a dress without relating to a body. That body does not only supply an anatomic support or morphological organization, since it is also fundamentally alive.

This intellectual framework does not agree with my experience as a student of architecture. Even when the teaching defined functions like sleeping, eating, living, as the starting point, functions were not conceived in relation to a body being present. When these functions were considered, they were seen from a mechanical perspective. The relationship with space was exclusively dimensional. It's not by chance that one of the most used texts was Neufert's exhaustive ergonomic research on the space in which we live.

Ergonomics is one of the most researched and legitimized approaches to design. However, it's more related to robotics than to living and perceiving.

There are no bodies to be seen in architectural journals, we will only find them to give a comprehension of scale. We must emphasize that, in general, in the presentation of the architectural design there is an absence of aspects that refer us to perception, with the exclusion of what is visual: fragrances and sounds never have the possibility of being present in a project. We also don't work with the surroundings and our capacity to change its spatial positioning. With the exception of what is visual, architecture in general has been thought about as something static, with the capacity to contain and isolate.

From this perspective, space seems like something somehow removed from the subject, nearer to the realm of dimension and construction than to living.

According to the Finish architect, Juhani Pallasmaa (*The Eyes on the Skin*): "Modern architectural projects shelter the intellect and the eye, but leave in the open the body and the rest of the senses".

This rupture between body and space refers to a way of conceiving the body. David Le Breton states: "The modern conception of the body implies man's separation from the cosmos and humanity. This involves the passage from a communitarian society to an individualistic one, where the body is the frontier with other individuals and even oneself. As if the body was something differentiated from being."

With this conflict as an initial issue, I decided to rethink my relation with architecture. I decided to approach public space from the garment as a first skin, connecting the successive spaces. This statement motivated a series of Workshops in different Latin American universities with the concept of design as skin and mediation. The notion of skin refers to making contact and continuity. From this perspective it's not possible to break the relationship between body and space, thus between the subject and the world. The skin is the frontier with which we make contact. We only perceive this frontier when we enter in contact with something or somebody. Contact makes us remember our exteriority, a frontier in incessant movement that provides the individual with the sensation of existence. Touching is the limit between our surrounding and us. The sway of this imprecise limit gives birth to identity, contention and bond. What's most interesting about this limit is its vitality, its capacity to recreate itself as well as the universe. It is a personal and collective experience that implies a community.

The results of these experiences have been highly stimulating with regard to the objectives established: to draw architecture near to everyday life, that is to life itself; to substitute the notion of frontier and rupture for border, gathering, tie and interaction; as a way of reconstructing the bonds of public space and social framework to alleviate social tensions. This is today one of the main challenges in Latin American cities.

Bibliography:

Antropología del Cuerpo y la Modernidad. David Le Breton, Ed. Nueva Visión, 2006. Original title: Antropologie du Corps et Modernité, Press Univertaires de France, 1990.

El Sabor del Mundo: Una Antropología de los Sentidos. David Le Breton, Ed. Nueva Visiòn, 2007. Original title: Le Saveur du Monde: Une Anthropologie des sens, Éditions Métailié, Paris, 2006

Los Ojos de la Piel: la Arquitectura y los Sentidos [The Eyes of the Skin]. Juhani Pallasmaa, Ed. Gustavo Gili, 2006.

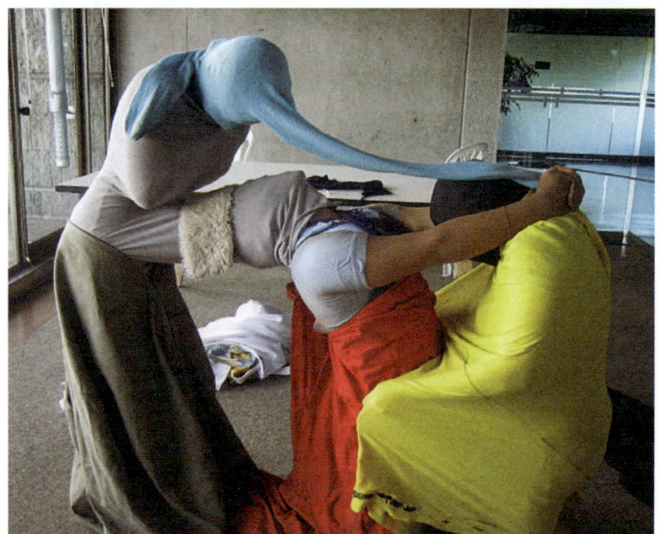

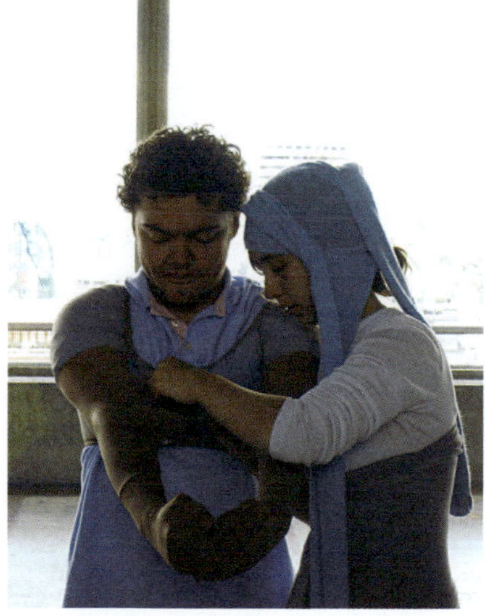

Image of the workshop Urban Skin developed at Universidad Javeriana in Bogotá, 2008 for Pei International Program: students' design explorations with clothing, involving spatial notions about the boundaries between self, you, them, us.

Dress for tree and body / Experimental design – Andrea Saltzman / Diana Cabeza / Joaquín Ardissone / Martín Huberman Architects – Buenos Aires, 2009

Images of the workshop Urban Skin developed at Universidad Javeriana in Bogotá, 2008 for the Pei International Program: Work on the transformation of space from the skin concept. Intervention with straws.

Entre Arboles [In Between Trees]. Exhibited at Casa FOA 2009 – Andrea Saltzman / Diana Cabeza / Joaquin Ardissone / Martin Huberman Architects. Buenos Aires, 2009

BODY / BODIES - Mar del Sur, 2015.
2015 _ Image especially composed for this book by Gustavo Suarez + Juan Andres Colicheo.

LISBOA 7
APARTMENT BUILDING

AT103
Mexico

Date: 2011
Project: Lisboa 7, Apartment Building
Location: Mexico City
Architecture: AT103, Francisco Pardo and Julio Amezcua
Design team: Margarita Flores, Tanya Martinez, Hanni Paz, Tiberio Wallentin, Jorge Vázquez, Arturo Peninche
Total floor area: 27,000 SF.

Mexico City's most important avenue, Reforma, is undergoing major changes of density including: Luxury apartments, retail and office spaces. The question is, what happens with what's left behind? The adjacent blocks in the different neighborhoods will be affected by these new developments and will act naturally as service areas for this new corridor. In order to avoid massive gentrification in the area and to take advantage of the empty sites left from the earthquakes, it is important to develop low and middle income housing as a counter balance to Reform's developments and avoid long commutes for people with lower incomes that work in this new area. These blocks have to serve as a symbiotic system all together, feeding from each other and not competing.

Our Project was able to identify a series of design variables that permit the housing to gain value over time and allow it to become part of the existing social fabric. We developed a dense building that is designed by cutting the maximum density allowed into six volumes. Each volume is 3.6 meters wide plus a 4-meter separation in between, which allowed each space to have cross ventilation and light. All the living spaces face west; the east side is closed almost entirely to have privacy between the units. When working with dense housing, the quality of the spaces is very important: natural light, ventilation and views when possible. The east elevation of each volume is a vertical garden to allow views for all the units.

The project has 60 modules; each has 36 square meters (the minimum area for housing in Mexico). In this exercise we incorporate a mix of different modular units, from 36 sqm (1 module) to 144 sqm (4 modules) giving the opportunity to include bank credits for minimal housing for workers. The building has 5 levels with only 2 corridors, on the 2nd and 4th floor, the units are accessed on the same floor, and each unit has 1 to 3 floors interiorly, understanding this more as a little house rather than an apartment. Each module has an open plan and a service area for either kitchen or bathroom that could be programmed as needed. The materials are basic construction materials with no further finishes, cinder block and exposed concrete for the structure.

CORTE 01

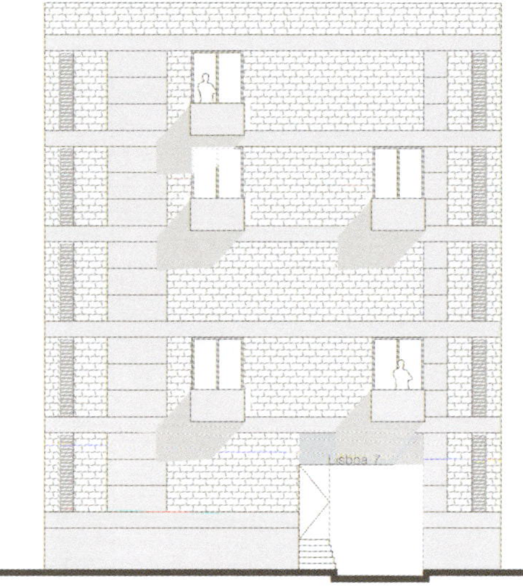

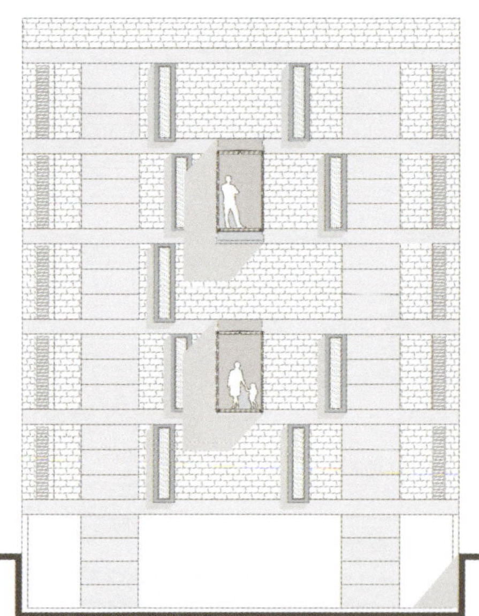

AVE FENIX FIRE STATION

AT103
Mexico

Date: 2007
Project: Ave Fenix Fire Station
Location: Mexico City
Architecture: AT103: Julio Amezcua and Francisco Pardo, Bernardo Gómez Pimienta, Hugo Sánchez
Team: Tiberio Wallentin, Jorge Vázquez, Margarita Flores, Daniel Ramírez
Collaborators: GLM
Contractor: Sare, Hermeregildo Acoltzin
Total floor area: 45,000 SF.

The English writer Thomas Quincy talked in his classic (Confessions of an English Opium-Eater) of the pleasure that, after making sure all possible victims and risk were absent, a burning building can provide. One century later, Austrian pyromaniacs from Coop Himmelb(l)au used fire as a material in their firsts architectural interventions, and the Swiss architect Bernard Tschumi theorized, radically, architecture that produced a pyrotechnical pleasure as useful, he stated, as 'lighting matches'.

Reality, tragic in itself, provides us with less extreme pleasures than those written by the confessed opium eater Englishman and the neo avant-garde European architects, but probably more useful. Without avoiding some justice symbolism, state and municipal officials in Mexico City have decided to build, in the same site left by a terrible fire that left behind no good memories, a fire station. They have also wisely selected the project through an invitation-only competition. To that symbolic gesture we have to add the usefulness of intervening on *Insurgentes Avenue*, one of Mexico City's most important, with urban facilities that, again – after many years of, in the best of cases, aesthetic neglect – have been proposed as a contemporary architectural gesture that is conscious of its conditions and its possible effects.

Due to the site's conditions and the program, which includes – in addition to the fire station – a space meant for capacitating and consulting for the general public, the chosen project for the station presents itself to the exterior like a simple elevated box that almost disappears behind a façade that appropriates its context in a game of reflections, floating over the maneuver and tank-truck area. The latter area extends towards the street or, in an inverse reading, incorporates the urban space while generating it throughout the analyses of the trucks' movements.

Inside the chromed box, both uses alternate and complement each other, organizing themselves through planes with perforations that vary in size, providing light sources as well as communication between floor levels, plus the classic steel poles the firemen slide down during an emergency. That way, making them share space thanks to the crossed sights in the patios, but without mixing them, the proposed solution manages to intertwine both uses – the station and the curiously named 'bomberoteca' (library for fire men) – also connecting them, thanks to the height of the first level, to the street and whatever happens there. Once the fire station is built, and emergency calls will begin coming in and, with less guilty pleasure than the one Thomas Quincy had watching a burning house, we will observe with delight the complete and complex performance of this urban piece that takes the most-needed urban facility as a theme for reflection and architectural action.

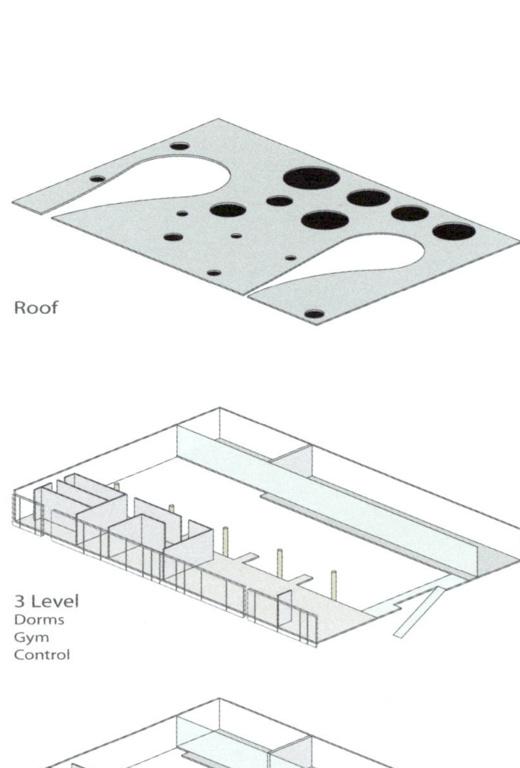

Roof

3 Level
Dorms
Gym
Control

2 Level
Dorms
Class Rooms

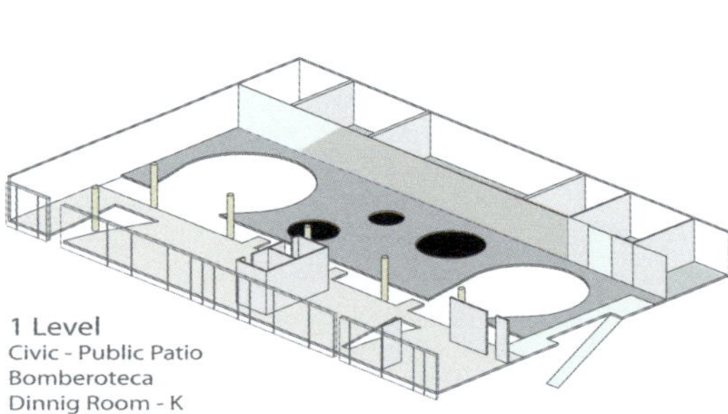

1 Level
Civic - Public Patio
Bomberoteca
Dinnig Room - K

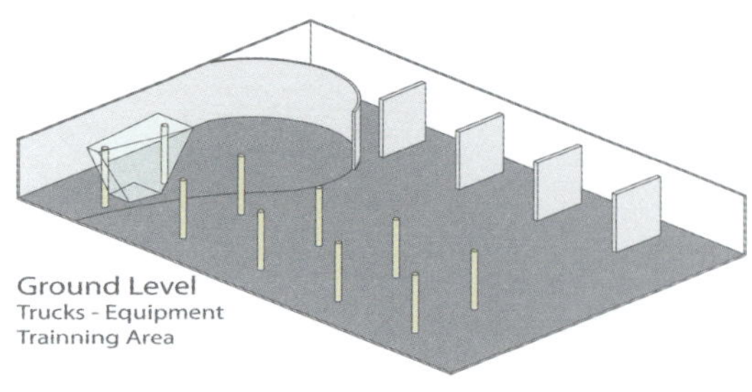

Ground Level
Trucks - Equipment
Trainning Area

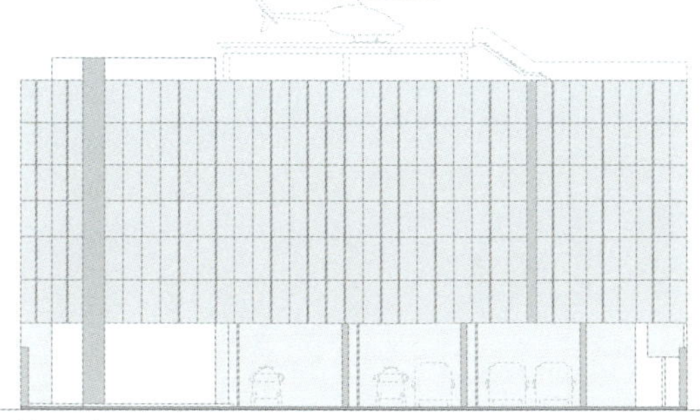

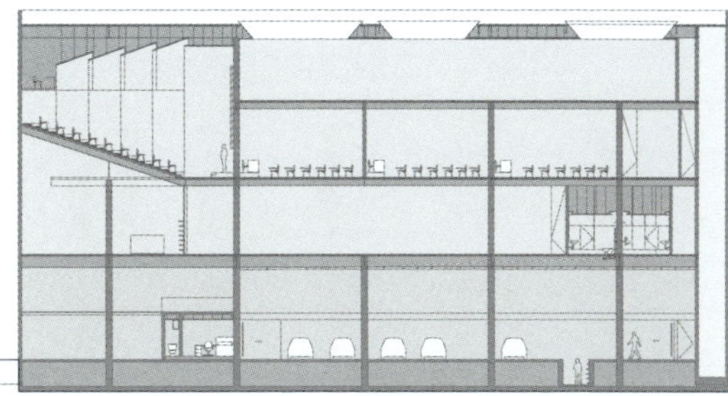

Libretto Latin
arquitectura

Book-Exhibit at the Recoleta Cultural Center [Sept 21 – Oct 20, 2013] Buenos Aires, Argentina by Ana de Brea. Collaborators in Buenos Aires: architects and professors Alejandro Stoberl + Fernando Fritz. Collaborators in the USA: students Abe Arregui + Sasha Mballa-Ekobena. The show was part of the international exhibitions at the BA13 XIV Buenos Aires International Biennale of Architecture directed by architect and professor Carlos Sallaberry, and coordinated by architect Enrique Cordeyro.

to Latinoamericano
tecturas siglo 21

Libretto Latinoamericano
arquitecturas siglo 21

Libretto Latinoamericano
arquitecturas siglo 21

Libretto Latinoamericano
arquitecturas siglo 21

NESTLÉ CHOCOLATE MUSEUM

Michel Rojkind
Mexico

Date: 2007
Project: Nestle Chocolate Museum
Location: Toluca, State of Mexico
Architecture: Rojkind Architects / Michel Rojkind [Design Principal]
Program: Cultural and educational
Project team: Agustín Pereyra (Project Leader), Mauricio García-Noriega, Moritz Melchert, Juan Carlos Vidals, Paulina Goycoolea, Daniel Dusoswa, Matthew Lohden
3D massing: Juan Carlos Vidals
Traqs: Luis Araiza, Jesús Gonzáles, Agustín Villegas
Efficiency factor: Fermín Espinosa, Francisco Espinosa, Carlos Juárez, Ricardo Brito, Francisco Villeda, Ana Isabel Morales, and Verónica Jaimes
Structural engineer: MONCAD (Jorge Cadena)
Lighting design: Noriega Architectonic Illuminators (Ricardo Noriega), Fernando Gonzáles
Landscape design: Ambiente Arquitectos y Asociados, [Fritz Sigg, Juan Guerra], Erick Flores
Total floor area: 6,340 SF.

What might seem like a capricious form is the fruit of diligent design explorations and an intuition about what the place should express. A playful folding shape that is evocative for kids, of an origami shaped bird, or maybe a spaceship, or could it be an "alebrije"? The spectacular result is as firm as the faceted shapes which sustain it.

THE RED ALEBRIJE

Miquel Adrià

Architecture as an experience. Sensory architecture, experienced through the architectural tour, through the surprises, the turns and the bends. Architecture as a challenge. The forms and spaces contained, as well as the times, are pushed to the limit. Complexity and record time: three months to design and build. Dramatic and expansive architecture that reflects the frozen instant of trains crashing in the air.

Located over the side lane of the highway in the entrance to Toluca, at the edge of a 300-meter-long insubstantial industrial installation that used to pass unnoticed, the new object appears with the spectacular nature of a window display. Halfway between Mathias Goeritz's "The Snake" and Munch's "The Scream", this zigzagging origami rises from the garden level and becomes the entrance to a magical world, to the tour of the chocolate factory that rivals Tim Burton's imagination.

The six hundred square meters of new construction standing over the garden house: a reception area; a theater that prepares young visitors for the trip to the world of chocolate; the entry to the existing tunnel that circles around the production areas in the inside of the factory; and the chocolate and gadget store at the end of the tour.

And so, a back staircase engulfs the groups of scholars with a trumpeted and faceted prism. The triangles of the unfolding kaleidoscope are made out of different shades of white to accentuate the different planes. The lobby opens up over an insipid view of high-voltage cables, billboards and highway to give way to the groups of visitors between the information desk and the chocolate-bar shaped sofas. The theater in this little EPCOT encloses the visitors for a few minutes to introduce them virtually into the liquid world of candy. From there, the tour begins through the corridors, tunnels and observation decks over the halls of the factory. Before leaving, a store invites us to perpetuate the moment with objects to take home and thrones that transform us into royalty for an instant. This urban-scale toy invites us on an emotional tour. The new *alebrije*, red on the outside and white on the inside – made from urgent origami, bursts out like a unique icon in the Tolucan periphery.

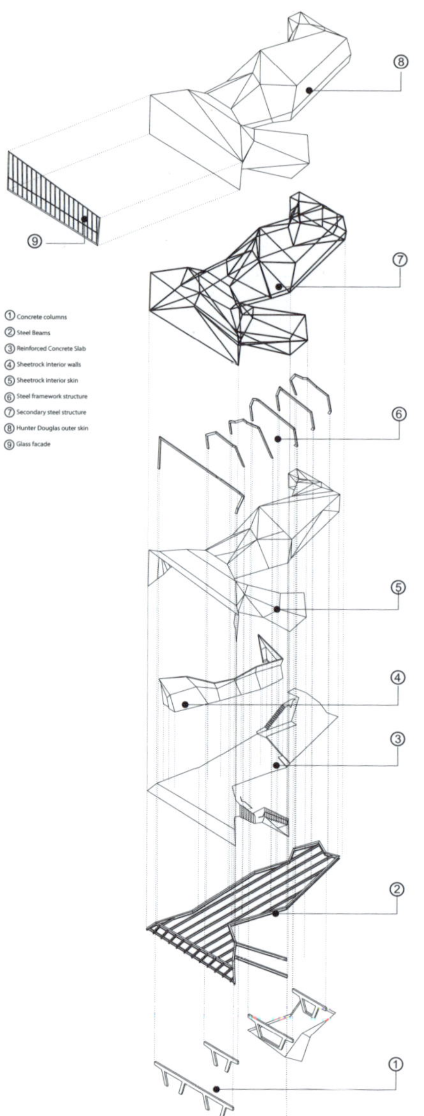

Composition of the volume

Ⓐ East View

Ⓑ North View

Ⓒ South View

Ⓓ West View

Ⓐ

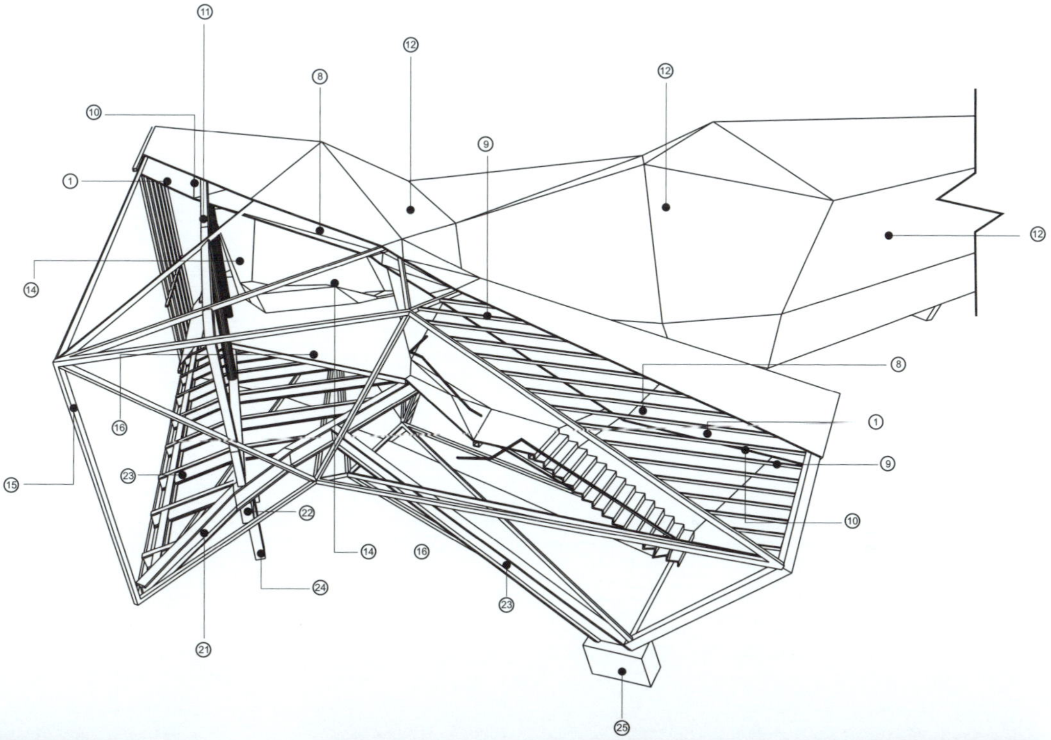

Construction process

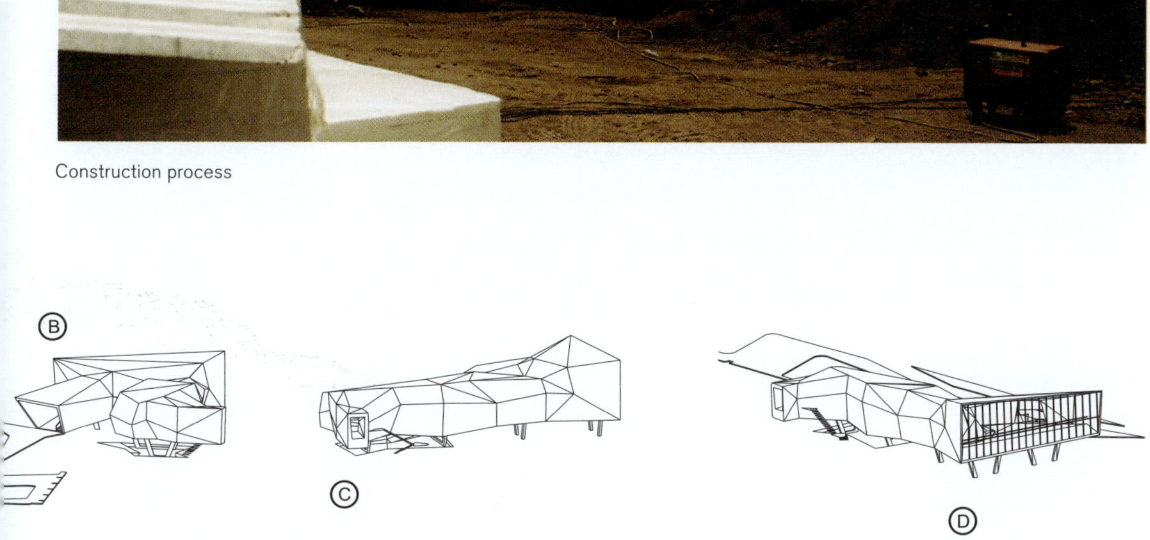

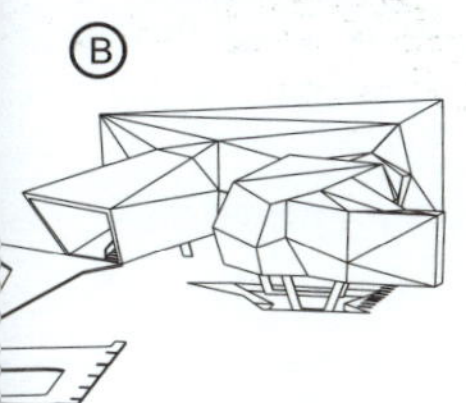

B

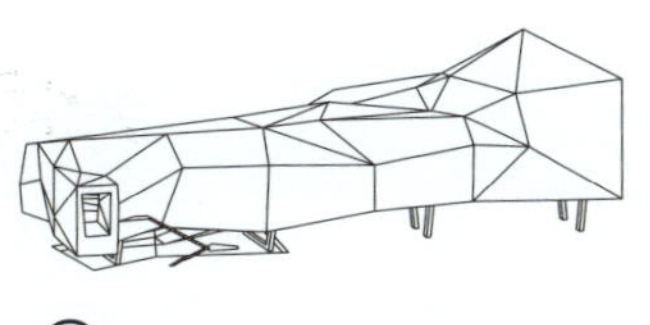

C

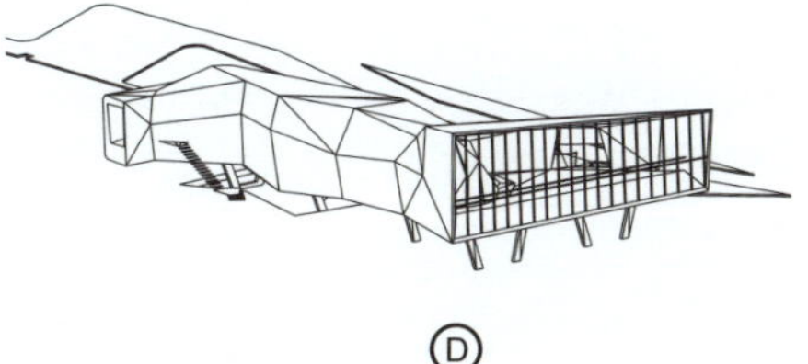

D

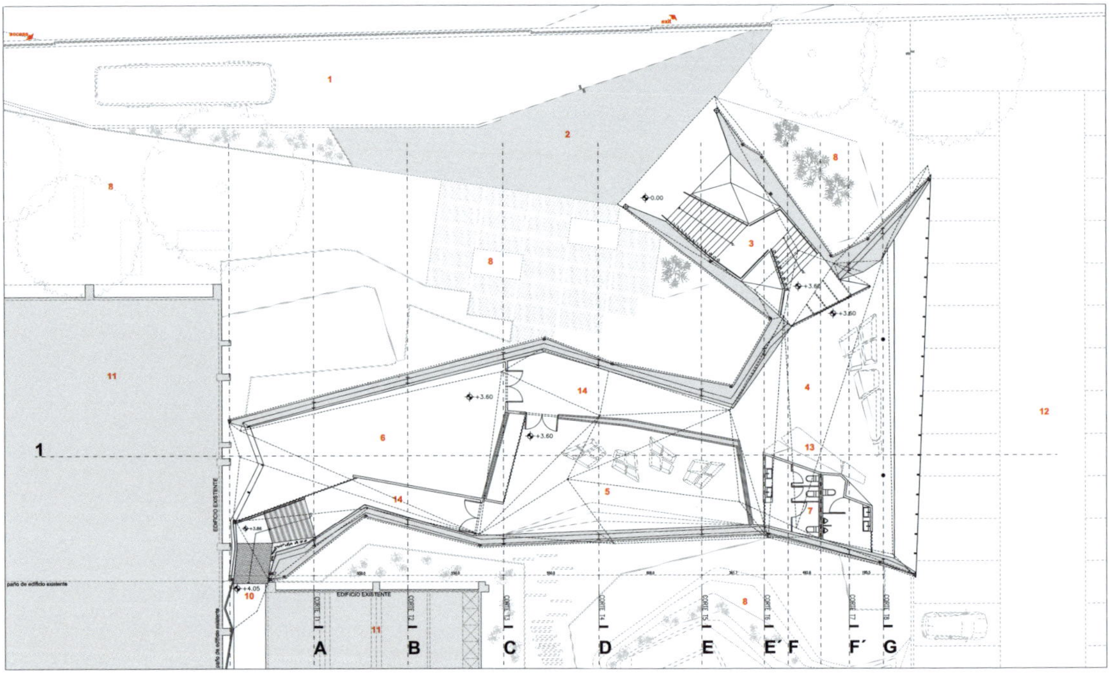

Nestlé

0 1 2 3 4 5 10

first floor plan

1 motor lobby
2 drop off
3 acces
4 lobby
5 auditorium
6 museum shop
7 restrooms
8 landscaping
10 acces to tunnel
11 existing chocolate factory
12 employee parking
13 reception
14 hallway

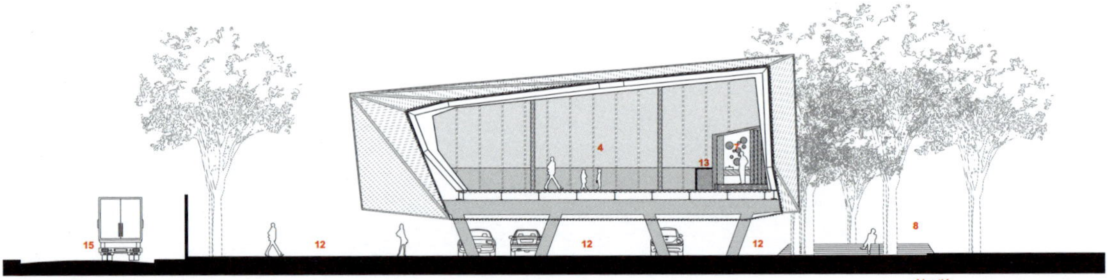

4 lobby
7 restrooms
8 landscaping
12 employee parking
13 reception
15 Leonardo DaVinci street

Nestlé

1 2 3 4 5

section T7

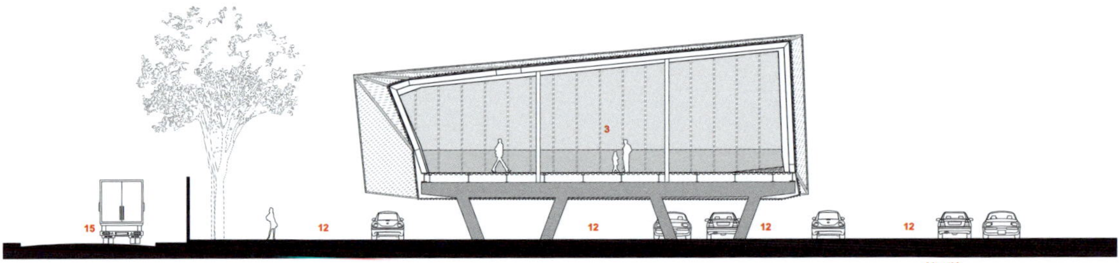

4 lobby
12 employee parking
15 Leonardo DaVinci street

Nestlé

1 2 3 4 5

section T8

Rojkind Architects

Kuwait Cultural and Educational Center, 2006

Falcon Headquarters, 2004

PR34 House, 2003

From top to bottom, left to right: 'Shelter' Installation artwork at Magneet festival, Amsterdam, Netherlands, September 2013. Artwork & Photograph by María de Brea
"Textile hunters," Art-Installation at CBK, during Museum Nacht, Amsterdam Netherlands, 2014. Artwork: Caroline Lindo and María de Brea. Photograph: Parcifal Werkman
"Indolent [1]. Fashioning [plastic] into," Functional-art/Settee by A.deBrea with students Emily Zizelman and Maya Bird-Murphy exhibited at Muncie Makes Lab, USA_2014
"Oink," artist in residence final exhibition at Dokhuis Galerie, Amsterdam, Netherlands, March 2013. Artwork & Photograph by María de Brea. Show curator: A. de Brea

AUTHORS OF THE SELECTED PROJECTS & ESSAYS

Al Borde
This office is a multidisciplinary collective, established in 2007 (Quito, Ecuador) by David Barragán (Quito, Ecuador, 1981) and Pascual Gangotena (Quito, Ecuador, 1977). It focuses on researching architectonical and constructive strategies for optimizing available resources, developing works with a sustainable perspective seeking a balance between economic, social and environmental issues. The explorations have taken AL BORDE to engage in the participative design of community projects, building with volunteers, and interdisciplinary collaborations. They understand architecture neither as a luxury item nor as a status icon. AL BORDE considers that all people, especially those who have less, must have access to quality spaces. We consider both sustainability and environmental issues as inherent topics in our profession. No matter the budget, scale or the location, they are always looking for resource optimization and to enhance local materials. In addition to revaluing local building techniques as a method for reach their goals.

Alejandro Haiek Coll (Miranda, Venezuela, 1970)
Alejandro graduated in Architecture from the Central University of Venezuela (UCV) where he earned an Honorable Mention for his M.S. in Architectural Design. He is a profesor and researcher at PUC, Chile and UCV, Venezuela. He works as a guest professor for the Technological Master's at UNAB, Chile. He has lectured at the Venezuelan Consulate in New York, The University of the Arts Philadelphia, at the Instituto Tecnológico de Costa Rica as well as at the XVII Quito Architecture Biennale. His work has been exhibited at several architecture biennales (Venice, Santiago de Chile, among others) and at the International Cultural Center in Antwerp. He has been widely awarded for his work; he is co-founder and director of LAB.PRO.FAB.

Alejandro Stöberl (Buenos Aires, Argentina, 1963)
He is an architect and artist; he is an assistant professor at Buenos Aires University UBA, and principal of Alejandro Stöberl Architects, a firm has carried out different design work as well as residential and commercial architecture projects. Many of these projects have been published in Argentina, Japan, France, Spain, and the United Kingdom; most of them also have been awarded in national and international competitions. Alejandro has participated in numerous architecture and art exhibitions; as an example, from 2003 to 2006 the work of the office was part of the Strangely Familiar exhibit, organized by the Walter Art Center in Minneapolis which later toured several American and European cities. In 2005 the firm participated in the international exhibition Absoluut Architectuur in Brussels, and in 2007 it was part of HEX / Contemporary Architecture Argentina at the Spain Cultural Center in Buenos Aires. It has also participated in many architecture biennales: Buenos Aires, Venice, Sao Paulo, and Miami, among others.

Ana Fernández (Buenos Aires, Argentina, 1962)
She obtained her architecture degree from the University of Buenos Aires. She has had an extensive international career, developing projects in Argentina, France, and the United Kingdom, but she carries out her work primarily in Holland and Spain. She was the head of design at KAW Architecten in Groningen, Holland, from 1992 to 2000, and currently runs the KAW Arquitectura office in Barcelona, Spain.

Ana Rascovsky (Buenos Aires, Argentina, 1972)
Ana is an Argentinian architect, who earned her degree from University of Buenos Aires (FADU-UBA, 1996); she received her Master's Degree from the Berlage Institute Rotterdam (Netherlands, 2002) and L'Ecole d'Architecture in Versailles (France, 2001). She also works as a lecturer and guest professor at several universities. Her work has been published worldwide. She is a founding member of Supersudaca – Think Tank for international architecture and urban planning. In several architecture, design, and landscape projects Ana Rascovsky has worked together with the architects Irene Joselevich and Florencia Moralejo.

Andrea Laura Saltzman (Buenos Aires, Argentina, 1958)
She is an Argentinian architect, currently chair and professor at the Department of Fashion and Textile Design, School of Architecture, Design and Urbanism, Buenos Aires University FADU UBA. Her recent book El cuerpo diseñado (*The Designed Body* – Editorial Paidos 2004) was result of the National Endowment for the Arts fellowship (Fondo Nacional de las Artes).

Angelo Bucci (Orlândia, Brazil, 1963)
He is an architect from FAU USP Sao Paulo University, 1987, has been dedicated to both teaching and practicing. Master's in 1998 and PhD in 2005. He has taught studios at FAU USP and also as a visiting professor in Argentina, Chile, Ecuador, Italy [IUAV, Venice, 2008 and 2009] and the United States [ASU, 2005; UC Berkeley, 2006; GSD Harvard, MIT, 2008; UT Austin, 2010]. Founder and principal in charge since 2003 of SPBR architects, www.spbr.arq.br, based in São

Paulo, Brazil. Some of his buildings have been widely exhibited and published. He has been a visiting professor at the Massachusetts Institute of Technology, Graduate School of Design Harvard, University of California, Berkeley and Arizona State University (USA), Università IUAV di Venezia (Italy), Torcuato Di Tella (Argentina), University of Cuenca (Ecuador) and Andres Bello (Chile). Angelo Bucci was recognized with an honorary fellowship from the American Institute of Architects (AIA) in 2011 for his contribution to the profession. He received the Holcim Silver Award for the Latin American region in 2008 for his project Low-Energy University Mediatheque, Rio de Janeiro, Brazil. He was a member of the Holcim Awards jury for the Latin American region in 2011. Since 2003, he has led SPBR, architectural office located in São Paulo.

Antonieta Angulo (Lima, Peru, 1957)
She holds a professional degree in architecture from Ricardo Palma University in Lima-Peru (1980) and a doctoral degree from Delft University of Technology in The Netherlands (1995). Her professional career comprises the design of residential and commercial projects in Peru, including healthcare facilities and the passenger terminal of the Chincheros International Airport in Cusco. Her academic career includes teaching and research activities at Texas A&M University (1995-2007), where she was awarded the 2005 college of architecture teaching excellence award. She is currently an Associate Professor of Practice at Ball State University teaching graduate and undergraduate studios as well as traditional and digital media courses. Her research is focused on the application of emerging media in the teaching and practice of design.

Arquitectura X
Adrián Moreno (Quito, Ecuador, 1972), María Samaniego (Quito, Ecuador, 1972). They have worked in architecture, urban, interior and furniture design in various cities in Ecuador since they started Arquitectura X in 1996. They are currently working on private and public projects of various scales. Their work has received a number of awards in urban design and architecture, among others: National Architecture Award, 10th Architectural Biennial, Quito, 1996; Winners of the National Urban Design Competition for El Barranco, Cuenca, 2003; Finalists 5th BIAU (Bienal Iberoamericana de Arquitectura y Urbanismo), Montevideo, 2006; First Runner-Up for the Urban Cooperation Award, Santiago de Compostela, Spain 2007; Third Place National Urban and Architectural Design Competition for the National Assembly Complex in Quito, 2010. Currently they both teach at the University of San Francisco de Quito and have taught and given lectures at different universities and academic events in Ecuador, Colombia, Bolivia and the U.S., where Adrian Moreno was invited (together with José María Sáez) to teach at the University of Texas, School of Architecture during the fall semester of 2011 and for the Latitudes 4 conferences in 2012. Arquitectura X's work has been exhibited at national and international events in Quito, Cuenca, Montevideo, Cartagena, Madrid, the London Festival of Architecture 2010 and the "Post Post Post" exhibition in Buenos Aires, Medellín and Montevideo, and featured in publications in South and North America, Asia and Europe such as Architectural Review, Revista Escala, AU Magazine or the Phaidon Atlas of 21st Century World Architecture.

AT103
The fast technological unfolding that ruled the last decades has caused designers to reflect on their creative processes, leading them to fortify multidisciplinary work. Founded with the clear intention of investigating and creating new techniques for architecture in the contemporary city, a multidisciplinary group shares the need for integration among the capacities of logistics and the multiplicity of knowledge. Each member contributes within his or her particular field of experience, together with the dedicated commitment to innovation. This methodology of associations tries to identify specific modes of action, using MEDIA as a tool that allows for the understanding of TIME and SPACE. Architectural typologies are in constant mutation in order to survey on the idea of a SKIN as a surface that, within its space, permits the existence of a BODY. To explore the relationship between two autonomous but interrelated systems: surface and program, as instruments of negotiation. Through MEDIA "Low-Tech High-Resolution" effects can be achieved; the set of relationships rules the materiality of the projects: skin becomes the outfit that protects the body while the body contains all programmatic activities. The focus is placed on the relationship between the various spaces and their changeability over time, rather than in the spaces themselves. Julio Amezcua / partner (Mexico City, Mexico, 1974) graduated in architecture from the Anahuac University with honors (1999), and with a Master's Degree from Columbia University (2001). Francisco Pardo / partner (Mexico City, Mexico, 1974 graduated in architecture from the Anahuac University with honors (1998), with a Master's Degree from Columbia University (2000). He began his professional practice at TEN Architects (1995-2000); CHOSLADE Architecture in New York (2000-2001).

Barclay & Crousse Architecture

Sandra Barclay (Peru, 1967) and Jean Pierre Crousse (Lima, Peru, 1963) both studied at Ricardo Palma University in Lima, Peru, and obtained further degrees at Paris-Belleville School of Architecture and at Politecnico di Milano, respectively. Barclay & Crousse was founded in 1994 in Paris, France, where they lived and worked till 2006. In that year, they moved to Lima and opened a new studio, while activity in France continued under the name Atelier North-South. Currently, they both teach at the Pontifical Catholic University of Peru since 2006. Jean Pierre Crousse has also taught at l'Ecole d'Architecture de Paris Belleville (France, 1999 to 2006), and has been a visiting professor in Italy and Latin America.

Blinder Janches Architects

Ricardo Blinder (Buenos Aires, Argentina, 1961) & Flavio Janches (Buenos Aires, Argentina, 1961). Based in Buenos Aires, since 1985, the office has been working in the areas of project management and urban design. They have participated in more than fifty international and national competitions and awarded in twenty-four of them. Blinder and Janches have lectured, taught, and conducted research at different international universities such as TU Delft, The Netherlands, Harvard University, TU Delft Amsterdam, the University of Buenos Aires, Palermo University, the University of Belgrano, and at the Pontifical Catholic University of Ecuador in Quito. In 2007 Playspace foundation, (based in Rotterdam, the Netherlands) was created with the main goal of improving the life of children in slums. Since then, B&J coordinates several projects in Villa Tranquila, a slum located in Avellaneda, Buenos Aires. In 2010 they also opened the Argentinean Playspace foundation office.

Camilo Restrepo (Medellín, Colombia, 1974)

He has a degree in Architecture from the University Pontificia Bolivariana, 1998; and a Master's in Architecture, Urban Planning and Urban Culture from the Metrópolis program at UPC and CCCB, Barcelona. He is specializing in Geopolitics at EAFIT University. His architecture firm is located in Medellín, Colombia since 2000. Its main interest lies in the display of built and unbuilt policies for administration, production and management of space. They understand architecture and design as the design of relationships in space. They practice as a third order, which is capable of producing a theoretical practice and a practical theory. They believe that collaboration is the best way to exchange information, to test our research approaches and, above all, to learn. Cooperation Award, Santiago de Compostela, Spain 2007, Third Place "National Urban and Architectural Design Competition for the National Assembly Complex in Quito", 2010.

Carlos Campos (Buenos Aires, Argentina, 1963)

Carlos Campos is a contemporary musician, architect (1988), and Doctor of Architecture (2013) from Buenos Aires University. He teaches as a full professor at FADU UBA, and was an invited visiting professor at the University of Florida, Dessau Institute of Architecture (Germany), Università IUAV di Venezia, VIA Vicenza Institute of Architecture, UniRC Università Mediterranea di Reggio Calabria, UniNa, Università di Napoli, and Università di Napoli II, in Italy; and invited professor at the Pontifical Xavierian University of Colombia. Founder of CCYZA ARCHITECTS, together with Yamila Zÿnda Aiub (Argentina, Architect and Contemporary Ballet dancer) they develop architectural and design projects with a focus on culture and urban performance. Designer and curator of the Argentine Pavilion at the XI Biennale di Architettura di Venezia (2008), the office was nationally and internationally recognized. Among other awards the studio obtained the 1st Prize in the international competition Argentina Bicentennial (2010), the 1st Prize in the Ternium Siderar Competition (2008), 1st Prize for the Argentine Pavilion at the XI Biennale di Architettura di Venezia (2008), 4th Prize in the LAGI International Competition, Dubai, EAU, 4th Prize OISTAT Theatre Architecture Competition, Prague (2011), and the 3rd Prize for the Opera al Muro, Milan (2011).

Castillo - Kogan Architects + Leonardo Cabral

Paz Castillo (Buenos Aires, Argentina, 1970) and Carolina Kogan (Buenos Aires, Argentina, 1980) are principal partners at Castillo Kogan Arquitectas. Among others, they have won the First Prize in Plaza Boedo Contest run by the Buenos Aires government GCBA. Paz Castillo obtained her architecture degree from Buenos Aires University UBA (1994), where she taught until 2005. She also graduated in History and Culture of Architecture and Cities from Torcuato Di Tella University (2004). Her academic career continues at Palermo University (since 2001) and at USAM (since 2014).

Carolina Kogan (Buenos Aires, Argentina, 1980) obtained her architecture degree with Honors from Buenos Aires University UBA (2006), where she taught until 2007. She graduated in Visual Arts from the National Institute of Art (2010). She is currently finalizing her Master's Degree in History and Culture of Architecture and Cities at Torcuato Di Tella University. She teaches at UP and USAM. Since 2012, she is part of the research group Contemporary Archeology, Space Culture and Politics at the Río de la Plata City coordinated by Aliata-Silvestri Architects at La Plata National University.

Leonardo Cabral (Buenos Aires, Argentina, 1965) obtained his architecture degree from FADU UBA (2002) where he teaches history courses; he also teaches at Flores University, adding experience to his many years as an academic. His postgraduate degree in History and Criticism was awarded in 2003 by UBA. Since 2005, he works at LC studio, designing and leading construction management; their project for Plaza Boedo (together with Castillo-Kogan) is published in this volume.

Claudio Ferrari (Buenos Aires, Argentina, 1959)

He obtained his architecture degree from the University of Buenos Aires in 1986. He has been professor at the School of Architecture (FADU) Buenos Aires University, is currently the director of the department of architecture at USAM San Martin University, and principal partner at Becker-FerrariArchitects. He has taken part in several emblematic designs for the Argentinian government: The Bicentennial Cultural Center in Buenos Aires (B4FS, 2010), formerly Palace of the Central Post Office; The Government House Museum (2011), former "Taylor's Customs house;" The Missing Persons Memorial, with BLV Architects (1998), and The Central Park in Mendoza (First Prize National Competition Design + Project 2000/2005) in Western Argentina, among the most recent projects. Some of the awards he has obtained include: the Vitruvius Prize of the Argentine Museum of Fine Arts (1998); the BA Buenos Aires International Biennial of Architecture (1998); the Gold Medal in the Miami Biennial (USA, 2000). He is a founding member of Paralelo 35, a group for reflection and critique of architecture, art, and design. He was part of the head-committee of post-graduate studies at the School of Architecture for the University of Palermo in Buenos Aires; and he was an associate researcher at the Metropolitan Architecture

Laboratory directed by Alberto Varas; he is currently a tutor in the Architecture Master's Program at the University of Buenos Aires.

Claudio Vekstein (Buenos Aires, Argentina, 1965)
He is an Argentinean architect graduated from the School of Architecture, Design, and Urbanism, Buenos Aires University. He became a disciple of South American master architect Amancio Williams and completed graduate studies at the Frankfurt Art Academy Städelschule in Germany under professors Enric Miralles and Peter Cook. Since 2002 he has been teaching at Arizona State University, where he is a tenured professor at the School of Architecture and Landscape Architecture. He has run his practice specializing in the architecture of public works and urban infrastructure, both in Buenos Aires Argentina (since 1996), and in Phoenix Arizona (since 2002).

Craig W. Hartman (Indiana, USA, 1950)
FAIA, he is the Design Partner for SOM San Francisco. His work ranges from entire urban districts to singular works of architecture, addressing issues of contemporary place and time, the poetics of light, and the sustainability of urban and natural ecologies. His work has been recognized with over 120 interdisciplinary design awards, which, in addition to 8 national AIA Honor Awards for Architecture, Interior Design and Urban Design, includes California's Maybeck Award for an individual oeuvre, of which he is the youngest recipient. In 2009 he received an Honorary Doctor of the Arts degree from his alma mater, Ball State University. During the dedication ceremony for SOM's The Cathedral of Christ the Light, Hartman received the Vatican's Knighthood for Service to Society.

Daniel Bonilla (Bogotá, Colombia, 1962)
He is a Colombian architect graduated from Los Andes University, Bogotá, and Master of Arts in Urban Design at Oxford Brookes University, England. Lecturer and professor at local and international universities, he has received multiple awards and distinctions in several biennials, architectural design awards and competitions. Designer of diverse scale projects such as the Colombian Expo Hannover 2000 Pavilion, the Chapinero Chamber of Commerce of Bogotá Building, the International Convention Centre of Medellín, and Los Andes University Julio Mario Santodomingo building, as well as urban furniture for Bogotá, Los Nogales School Chapel and La Milagrosa chapel at La Calera, among others.

Daniel Miranda (Buenos Aires, Argentina, 1956)
He is an architect graduated from the University of Buenos Aires (UBA) in 1979. He has extensive experience in Landscape Architecture as Project Leader in APN National Parks Administration. He has taught at the National University of Lomas de Zamora and is currently leading his own studio Miranda Workshop at FADU UBA, where he also acted as associate dean from 2009 to 2013.

Dellatorre-Oubiña-Shanahan-Valverde
Diego Dellatorre (Buenos Aires, Argentina, 1958) obtained his architecture degree from the University of Buenos Aires in 1983. He is professor at the School of Architecture (FADU) Buenos Aires University, and principal partner in Dellatorre Shanahan Architects.
Daniela Oubiña (Buenos Aires, Argentina, 1971) obtained his architecture degree from the University of Buenos Aires in 2000.
Marcelo Fernández-Shanahan (Buenos Aires, Argentina, 1960) obtained his architecture degree from the University of Buenos Aires in 1983. He is professor at the School of Architecture (FADU) Buenos Aires University in Catedra Sudamérica [South America Class], and professor at Torcuato Di Tella University (UTDT) as co-chair of Constructions 1 and 2 [with Mariano Clusellas]. He is principal partner at Dellatorre Shanahan Architects.
Juan Ramón Valverde (Buenos Aires, Argentina, 1964) obtained his architecture degree from the University of Buenos Aires in 1989.

Dellekamp Architects
Derek Dellekamp (D.F., Mexico, 1972) is a graduate architect from the Ibero-American University (UIA), Mexico, 1997. Derek has also studied at SciArc, Los Angeles, and has taught architecture at different universities in Mexico City. In 1999, Derek founded Dellekamp Arquitectos where he continues to be the creative mind behind each of the office's projects. He is also the director of MXDF, a Mexico City-based urban research workshop, co-founded in 2004 with Tatiana Bilbao, Arturo Ortiz and Michel Rojkind. One essential part of Dellekamp Arquitectos' philosophy is to maintain a connection between work and academia, which Derek sees as reciprocally dependent. As both a professor and a lecturer, academia is a part of his daily work. These interests are additionally evident in his projects and a recent research project to study concepts of social housing.

Diego Petrate (La Plata, Argentina, 1969)
He studied architecture at the National University of La Plata, attended the StaedelSchule Frankfurt as a guest student of Enric Miralles and Peter Cook. He received a Master's Degree in architecture from UCLA, with Gregg Lynn as his thesis advisor. He was a recipient of the Fulbright scholarship, as well as grants from the Argentine Ministry of Education and the Austrian Academic Exchange Service. He is principal at Florencia Wynne & Diego Petrate Architects and partner at GIGO based in La Plata, Argentina. His work ranges from built projects, including architecture, furniture and graphic design, to more speculative research-driven projects based on design related to digital computation and fabrication. With an academic and professional background from Argentina, Europe and the U.S., he has worked for more than six years for Frank O. Gehry on buildings, design competitions and exhibitions.

Dieguez-Fridman Architects & Associates
Tristán Dieguez (Buenos Aires, Argentina, 1972) graduated as an architect from the University of Buenos Aires in 1997, obtaining the Sociedad Central de Arquitectos–Consejo Profesional de Arquitectura y Urbanismo award for the best architecture student's project in 1993 and the CPAU award for the best architecture career in 2000. Between 1996 and 1998 he worked in Luis Bruno Arquitectos and between 1998 and 2000 with Cesar Pelli and Associates in New Haven, CT, USA.
Axel Fridman (Buenos Aires, Argentina, 1971) graduated as an architect from the University of Buenos Aires in 1997. Between 1994 and 1997 he worked as a designer for Berdichevsky-Cherny Architects and between 1997 and 1999 in M/SG/S/S/S arquitectos. In 1998 he began the Master's in Advanced Architectural Design at Columbia University, NY, USA, graduating with honors in 1999. In 2000 both principals returned to Buenos Aires and began their independent practice Dieguez-Fridman Architects, building several residential and

commercial projects. Since 2004 they have won many competitions, and their work has been published internationally. They teach design studios at the University of Buenos Aires, and at Washington University in St. Louis, USA.

Dutari - Viale Architecture
Office established since 1997.
Ian Dutari (Córdoba, Argentina, 1963) studied Architecture at the National University of Cordoba and he graduated in 1990. In 1992 he won the "Park of the Nations" competition, in San Luis, Argentina, which was built during the following four years. In 1996 he obtained the "Vitruvius Award." In 2006 he published his book Initial Architecture [Cordoba Catholic University Press]. Since 2008 he is the Dean of the School of Architecture of the National University of Córdoba, Argentina. He has participated in numerous competitions and was awarded in many of them. In addition to his professional practice, he has lectured at different universities throughout South America, China and Italy. Many of his works have been distinguished in different biennials and competitions.
Santiago Viale (Córdoba, Argentina, 1967) obtained his degree from UNC in 1994.

Felipe Mesa (Medellín, Colombia, 1975)
He is an architect and co-founder of the architecture practice, plan:b. He studied architecture at the Pontifical Bolivarian University (UPB), Medellín, in 1998 and was awarded a Master's Degree in Architecture: Criticism and Design from the ETSAB, Barcelona, Spain in 2000. He has taught at the Pontifical Xavierian University (PUJ), and the University of Los Andes in Bogotá. He has also been an invited professor for workshops and lectures in numerous countries in Latin America, Norway, Spain and the U.S.
Founded in 2000 by architects Felipe Mesa and Federico Mesa, plan:b is interested in material practices as eco-social areas of convergence and as partial agreements with the potential to transform our environments.

Fernando Fritz - Eric Fritz Architects
Fernando Fritz (Buenos Aires, Argentina, 1974) graduated as an architect from the University of Belgrano in 1998. In 2002 he obtained a Master's Degree in Advanced Architectural Design from Buenos Aires University. Between 2001 and 2002 he collaborated with Dieguez-Fridman Architects & Associates in several competitions, winning together the second prize in the Republic Square Redesign Competition (Buenos Aires, 2001) and Great Egyptian Museum (Egypt, 2002). He is currently assistant professor for the School of Architecture, Design, and Urbanism at Buenos Aires University. In 1998 he began together with his brother Eric Fritz (Buenos Aires, Argentina, 1971) their independent practice, establishing Fritz + Fritz Architects and developing a number of residential projects and participating in national and international competitions.

Gerardo Caballero - Maite Fernández Arquitectos
Gerardo Caballero (Totoras, Argentina, 1957) finished his undergraduate studies at Rosario National University in 1982 and his graduate degree at Washington University in St. Louis in 1986. From 1983 to 1985 he was senior designer at the architectural office Corea-Gallardo-Mannino in Barcelona, Spain. At that time he worked on the waterfront renovation of the City Hall in Badalona, Spain. He has been professor of architectural projects at the University of Palermo in Buenos Aires and also a visiting professor at Washington University, the University of Arkansas and Kansas University, and lecturer at several universities in the USA, Spain, Argentina, Bolivia, Brazil, Chile, Uruguay and Mexico. Since 1993 he teaches the Barcelona summer Studio (Washington University) in Spain. He was visiting professor at GSD Harvard University in the spring 2002. From 1996 to 1998 he was in charge of the Architectural projects and Urban Planning office of the Planning Department at the Rosario City Hall. He participated in the exhibits: Argentinian Emerging Architecture, Berlin 1993; Argentina Architetture 1880-2004, Rome 1996; 10 Arquitecturas Iberoamericanas, La Coruña, Spain, 2001, and Argentina Recent Architecture, Holland 2002. Maite Fernández (Buenos Aires, Argentina, 1967) graduated in Architecture from Rosario National University in 1992. She worked at Villafañe/ Farruggia and Rafael Iglesia architectural offices.

Giancarlo Mazzanti (Barranquilla, Colombia, 1963)
Giancarlo graduated as an architect from Javeriana University, Bogotá, Colombia (1987). He received a postgraduate degree in architecture history and theory studies as well as industrial design postgraduate studies, both at the University of Florence, Italy (1991). Most of his architectural work has social values at its core, and features projects which empower transformations and build community. His most relevant projects are the Convention Center, the Biblioteca España and the South American Games Coliseums in Medellín, Colombia; the Tercer Milenio Park and, more recently, Jardín Social Porvenir in Bogotá; Jardín Social Timayui in Santa Marta; and the Velodrome in Medellín. Mazzanti has taught at various Colombian universities and at some of the most prestigious American universities, such as Princeton University and Harvard Graduate School of Design. He has received several national and international awards and distinctions.

GSH Gonzalo Sánchez Hermelo Architects
Office established in 1991 as Estudio Sánchez Hermelo and Associates. Managed by Gonzalo Sánchez Hermelo (San Carlos de Barichole, Argentina, 1963), graduated as an architect from National University of Rosario, giving his work a large range of design topics since the beginning. Since then, he has developed close to 900 design projects with a surface of 4.200.000 m2 that support his career. The work realized by the office covers a wide range of commercial and branding projects, single-family and collective housing, country clubs and gated communities, spread all over the country. Moreover, the office also takes part in several investment-developments managing projects in Uruguay and Argentina.

GrupoSP
Alvaro Puntoni (São Paulo, SP, Brazil, 1965) has a degree in architecture and urban design (1987) and a Master's Degree (1999) both from FAU USP; in 2005 he obtained his doctorate from the same institution. Partner and founder of Escola da Cidade since 2002, where he also teaches since 2002. He worked with Ângelo Bucci from 1987 to 1996, with whom, between 2002 and 2004, he founded SPBR Architects. SPBR has been a part of several national and international competitions winning several first prizes – the Brazilian Pavilion for Expo92 in Seville, the "Memorial à República" in Piracicaba, the SEBRAE Headquarters, among others. Puntoni has participated in various collective architectural exhibitions showing at different, international, architecture venues. He is part of gruposp since 2004.

João Sodré (São Paulo, SP, Brazil, 1978) has a degree in Architecture and Urban Design (2005) and a Master's Degree (2010) from FAU-USP. He won the First prize EX-AEQUO Student Competition at XVII Brazilian Congress Competition (2003). He was a finalist in the Elemental Architecture World Competition (2003) and Petrobrás Headquarters Vitória-ES (2005). He earned an honorable mention at Capes Headquarters Brasília (2007). He has directed the documentary film "3.5 Overpass", winner of the "É Tudo Verdade / It is All True" festival in 2007. He is part of gruposp since 2004. Jonathan Davies (São Paulo, SP, Brazil, 1975) has a degree in Architecture and Urban Design (2003) Facultade de Belas Artes de São Paulo - FEBASP. He has specialized in environmental design and energy conservation at FUPAM-USP (2005). He took part in the National Competition for International Airport of Florianópolis, Finalist at Elemental Architecture World Competition and Petrobrás Headquarters Vitória-ES (2005). He was awarded an honorable mention at Capes Office (2007) MBA in Real Estate Development, Fupam-USP (2009). He is part of gruposp since 2004.

g+ Marcelo Gualano - Martín Gualano Architects
Marcelo Gualano (Montevideo, Uruguay, 1967) and Martin Gualano (Montevideo, Uruguay, 1969) received their architecture degrees from the School of Architecture at the University of the Republic, Uruguay. They established their own office gualano+gualano in 1999. At the same time, they teach at Scheps Drafts Workshop for the School of Architecture at the University of the Republic. They have obtained several awards in Uruguay, Ecuador and Portugal. Their work has been published and they have lectured worldwide – in Argentina, Brazil, Chile, Colombia, Costa Rica, Nicaragua, Perú, Portugl, Spain, and Venezuela among others.

Harry Gugger Studio
Harry Gugger (Grezenbach, Switzerland,1956) started his professional career as a toolmaker's apprentice from 1973 to 1977. From 1984 to 1989 he studied architecture at the Swiss Federal Institute of Technology in Zurich (ETHZ) with Flora Ruchat and at Columbia University, New York with Tadao Ando. He received his degree in architecture from ETH Zurich in 1990. In the same year he began his collaboration with Herzog & de Meuron (HdeM), when he was their assistant at the summer school in Karlsruhe. From 1991 to 2009 he was a partner of the firm. Harry Gugger established his studio in 2010, after nineteen years of partnership at Herzog & de Meuron, where he was in charge of the Tate Modern in London, the Caixa Forum in Madrid, the Schaulager in Basel, among many other museum projects. Drawing from this experience, Harry Gugger Studio (HGS) emphasizes the singularity of each project and explores its research potential by working closely with the client. In questioning the traditional role of the architect as the sole author of a building, HGS initiates a collaborative process that engages clients, other designers, consultants, and relevant experts. The firm's highly professional structure is complemented by the cultivation of "dilettantism," an approach that allows the design team to discover and capitalize on the unique characteristics of each commission.

Horacio Torcello (Buenos Aires, Argentina, 1948)
Horacio Torcello is an architect, graduated from Buenos Aires University 1972. His experience spans a range of projects, many as award-winner of competitions: International Airport Asunción; Urban Bridges Viedma-Patagones; Art Museum Neuquén; World Bank Public Hospitals; Residential buildings; Salta judicial power headquarters; Prision Buenos Aires, Mental health centers Buenos Aires; Cultural Centre Concordia. Also he has participated in competitions for Archeological Museum Egypt; Moscow Central Government, Acropolis Museum, and the Master Plan for Rio 2016.

José Cubilla & Associates
José Cubilla (Asunción, Paraguay, 1969) obtained his professional degree from FADA-UNA, School of Architecture, Design and Fine Arts in Paraguay, and a Master's Degree in Contemporary Architecture from UCA, as well as a degree in project experimentation from the School of Architecture and Urban Planning, National University of the Northeast, Argentina He established his own professional practice in Asunción (Paraguay) in 2002. The work of the office is focused on single housing projects, most of them awarded at several architecture venues around Latin America. The office's current partners are: Dahiana Núñez (Asunción, Paraguay, 1981), Paulina Aguilar (Guadalajara, Mexico, 1981), Celeste Sakoda (Asunción, Paraguay, 1980), María Paz Gil (Asunción, Paraguay, 1989) and Solano Benítez (Asunción, Paraguay, 1990).

José María Sáez + David Barragán
José María Sáez Vaquero (Ávila, Spain,1963 is an architect graduated from the Polytechnic University of Madrid; he has specialized in environmental and bioclimatic architecture for architecture rehabilitation. Sáez Vaquero was awarded first prize in the VI Ibero American Architecture and Urbanism Biennale of Lisbon (2008) for the Pentimento House, the same project also received the national award at the XV Pan-American Architecture Biennale of Quito in 2006. Designer and builder, known for the rehabilitation in Quito of his own house, he also obtained the Heritage Award for Architectural Restoration in the Historic Center of Quito in 2005, and a number of national and international recognitions. He is a founding faculty member at the School of Architecture, Design and Arts of the Catholic University of Quito, where he was chair from 2001 to 2002. Saez Vaquero has lectured at several universities in Ecuador, Argentina, Peru, Spain and the USA. David Barragán (See Al Borde Architects)

Jprcr Architects (Camilo Restrepo + J. Paul Restrepo)
Jprcr is an architecture agency located in Medellín, Colombia since 2000. Its main interest lies in the display of built and unbuilt policies for administration, production and management of space. The office understands architecture and design as the focuses of relationships in space. The firm considers their practice as a "third order," which is capable of producing a theoretical practice as well as a practical theory. The group believes that "collaboration is the best way to exchange information, to test research approaches and above all to learn from others."

Julio Arroyo (Argentina)
Julio Arroyo is an architect and professor at the School of Architecture, Design and Urban Planning, National University of the Littoral, Santa Fe, Argentina, since 1981. He is also Coordinator of the Urban Planning Office at Santa Fe Municipality. He has taught design, theory and city culture courses for more than 20 years. He was convened in 2008 by the local government to work in the planning office of the Santa Fe City Hall.

Lateral Arquitectura (Santiago, Chile, 2006)
Lateral is an architectural office run by Christian Yutronic, Sebastián Baraona, and Loreto Figueroa. The office was established in 2006; however these three Chilean architects have been working together since 1998. Their notable work includes: the Covintec Social Housing Competition in Valparaiso (2006); first place in the Gabriela Mistral Cultural Center competition (2007-2008, together with Chilean architect Cristián Fernández Eyzaguirre, Santiago, 1960), and the first place in the competition for the design of the new stadium Luis Valenzuela Hermosilla in Copiapo (2009).

Marcelo Villafañe (Rosario, Argentina, 1951)
He obtained his architecture degree from the National University of Rosario in 1975. During 1977, he become partner in Studio Jaime Bruguera y Asociados and won the first prize for the Junta Nacional de Carnes Stand competition. In the same year he opened his own office and started his first projects. He was one of the founding members of Grupo R and, in 1992, he made an art exhibition in the Castagnino Museum. He has won many architecture awards. He was invited professor at the National University of Rosario, and at the International Union of Architects UIA Conference / Barcelona UNR. In 1998 he became co-director of the magazine 041 and director from 1999 until 2011. He has been keynote speaker at several national and international conferences. His work has been awarded and published extensively. Currently, he is working at his own office on several projects of soft geometrical shapes and roofs shaped by the wind blowing across the Pampas.

Marco Rampulla (Córdoba, Argentina, 1970)
He obtained his Architecture degree from the National University of Córdoba, 1996. During his studies at university he worked for the architects Soneira, Luciani, Zanoni, and for his father, the architect Antonio Rampulla, on different projects, works and several National Architecture competitions. From the year 1994 to the year 2006 he worked with Portuguese architect Alvaro Siza as the coordinator of different projects and works such as The Faculty of Communication Sciences of Santiago de Compostela; The Caixa Galiza-Pontevedra Foundation; The Southern Municipal building of Rosario in Argentina; and The Sportscenter of Cornellà de Llobregat in Barcelona, among others. Currently living in Córdoba, he now works as an assistant professor of the Architectural Design chair at the Catholic University of Córdoba and on different works and projects in his own firm.

Martha Kohen
Martha Kohen (Montevideo, Uruguay, 1947) is a Uruguayan architect, and since 2003 a professor and former director (03-08) for the School of Architecture at the University of Florida; she is currently teaching research methods in Architecture, Sustainable Urbanism, and Advanced Graduate Studios. She co-directed her architecture office, MKRO, with Rubén Otero, in Montevideo from 1986 to 2003, with work in urban design, landscape architecture, housing and public buildings. The office obtained the First Prize at the Sao Paulo Architecture Biennale in 2004.

Mauro Bianucci (Buenos Aires, Argentina, 1972)
Mauro Bianucci graduated with a Master's of Architecture in 1997 from Buenos Aires University. He moved to New York in 2000 to work on residential and commercial projects before relocating to Barcelona in 2007. There, he established The Workshop of Mauro Bianucci, a firm focused on providing design solutions to clients with wide-ranging needs: from architecture to graphic, industrial and interior design. He is also the founder and designer of *Carga, an international brand that manufactures bags and accessories bringing unusual materials, techniques and construction methods to the fashion world.*

Maxi Spina (Rosario, Argentina, 1976)
He studied at the National University of Rosario (BArch 2001), where he graduated with honors, and Princeton University (MArch 2005). While in Argentina, and until 2002, Maxi was an associate architect at P-A-T-T-E-R-N-S. In 2001 the firm's work began to achieve considerable recognition, most notably through the Jujuy 2056 apartment building, Maxi's first-built project, which has been published since then in numerous journals, including Casabella, Praxis, Summa+, Bio, Architectural Record, L'Arca, Metalocus and A+U. Jujuy 2056 has also appeared in the book Rosario: Architecture with Identity from 1998 to 2003, and was part of the exhibition "Urban Life: Housing in the Contemporary City" at The Architectural League of New York. After his postgraduate studies at Princeton, Maxi moved to New York and held a senior designer position at Studio Daniel Libeskind from 2005–07. He participated in a wide range of projects, including the in-progress Zlota 44 Tower in Poland, for which he was project architect.

Michel Rojkind (Mexico City, Mexico, 1960)
Michel Rojkind began his studies of Architecture and Urban Planning at the Ibero-American University (UIA) (1989-1994). In 2002 he established *rojkind arquitectos* with the idea of exploring new challenges that address contemporary society, of designing compelling experiences that go beyond mere functionality, and of connecting at a deeper level with the intricacies of each project. He has been short-listed to participate in several large-scale international projects, in countries including Mexico, Canada, Kuwait, China, Dubai, Singapore, and Spain. He has been a guest professor at SCIArc in LA and at IACC in Barcelona, and has participated as a juror at several international competitions and lectured in many different countries. Besides being a member of the "SCI-Arc Future Initiatives Network", Rojkind was selected among the "Emerging Voices," New York, 2010. Recent recognitions include "Architectural Record's Innovation," in 2011; "TEDx," and "3rd Holcim Forum for Sustainable Construction" both in 2010. Two years ago Michel Rojkind was included by the Los Angeles Times among the "Faces to Watch." Also, he was named one of the country's "Treasured Architects" by the Mexican Civil Registry and was featured by ProMéxico Magazine as one of the "50 Mexican Names in the Global Creative Scene". In 2011 Wallpaper* Magazine called Rojkind "one of the 150 movers, shakers and makers that have rocked the world in the last 15 years".
Miquel Adrià (Barcelona, Spain, 1956) – cited by M. Rojkind to relate to his work, is an architect from Escuela Técnica Superior de Arquitectura de Barcelona, who moved to Mexico in 2004. He was established as Adrià+Broid+Rojkind from 1998 to 2002. He has served as a jury member in several international contests. Nowadays, he runs Arquine magazine.

Miguel Mesa, Luis Callejas, Camilo Restrepo
Miguel Mesa (Medellín, Colombia, 1975), architect, leads Mesa Publishers and has been part of plan:b architecture.
Luis Callejas, architect, leads LCLA office since 2011. The firm is positioned at the intersection of architecture, landscape and urbanism, oriented toward new forms of engagement with

the public realm through territorial operations. Luis Callejas is a faculty member at Harvard University Graduate School of Design since 2011, where he is engaged in graduate level design instruction as part of the Architecture and Landscape Architecture departments. Camilo Restrepo (See Camilo Restrepo)

MMBB Architects
The group came about in 1990 as a result of the association of the architects Fernando de Mello Franco (São Paulo, Brazil, 1964), Marta Moreira (São Paulo, Brazil, 1962) and Milton Braga (São Paulo, Brazil, 1963). Previous experience provided by their capacities as collaborators in Brazilian and foreign companies was gathered in one common organization, consolidating a comprehensive professional performance which has stood out for the development of public and institutional designs in the areas of building and urbanism.

Néstor Bottino (Buenos Aires, Argentina, 1955)
He is a partner at Holzman Moss Bottino Architecture, a New York City-based architecture and interior design firm. He is also a partner at ForeSite, specializing in facility programming and master planning of cultural projects. He received a Bachelor of Environmental Design from Texas A&M University in 1977, and a Bachelor of Architecture in 1983 from the University of Texas at Austin. Between 1977 and 1985 he worked in the studios of Bruce Goff, author/architect Michael Benedikt, and Architektburo Szyszkowitz-Kowalski in Austria. In 1986 he joined Hardy Holzman Pfeiffer Associates and was named Principal in 2002. From 2004 to 2008 he led the New York studio of Bottino Grund Architects. In 2008 he joined Holzman Moss Architecture, which in 2010 became Holzman Moss Bottino Architecture.

Nicolás Campodonico (Rosario, Argentina, 1973)
He graduated with a silver medal in Architecture from the National University of Rosario. During his studies he obtained a scholarship for an international student exchange with the ETSAV, Valladolid, Spain. In 1996 he collaborated at the office of Mario Corea & Francisco Gallardo in Barcelona. In 1997 he designed his first work. In 2000 he established his professional practice in Rosario city. He has participated in numerous competitions, being awarded in many of them.

over,under
over,under has worked with cultural and educational clients since the firm's founding in 2006, most recently for the Boston Society of Architects, deCordova Sculpture Park and Museum, Massachusetts College of Art and Design, and Qatar Foundation. The firm's principals have staged and curated more than three-dozen exhibitions in Boston, Chicago, Los Angeles, Miami, Pittsburgh, Caracas, Doha, and Vancouver. They have designed buildings and urban places across Central America and the Middle East. The practice's approach emphasizes the coherent relationship of design across scales and disciplines, from exhibitions and graphics to architectural and urban environments. over,under principals are: Roberto de Oliveira Castro (Bogotá, Colombia, 1976), Rami el Samahy (Asyut, Egipto, 1970), Chris Grimley (London, United Kingdom, 1972) and Mark Pasnik (Morristown, New Jersey, United States, 1970)

P-A-T-T-E-R-N-S
Marcelo Spina and Georgina Huljich, born in Argentina, are architects and educators. They are the co-principals of P-A-T-T-E-R-N-S, a design research architectural practice based in Los Angeles. Its original approach to design and architecture integrates sophisticated digital tools and techniques in the understanding and conception of form, tectonics and materials. In pursuit of a synthetic real, their architecture operates in close proximity to the material forces that influence and give rhythm to the life of the body and its physical environment. Part of a so-called digital generation, what sets P-A-T-T-E-R-N-S apart is not only its overt ambition to control materialization, but the quality and extent of the built work.

plan:b
Felipe Mesa (Medellín, Colombia, 1975) + Federico Mesa (Medellín, Colombia, 1979). Plan:b is an architectural office that defines its work through a practice in which equal attention is paid to dialogue, drawing, travel, layout, models, construction, professional + academic situations, publications, and more. Plan:b works collaboratively; the office believe in teamwork – either local or worldwide. Since 2000 to 2005, architects Felipe Mesa and Alejandro Bernal led the office; Felipe Mesa was head of the office from 2006 until 2010. Currently Felipe Mesa and Federico Mesa are principal partners. The work of plan:b is generated primarily through participation in international architectural competitions and also collaborating internationally with other professionals in a variety of projects.

Polidura - Talhouk Architects
Antonio Polidura (Santiago de Chile, Chile, 1976), Marco Polidura (Santiago de Chile, Chile, 1971) and Pablo Talhouk (Viña del Mar, Chile, 1973), graduated in Architecture from the Central University of Chile. After working at several offices, they established Polidaura-Talhouk in 2002. They have developed public and private projects. Their work has been selected by I Architectural Triennial of Libon 2007, XV and XVII Biennial.

Quilian Riano (Bogotá, Colombia, 1979)
Quilian Riano is a designer, writer, and educator currently working out of Brooklyn, New York. He founded DSGN AGNC and collaborates on a variety of architectural design and research projects with other groups. Quilian's current interests and research are focused on the study and implementation of flexible and hybrid designs and processes at a variety of scales to address urban, landscape, architectural, ecological, and social systems.

Rafael Iglesia (Concordia-Entre Ríos, Argentina, 1952)
He has a degree in architecture from the School of Architecture, Design and Planning, National University of Rosario (1981). He has taken part in several national and international workshops, conventions, competitions, conferences and exhibitions, in which his professional and research work has been recognized by the most important architecture venues. He has lectured all over the world, and his work has been internationally awarded. He is a founding member of Grupo R since 1991.

Ricardo Blanco (Buenos Aires, Argentina, 1940)
He obtained his professional degree in architecture from Buenos Aires University in 1967 and his PhD in 2011. He chaired the architecture and industrial departments at Buenos Aires University, where he has taught design studios. Based in Buenos Aires, and since 1965, Blanco has run his own practice, and his work and investigations have been published as well as awarded internationally. Since 2010, RB is the president of the Argentinean Fine Arts National Academy (Academia Nacional de Bellas Artes).

Roberto Amette (Buenos Aires, Argentina, 1959)
He obtained his architecture degree from Buenos Aires University in 1984. From 1986 to 1989 he worked in Alemparte & Barreda Arquitectos, Santiago de Chile. From 1994 to 2004 he was principal partner in Amette-Busnelli Arquitectos. In 1989 he returned to Buenos Aires and began teaching, from 2006 he has been a full professor at the Buenos Aires School of Architecture (FADU UBA). From 2005 to 2008 he was the director of the architecture courses at FADU UBA. He has participated as visiting professor at the University of Palermo. He has obtained many awards in urban and architecture competitions and his work has been published in many specialized magazines. From 2004 to 2006 he participated as the project manager for the Dirección General de Desarrollo Urbano, City Hall Buenos Aires. Until 2014, he was principal partner in SEGGIARO Arquitectos. Currently, he leads with his daughter Francisca Amette, Amette Arquitectos.

Roberto Busnelli (San Miguel de Tucumán, Argentina, 1966)
Roberto Busnelli obtained his architectural degree at the Buenos Aires University in 1993, and his post professional degree in the same school in 2005. He is currently teaching at FADU Buenos Aires University and UP Palermo University (Buenos Aires). He was invited professor at Torcuato Di Tella University (Argentina), UNIS University (Guatemala), Shinshu University (Nagano, Japan), and Tokyo Science University (Tokyo, Japan). He worked with John Hejduk at the Theatre Mask experimental architecture instalation at La Boca, Buenos Aires, with the Torcuato Di Tella University and PROA Foundation (1994 – 1996). Principal partner at Busnelli Arquitectura he has taken part in several designs in Argentina, Uruguay and Spain. Some of the awards he had obtained included: Ayutun Hue House (Patagonia Argentina) World Community Award Seven Cycle, First Prize for Emerging Architects at Buenos Aires Architecture Bienal, First Prize at Bahia Blanca Urban Design National Competition, Second Prize IFIByNe National Competition, among others. He was the curator for the Argentine Pavilion at Sao Paulo International Bienal in 2005 and in 2007, and at the 2010 Venice International Bienal.

Santiago Cirugeda (Sevilla, Spain, 1971)
He graduated in architecture from ESARQ (Universitat Internacional de Catalunya) in Barcelona. As an architect he has developed architectural projects as well as written essays and has taken part in many debates, discussions, congresses and architectural biennales. Santiago Cirugeda's practice tackles urban reality in terms of temporary installations, recycling, occupation strategies and urban intervention by adding prostheses to existing buildings, and citizen participation in the decision-making processes regarding urban issues. He is known as a social architect who takes advantage of legal gaps to the benefit of the community. He develops protocols, which may be used by groups of citizens and individuals regarding legal boundaries that arrange the city. These "Urban Prescriptions" (www.recetasurbanas.net) describe tips to take advantage of regulations, which allow for temporary installations in public spaces and scaffolding on roofs in order to create living extensions. A network called "Arquitecturas Colectivas" is the result of working with several groups focused on urban habitats (hackers, urban planners, architects, activists, etc.).

Sergio Forster (Buenos Aires, Argentina, 1960)
He obtained his architecture degree from Buenos Aires University and his PhD in 2011. Currently he chairs the architecture undergraduate program at the Torcuato Di Tella University, where he also teaches design studios. Between 2000 and 2006 he taught theory and design courses in the graduate and undergraduate programs at the School of Architecture, Design, and Urbanism, Buenos Aires University. Since 1987 Forster has run his own architecture practice in his office in Buenos Aires.

Simon Bussiere (Massachusetts, USA, 1982)
He is an Assistant Professor of Landscape Architecture and a Faculty Fellow with the Global Health Institute at Ball State University's College of Architecture and Planning. His research and teaching focus on critical issues at the intersection of informality in the Latin American community and public realm design, ecological urbanism and representation technology in contemporary landscape architecture.

Tatiana Bilbao (Mexico DF, Mexico, 1972)
She graduated in Architecture and Urbanism from the Ibero-American University in 1996; in 1998 she won an honorable mention for her career and also appreciation for the best thesis of the year. Advisor for Urban Projects at the Urban Housing and Development Department of Mexico City (1998-99). As advisor for the government, Tatiana was member of the urban council of the city. In 1999, she joined and co-founded LCM S.C. In 2004, she started Tatiana Bilbao S.C. with projects in China and Spain, France and Mexico. Also in 2004, she founded mxdf along with the architects Derek Dellekamp, Arturo Ortiz and Michel Rojkind, an urban research center, addressing the production of space, its occupation, its defense and control in Mexico City. In 2005, she became a design professor at Ibero-American University.

Tres Arquitectos + Masif + Camilo Restrepo
Tres Arquitectos is a multidisciplinary office located in Medellín and led by Jorge Gómez (Ríonegro, Colombia, 1983), Juan Pablo Ramos (Medellín, Colombia, 1980) and Juan José Ochoa (Medellín, Colombia, 1983), architects graduated from the Pontifical Bolivarian University, Medellín (Colombia), 2007. Masif Design Affairs is an office focused on Art Direction, Graphic Design and Branding, established in Medellín (Colombia) since 2008. Camilo Restrepo (See Camilo Restrepo + Jprcr)

Una Arquitetos, Brazil
The firm was founded in 1996 as the association of architects graduated from the School of Architecture and Urbanism at São Paulo University (USP). Since its formation it has developed projects on different scales and programs, like facilities for public transportation as well as urban projects such as cultural centers, schools, commercial buildings and residences. Una has chosen to work in association with engineering firms and consultants, thus assuring a space for a comprehensive and multidisciplinary discussion with a focus in architecture and urbanism. The office has received several awards for projects and for finished construction works. Among them, several were awarded by the Institute of Architects of Brazil, having received in 2008 the top prize from this institution, the Carlos Milan Award, for the project of the New Piqueri Train Station. The studio was awarded in the Fifth International Architecture Biennial of São Paulo for the project of the

Centro Universitário Maria Antonia – USP (Universitary Center Maria Antonia-USP) and Instituto de Arte Contemporânea (Institute of Contemporary Art). The partners are: Cristiane Muniz (São Paulo, Brazil, 1970), Fábio Valentim (São Paulo, Brazil, 1970), Fernanda Barbara (São Paulo, Brazil, 1967) and Fernando Viégas (São Paulo, Brazil, 1971). Between 1996 and 1999 the office also had as partners Ana Paula Pontes and Catherine Otondo.

Vila-Sebastián Architects VSA
Marcelo Vila (Buenos Aires, Argentina, 1959) graduated in Architecture from Buenos Aires University in 1986. He is a professor at Buenos Aires University and a visiting professor at Escola da Cidade de Sao Paulo, Brazil, and at Córdoba Catholic University, Argentina. He is the honorary Director of Urban Planning and Design of the Cities, Chizou, China. Adrián Sebastián (Buenos Aires, Argentina, 1963) graduated in Architecture from Buenos Aires University in 1991 and earned a Master's Degree in Policies, Project and City Management at Les Heures - Universitat de Barcelona. VSA is based in Buenos Aires. Vila Sebastian Architects works in different thematic areas including the development of projects for public space, large-scale buildings and housing.

Wes Janz (Wisconsin, USA, 1953)
He is a professor of architecture at Ball State University. He received his BS in Architectural Studies and his Master's of Architecture from University of Wisconsin-Milwaukee and earned his PhD in philosophy from the University of Michigan. In 2006, he was the recipient of the university's Outstanding Teaching Award. Wes has worked and traveled in Argentina, China, Ethiopia, Finland, India, Panama, Russia, South Africa, Sri Lanka, Thailand, Turkey, and UAE; the Gulf Coast five times post-Katrina, and cities throughout the U.S. Rust Belt. Janz believes that people, in general, no matter how poor or apparently disadvantaged, are fully capable of making their way and that it is often the case that the interventions of well-intentioned persons bring both opportunity and harm to the lives of locals. His beliefs are integrated into all facets of design including research, programming, technology, function, human behavior, scheduling, time management, communication, use of materials, and systems. Janz is the founder of *onesmallproject*, a collection of local initiatives from around the world, the U.S., and Indiana that highlights the lives of people that many observers consider to be in-need or at-risk. In 2008, Wes was a finalist for the Curry Stone Design Prize, which is awarded to breakthrough projects that "engage communities at the fulcrum of change, raising awareness, empowering individuals and fostering collective revitalization."

Zas - Lavarello Architecs
Founded in 2006, the office is the reunion of two complementary and creative designers Javier Zas (Buenos Aires, Argentina, 1960) and Paula Lavarello (Rosario, Argentina, 1958); the firm is committed to development and innovation in architecture, interior design, and urban planning. Expertise, dedication, and passion for the making of space, the office is framed by sustainable, social commitment and responsibility. The versatility of its team members approaches with equal intensity a variety of project types. In a recently started international stage Zas Lavarello Architects is developing together with the prestigious firm Fow & Fowle Architects, New York, a proposal for an urban office "building LEED" which again shows the focus on sustainable design.

01ARQ
Office established in 2004. The office has developed projects mainly in Chile; some of them have been selected for the Chilean Biennale of Architecture and published in several international books and magazines. Pablo Saric (Santiago de Chile, Chile, 1971) is a partner at 01ARQ. He received his degree in architecture from Central University of Chile in 1997, doing his professional practice at KPF New York. In 1998 he was awarded with the "Presidente de la República" de Chile and the Fulbright scholarships to continue his studies at Columbia University, obtaining the degree of Master of Science in Advanced Architectural Design in 1999. In 2000 he received the degree of Master in Architecture from the Polytechnic University of Catalonia (UPC). Between the years 2000 and 2002 he worked at *Carme Pinós Studio* and joined the PhD program in the Department of Architectural Design at the Polytechnic University of Catalonia (UPC) where he is now developing his dissertation on Modern Architecture. Currently he is a studio teacher at the Catholic University's Magister in Architecture, Universidad Mayor and visiting professor at Andrés Bello National University, also in Chile. Cristian Winckler (Osorno, Chile, 1971) is a partner at 01ARQ. He received his degree in architecture from the Central University of Chile in 1997. In 1999 he continued his studies at the Polytechnic University of Catalonia, obtaining the degree of Master in Architecture. Currently he is a studio teacher at Universidad Mayor and visiting professor at Andrés Bello National University, also in Chile. Felipe Fritz (Santiago de Chile, Chile, 1978) is a partner at 01ARQ. He received his degree in architecture from Chile's Universidad Mayor in 2007. Currently he is teaching as a studio professor at Universidad Mayor and the Catholic University, both in Chile. Projects developed by 01ARQ seek to provide a comprehensive solution to the needs of users. Design alternatives developed include a broad spectrum of programs and scales: public and private large-scale buildings, restaurants and retail design, collective and individual housing, and urban master plans.

26-26-26-25
Group of designers who, through selected projects, continually question the role of the architect, the global-citizenship, commercial-centric design, and traditional notions of beauty. The group is composed by Wes Janz (See Wes Janz), Jerome Daksiewicz (BArch '00), Adam Janusz (BArch '00) and Devin McConkey (BArch '00).

PAUSES CONTRIBUTORS

Adam Pruden (Indianapolis, USA, 1984)
Adam Pruden's greatest passion is floating media. From fireworks to flying LEDs, he explores the vast possibilities of airborne communications and their cultural impact on society. He recently completed a research fellowship MIT's SENSEable City Lab, where he supported projects on spatial and pervasive media, volumetric scanning and sensor technologies. He was team leader for Flyfire – a project that aims to transform any ordinary space into a highly immersive and interactive display environment. He also led the following projects at SENSEable City Lab: Floating Pixels – a workshop with Google data artist Aaron Koblin, where participants built low-tech 3D light scanners; Dancing Atoms – a 3D scan, motion capture and pixel animation of Roberto Bolle – étoile ballet dancer; Pixel Vision

– 3D volumetric capture with Microsoft Kinect and Processing. Before joining MIT, Adam graduated from BSU with a B.A. in Architecture. While at Ball State, he participated in America, the North and the South: a semester-long research and design seminar about North and South American art, architecture and culture. Adam also participated in CAP Americano Sur 2007 / Argentina, Chile and Uruguay. This program included a workshop with Craig Hartman of SOM to redesign shipping 'cranes' at Puerto Madero [the most recent official neighborhood in Buenos Aires] into unique dwelling spaces. Adam received his M.S. in Visual Communications and Digital Design from Pratt Institute (2010). He has worked in both architecture and graphic design firms and shared his research and projects at AIGA, TED, SXSW and Oslo Lux.

AMORIR alonso+craciun collective
Sebastián Alonso (Montevideo, Uruguay, 1972) and Martín Cracium (Montevideo, Uruguay, 1980) graduated in Architecture and Urbanism from Farq, UDELAR. They established themselves as alonso+craciun collective in 2003. The office works on projects linking art, architecture, thought and social practices but they also have continued their own private careers in parallel to their joint creative adventures.

Gina Stahl (Indianapolis, USA 1984)
Gina graduated with a Bachelor of Fine Arts degree in Photography from Ball State University in 2006. Since college, she has worked as a professional photographer in both Indianapolis and New York City. Her work has been exhibited in various shows and has also been published in several books. Her unique vision and expertise have been recognized and published in several publications, mainly in the Americas.

Gustavo Suárez (Buenos Aires, Argentina, 1959)
Gustavo is an architect and designer from Belgrano University, Argentina. He was awarded as an educator in academic teaching as well as a yogic-therapy professor. Since 1984 he has been a professor at Buenos Aires University (UBA). He is a principal at GZOO Architecture & Design, where he has developed a series of design projects and competitions, a number of them widely awarded nationally and internationally. He was the author of "Los Pleyadianos," first published at El Cronista newspaper's Architecture & Design weekly supplement as the main icon of the sequence of interviews by Ana de Brea [1999-2000], seminal work for her later book 10x50_Terreno de Arquitectura. One of Gustavo's several special contributions for this publication "Los Pleyadianos(2)," is part of the graphic composition of the book-cover.

Juan Andrés Colicheo (Patagonia, Argentina 1977)
He is a philosophy and psychology professor mainly focused on thought and ways of thinking; he has been practicing at several schools – for young and adult students. One aspect of his teaching methods shows the association of different artistic disciplines (especially photography) to the world of philosophy and cognitivism.

Isaac Bracher (Huntingburg, Indiana, USA, 1981)
He is a 2004 graduate of Ball State University, and is an architect with OPN Architects in Des Moines, USA. The Ball State University College of Architecture and Planning Alumni Society Board of Directors recently named Isaac Bracher, AIA, as a recipient of its 2013 Outstanding Achievement Award.

Jason S. Johnson (Minnesota, USA, 1973)
He obtained a Bachelor of Architecture degree from BSU in Indiana, USA and a Master of Architecture and Urbanism from the Architectural Association (AADRL) in London. He has practiced and taught architecture in the U.S., Europe and South America, and currently teaches architecture at the University of Calgary (EVDS), and he is the co-director of the Laboratory for Integrative Design. Jason S. Johnson founded MINUS ARCHITECTURE as a collaborative research and design studio. The office works with designers, fabricators, engineers, programmers, material scientists and any number of allied disciplines based on the needs of the project.

Kevin R. Klinger (Texas, United States, 1968)
He is director of the Institute for Digital Fabrication at Ball State University, associate professor of architecture, and director of the Post-Professional Master of Architecture program in the College of Architecture and Planning. Kevin was responsible for developing a Certificate for Digital Design and Fabrication for Ball State University. He has also served as a two-term President (03-05) of the Association of Computer Aided Design in Architecture (ACADIA), an international organization devoted to studying the advances in architecture resulting from the influences of digital technology. The digital exchange of information is central to this innovative process of architectural production and demands new forms of collaboration with industry for the future of the discipline through-production process.

María Agustina de Brea Dulcich (Buenos Aires, Argentina, 1983)
She is an audiovisual designer from the School of Architecture, Design and Urbanism, Buenos Aires University, FADU UBA 2009. Maria has participated in several design projects and design exhibits nationally and internationally. Among others, she has been principal assistant for the exhibit "No Tango" (Germany, 2004) as well as invited exhibitor of the collective art exhibition "XXL" at "Champion Breakfast" (La Boca, Argentina 2011). In parallel to her design career and her creative work in photography, drawings, and paintings, she has participated as an actress and performer in several broadcasting commercial-films and advertisements for different international companies. After being accepted in 2012 for the AIR program in Kanaal 10 Guest Studio, Amsterdam, Holland, she has developed a year-long artistic residency in that city, bringing the visual components to the three dimensions through knitting and weaving design. Two years later still in Amsterdam, Maria has put on display a series of assorted shows, "OINK" among others. Currently in Buenos Aires, Argentina, she is coordinating the process to produce the film "Al Ver, Veras," working together with producers and script author Luis de Brea.

Marisela Echeverría (Buenos Aires, Argentina, 1964)
She is a photographer, video editor and drama theater producer. Marisela's artistic agenda focuses on capturing and communicating social issues and equal rights.

Matt DeLoughery (Indiana, USA, 1986)
He graduated with a Bachelor of Arts in Architecture from BSU in 2009, and he developed graduate studies at Arizona State University. Finishing a Masters of Architecture and a Masters of Science in the Built Environment, he devoted his studies to a focus on building energy science. His academic work

emphasizes social, environmental, and economic sustainability and has been included in publications and design exhibitions internationally.

Nicolás de Brea Dulcich (Buenos Aires, Argentina, 1985)
He is a social anthropologist from Buenos Aires University (UBA). His research is focused on Latin American studies. He has worked as an educator at the Juan B. Ambrosetti Ethnographic Museum (Faculty of Philosophy and Literature, University of Buenos Aires) and since 2013 he develops the role of coordinator of exhibits and bilingual educator at the Casa Nacional del Bicentenario, also in Buenos Aires, Argentina.

Oscar Padrevecchi (Buenos Aires, Argentina, 1955)
He is a visual artist and architect FAU-UBA (1984). He has over 20 years of professional experience in ideas, art and design for projects of architecture and urbanism. He has received prizes and special mentions in national and international competitions. He is a professor of architecture and drawing at FADU and UP in Buenos Aires. His work has been published in specialized media and more than 3.550.000 m2 of developed blueprints. He has worked in collaboration with the architects Clorindo Testa and Justo Solsona. Today from his studio/workshop Padrevecchi_DesignArquitectos he concentrates his professional services as a Consultant of Art and Design in Architecture and Urban Landscape for public and private companies.

Paul Puzzello (Illinois, USA, 1964)
He received his Bachelor of Architecture degree from Ball State University, Muncie in 1992, and a Master of Architecture from Cranbrook Academy of Art, Bloomfield Hills, Michigan in 2006. Prior to forming Puzzello Architecture Practice, Paul worked in large architecture offices specializing in health-care design and academic buildings as well as co-owning his own architecture practice in Bloomington, Indiana for nine years. In addition to exhibiting work as a designer, Paul continues to be a reviewer and juror of student design work at art, architecture, and design schools internationally and has formally held faculty positions in architecture and design at Indiana University; Lawrence Technological University in Southfield, Michigan; Ball State University; and currently at the Herron School of Art in Indianapolis. Paul is an active board vice-president for People for Urban Progress in Indianapolis, working in urban and public design and product development. He is NCARB certified, NCIDQ certified as an interior designer, and is a registered architect in Indiana and Ohio. Paul is also a licensed contractor in Indianapolis. His work explores materiality, making, and the broader social and cultural arrangements that make up human lives.

Roberto Frangella (Buenos Aires, Argentina, 1942)
Roberto is a South American Architect, who obtained his professional degree from FADU UBA in 1968. He has formed himself in the architecture of the Modern Movement. He grew up in the surroundings of the Rio de la Plata River, and he has been always worried about finding possible answers reflecting on his South American roots. He is very enthusiastic about drawing, and the artistic expression that, in most occasions, observe social aspects of the reality of disadvantaged people. Roberto reflects upon how those people – the "deprived," live; he does appreciate their courage to build a better society. Roberto believes South America is a young land, where architects and other creative groups must practice and work looking for a better reality to be constructed.

Supersudaca
It is a network of architects (mostly Latin and all friends) who have managed to keep working together after nearly 10 years despite being dispersed in several countries. Supersudaca (a word combination of virtue and immigrant insult for Latin people) through all these years has built a profile that is increasingly diverse in subjects affecting the environment while embracing a main question: how to be hopeful against world crudeness? Supersudaca advocates the use of different formats for each topic and uses humor and attitude to talk about serious matters. Caribbean Tourism, China's exports, Direct Actions in Public Space, and Housing for All are some of the recurrent themes being explored from Tokyo to Talca, from Cancun to Cambodia, from Ceuta to Yiwu to mention a random sample. Among other appreciations, Supersudaca was recognized with the Best Entry Award at the II International Biennale of Rotterdam (2005) and the Best Research Project at thei Bienal Iberoamericana (2004). The architectural work done by Supersudaca has been published in renowned architecture journals such as Volume, Architecture Design, Arquine, Icon, Praxis, and Summa+. In the architectural realm, Supersudaca has obtained first prize in i the international competitions for the Museum of Modern Art of Medellin andi the experimental social housing project in
Ceuta, Spain.

Taylor Henderson (Michigan City, USA, 1992)
She is a graduate architecture student at Ball State University, from where she obtained her undergraduate and honors degrees in 2014. She values travel and cultural understanding as a means of broadening her perspective and influencing her designs.

Tessa Pobanz + Mishayla Binkerd
Tessa Pobanz (Jacksonville FL, USA 1987) obtained her Bachelor's degree from BSU and her graduate degree from Honolulu University, Hawaii. She works independently as a creative designer, and as an intern at Walt Disney World, Theme Park, Orlando, FL USA. Mishayla Binkerd (Logansport IN, USA 1987) obtained her Bachelor's degree from BSU and her Master in Architecture from the University of Michigan, Ann Arbor MI USA. She lives and works in San Francisco, California. Both Tessa and Mishayla have creatively collaborated in this book; one of their pieces is a part of the cover.

Wil Márquez (Indianapolis, USA, 1977)
He is principal of wpurpose based in Indianapolis and co-founder of Design Bank, a unique design center focused on entrepreneurship, community, and design. A graduated of the University of Michigan with a Master of Architecture, Marquez's philosophy is centered on the belief that "it is imperative for creative designers to seek out new solutions if they want to contribute to meaningful and relevant environments to society." Marquez has worked and lectured internationally, including in Abu Dhabi, Buenos Aires, and Chihuahua.

CREATION IS A PATIENT SEARCH / Tribute to Le Corbusier. Collage. IMA Indianapolis Museum of Art. 2009_Image especially composed for this book by Ana de Brea.

ACKNOWLEDGEMENTS

I must say any single project as stupendous as this makes necessary the significant enthusiasm and congenial passion of a great number of people, for their contribution with inquiries, suggestions, academic and/or professional work, exchanges, discussions, etc. And, yes, that is an absolutely honest affirmation. It is also very sincere to note that it would be almost impossible to list all the names here with absolute certainty, so first and foremost my deep thanks to everyone who in one way or another has related to each of these years of ideas, pre-production and making.

This project is those people's project since the very beginning of 2009; every contribution has made the completion of this large first step possible and, all together, they reveal themselves as the source for restarting with the next moves, including the publication of the book in the Spanish language – currently in progress and already considering the addition of a few contrastive ventures.

My gratitude to each of the members of Actar, who from the earliest moment have believed in this project and supported it as it was originally conceptualized and dreamed up; especially beginning with Ricardo Devesa, always – always, with a positive standpoint and tactful encouragement.

The helping hand offered by architect Doug Shoemaker as well as by Patricio Ramos for the very conscious reviews of translations of English and of Spanish, and the patience demonstrated with my concentrated objective of finding a mode of expression – discursive text + graphic ingredients – capable of transcending the regular analysis of an architectural book. Both Doug and Patricio have been openly receptive to each of my detailed action-points, allowing me to observe and discover a very extraordinary approach to team working.

I also want to inform that with the release of Total Latin American Architecture / Libretto of Modern Reflections and Contemporary Works, a new scenario is being organized in the form of a topical expedition-tour to perform a number of international talks, travelling exhibitions, discussion panels, exchanges of viewpoints, theoretical explorations – among other formats – to serve, to the extent possible, as a thought-provoking tool for a more intense global-discussion.

From earlier stages, we should note the most ceremonial presentation of the book-project in Argentina, which took place at the National Library in December 2014, with Carlos Campos and two collaborators playing architectural music introducing the gathering, and Claudio Ferrari and Martha Kohen as invited speakers. Particularly, because of their generous, unconditional assistance I want to extend thanks to architect Laura Gamberg and to Gabriel Saie, audiovisual designer, as well as to the essayist and director of the library, Horacio Gonzalez, for believing the project could be part of the cultural agenda of the institution, coinciding with an homage to Clorindo Testa, with its very diverse audience – Roberto Amette, Oscar Padrevecchi, Ian Dutari, Horacio Torcello, German and Gustavo Suarez, Marcelo Vila, Paz Castillo, Carolina Kogan, Claudio Vekstein, Barbara Gotheil, Liliana Bortolin, Alejandro Stoberl, and Berto Gonzalez Montaner, among others, and of course a numerous group of family and friends.

The event at the Library was also the first evidence of a series of moments that have challenged me to combine the essential parts of the book process and the actual publication itself – as well as the interesting aspects of currently rolling the project to incorporate new knowledge. I certainly like to promote the entire experience for the book as an open project, incessantly inviting a potential, circular string of actions in the future.

The vigorous academic advice and emotional friendship of Dr. Carol Flores has been one of the strongest forces of inspiration; Carol knows the real meaning of tolerance and diversity; we both also love contemporary art and architecture so, easy to say, it has been a pleasure at all times. For the same long, seductive conversations as the ones shared with Carol over dinner or over coffee and chocolates, my eternal thanks to Dr. Alfonso Corona Martinez who accepted from the very beginning to be a continual reviewer – in English and in Spanish, of every phase of the book process, and invariably tried to be the most accurate interpreter of what I wanted to communicate; I would like to express that it was a unique experience to work with Alfonso: a fabulous and philosophical learning process which both of us fervently enjoyed.

The association with students, professors, critics, and staff at all the international universities involved in the book has not been less enjoyable; I like to believe the readers will be able to identify the members and connections of that enormous group by associating projects and academic experiences through the distinct segments of the book. Just to mention a few names of that network – probably many of them will have a more active presence in future editions of this publication – I thank architect and professor Paul Millet for sharing my visit with/without students to Porto, Portugal, helping me/us to map the tradition of the city, the great work by Alvaro Siza, and the guidance in terms of urban, local transportation; for the collaborative workshops and lectures at the National University in Cordoba, thanks also to architects and professors Carolina Vitas, Lucas Ruarte, Matías Dinardi, Iván Ravnik, Pablo Carballo, Daniel Huespe and Ignacio José Imwinkelried; for the constructive initiative of inquiring into Latin American architecture in Washington through semester-long lectures+discussions, additional thanks go to professors Terrance Williams – FAIA, who retired in 2014, Carlos Reimers and Julio Bermudez; for continuing efficiency and encouragement I am grateful to architect Diego Fratini from Rosario, Argentina; for the recollection of names, visits, images, and more that benefited the book significantly my thanks go to former students today professionals Michelle Doyle, Jen Worley, Karli Molter, Joe Bohn, Adam Miller, Adam Pruden, Michael Gastineau, and Julieta Rosa.

For similar reasons, I am extremely thankful to the people, generally designers, with whom I have completed and/or shared my functional art pieces at different, international encounters helping me to better understand contemporary aspects and notions that the modern world brings to the design and architecture disciplines.

I cannot fail to mention Pam De Hart and Christine Kotch, because of their support in complicated circumstances; there has been an essential synergy that allowed me to learn about two very good friends. It is also important to say that Jami Spice can be seriously seen as "an energy-producer" for those several times in which any large project gets complicated. Honorable mention to my family and to my very close friends – and to Paula Rosa, Nicolas de Brea Dulcich, and Eric Tulle, for the infinite set of ways they explore in light of helping me to continue walking, for being influential stimulation to persist in the search of the best processes possible to reach my objectives, and for paying full attention to my inquiries, without judging and giving me freedom instead. They are special; they share their findings, their questions, and always more.

For Checha and Salvador, my parents.
Thank you all.

Ana de Brea
November 2015

Ana de Brea

Graduated with a Diploma in Architecture from the School of Architecture, Design, and Urbanism, Buenos Aires University FADU UBA in 1986, Ana de Brea is an architect and an artist as well as a critical observer of contemporary architecture and the design disciplines.
Her background describes an extensive teaching experience performing at different institutions such as Buenos Aires University UBA, J. F. Kennedy University UK, as well as Argentinean Catholic University UCA where she taught design studios and architectural theory seminars. Ana is currently an associate professor of architecture at Ball State University, USA, where she was granted tenure in 2009 to teach classes based on the relationship between art and architecture.
Since 2004 professor de Brea has directed the BSU CAP Americano Sur Program, a five-week study abroad on Latin American architecture and culture that has taken students of different nationalities to visit well-known architecture offices, colleges, and projects in Argentina, Bolivia, Brazil, Chile, Ecuador, Peru, Portugal, Spain, and Uruguay. Ana was among the founders of *Paralelo 35* in Buenos Aires and Grupo R in Rosario as well as an invited professor, international guest speaker and exhibitor mainly in Europe and the three Americas – Argentina, Canada, Chile, Brazil, Ecuador, Germany, Holland, Spain, the United States, Uruguay, and Venezuela are included.
Ana de Brea's teaching, artwork, and research are focused on the meaning of geometrical bodies and the significance of materiality in contemporary, modern, global design predominantly in Latin America.
In parallel to her work as an educator and her professional practice, Ana worked for more than fifteen years as a design-columnist in some of the most significant newspapers in the Spanish language – with global, weekly editions, in which she published a great number of articles and held interviews with renowned architects and designers from all over the world. Her published work includes *Señores Arquitectos... Dialogos con Mario Roberto Alvarez y Clorindo Testa* (with Tomas Dagnino, 1999) and 10x50: Terreno de Arquitectura (2001) –both books in the Spanish language, launched and exhibited at the Buenos Aires Museum of Modern Art.
As part of her present-day activities Ana is continuing a series of international workshops and presentations that have been developed in correspondence to the publication of this existing book-project on Latin American architecture, her first volume in the English language.
The Buenos Aires National Library in Argentina, the UF Center for Latin American Studies and the CUA School of Architecture and Planning both in the United States, as well as the most recent international, architecture biennales in Rosario and Buenos Aires, among other intercontinental institutions and conferences, have been involved in a plan of action that unites travelling exhibitions and lectures intended to stimulate an open, wider discussion in connection with architectural discourse.

IMAGE CREDITS

T top; M middle; B bottom; L left; R right; A all

Alejandro Haiek (277, 278, 279)
Alberto Fonseca (194LT, 314, 317A)
Alejandro Peral (184,185)
Alejandro Stöberl (203)
Ana de Brea (042B, 307A)
Ana Rascovsky Architecture (266, 267A)
Andrés Arenas (195LB, 195RM, 195RB)
Antonieta Angulo (300, 301)
A. Tellez (315)
Aryeh Kornfeld (096, 097A, 99A, 100, 101A, 102A, 103A, 321A)
Axel Fridman (411T)
Barclay & Crousse (346T)
Becca Staley (176, 177, 178, 179)
Blinder Janches Architects (282, 283)
Camilo Restrepo (058, 059)
Carolina Kogan (370, 371T, 372T)
Claudio Ferrari (205, 338, 339A)
Claudio Vekstein (240A, 241A)
David Barragán (104, 105, 106, 108, 109, 110, 111)
David Franzen (188LT, 189RT, 189LM, 189RM)
Daniel Bonilla Architecture (195T)
Daniela Macadden (036A)
Dieguez Fridman (136, 137, 139A, 382, 385A)
DSH (080, 081, 082, 083, 084, 085)
Eduardo Sauce (272, 274, 275, 278, 279)
Enmanuel Cardozo (277)
Eric Lawler (042LT, 042RT)
Fito Pardo (401, 402A, 403A)
Google Images (187RT, 231A, 232A, 233A)
Guido Torres (409, 411M)
Gustavo Frittegotto (131,133, 134A, 140,140A, 144A)
Gustavo Sosa Pinilla (081,082T,083T)
Hester+Hardaway (189B)
Holzman Moss Bottino Architecture (189LT, 189LB, 189RB, 190LT)
Ileana Pita (272, 274, 275)
Iwan Baan (169A, 358A, 359A, 360A, 361A)
Jaime Navarro (411B)
Jason Klinker (176, 177, 178, 179
Jerome Daksiewicz (270, 271A)
Jorge Gamboa (162, 163A, 194RT)
José Cubilla&Associates (124,125)
José María Sáez (114,115,116,117)
J. P. Crousse (342, 344,345A, 346B, 347A)
J.Paul Restrepo (058, 059)
KAW (201A)
Leonardo Finotti (086, 087A, 088A, 089A, 090, 091, 092, 093)
Lucas Carranza (374, 375)
Madelon Vriesendorp (247)
María de Brea Dulcich (039, 045, 051)
Mauricio Fuertes (320, 322, 323, 324, 325A)
Mauro Bianucci (215)
M/SG/S/S/S (048A)
M. Spina (062, 0653, 064A, 065A, 067)
Nelson Kon (074, 075A, 076A, 077A , 250,251,252,253A, 334, 335A, 336A, 337)
Nicolás Campodonico (175A, 182A,183A, 308,309A)
Pascual Gangotena (104, 105, 106, 108, 109, 110, 111)
Paúl Rivera (406, 407, 408A)
Pelli Clarke (009)
Philippe Ruault (225A)
Quilian Riano (290)
Quiroga Caraffa (118, 119A, 388, 389A, 390, 391)
R. Alvarado (343)
Raed Gindeya (104, 105, 106, 108, 109, 110, 111, 114, 115A, 116A, 117A)
Rafael Gamo (398, 399A, 400A)
Ramiro Rodríguez Barilari (326, 327RT)
Roberto Busnelli (310, 311, 312A)
Rodrigo Dávila (161A, 193A)
Roger Bertame (330M, 331LB)
Sandra Pereznieto (151, 152A, 157A)
Sebastián Crespo (054, 055, 056, 057)
Sergio Forster (217A)
Sergio Gómez (159A, 194RB, 194LB, 194RB, 261, 263)
Studio R. Iglesia Architect (172, 173)
Studio Amette (060, 061A)
Taller 301 (164, 165)
Tatiana Bilbao Architecture (357A)
Teresa Margoles (356)
Tom Kessler (188RT, 188LB, 188RB)
Viale-Dutari (329, 330T, 330LB, 331RB)
Victoria Montero (371B, 373A)
Walter Salcedo (120, 121A, 122A, 145)
Wes Janz (219A)
Zas Lavarello Architects (070, 071A, 072A,073A)

Author
Ana de Brea

Editor
Ricardo Devesa

Graphic Design
Marga Gibert

Copyediting
Angela Kay Bunning

Editorial coordination
Marta Ariza

Publishers
Actar Publishers, New York,
Barcelona, 2016
www.actarpublishers.com

Distributed by
Actar D Inc.
New York
355 Lexington Avenue, 8th Floor
New York, NY 10017
T +1 212 966 2207
F +1 212 966 2214
salesnewyork@actar-d.com

Barcelona
Roca i Batlle 2
08023 Barcelona
T +34 933 282 183
salesbarcelona@actar-d.com
eurosales@actar-d.com

ISBN 978-1-940291-47-5
Library of Congress Control Number:
2015940111

A CIP catalogue record for this book is available from the Library of Congress, Washington D.C., USA.
Printed and Bound in China

The author and Actar Publishers are especially grateful to these image providers. Every reasonable attempt has been made to identify owners of copyright. Should unintentional mistakes or omissions have occurred, we sincerely apologize and ask for notice. Such mistakes will be corrected in the next edition of this publication.

Thanks to: